A KILLING IN

CAPONE'S PLAYGROUND

ABOUT THE AUTHOR

For nearly twenty years, public safety professional and historian Chriss Lyon has not only walked the beat, but shot the most famous Thompson submachine guns in the world, all while documenting and researching the historic era of the "The Roaring Twenties." Using techniques of forensic genealogy combined with investigative research, she has been able to uncover little known facts about the people and events surrounding the St. Valentine's Day Massacre, revealing them at presentations at schools, museums, genealogical, and historical societies. Her passion in Prohibition-era gangsters, maritime, and aviation history as well as historical weather has afforded opportunities to write articles for various magazines and journals and assist other authors with historical research. A graduate of Grand Valley State University's Film/Video School, Chriss began working behind the scenes at CNN Headline News but now is out in front of the camera. She has appeared in an episode of the PBS series, "History Detectives" as well as documentaries on the National Geographic Channel, Travel Channel, and Investigation Discovery Channel.

St. Joseph, Michigan Police Officer Charles Skelly in 1929.
Courtesy of The Heritage Museum and Cultural Center.

A KILLING IN CAPONE'S PLAYGROUND

THE TRUE STORY OF THE HUNT FOR THE MOST DANGEROUS MAN ALIVE

Rich—
Thank you for your support! Capone was here!

Chriss L

CHRISS LYON

Photographs
As credited and used with permission.
Cover Images: St. Joseph Police Officer Charles Skelly in 1929, Heritage Museum
and Cultural Center Collection. Mugshot of Fred "Killer" Burke in 1931, State of
Michigan Archives. Scene of downtown Benton Harbor, Michigan, circa 1930,
Heritage Museum and Cultural Center Collection. Front page of *News Palladium*
after Charles Skelly was killed.
Rear cover: Chriss Lyon holding one of the Thompson submachine guns used in
the St. Valentine's Day Massacre and photo of St. Valentine's Day Massacre victims
from author collection.

Published
In the United States of America by In-Depth Editions, 2014
www.in-deptheditions.com
18 17 16 15 14   5 4 3 2 1
First Edition

Publisher Cataloging-in-Publication Data
Lyon, Chriss.
A killing in capone's playground:
the true story of the hunt for the most dangerous man alive

384 p. : 94 ill.
Includes bibliographical references (349-363) and endnotes
ISBN 978-09889772-0-4 (pbk: alk paper)
1. Skelly, Charles 1904-1929. 2. Burke, Fred "Killer" 1894-1940.
3. Gangsters—Illinois—Chicago—Biography 4. Capone, Al 1899-1947.
5. Organized crime—Illinois—Chicago—History.
6. United States History—20th Century.
7. Michigan—History.
I. Title. II. Author.

2014
364.1 Lyo   2014940471

Dedicated to my grandmothers,
Macille A. (Betz) Kline and Elsie G. (Markwart) Lyon,
for inspiring and unlocking the curiosity of a child.
To the late Rick Mattix, for opening the door, and
to the late Berrien County Sheriff's Deputy Michael Moore,
for proving that laughter and tears often occur simultaneously.

Fred "Killer" Burke in custody at the Berrien County Jail in St. Joseph, Michigan, March 30, 1931. *Author's collection.*

"I DON'T KNOW ANYTHING ABOUT THIS ROBBERY. I WAS IN ST. JOSEPH, MICHIGAN, AT THAT TIME."

- Fred "Killer" Burke, 1931

CONTENTS

PART III CONSEQUENCE

Alphonse Capone, "The Big Guy."
Author's collection.

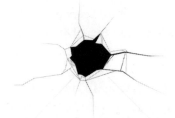

AUTHOR NOTES

MY EARLIEST MEMORY WAS OF STANDING IN THE KITCHEN watching my mom wash dishes, when I tugged on her shirt and announced, "I'm three years old." While I was confident about my age in 1971, I did not understand the world yet and was curious about everything. From an early age, I had a bond with both my grandmothers. On the paternal side, Grandma Lyon and I were very close, and family members commented on how much I resembled her. At first, I thought that was what bonded us, but later I found that we had a strange sense of presence in each other's lives; she would think of me and I would subconsciously know it, and vice versa. Grandma Lyon taught me about sacrifice, about death, and about being strong and independent. I remember her words of advice: "Never bring shame to your family name." I wanted and needed her to be proud of me.

On the maternal side, I was the first grandchild for Grandma Kline, who doted on me much differently. She was a storyteller and artist, who was probably most proud of her military service as a Navy WAVE. When I was six or seven years old, I remember listening to her tell the true story about a gangster who shot a police officer in downtown St. Joseph. Her passionate interest in local history ignited me without my even realizing it. At the time, Al Capone was the only gangster I had ever heard of and I could only envision scenes from a few black-and-white movies that I had watched on WGN-TV out of Chicago. This was when there was only one television in the house, a rather large console that resembled a piece of furniture, and the television captivated me. The gangsters all wore dressy long coats and hats, held guns at their waists, and drove always drove black cars. I wondered why a gangster would be in a small town like St. Joseph. Over the years, I learned that the gangster was Fred "Killer" Burke and the police officer was Charles Skelly.

Once I fully embraced my genetic disposition to pursue historical research and genealogy, I studied the Skelly/Burke story first told to me as a child. I was not the only one, though, because I learned that my uncle, Mike Kline, had the same interest. Only 10 years my senior, Mike was more of an older brother than an uncle, and in the 1990s we both wound up working at the Berrien County Sheriff's Department, he as a jail deputy and I as a 911 dispatcher.

Over the next 10 years, Mike and I met quite a few "gangsterologists," people who live and breathe the gangster era. We were in great company because our new friends wanted to preserve the legacy of the era not for fame or money, but out of pure historical passion. In 2000, Mike was promoted to quartermaster at the sheriff's department, which meant that the most famous Thompson submachine guns in the world became his responsibility. After years of researching and reading about the St. Valentine's Day Massacre and Charles Skelly's run-in with Fred "Killer" Burke, I began to see that there was much more written about the gangsters than the police officers. Of course, that did not sit right with me, having taken up a career in public safety. I felt compelled to write a complete, detailed, and accurate portrayal of what occurred that tragic night, what instigated it, and the aftereffects. Previous attempts to tell the story had skimmed over details and quoted only newspaper articles, including some I found to be inaccurate. My goal was to find the original sources: police reports, court records, autopsy reports, and other governmental records. To understand the era, I needed to go beyond that fateful night when Skelly was killed and explore the atmosphere of Prohibition, community temperaments, and political agendas. I had to learn what was going on in society at the time and look at the key players in more detail. A few members of Al Capone's inner circle owned property in Southwestern Michigan and Northern Indiana, but this was in no way a local story.

What I was able to find in terms of official documentation was much more than I ever could have imagined. Reading the actual police report taken by the Michigan State Police, the testimony of witnesses, and the hundreds of interviews conducted by detectives gave a much more analytical portrayal of what had occurred, quite different from what most of the newspapers reported. History is about the truth; history does not have an opinion. I soon realized that I needed to do a lot more research, but most of it was right in front of me.

As luck or as unusual coincidence would have it, the two key people who gave Skelly his first police job were Fred Alden and William Barry, and their grandson/nephew was my boss, David Agens. From discussions with him, I was given a three-dimensional view of each man, much different from the flat descriptions given in the newspapers. Then, I happened to reconnect with a former classmate I had known since kindergarten and learned that his father was the nephew of Steve Kunay, one of Burke's carjack victims. Next, I tracked down cousins and a niece of Charles Skelly, who gave me a much clearer picture of the hero in this story. No less exciting was connecting with a cousin of Fred Burke, who had an equally coincidental occurrence with me, in that she somehow knew I would be contacting her. However, most touching was meeting the last living person who was present when the shooting occurred. Joyce Kool Ender was the three-month-old baby in the car that crashed with Burke's car. I was astonished at how real this event was for so many people and how it had become something much more to me than historical research and documentation.

The old saying, "never assume anything," was put to the test immediately during my research. With my knowledge of criminal investigations and scene security from almost 20 years in the public safety field, I found that procedures were less evolved, or absent, during the early and mid-twentieth century. I learned that the Michigan State Police had been established and had operated under several different names: Michigan State Troops Permanent Force, Michigan State Constabulary, Michigan State Police, Michigan Department of Public Safety, and the Michigan Department of State Police. In addition, the head of the department was called commissioner from 1921 to 1965, and was a plainclothes position. The sheriff of the county was not always someone from law enforcement but an elected position usually filled by a businessman or farmer. While jurisdictional boundaries existed, I did not get a sense of sole responsibility by each municipality, but more so a cooperative effort among local, county, and state authorities. In an effort to keep true to the time in this book, I have referred to the authorities in their proper titles at the time. Some highway designations and road names have changed significantly as well, but I have kept them as they were for the time, which sometimes differ from their names today.

Interviews with the family members of participants in this story proved to be a challenge. In a few cases, what I was told did not match up with the public record. I set out to confirm what I considered family legends, but found that some timelines could not be corroborated with the events. While I valued the additional viewpoints and possibilities of other versions, I tried to stay with what was the most widely accepted, logical, and proven sequence of events.

Discovering documents and police reports with actual witness interviews led to my decision to write in the narrative form. I used the actual dialogue as reported in newspapers, police reports, court records, newsreel films, and interviews, and I developed dialogue from some first-person accounts.

Throughout the writing process, I became very attached to the characters. I laughed and I cried. This is the story I was meant to write. From every strange coincidence to the thousands of pages I have collected, here is my version of the true story. For the children and grandchildren I never had, this is my gift to you.

- Chriss Lyon, 2014

Bloody scene of the St. Valentine's Day Massacre at 2122 N. Clark Street, Chicago, Illinois, February 14, 1929.
Courtesy of William J. Helmer.

FOREWORD

EXACTLY **10** MONTHS AFTER THE MASSACRE IN CHICAGO on St. Valentine's Day in 1929, the small town of St. Joseph, Michigan, felt the aftershock of that violent gangland event. Unlike that tragic day where witnesses were few and those coming forward even fewer, a profound voice would emerge on the evening of December 14, 1929, one that collectively enabled a cleansing of polluted public apathy and served as a catapult of scientific advancement. However, it would come at a heavy price.

St. Joseph began as a small village in 1834 within the county of Berrien in Southwestern Michigan, and graduated to city status in 1891. Lying adjacent to Lake Michigan at the mouth of the St. Joseph River, St. Joseph served as a major hub for commercial maritime transportation. Benton Harbor, its sister or "twin city," as it was popularly called, was separated by the winding river just to the northeast. Away from the heart of each city square filled with shops, the branches of dirt roads led in all directions to rural farmlands primed for fruit crops. The rich soil and climate made the area ideal for growing apples, peaches, grapes, strawberries, and blueberries, which were often exported to Chicago via ships and, in later years, by trains and motor vehicles. With the finest commodities of Southwestern Michigan's Fruit Belt being served up in kitchens all over Chicago, exports from Chicago to Southwestern Michigan were not always of the same quality. An influx of immigrants with the inevitable cultural and political clashes, and a growing industrial age, led to a build-up of tension and crime, one that would expand beyond Chicago's city limits and into the rural heartland.

PROLOGUE

"MERRY CHRISTMAS, OFFICER SKELLY," BELLOWED Santa Claus, the treasured character aptly portrayed by a local merchant. It was a Saturday evening, December 14, 1929, in downtown St. Joseph, Michigan. Police officer Charles Skelly smiled and waved at the well-padded jolly man in red. It was just above freezing and clouds hid the fiery sun sinking into Lake Michigan. Officer Skelly had bundled up in his duty coat to stave off the elements. Southwesterly winds blew in from Chicago, much different from the "pea soup" treachery of the previous two days.[1] Dealing with the elements was part of Skelly's job. Most recently, the elements were in the form of fire and water, since he had been serving as the assistant chief of the St. Joseph Fire Department during the last year. Deep down he was a boy in blue, so when the opportunity arose in June, Skelly stepped off the fire engine and onto a motorcycle. That winter night, though, he was on foot, walking his beat, passing by garland-decorated lampposts and shoppers struggling to carry bulky packages.

Christmas was on the minds of everyone, and maybe a few other things, too. That night was the opening of the Class D high school basketball season for Benton Harbor's St. John's Irish who faced the Gaels of the Berrien County community of Galien. Those seeking to cozy up at home could listen to WGN Radio's "Radio Floorwalker" at 8:00 p.m. News around the state showed that liquor law violations were down, and Detroit's new police radios were proving to be highly successful in the fight against crime.[2] Nationally, the U.S. Senate was about to pass a 1 percent income tax cut resolution, and the date marked the 130th anniversary of George Washington's death.[3] There was so much to celebrate and be grateful for. It was Christmastime and almost the end of a decade.

Among the crowds on the streets and sidewalks were people familiar to the young officer. Fred and Leona Ludwig noticed Officer Skelly when they exited one of the downtown stores.[4] Mingling for a moment, the three continued walking for the distance of a pleasant conversation and then went their separate ways, offering a wave to each other as they did. At 25-years-old and still a bachelor, the ruggedly fetching Charles Skelly worked 12-hour shifts, sometimes seven days a week, which made romance difficult. Bevies of beauties were always within sight around a man in uniform, yet Skelly had become aware of a special girl, Mildred Thar, a 20-year-old brunette with a smile that could make any male "dizzy with a dame." Mildred shared an apartment with her sisters, Belle, Caroline, and Gladys, at 607 Broad Street in the Freund Building, across from the police and fire station.[5] Skelly could not help gazing at Mildred any time she was around. The attraction must have been mutual because the two began a courtship. Mildred worked at the Williams Box Factory just a few blocks away and looked forward to running into her handsome boy in blue. On that busy night, he walked his beat, the ashy flame from his cigarette visible as he took sight of others walking hand in hand. He may have thought about the day when he would marry…maybe Mildred.

The atmosphere of downtown St. Joseph was magical that night. A Christmas tree adorned the corner of State and Pleasant Streets where Santa Claus hollered his greetings. Storefronts displayed the latest fashions to entice the ever so tempted consumer. Men in overcoats and fedoras noticed a group of young women who were pointing out the newest lingerie that you "step into." Who could resist the "silken wisps of loveliness," as Gilmore Brothers described their stockings? They cost $2 a pair.[6]

By 7:00 p.m., darkness covered the city, but flickers of candlelight and sidewalk lamps lit up the streets. The whistling wind wafting around lampposts created dust swirls on the sidewalks and ripples over the wool-adorned shoppers. A jettisoned piece of velvet ribbon floated to the ground and curled, as if seeking a package to adorn. The dull roar of Lake Michigan only two blocks away grumbled like a machine, dark and ominous. Officer Skelly kept watch, like the lighthouse stationed at the end of the pier to keep all who enter the harbor safe. He lifted a cigarette to his lips and inhaled, the bright amber glow reflected in the store window on the corner where he stood, just as the lighthouse beacon illuminated the harbor. Skelly heard the giggles of several young boys and girls approaching. He pointed out Santa Claus, much to their delight and his own.

As the clock hands pointed to 25 minutes past seven, the sudden blaring of a car horn drowned out the distant sounds of sleigh bells. Skelly turned toward the sound and saw a man driving a Chevy Coach, hailing his assistance.

The vehicle pulled up along the southeast corner of State and Broad Streets where Skelly had been walking his beat. Listening to the excited story of the driver, Skelly had no idea he had just stepped into a role in a Shakespearian tragedy about to unfold.

Skelly approached the car and leaned in to the driver, who rambled the numbers six, five, seven, one, zero, six. While reaching for his notepad, Skelly interrupted, "Sir, please calm down and start at the beginning."

The man explained that they had been involved in a fender bender on U.S. Highway 12 back by Cleveland Avenue and said the man driving the car that hit them was very drunk. Taking notes, Skelly interrupted once again to ask some basic questions. The driver finally identified himself and the occupants of the car, apologizing for being flustered.

"I'm Forrest Kool from Buchanan and this here's my wife, Laverne, with our three-month-old daughter, Joyce," he said, while gesturing in the direction of each person. "In back is my mother-in-law, Hattie Carlson, and brother-in-law, Harold."

Skelly took note that Harold was only about 10 years old. He nodded and then asked Kool to tell him what happened.

The 22-year-old Kool explained that they had been Christmas shopping and were on their way home to rural Weesaw Township, driving south on U.S. Highway 12, when he noticed a Hudson coupe driving toward them in the same lane, near the intersection of Cleveland Avenue. Seeing that the oncoming vehicle was not moving back into its own lane, Kool abruptly swerved his Chevy off onto the shoulder but still took a direct impact in the side rear fender, jarring his passengers. After making sure everyone was safe, he turned around to see the Hudson slow and pull over about a quarter mile down the road behind them. Kool managed to pull his car, which was no longer drivable, into the driveway of the home belonging to Dr. Charles W. Merritt. Kool got out of the car and waved down a couple in a passing Chevy, who he figured had seen the accident. The driver pulled over and introduced himself as Edward Rupp of Union Pier. Kool hopped onto the running board of Rupp's Chevy and they drove the short distance to the Hudson, which had come to a stop near the St. Joseph Auto Camp, across from LaSalle Street.

Rupp pulled in front of the Hudson and Kool stepped off the running board. The Hudson appeared to be new, and Kool took note that it had an orange Indiana license plate, number 657-106. The car had slight scuffing and a small dent in the front quarter-panel, where it had hit Kool's fender. He walked up to the driver's side, boldly opened the door, and confronted the man sitting inside, "What do you mean by running into me like that?"

"Hit your car?" the man slurred, looking puzzled. Kool realized the driver was clearly intoxicated. "Well, why don't you drive it over here so I can look at the damage," he mumbled.

"Well, the fender is bent in against the tire so I can't drive it," Kool explained. "Why don't you come with me and see for yourself?"

The intoxicated driver attempted to get out of his car but hesitated for a moment as if getting his bearings. It was then that he apparently noticed Rupp standing next to Kool. This seemed to make him nervous because once again he asked Kool, "Why don't you drive yer car over?" apparently forgetting that he had already suggested that.

Not interested in dealing with the intoxicated man, Rupp drove away. The man seemed quite relieved. Just then, another car slowed down and stopped. The driver, William Lohraff of Berrien Springs, asked if they needed any help. Kool waved him off, and Lohraff continued on his way.[7]

The intoxicated man managed to struggle to his feet. He took a few steps, stopped, and turned to look at his car for a moment, but then joined Kool, who was walking south toward his Chevy, where his family still sat. The intoxicated man seemed to stagger more than walk the quarter-mile distance. Kool took note that he wore a cap, light buff-colored sweater, and dark pants, but no coat. His face was rosy from inebriation and he reeked of alcohol. He was all of 200 pounds, tall, with a small dark mustache and manicured nails; he was well groomed but missing a front tooth. Kool thought the man acted polite, but noticed that he talked somewhat brokenly. Kool wondered if he was from another part of the country, but considered that perhaps the missing tooth was the cause.

The man then said, "You know, I was on my way to pick up my wife at the train station."

Trying to avoid being downwind of the foul-smelling man, Kool showed him where he had swerved and finally where the car ended up. Laverne and her mother peered through the car windows at the tall stranger. Their piercing shouts penetrated the windows, even when rolled up. Worried that they were agitating the man, Kool quickly interrupted, "Shut up. I've got this under control."

Looking puzzled, both women complied. The man glanced at the women as he tried to keep his balance but hardly reacted to them. He let out a belch and rocked back on his heels.

Both men looked over the damage. Kool asked the man if he would help pull out the fender so he could drive home. With a few tugs, they managed to wrench the fender from the tire.

"You know, there's a repair shop up the road," the intoxicated man managed to say. "I'll show you where. Follow me."[8]

Kool sighed, knowing that a repair shop would be closed on a Saturday night. "Look," he replied, "I'll have to get a new fender and probably a new tire, so I'll settle for $25."

Calling him to the side of the road near some trees, the intoxicated man reached into his pocket and pulled out a large roll of bills. He thumbed through them, telling Kool, "Sorry, but I don't have 'nuff small bills to make change."

Frustrated, Kool backed away from him. "If you're not interested in settling this, it really doesn't matter. Either way, you are not fit to drive in your condition and I am going to have to report this to the police."

"Do whatever you have to do," the man unsympathetically replied as he put the roll of bills back in his pocket.

Being a proper gentleman, Kool offered the other driver a ride on the running board, back to his Hudson, so that they could make their way to the police station. However, it became clear that the man was too drunk to manage that, so Kool was satisfied that he chose to walk. Kool turned his Chevy around, drove ahead of the Hudson, and waited. Once the intoxicated man reached his car, Kool watched as he fell into the driver's seat and—remarkably—was able to start up the vehicle and pull forward. Driving by the St. Joseph Auto Camp, he blew the horn, and then passed Kool's Chevy. Then he blew his horn again, apparently signaling Kool to pass. Kool pulled around him and turned onto State Street in hopes of finding a police officer, but the intoxicated man in the Hudson kept blowing the horn. Unsure whether something was wrong or the man had suddenly reconsidered paying for the damage, Kool stopped about two blocks south of the Caldwell Theater on State Street to find out what his problem was. Laverne urged him to stay in the car, but instead Kool got out and walked up to the driver's side of the Hudson. The window was already rolled down, and the stench of alcohol wafted out.

"You've been blowing the horn the last half mile," Kool said. "What's the problem?"

"I've been following you, I don't have any problem," the driver replied. He then gave a few toots of the horn and smiled as if amused.

Shaking his head, Kool returned to his car, but before he reached it, he saw the Hudson speed down a side street and vanish. He realized that the drunk had duped him.

A simple Christmas shopping trip to St. Joseph had become much more complicated for the Kool family. Now with a dented fender and a drunk driver on the streets, Forrest Kool hoped to notify the authorities so the family could be on their way home once again. He started blowing his horn at the intersection of State Street and Market Street in an attempt to find a policeman and spotted Officer Charles Skelly, just a block away, standing at the corner near Broad Street.

Just as he had finished explaining their misadventure to the police officer, Laverne Kool noticed the Hudson pass by. "There he goes," she blurted, while pointing to get the officer's attention.

Skelly looked up in time to recognize a familiar face behind the wheel. *He was the new guy in town,* Skelly realized. He grabbed hold of Kool's doorframe, hopped on the running board, and hollered, "Follow him."

Excited to be on a chase with a police officer, Kool drove north about two blocks on State Street and then came to a stop behind the Hudson at the intersection of Ship Street, where the driver had stopped for a red light. Skelly jumped off Kool's running board, ran a few car lengths to the Hudson, and climbed up on the driver's side running board.

Skelly leaned his head into the open window to confront the driver. "Better pay the money and save going to court," he suggested. This was routine business and Skelly knew the script.

Several people in the area had taken notice of the activity. Pere Marquette Bridge tender Lawrence Terry, standing in front of the Jefferson Poolroom at the corner of Ship and State, had heard Skelly blow his whistle and saw the Hudson come to a stop.[9] St. Joseph police officer Arthur Truhn, also on foot patrol, had watched Skelly jump off the Chevy and run toward the Hudson.[10] Phil Daly, Ted Lucker, and Adam Ehrenberg had all seen Skelly climb on the Hudson's running board.[11] Gustav Getz also saw what was taking place from his vantage point a few blocks away.[12] Just a cop doing his job, it must have appeared to all of them.

Allowing other vehicles to pass, Skelly signaled back at Kool, motioning for him to follow. Skelly would direct the man to the police station in order to sort this all out. When the traffic light turned green at Ship and State, the Hudson and the Chevy turned the corner heading east and then made a right on Main Street heading for the police station. They passed Charles L. Miller's Garage with Skelly still riding on the running board. The Kools followed behind by about 20 feet. As both vehicles approached the intersection of Main and Broad, just within sight of the Freund Building apartments where Skelly's gal, Mildred Thar, lived, the traffic light turned red.

Puffs of exhaust mixed with Skelly's breath as he glanced up toward her apartment. There in the second-floor window he saw her silhouette illuminated by a light. She must have heard the commotion. Mildred saw Charles and waved. Skelly smiled back, keeping his hands on the doorframe, but he lingered for a moment in her smile. Here he was in action for Mildred to see and he must have been proud. As the opposing traffic light transitioned from green to yellow, Skelly redirected his attention to the man behind the wheel. He pointed ahead, instructing him to pull over by the station just beyond the intersection. Mildred walked away from the window, probably impressed by the strapping Skelly.

When the light turned green, traffic began to move north and south, but the Hudson sat idling. Staring straight ahead toward the endless roadway, the driver loosened his grip on the steering wheel. Skelly bent down to look into the vehicle.

From a car length behind, Kool watched the man through the Hudson's large glass rear window, his head fully visible. *What is he waiting for?* Kool thought. He then saw the man lean to his left.

With eyes blurred from alcohol, his mind consumed with fear, the driver of the Hudson grabbed for his Colt .45-caliber pistol in the side pocket of the door and took aim at his obstacle to freedom.

Officer Charles Skelly found himself face to face with the barrel of a pistol and the cold eyes of a killer. A secret kept for the last 10 months was about to be revealed along the brick boulevard.

Mildred Thar, girlfriend of Charles Skelly, in 1929. *Author's collection.*

St. Joseph Police Department Officer Charles Skelly circa 1926.
Courtesy of the Berrien County Sheriff's Department.

PART 1

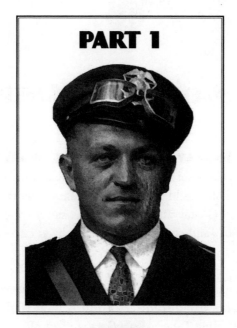

CRIME

*"Show me a hero, and
I'll write you a tragedy."*

- F. Scott Fitzgerald

First-Generation American

CHARLES SKALAY CAME INTO THE WORLD ON MAY 3, 1904, on a Danneffel Road farm in rural Bainbridge Township, Michigan, the second child of Gustav and Mary Schultz Skalay, both Germans from Russia.[13] Gustav and Mary had set sail for the United States on a cattle boat in 1901, and soon became naturalized citizens. Their passage was made possible through the generosity of the Prillwitz family, prominent farmers from Benton Harbor, Michigan, and graciously repaid through hard labor. Gustav's younger brother, William; his sister, Hattie; and his mother, Anna Schelley Skalay, had already settled in Benton Harbor, a year earlier. William had met Pauline Tober, also a German from Russia, who immigrated with her family the same year; they married in May 1903. Hattie married Rudolph Hoffman in December 1904.

German-Russian immigration into Bainbridge Township was much in advance of general German emigration to the United States.[14] The Midwest was a popular choice for these people, many of whom were farmers, because the region and climate very much resembled the place they were leaving behind. One such group was from Volhynia, Russia, an area located west of Kiev to the border of Poland within northwestern Ukraine.

By 1910, younger siblings Minnie and Richard had joined Charles and his older sister, Olga, and the family had relocated to 1121 Lavette in Benton Harbor; Gustav worked in the sidewalk construction business and Mary tended to their small fruit farm.[15] Gustav then began work as a machine molder at the Covel Manufacturing Company in Benton Harbor, which made hacksaws and saw-sharpening tools. The Skalay family kept growing and, over the decade, Mary gave birth to Walter, Ruth, Erven, and Elsie. Chuck, as his family referred to him, was proud of his heritage. As if almost instinctively, he took special care of his younger sister Minnie, who was deaf and suffered from a speech impediment.[16] Gustav stayed close to his brother William and his sister Hattie, especially after their mother, Anna, passed away on March 23, 1913.[17] As each of the families grew, they probably worried about the relatives left back in Russia when the start of what would become the Great War broke out there in 1914.

Loss reached the extended Skalay family once again on May 8, 1918, when Freda, the six-year-old daughter of William and Pauline, died from a heart defect.[18] This certainly would have touched Chuck and his siblings, who had grown up with their young cousin. Unfortunately, the Skalays would suffer even more tragedy within their immediate family in the months and years to come.

The Great War or World War I, as it was later referred to, reached the Skalay family in the form of the Selective Service Act, or the draft. Both Gustav and William were required to register and did so on September 12, 1918. Hundreds of local residents enlisted and went off to central Europe to serve in combat. Forty-nine men from Berrien County became casualties by the end of the war on November 11, 1918, known as Armistice Day. Compounding the impact of war was a deadly strain of flu virus that spread throughout the world between 1918 and 1919, later known as the Spanish Flu Epidemic, the deadliest in modern history. Globally, casualties from the virus may have reached up to 50 million; nationwide, casualties were about 675,000. In Berrien County 168 people died in the epidemic by the close of 1919. The Skalay family were relieved that the war ended and the epidemic passed without affecting their family, but any relief they felt would be short-lived.

Unfortunately, the next tragedy would hit closer to home. On November 21, 1919, Gustav's wife, Mary, died at 35 years of age, while delivering her ninth child. She began hemorrhaging late in her third trimester, causing premature labor. Although the baby was born, Mary died within three hours.[19] Gustav named the small, frail newborn girl Helen. She needed a great deal of medical care, so a doctor transferred her to the Michigan Children's Home Association in St. Joseph, just four days after her birth. Mary Skalay was laid to rest in Crystal Springs Cemetery in Benton Harbor on Sunday, November 23, 1919, as baby Helen struggled to live. However, on December 6, 1919,[20] the infant joined her mother in death. A monument inscribed with "SKALAY" would later grace the family plot. The young Skalay children now faced life without their mother and their baby sister. In order to help his father maintain the household, Chuck dropped out of school. He was learning what it was to love, lose, and sacrifice, all at the young age of 15.

While his younger siblings continued their education, Chuck's older sister, Olga, met and fell in love with 23-year-old hotel clerk Max Moulds, the son of William Moulds, who owned and operated the Moulds Brass Foundry on Ninth Street near the Michigan Central Railroad tracks in Benton Harbor. While their courtship carried on into the new decade, the United States government set about to divorce its citizens from what some touted as the evils of alcohol consumption.

Even though Michigan voters had approved statewide Prohibition in November 1916, going into effect on May 1, 1918, national Prohibition began on January 17, 1920, the direct result of the Volstead Act of 1919 and the passage of the Eighteenth Amendment. Prohibition made it illegal to manufacture, transport, import, or sell alcoholic beverages anywhere in the country. The "Dry Movement" had garnered strength from some religious groups, temperance societies, and progressives who saw a form of gluttony and moral upheaval due to alcohol consumption. Advocates believed that sobriety would help diminish crime to the point where police departments could cut staff, jails could close their doors, farmers could use their corn and grain for food products rather than in alcohol, poverty would end, and families could have a new gathering place within the church. Unfortunately, this idealistic thinking would have just the opposite effect.

In the first few months of the 1920s, Prohibition stopped few from drinking; instead, the era created a new allure. It made criminals out of otherwise law-abiding citizens. Forbidden spirits suddenly became liquid gold for anyone willing to pay for them. The duty of enforcing the law was given to the Bureau of Prohibition, part of the Internal Revenue Service of the United States Department of Treasury. Additionally, state and local authorities assisted the endeavor, which proved problematic for the government because violators outnumbered enforcers. The Great Lakes, which separated much of Canada and the United States, also separated "wet" and "dry" in terms of the manufacture of alcohol. Ontario had gone dry in 1916 under the Ontario Temperance Act, which banned the sale of alcohol in Ontario; however, the breweries and distilleries in Ontario could manufacture the product for export. Importing it into the United States, though, was illegal. This did not stop many. Detroit suddenly became a central distribution point. Criminal organizations already operating prostitution and gambling rings in the big cities discovered a new, lucrative business, one that would give birth to a new breed of criminal.

Evolving from early nineteenth-century neighborhood and ethnic gangs to part of an organized criminal empire, the gangster was born. Gangsters thrived during periods of weakened social order and governmental suppression, ensuring that an illegal product or service was available. In the days before gangster rule, murders were typically spontaneous actions, or the result of heat-of-the-moment behaviors; however, the new era of organized crime gave rise to intricately detailed planned killings with the uttermost brutality. Where a back-alley fistfight may have settled a score before, now murder, with its lack of adequate punishment, became the norm on the street. Gangsters established turfs within the organization and an infringement of turf by another gangster was sure to bring a violent end. Benton Harbor residents, however, knew little about criminal empires or gangs and less about gangsters in 1920; the talk of the town instead was the prize-fighting heavyweight champion pugilist, Jack Dempsey.

A Benton Harbor boxing promoter, Floyd Fitzsimmons, got the deal of a lifetime in April 1920, when he arranged to bring Jack Dempsey to Benton Harbor to defend his title. Considered the most successful sports promoter in the state, Fitzsimmons scheduled the bout for Labor Day, September 6, 1920, matching Dempsey with Billy Miske for a third career meeting in the ring. Chuck Skalay heard that Dempsey was coming to town, and like any other soon-to-be 16-year-old, he was elated. Chuck eagerly followed the latest news and might have even tried to wangle a way to see the fight himself.

The heavyweight champion, born William Harrison Dempsey in 1895, was a unique hero. Besides his ethnic mix of Scottish, Irish, Cherokee, and Jew, his rise from poverty to claim his first heavyweight championship title on July 4, 1919, resonated with the American public. Commercialism had not infiltrated professional sports, and athletes played merely for the love of the sport.

Bringing an event of this magnitude to Benton Harbor had been the dream of Floyd Fitzsimmons and the thrill of every prizefight fan with a means of transportation to the area. Dempsey liked and trusted Fitzsimmons, having first met him in Racine, Wisconsin, in 1918. The championship match would be held in a one-of-a-kind location, dubbed "Fitzsimmons Arena," located on the eastern edge of Benton Harbor on rural Britain Avenue and East Main Street, less than two miles from the Skalay home. The original Fitzsimmons property had begun as a ballpark in 1917 where the Benton Harbor Speed Boys became the inaugural team. In early 1920, a $100,000 boxing arena was added, set into a hollow of hard sand, then wetted and rolled until it baked in the sun, as solid as concrete; the highest bleacher point was only about five feet above the level land. The center of the ring was 115 feet from the last row of seats with three tiers of bleachers behind them.

Dempsey and his manager, Jack Kearns, arrived in Benton Harbor by train on August 15, 1920, having begun their journey in New York City.

Throngs of fans waited outside the train station to catch a glimpse of the larger-than-life Dempsey as he disembarked from the train. The "smiling hero of many" waved humbly to all those who greeted him. Fitzsimmons then escorted Dempsey and Kearns to their training camp. Dempsey started workouts the following morning and continued from that point by jogging along the area's rural roads, jumping rope, hitting a sandbag, and sparring in the ring with trainers. Dempsey ate steaks and other protein-rich foods to get to his desired weight of 188 pounds. Chuck Skalay may have caught a glimpse of Dempsey jogging along the road or otherwise training at the resort.

Newspaper reporters and sports enthusiasts followed Dempsey's every move before the match, which was now being hailed early on as the "Slaughter on Fair Avenue." When reporters asked about his impression of Miske, Dempsey commented, "He has a very snappy punch that is powerful enough to knock any one out. Of course, I expect to win, but I do not expect a cake walk or anything that resembles it."[21]

Dempsey's opponent arrived in Benton Harbor on August 21, 1920. Miske began his regimen of training at Eastman Springs Resort, three quarters of a mile up the road from the Fitzsimmons Arena. Appearing confident, Miske told reporters, "I didn't come to Benton Harbor to get licked."[22]

The public was not aware of it at the time, but Billy Miske was very ill. His doctor had given him a death sentence two years earlier for "Bright's Disease," or kidney failure.

In the week leading up to the fight, newspaper reporters speculated who appeared in better shape as each fighter's manager spoke out on the progress after each day's training. Fans clamored to catch sight of these larger-than-life men and the public could not get enough of the coverage. Chuck Skalay may well have been one of those fans. At times Dempsey himself donned a pair of overalls, picked up a hammer or a spade, and helped workers who were bringing in more bleachers for the arena. The foreman finally put his foot down because the workers were too distracted from watching Dempsey. The champion told the foreman, "I'd been glad many a time to get two dollars a day for this kind of work."[23] Dempsey never forgot where he came from.

The previously smaller Fitzsimmons Arena had been used for the first time on July 5, 1920, when lightweight champion Benny Leonard defended his title against Charlie White.[24] That night, Leonard had received some help from the unlikeliest of people, a gangster. Once Leonard signed on with Fitzsimmons, he began a regimen of training in Chicago. After one particular session, he retired to his hotel room for the night and was surprised to hear a rap on the door. Leonard opened it to find three brutes standing in front of him. The five-foot-five-inch, 130-pound Leonard knew what a hard guy looked like, and here were three of them. One of the men said, "Hey, Champ, the Big Fella wants to see you. We're supposed to bring you there."

Leonard knew this was more than a social visit. In fact, the only "Big Fella" he knew in Chicago at the time was Al Capone. There was plenty of talk on the streets and he knew well enough to go along with the three men. They arrived at another hotel, where the "Big Fella" himself awaited. Capone greeted Leonard warmly and invited him to have a seat in his office.

"I always wanted to meet you because I like the way you fight," Capone remarked, while puffing on his cigar. "You're a champ, and I'm a champ."

Leonard appreciated the acknowledgment, although he felt there was something more to the visit, but Capone ended the meeting when he stood up and added, "Look, champ, if you ever want a favor some time, come and see me."

Somewhat dismayed by the invitation, Leonard returned to his room and continued his training the following day. Not long before the scheduled match in Benton Harbor, Leonard got wind of a rumor floating around. Fitzsimmons always paid the fighters in cash taken directly from the box office, and if he won Leonard would get $40,000 cash. He heard that some hoods were planning to rob him of his prize winnings while he was on his way back to Chicago, and he began to worry that the rumor would prove to be true. He thought back to the offer Capone had given him and immediately decided to pay him a visit.

Here he was, face to face with the "Big Fella" once again; however, this time it was to take him up on his offer. Capone looked over Leonard steadily for a while and then said, "Look, kid, I'm gonna tell you something. There ain't gonna be no such hijacking and you have my word on that."

Feeling a sense of relief, Leonard went ahead with the fight in Benton Harbor on July 5, walking away with the lightweight championship title once again. After collecting his cash from Fitzsimmons, he returned to Chicago without a hint of trouble. Capone, it appeared, was a man of his word.[25]

The "Big Fella" was a syndicate apprentice who coincidentally shared his 21st birthday with the onset of national Prohibition. Although already quite notorious in New York, Capone had taken up an offer from Johnny Torrio, a former Five Points Gang member who had moved to Chicago to work under crime boss "Big Jim" Colosimo. Torrio invited Capone to the Windy City in 1918, where the experienced delinquent served as a bouncer at Torrio's headquarters, The Four Deuces, at 2222 South Wabash Avenue. The club offered booze, prostitution, gambling, and other vices. Impressed with the aspiring

Capone, Torrio quickly promoted him to manager, where he immediately established his presence and ruthless reputation in the racketeering business that Prohibition had ushered in.

On May 11, 1920, "Big Jim" Colosimo was taken down in gangland style, allowing for a division of turfs and new leaders. Torrio and his trusted lieutenant, Al Capone, took control of the South Side, while Dean O'Banion got control of the North Side. Capone established himself as a dedicated and trusted follower of Torrio, and took full advantage of the opportunity when he heard about the upcoming Dempsey-Miske fight. The city of Benton Harbor was now attracting big names, and not all of them were on the "up and up."

Capone made the trip to Benton Harbor in late August 1920, his first known appearance in the area. Here was one of Torrio's top lieutenants strolling along the same paths that the curious Chuck Skalay had taken to lay eyes on the champion. While Chuck could only view from afar, Capone created his own free rein in Benton Harbor.

Capone arrived at Dempsey's training camp wearing a wide-brimmed hat and short-sleeved white shirt. His bodyguards instructed reporters and fans to put away their cameras, saying "Mr. Capone don't want no pictures today."

Capone barged into Dempsey's personal dressing room where the unsuspecting Dempsey stood alone; he smiled and took the cigar out of his mouth. "You know who I am, Champ?" he asked.

"Sure, I know you," remarked Dempsey, as he looked around at the entourage of bodyguards.

"I'm a big fan of yours, Champ. I like boxing and I think you're a great fighter," Capone said while gesturing with his cigar. "I own a private club in Chicago and I want you to fight some exhibitions there for me." Capone then pulled out a roll of bills from his pocket and began thumbing through them. "Name your price and you've got it."

Dempsey, like Benny Leonard, was very aware of who Capone was and what he represented, perhaps recalling the fixed 1919 World Series, coined the "Chicago Black Sox Scandal," when eight players on the White Sox intentionally lost the World Series to the Cincinnati Reds for a payoff by New York Jewish gangster Arnold Rothstein.

Fanning the bills, "Champ, did you ever see so much money in your life?" Capone asked Dempsey.

This was indeed the most money Dempsey had ever seen, but his instinct kicked in and he thought about all that he had worked for up until now. Accepting any offer would mean fixed fights, Capone taking over as promoter, and shakedowns by thugs, killers, and bullies. Dempsey shook his head, "I can't do that. Thanks, Mr. Capone, but no."[26]

Still smiling with the cigar between his teeth, Capone folded up the wad of bills and quietly left the dressing room after Dempsey snubbed him. The act of standing up to Capone was a risky one; however, Dempsey found Capone rather interesting, and the snub would not keep him away.

As the Dempsey-Miske fight day approached, scores of visitors filled the hotels and eateries. "Standing Room Only" folding boards were set up at most businesses. Benton Harbor's city population of over 12,000 increased by about 5,000 in a matter of days. On September 6, the *New York Tribune* described the scene, "Down the bluffs that half circle the two cities by Lake Michigan, automobiles coasted by the dozens, and long before the fight, there was one of the largest assemblages of cars ever seen in the Middle West."[27]

Many fans had already been waiting overnight outside of the arena for a chance to buy tickets, even suffering through downpours. Prices started at $2 but the best seats went for between $25 and $30, which was more than a week's salary for most. By noon, all the bleachers had filled and only small sections of reserved seats remained. Sales had already reached the $90,000 mark.[28] Spectators numbered a reported 11,348.[29]

At 6:00 p.m., Miske entered the ring wearing a dark robe and immediately took his place in the southeast corner. Dempsey arrived just 12 minutes later, wearing a red sweater and white silk trunks. After the referee spent a few moments with each fighter, he called both men to the center of the ring. Dempsey saw a sick man standing before him and at that moment decided to finish the match as quickly and painlessly as possible. The clang of the bell signaled the start of the 10-round match. Within 90 seconds in the first round, it was clear Dempsey had the lead and, ultimately, the prize. Dempsey was happy, but not elated, because he approached the fight as a job, admiring Miske for his tenacity in fighting when he was so ill. Dempsey later wrote, "I knocked him out because I loved the guy."

Miske would succumb to his disease three years later.

For retaining his heavyweight championship status, Dempsey received $55,000, while Miske received $25,000. Receipts at the Benton Harbor match totaled $134,904, but deductions for state and war taxes brought the amount down to $109,376.[30] For those lucky enough to witness the fight, it was the most exciting day in Benton Harbor history.

Chuck Skalay probably wished he could have seen Dempsey fight in person but would have figured there would be another time. Champions always defend their title and maybe then he would be able to sit ringside.

Benton Harbor, Michigan, boxing promoter Floyd Fitzsimmons (left) with Heavyweight Champion Boxer Jack Dempsey. *Author's collection.*

A New Blue Coat on the Beat

PUBLIC SENTIMENTS ABOUT PROHIBITION CONTINUED TO fill newspapers with both "wet" and "dry" propaganda, but on September 25, 1921, almost two years after the law was written, the head of Chicago's police department added his assessment: "Prohibition enforcement in Chicago is a joke," slammed Chief Charles C. Fitzmorris. In his interview with the *New York Times,* he went on to say, "That statement not only goes for the police department, but for the citizenry. Thousands of Chicagoans are interested in violating the Prohibition laws every day. In Chicago, there is more drunkenness than ever, more deaths from liquor than before Prohibition, more of every evil attribute to the use of liquor than in the days of before the so-called Prohibition laws became 'effec'tive.'"

Fitzmorris learned that literally half of the police force of over 5,000 officers might have violated liquor laws. He intended to dismiss every man implicated in the crimes and fully cooperated with the United States district attorney during the investigation.[31]

"Chicago is like a dry farm needing water," related Fitzmorris, "and the Prohibition Enforcement Office is as futile as any group of men would be who tried to stop the rain and prevent the ground from soaking up the moisture. The only way to make Prohibition an actuality here or anywhere else is to stop the liquor at its source."[32]

CHUCK SKALAY PROBABLY HAD little knowledge of what was taking place in Chicago because schoolwork and family took up all of his time. In fact, his sister Olga had married Max Moulds on July 24, 1920, one month before the Dempsey fight.[33] Chuck had been preoccupied with the sports section of the newspaper and hardly noticed Olga's absence from the house. On July 9, 1922, almost exactly two years after the marriage, a beautiful baby daughter came into the world. The couple named her Mary Emma Moulds, certainly in honor of the grandmother she would never know. Mary Emma quickly became the apple of Uncle Chuck's eye. His little niece fascinated him and he loved to hold her. As she grew into a young girl, Mary Emma always anticipated Sunday afternoons with Uncle Chuck. He would take her for long rides in his convertible, watching her giggle at every sharp turn. When Chuck finally brought Mary Emma home, her pockets were overflowing with candy and toys. Olga loved the expression on Chuck's face every time he was with Mary Emma and she knew he would make a doting father someday.

Widower Gustav Skalay continued to support the household by working extended hours, but he did not let that stop him from getting out and sharing with the community. On a frigid day in January 1923, Gustav took the students and teachers of River School in Sodus out for their first sleigh ride of the season, spending two hours enjoying the snow-filled scenery of Kings Landing and the surrounding Sodus farmland they all knew so well. Afterward, the owners of the Peterson Resort opened up the facility and treated everyone to sandwiches and hot chocolate.

After a respectful time of mourning, Gustav decided to remarry. On a blustery cold March 31, 1923, he and Bertha Krause Schonert[34] took their vows at the Church of God in St. Joseph, with the Reverend Gustav Butgereit officiating.[35] The new Mrs. Skalay was a 32-year-old German who had immigrated to the United States in 1921, bringing along her daughter, Alice, from a previous marriage.[36] Both Alice and the youngest Skalay sibling, Elsie, were five years old. While all seemed well at first, the tight family bond would become splintered over the next few years when stepmother Bertha exposed the Skalay children to violent outbursts.

As Chuck Skalay grew from his adolescence, he saw a world full of opportunities in the prosperous post-war era. In June 1923, at the age of 19, he ventured out and began working as a driver for the Yellow Cab Company, located at 20 West Main in Benton Harbor. The company proprietor, 21-year-old William Barry, took an immediate liking to Chuck. The two young men often encountered city officials, tourists, regular townsfolk, and even seedier characters among their clientele. Chuck soon found this aspect of the job exciting. The two would share stories of who rode in the cab each day and all the latest town gossip, and when business was slow, Barry would spend time hanging around the Berrien County Sheriff's Department and partaking in the bull sessions. Listening to the deputies replay tales of liquor raids and bank robberies piqued his interest.[37] Barry could imagine himself as a police officer and he would soon get that chance.

Chuck took to his new job, and quickly became accustomed to the long hours and the sometimes-questionable characters in his cab. On the night of July 3, 1923, he summoned the police when two drunken Chicago men began fighting with him near the Graham & Morton boat docks along the Morrison Channel. Chuck might have envisioned Jack Dempsey in the ring as he defended himself against the drunks. When Benton Harbor officer Ernest Hardke and night chief Clyde Sink arrived, they arrested and lodged the agitated Chicagoans at the Berrien County Jail. By this time, Chuck realized there were plenty of people who did not take Prohibition seriously. The news that circulated in the papers confirmed that there was no shortage of alcohol anywhere in the Twin Cities or in the rest of the state.

Chuck likely read in the *News-Palladium* that on September 25, 1923, opening statements in the State of Michigan *vs.* Alex Goldbaum trial had begun in Berrien County Circuit Court. Goldbaum faced second-degree murder charges for selling poisonous alcohol to a 21-year-old Hotel Benton clerk, Lawrence Vincent Murphy. This was the first case of its kind in the state. Prosecutor Charles W. Gore accused the former Regent poolroom proprietor, Goldbaum, of selling four pints of moonshine liquor to Murphy, which had resulted in his death on August 20, 1923. Physician Carl A. Mitchell had determined that Murphy's death was due to wood alcohol poisoning. An investigation revealed that Murphy drank a small amount of the liquor to ease some stomach trouble he had been having. He was working as the desk clerk at the time and when the liquor seemed to worsen the pain, he called his boss and asked if he could go home. Once there, his condition further deteriorated until he collapsed and died. This occurred on the heels of a police raid on August 6, which closed the Regent's doors for operating a business without a license. Working as a taxi driver, Chuck surely knew where the Regent was, and may have even encountered Goldbaum and Murphy.

In reaction to the case of using bootleg liquor to treat general ills, Dr. Mitchell cautioned the public, telling reporters, "Liquor these days is becoming more and more poisonous. To take only a small quantity for supposedly medicinal purposes is flirting with the undertaker."[38]

The four-day trial featured a pathologist and chemist from the University of Michigan and other key witnesses. Defense counsel John J. Sterling acknowledged that Murphy died from drinking liquor, but adamantly denied that the liquor sold to him by Goldbaum was responsible for his death. Prosecutor Gore could not prove the case and the state dropped the murder charges. Goldbaum pleaded guilty to liquor law violations.

Although Chuck Skalay never considered taking a drink from a bootlegger, others in the area certainly did. The Goldbaum case had little effect on curbing what was becoming a widespread epidemic. Alcohol was making its way through each community, and law enforcement officials had the daunting task of trying to seal off the pipeline. As the number of rumrunners increased on the Detroit River, Commissioner Oscar G. Olander, head of the Michigan Department of Public Safety, attempted to quash the activity through the "Dry Navy" and "Sponge Squads," specialty teams of officers devoted strictly to enforcing the liquor laws. The city of Detroit was the conduit for 75 percent of all the beer and liquor that entered into the United States from Canada.[39] While many officers guarded the crossing points, others did what they could to get rid of the product within their jurisdictions.

As the hooch trade thrived in Southwestern Michigan, despite the laws banning it, the Yellow Cab Company faced fierce competition from other taxi services over the next year and William Barry's business declined, eventually forcing him to close his company. In early 1925, Barry's interest in police work paid off when he accepted a job as a county truancy officer with the Berrien County Sheriff's Department. He joined Benton Harbor's truancy officer, 37-year-old Edith B. Crowhurst, who started in 1924 as the first female police officer within the department. Barry had married his sweetheart, Helen Lutter, in November 1923 and was happy to have a more stable job. He kept his equally curious pal, Chuck, informed about his new job as Chuck sought out a new job for himself.

Barry soon transitioned from truancy officer to the police force when, in early 1926, he was sworn in as a deputy sheriff.[40] No one was more excited than Chuck because now he would be able to hear all the stories about liquor raids, fights, arrests, and more from someone who knew. *What a thrilling job*, Chuck must have thought.

Barry realized that Chuck's curiosity and drive were much the same as his own. Chuck was certainly on the straight and narrow path. He was also persistent and compassionate, levelheaded and fair, and he could take care of himself in a fight. He had the right combination of characteristics to work in law enforcement. Barry suggested that Chuck approach Chief Fred Alden at the St. Joseph Police Department. As Chuck pondered the idea, he realized that could be the opportunity of a lifetime. Barry then revealed a little secret to Chuck: Chief Alden was actually his uncle, and Barry assured the eager 22-year-old that the job would be his if he wanted it.

It did not take Chuck long to find himself at the steps of the St. Joseph Police Department and even less time for Chief Alden to hire him. The new career prompted a new identity. Wanting to have a more pronounceable name, Chuck dropped "Skalay" and adopted the Americanized version of

"Skelly," a spelling his siblings would also choose, while his cousins opted to change their name to "Skelley." Only patriarchs Gustav and William retained the Skalay spelling. Charles Skelly emerged in early April 1926, becoming a member of the police department, or rather a "blue coat," as they were known. The St. Joseph Police Department had only employed three full-time paid officers since 1900—John Karstens, Ben Phairas, and David Hunter—and Skelly made history by becoming the fourth. They had no squad cars or radios, just pairs of well-worn boots with plenty of miles on them. Officers normally worked 6 a.m. to 6 p.m., seven days a week, while their counterparts at Benton Harbor had one day off. Skelly, like the other St. Joseph police officers, was paid $125 per month; they were all required to purchase their own uniforms and accessories, including Sam Browne belts (thick leather belts with a cross strap), puttees (long narrow strips of cloth that wound tightly over ankles and calves for protection), guns, ammunition, handcuffs, and blackjacks (leather billy clubs).

Soon, Skelly settled into an apartment at 212½ State Street in downtown St. Joseph, excited to be on his own. A bond immediately formed under the leadership of Chief Alden. The young Skelly looked up to 62-year-old Alden, 40 years his senior, and learned all he could from the man who would become his biggest advocate. Skelly probably welcomed the guidance, knowing that his own father had a new wife who demanded most of his attention. Alden never had any children himself and saw Skelly much like a son.

Fred Eugene Alden was born in 1866 to one of Berrien County's pioneer families, and he felt a dedication to public service from early on. Alden began his career as a member of the St. Joseph Life-Saving Station, the precursor to the United States Coast Guard. The maritime rescue season typically spanned April 1 to November 30, and the seven crewmembers and one captain trained rigorously in their rowboats. His physical ability and stance had impressed not only Mary Ryan, whom he married in December 1896, but also a well-known sculptor who was in search of the perfect model.

In honor of five St. Joseph firefighters who tragically lost their lives in the Yore Opera House fire on September 5, 1896, the department had raised money to erect a monument affixed with a bronze statue depicting a heroic rescue by a firefighter. Alden modeled for the New York architect and sculptor W. Liance Cottrell, who personally selected him for his brawny form. He replicated the pose of a firefighter while holding five-year-old Mabel Schneider, also of St. Joseph, in his arms. The American Bronze Company of Chicago then cast the statue and the Harrison Granite Company of Vermont constructed the base. The monument was unveiled on September 5, 1898, two years to the date after the tragedy, and it would still be standing more than a century later.

His work on the Life-Saving Service had led Alden to a position in the police force. In 1903, the mayor of St. Joseph appointed him as "special police without pay." His outstanding performance and dedication during the next several years set him on a journey that would lead to his promotion as a paid chief in May 1912,[41] in fact, the youngest chief at the age of 48. The department consisted of Alden and two other officers, 34-year-old Delwin Fisher and 56-year-old David Hunter. A month later, Alden became the first police chief in Berrien County to carry a gun while on duty—a Smith and Wesson .38-caliber pistol. He was especially noted for his compassion. Alden believed in taking youthful offenders into his office for a fatherly talk rather than sending them to reform school. He felt that jail was a last resort, if all else failed.

Skelly and Alden may have become close because they both had dealt with so much grief. In 1909, Alden's 11-year-old nephew, Victor, was accidentally shot and killed in a hunting accident. Then his sister-in-law, Nora Ryan, died in 1914 after extended health problems. He experienced more loss when two brothers died: Arthur in 1922 and Ola in a 1926 car accident. Despite his losses, or maybe because of them, Alden became a philanthropist. In 1914, he began going to all the downtown merchants at Christmastime, collecting donations to purchase candy and trinkets for Santa Claus to distribute to children on Christmas Eve at the brightly lit center attraction on State and Pleasant Streets. Alden continued this festive tradition for many years. Skelly knew that Christmas was a joyous time in St. Joseph, Michigan, and quickly offered his hand at ensuring it always would be.

By the close of 1926, Skelly had racked up 35 arrests ranging from traffic violations to drunkenness; he had even arrested a few prominent citizens in the area. His dedication to enforcing the law equally for all earned him the utmost respect from the community. Alden was proud of the young man he had hired and trained, believing that Skelly would have a long career in law enforcement ahead of him.

Charles Skelly as he appeared working for the Yellow Taxi Company in Benton Harbor, Michigan, circa 1925. *Courtesy of the Berrien County Sheriff's Department.*

Firemen's Monument in St. Joseph, Michigan, depicting a heroic firefighter as modeled by St. Joseph Police Chief Fred Alden in 1896. *Author's collection.*

BOOTLEGGERS AND BAD GUYS

AS THE VICTORIAN-ERA IRISH PLAYWRIGHT AND POET
Oscar Wilde once said, "You can't make people good by an act of
Parliament." In the Prohibition Era, his statement still had compa-
rable meaning. Bootlegging operations were alive and well within Michigan
and the boundaries of Berrien County during the 1920s, just as they were
around the nation. The industry flourished in spite of laws banning it. Some
people had ventured into the liquor trade from the moment it became illegal,
while others saw those advantages only in later years. The sight of clogged
exhaust vents on roofs used to disperse the dangerous gases and the sound of
constant running water to keep still coils cool became more prevalent. Many
farmers began dabbling in the bootlegging trade. The temptation of high
profits was just too great when times were tough. Corn as a food product
had been selling at about a dollar per bushel, while the same amount of corn
sold to a distillery could bring in multiples of that amount. The conditions
in Southwestern Michigan were ideal for corn and fruit harvesting, resulting
in abundant produce for not only consumption but also for bootleggers in
the region, especially those in Chicago, which began to cast dark shadows on
what had previously been peaceful communities.

Undoubtedly, bootlegging activities brought about a surge in violence. In
1926 alone, the city of Chicago recorded 510 homicides, making it the murder capital of the country. That same year, Detroit reached 313 homicides,
while New York City, the most populous city in the nation, had 340. Even
the smaller metropolitan areas experienced violence: Jacksonville, Florida,
had 104 homicides; Memphis, Tennessee, 75; and Grand Rapids, Michigan,
2. In mid-December 1926, after an increase in homicides for the year, police
departments within Wayne County, Michigan, including Detroit, Highland
Park, and Hamtramck, began a cycle of 12-hour shifts with more officers
under Commissioner William P. Rutledge. Highland Park outfitted its squad

cars with 10-inch-long shotguns, which fired like revolvers in both 12 and 20 gauges. Violence became a byproduct of Prohibition and only some authorities attempted to counter it.

In Southwestern Michigan, the Berrien County Sheriff's Department conducted liquor raids all over the county, targeting "blind pigs," or speakeasies, such as Benton Harbor's Higman Park Inn, The Yellow Cat Lunchroom, The Belmont Soda Shop, Casey's Place, Stevensville's Spaghetti Inn, and Dad's Lunch Stand in Bridgman, because law enforcement authorities knew these businesses sold alcohol illegally. Some bootleggers kept a lower profile. Italian-born, Benton Harbor farmer Tony Domingo saw no choice but to venture into bootlegging as a means to provide for his wife, Mary, and their daughter, Matilda. His brother-in-law, Frank DiMaria, had already launched an illegal alcohol production business. In July 1925, Berrien County sheriff's deputies found a 50-gallon still at the DiMaria residence, 418 Riford Street in Benton Harbor. After he posted the standard $500 bond, DiMaria was allowed to remain free until his court appearance, but his criminal self-interests would serve up the necessary justice in another form.

On December 31, six-year-old Matilda Domingo spent the day at the Riford Street residence of her grandparents, along with her 10-year-old uncle, Leo DiMaria. While playing in the living room, Leo found a .38-caliber nickel-plated revolver hidden in the cushions of a couch. Without any warning, the gun fired and Matilda suffered a fatal wound.[42] Leo told the police that the gun belonged to a Chicago man who had visited the day before, undoubtedly an underworld associate of Frank DiMaria and Tony Domingo.

Bootlegging turned tragic for the family again in August the following year, while Frank DiMaria and his younger brother, Sam, were working in the Domingo barn. Sam fell into the giant vat filled with sugar corn mash. He cried out for help and his brother climbed to the top to pull him out, but Frank too fell in and the men slowly became incapacitated by the ethyl alcohol vapor. Inhaling the poison depresses the central nervous system and irritates the respiratory tract. The brothers eventually slipped into unconsciousness and died. Sam and Frank DiMaria's double funeral was a grand affair. A brass band marched from St. John's Catholic Church with Father F. A. Lewis in the lead to Calvary Cemetery, a distance of five miles.[43]

Despite these high-profile accidents, illegal alcohol production in Benton Harbor did not wane. The city of St. Joseph, however, had more problems with alcohol consumption than its manufacture. Working to end the problem were Chief Alden and Officer Skelly, who operated in partnership on the job like a well-oiled machine. This would come in handy when Earl

Wood, owner of the Neighborhood Coal Company on Niles Avenue, took a few too many spirits on the eve of St. Patrick's Day in 1927. He caused quite the scene with his canine companion at the corner of Broad and State Streets. Alden and Skelly managed to escort the man to City Hall with some of his celebratory fanfare left to express. The dog may have sensed his own marked time, considering that he latched hold of Skelly's pant leg during the arrest process. Nevertheless, the drunken man and his dog shared a cell together. Wood seemed content, but suddenly he felt the need to express himself vocally while a city council meeting was taking place on the floor above.[44] Skelly would have let out a chuckle had he heard the bellows of Wood and howls of his furry best friend interrupting the official meeting. The city leaders probably were not laughing.

Skelly had to deal with his share of seedier citizens, but even the well-bred caused problems. In April 1927, when the affluent Robert J. Watts referred to his equally affluent associate, Conant H. Hatch, with a derogatory name, the simple act of character assassination turned into fisticuffs. When Hatch demanded an apology and did not receive one, he poked Watts in the nose. The two men began punching each other in front of passing motorists and pedestrians. Officer Skelly had to intervene to separate them. After straightening his jacket and composing himself, Watts filled out the paperwork for an assault charge, while Hatch was sent over to Justice Joseph R. Collier's court, where he paid a fine of $5. Whether he was investigating a mugging or dealing with the plethora of drunken and disorderly townsfolk, Skelly was always the consummate professional.

Meanwhile, in rural Benton Harbor, Tony and Mary Domingo continued their bootlegging ventures, unaware that the tragic vat accident on their property had brought them some newfound attention, most notably from the Berrien County Sheriff's Department. Fred G. Bryant, a 19-year law enforcement veteran from Benton Harbor and newly elected sheriff of Berrien County as of New Year's Day 1927, kept a close watch on the Domingos. He knew their bootlegging operation was the largest in Berrien County, as well as one of the largest in the state at the time. He launched an investigation of the DiMaria brothers' vat deaths and conducted two more raids in April 1927, one at the Domingo farm and the other at a distillery hidden on a hilltop farm near an area known as Twelve Corners. Bryant and fellow deputies took Domingo into custody and recovered 118 gallons of sugar moonshine in five-gallon tin containers, 13,000 gallons of mash in barrels, three 80-gallon stills, and other distillery equipment consisting of 11 1,000-gallon vats, a number of barrels used for mash, a huge upright boiler, and a stove. The officers noted that the stove was warm when they arrived and the fire stoked. The hilltop farm distillery, they estimated, was capable of producing 240 gallons of liquor daily and Sheriff Bryant believed that this raid had just cut off the major supplier of liquor in Berrien County. Not even the senseless deaths of his young brothers-in-law or his own daughter had stopped Domingo from engaging in this lethal and illegal profession.

Two months later, a routine day of patrols in St. Joseph turned deadly when 23-year-old St. Joseph Police motorcycle officer Francis LaMunion was involved in a serious traffic accident. On the job for just over a month, Officer LaMunion was attempting to stop a speeding motorist when he collided with a Barlow Laundry delivery truck at the corner of Court and Ship Streets, hurling LaMunion onto the pavement. Although the speeder escaped apprehension, the officer and delivery truck driver, R. J. Lavanway, appeared fine so both men went home. However, the next day, on June 23, LaMunion was not fine. Family members rushed him to St. Joseph Sanitarium, where surgeons performed an emergency operation and determined that he had suffered massive internal injuries. Before he lost consciousness, the officer exonerated the delivery driver of any blame. Sadly, Officer LaMunion did not survive and became the first St. Joseph police officer to die in the line of duty. Skelly's loss of a friend and coworker probably disturbed him immensely, since they were the same age. Another grim reminder of how short life could be may have inspired Skelly to take advantage of the opportunities before him.

More tragedy would come to the Domingo family because of their involvement in bootlegging. On October 22, 1927, just six months after the raid, at about 9:00 a.m., the Domingos were returning to their farm from a trip into Benton Harbor. Domingo was driving the truck while his wife, Mary, followed behind in the Ford coupe. About a mile from their family farm, the Ford exploded into flames. Domingo slammed on the brakes, turned the truck around, and rushed back to the scene. He spotted Mary's lifeless body lying near the burning wreckage, so bloody and mutilated she was barely recognizable. Hardly anything remained of the car. Parts of the vehicle had landed as far as 500 feet away while torn pieces of Mary's clothing and automobile upholstery were hanging in the uppermost branches of nearby trees. A tire landed on a nearby farm, 500 yards away from the rest of the vehicle. The grief-stricken Domingo fell to his knees and cried out, "O, mama, mia," repeatedly, as he tugged at his hair.

The chief deputy, Ray Hall, and coroner George Slaughter soon reached the scene, and after studying the wreckage, they determined that someone had placed a bomb under the hood. The wiring went straight to the manifold.[45] Once the manifold got hot, the wire melted and set off an explosion so severe that it gouged out a large section of pavement. When Hall questioned Domingo about possible suspects, he said very little.

Authorities had barely cleared the scene and returned to the department when a hail of gunfire rang out in Benton Harbor's Little Italy district. With the help of his 17-year-old brother, Sebastiano, and repeating shotguns, Domingo shot at Benton Harbor grocer Louis Vieglo,[46] who was socializing at the Fourth Ward Republican Club on Territorial Road. Sebastiano missed a direct shot. Vieglo scrambled into his Oakland coupe parked near the curb and fled down an alley to Miller Street. Curious Italian residents peered out their doors with guns in hand, ready if needed. As Vieglo fled, Domingo sobbingly accused him of murdering his wife.[47] The bullet-filled frenzy in Little Italy did nothing more than stir up anger and bitterness as the Domingo brothers were hauled away to the Berrien County Jail by Chief Deputy Hall and Deputy Charles Andrews. They were booked on the vague charge of "suspicion" and released the next day.[48] Vieglo immediately left town.

The bombing and subsequent attack were the talk at the police departments as Skelly and the other officers tried to make sense of the violence erupting before them and the flow of criminal elements into the once quiet, rural area. They would later learn that there was much more going on behind closed doors.

The attraction of visitors to the eastern side of Lake Michigan had to do with convenience. U.S. Highway 12 connected Chicago and Detroit through Southwest Michigan. The highway got its start as an important travel corridor built over the Native Americans' Great Sauk Trail. The southern and eastern edge of Lake Michigan was alluring to not only the sightseer, but also to those who wanted to disappear for a while. With the rise of Al Capone and his syndicate, rural hideouts and retreats peppered the area amid the sprawling beaches and fruit farms.

Capone had been ruling the south side of Chicago ever since Johnny Torrio retired in 1925. Earl "Hymie" Weiss took over control of the north side in November 1924 after Dean O'Banion was knocked off. Bitter feuds brewed among the gangs, but ultimately Capone proved more durable after multiple attempts on his life. A small vestige of revenge came to Capone when he had Weiss gunned down on October 11, 1926, in front of Chicago's Holy Name Cathedral. Vincent "The Schemer" Drucci then took on the leadership of the North Side Gang for about six months, before Chicago Police detective Daniel F. Healy killed him on April 4, 1927. Then the door opened for George "Bugs" Moran to establish himself as the sole ruler of the North Side Gang.

Quite unexpectedly, the streets of Chicago calmed down somewhat after this, but only for a short while. Meanwhile, the residents of Williamson, Jackson, and Franklin Counties in southern Illinois spoke out about the caustic and unfavorable criticisms hurled toward the state of Illinois for the bloodshed that had been taking place in Chicago. Certain people in Williamson County even offered to start up a fund "to help clean up the dirty blot on the state of Illinois–Chicago." The public urged Chicago to eradicate the problem.

Having garnered a following by the morbidly curious media, Al Capone reveled in the opportunities to cast his own image on the American people, one less about murder and more about public service. Oddly enough, Capone held a press conference in mid-December 1927 expressing his dissatisfaction with how the media portrayed him.

"I'm going to St. Petersburg, Florida, tomorrow. Let the worthy citizens of Chicago get their liquor the best they can. I'm sick of the job — it's a thankless one and full of grief. I don't know when I'll get back, if ever… I've been spending the best years of my life as a public benefactor. I've given people the light pleasures, shown them a good time. And all I get is abuse…I guess murder will stop. There won't be any more booze. You won't be able to find a craps game even, let alone a roulette wheel or a faro game… Public service is my motto. Ninety-nine percent of the people in Chicago drink and gamble. I've tried to serve them decent liquor and square games. But I'm not appreciated. It's no use…My wife and my mother hear so much about what a terrible criminal I am. It's getting too much for them and I'm just sick of it all, myself… Today I got a letter from a woman in England. Even over there I'm known as a gorilla. She offered to pay my passage to England if I'd kill some neighbors she's been having a quarrel with… I wish all my friends and enemies a Merry Christmas and a Happy New Year."[49]

ON MARCH 1, 1928, the St. Joseph Fire Department made a significant advancement by officially becoming a fully paid department. Up until this point, firefighters were volunteers from within the community, with little or no experience, led by a minimally compensated chief. Now volunteers would serve to supplement the full-time firefighters, improving response time and increasing the overall quality of fire suppression. Fire Chief William Hudson Mitchell needed an assistant to help manage the department and Charles Skelly was an obvious choice. He offered him the position. After pondering the offer for several days, Skelly decided to accept. He turned in his blue coat on March 6, 1928.[50] As second in command at the fire department, he led with the voracious work ethic instilled by his father. His blue coat comrades were never too far away. In fact, both the police and fire departments occupied the same building, so Skelly still heard about the raids and drunken brawls. His pal, William Barry, dealt with the same on a much wider scale by working at the Sheriff's Department. There would be many more incidents to come.

Those choosing the safety and peace of rural Berrien County over the big cities often found themselves no better off in the end. Violence even lurched into quiet recreational areas. Shortly after 9:00 a.m. on September 9, 1928, youngsters Kenneth Surger and Leland Kerr were walking along the Mizpah Park Beach just north of Benton Harbor when they stumbled across the lifeless body of a man, fully clothed and lying partly on a raft on the shore of Lake Michigan. The boys immediately ran home and alerted their parents, who notified Undersheriff Charles Johnson. He dispatched Deputies Charles Davis and John Lay to the scene, who then summoned the coroner, George Slaughter. A German Mauser pistol lay next to the body. Slaughter determined that the man, whom he believed to be Italian, had died from a dumdum, or hollow-tipped bullet, wound to the head.

Later that night, police found a torched 1926 Willys-Knight sedan on the Wickwire Bridge over the Paw Paw River, only a couple of miles from Mizpah Park Beach. The license plates were missing and authorities found a cap to a gasoline container on the ground next to the car and an empty gasoline can about a half mile down the road. In an attempt to locate the owner of the vehicle, Sheriff Bryant sent a wire to the Willys-Knight Automobile Company in Cleveland, Ohio. The only parts of the vehicle that contained a unique identifiable serial number were the engine and the chassis. The inquiry revealed that the owner of the vehicle was Chicagoan Frank Viscuso. The sheriff contacted Chicago's chief detective, John Stege, who told him that Viscuso had reported the car stolen early Sunday morning.

With the help of Detective Stege, Berrien County authorities concluded that the dead Italian man and burned car were tied in with a murder that had occurred two days earlier in Chicago. On September 7, one of Capone's top lieutenants, Antonio Lombardo, was gunned down during rush hour in Chicago's Loop. Two dum-dum bullets fired at close range pierced his brain. The body found on the beach in Benton Harbor fit the physical profile of the man seen running from the scene with a smoking gun in his hands, and the Mizpah Park location matched the vicinity of many syndicate retreats.

Sheriff Bryant knew that Capone and a few of his associates, gambling opera-tor Anthony "Mops" Volpe and chief gunner "Machine Gun" Jack McGurn, had visited Benton Harbor two weeks earlier. He theorized that perhaps the Italian whose body had been found had come to the area looking to get even with Capone, but was then spotted and "taken for a ride."[51] "An eye for an eye, and a tooth for a tooth," fit the gangland code.

Chicago authorities sent officers to the Slaughter Undertaking Parlor at 112 Pipestone Street in Benton Harbor, where they took fingerprints and Bertillon measurements of the body.[52] Alphonse Bertillon, a French crimi-nologist, had developed anthropometry in France during the 1800s. His technique based identification on common morphological characteristics: the specific shapes and measurements of the different parts of the body.[53] Fingerprinting had now become a long-overdue replacement for the compli-cated Bertillonage system. Using the Henry Classification System, each of the 10 fingerprints was assigned a value based on whorls, loops, and arches pres-ent, and then filed accordingly using these values. Older criminal records only contained Bertillon data and therefore both identification systems had to be used.

Chief Deputy Hall and Deputy Dave Tyner, both identification experts, also took a set of fingerprints and photographs for Berrien County. Unfor-tunately, after a thorough search of records Detective Stege informed Sheriff Bryant that the deceased did not match up with any known criminals on file. Criminal records were also checked in New York City and through the Bureau of Investigation.[54] No data ever surfaced tying to identify the Mizpah Beach body, as it was called, or tie the victim to the Lombardo murder.

The unsolved murder in Benton Harbor was filed away, for the time be-ing, while bootleggers turned up the heat in other parts of the county. On October 10, 1928, a suspicious fire in Bertrand Township, near the Indiana state line, uncovered yet another record liquor haul in Berrien County: a 500-gallon still, kettles, coils, 10 oil burners, and the remains of at least 68 sugar barrels.[55] With the nation deep into Prohibition, it seemed that few let their thirst for the fermented beverages diminish. Although a battleground raged between bootleggers and law enforcement, a playground had since emerged right in the heart of Southwestern Michigan and Northern Indiana.

CAPONE'S PLAYMATES

WHEN CHICAGO GANGSTERS AND THE CRIMINALLY noteworthy began to notice the amenities of St. Joseph and Benton Harbor, many purchased vacation homes there. Southwest Michigan and Northern Indiana became Capone's new playground.

Jake "Greasy Thumb" Guzik set himself up in an eight-room, two-story frame house with a barn, located on Lincoln Avenue near West Linco Road in Berrien County's rural Lincoln Township. Old-timers knew the cozy retreat as the William J. Taube place, but when Jake and his brother, Harry, bought it, they renamed it the "G and H Farm."[56] Guzik was a Jewish Russian immigrant who served as Capone's moneyman and ran the lucrative whorehouse industry within the syndicate. He was one of Capone's most trusted confidants, known as "The Fixer," "The Greaser," as in greasing the political wheels, and the "Treasurer of the Capone Gang," cultivating the highest respect from within; however, his financial power over more than just the syndicate may have provided another level of respect from authorities—that being the almighty dollar. He regularly made payoffs to anyone who tried to interfere with Capone's operations. After one of Guzik's arrests in Chicago, detectives asked him to take a lie detector test. "If I took a test," Guzik warned, "twenty of Chicago's biggest men would jump out of windows."[57]

Another dweller in the area was Capone bodyguard Louis "Little New York" Campagna, who in 1926 purchased an 80-acre estate along the St. Joseph River in Berrien Springs. He began raising cattle and hogs but eventually settled on growing alfalfa. Campagna was born in 1900 in Brooklyn, New York, leaving home at the age of 15 to join a theater group that toured Texas and California before eventually winding up in Chicago. He began work as a waiter and then as a member of the Teamsters Union. His small stature, at five-foot-five-inches tall, did not hamper Campagna's criminal career, which ranged from vagrancy and bank robbery to, allegedly, murder.[58]

Fierce Dobermans patrolled the Campagna property, which was surrounded by a 10-foot-high fence. The nameplate, "LA. BRUNS FARM," adorned the exterior wall. The house was one of the first in Berrien County to have a 110,000-gallon, in-ground tile swimming pool and bathhouse which, according to neighbors, purportedly was built by the Chicago Public Works. The main house featured four bedrooms, several bathrooms, a wraparound sun porch, study, and spaces for three cars. The study was the nerve center of the estate, equipped with remote controls for the yard lights, gates, floodlights, and an intercom network. The living room library was stocked with law books, one of Campagna's favorite topics. The property also had an underground sprinkler system, guesthouses, and stables. The estate became more of a summer retreat after Campagna purchased an 800-acre working farm in Fowler, Indiana, about 135 miles south of Berrien Springs and very close to the Illinois state line.

Edgar Kesterke, a young man, delivered meat to the estate when he worked at the Royal Blue Grocery and Meat Market. He would come in through the creaky iron gates and Mrs. Charlotte Campagna would hand him a $5 tip. Although he never saw Capone at Campagna's estate, Kesterke did recognize Charles "Cherry Nose" Gioe, a syndicate member who later served as lieutenant under Frank Nitti, Capone's successor.

Another Capone bodyguard, Phil D'Andrea, purchased a farmhouse on 10 acres in St. Joseph overlooking the St. Joseph River,[59] in an area known as Irish Hills.[60] This was D'Andrea's replacement retreat for the previous one just north of Benton Harbor, which burned to the ground one night.

Born in 1889 in Buffalo, New York, Philip Louis D'Andrea was a proud Italian standing five-feet-six-inches and weighing 165 pounds, with jet-black hair, a mustache, and glasses. He always dressed like an executive. D'Andrea had been with Johnny Torrio's gang since the early 1920s and had stuck with Capone when Torrio retired and leadership peacefully changed hands. He claimed to have attended the Hamilton School of Law in Chicago, but his experience ranged from selling insurance, the newspaper business, and the cartage business, to affiliating himself with the Teamsters & Truckers Union, as well as the Carriers Union in Chicago. When in Chicago, he stayed at the syndicate headquarters located in the Lexington Hotel, but regularly vacationed at his St. Joseph home. D'Andrea handled the bribes and payoffs, making sure that money kept law enforcement and any other officials content.

Deputy William Barry, Charles Skelly's pal, heard that D'Andrea was selling beer illegally out of his St. Joseph estate. He learned that someone would drive up to the gate and flash the car's dome light on and off to signal his arrival. A man would emerge from the house and place a couple sacks of beer into the vehicle, like an early form of the drive-in.

Besides Capone's inner-circle playmates, several other associates flocked to the area. St. Joseph and Benton Harbor became popular hangouts, but the villages of Lakeside and Union Pier, Michigan, also saw their share of activity. Capone himself spent time at the Lakeside Inn, where he would enjoy a game of cards with his entourage.[61] Chicago mayor Anton Cermak kept a summer home in Union Pier and frequently visited the Lakeside Inn before his untimely assassination in Miami in 1933.[62]

Within the winding lanes of Long Beach, Indiana, the beachside community just south of the Michigan and Indiana dividing line, wealthy Chicagoans from both sides of the law built their vacation homes. Cicero politician and racketeer Edward Konvalinka, a friend of Capone and his brothers, purchased a Spanish-style home there and named it "Belle Casa." He and his wife, Rose, often played golf, their favorite pastime, at the Long Beach Country Club.[63] Rose eventually opened up beauty shops in New Buffalo, Union Pier, and Three Oaks, Michigan, while their only son, Robert, attended the Culver Military Academy in Indiana. Although they seemed to fit in well with others in the community, the Konvalinkas reportedly invited outsiders into the area who may not have otherwise been welcome.

Edward Konvalinka's career started behind the counter of a soda shop, but he had political aspirations. As a Republican committeeman during the volatile 1924 Cook County, Illinois, elections, Konvalinka had made an offer to Johnny Torrio and Al Capone: If they could ensure that Cicero mayor Joseph Z. Klenha was re-elected, then he would allow the Torrio-Capone organization to set up operations with protection in Cicero. The election turned out to be one of the most violent and corrupt on record, even resulting in the death of Salvatore "Frank" Capone, Al's older brother. A favorite saying arose after the explosive election: "If you smell gunpowder, you're in Cicero."[64]

Paul "The Waiter" Ricca, a member of Capone's syndicate, also took up residency in the small village of Long Beach. Ricca was born as Felice DeLucia in 1898, in Italy. He immigrated to the United States in 1920 and became the manager of a restaurant located at 905 South Halstead Street in Chicago.[65] He often associated with D'Andrea, Gioe, Campagna, and others in his large, Tudor-styled mansion on four acres. The estate featured a tennis court, a semi-underground parking garage, a swimming pool, staff quarters, and a grand view of Lake Michigan.[66] He even had a house designed and built in the shape of a gun at 3001 Northmoor Trail for his sister, Mrs. James Nuzzo. Eventually, Notre Dame's football coach, Frank Leahy, purchased the home.[67]

The former assistant Illinois state's attorney, John F. Tyrrell, also had a vacation home in Long Beach. Known for his role as a prosecutor during the Chicago "Black Sox" scandal of 1919, Tyrrell worked for a Chicago law firm and had taken on clients affiliated with Capone. On January 9, 1929, this dangerous association came directly to him when an early morning explosion rocked the home, leveling the structure and hurling wooden boards into Lake Michigan some 200 feet away. No one was home at the time, but authorities determined that the explosion was the result of a bomb placed in the basement, likely tied to gangster activity. However, Tyrrell suggested that a kerosene stove was the cause of the explosion, probably to take the focus off of gangland and prevent further attempts on his life.

With so many playmates and favorite pastimes within close proximity, Capone's Playground was in full operation, featuring the lavish Whitcomb Hotel in St. Joseph, Hotel Vincent in Benton Harbor, the Berrien Hills Country Club, and the Twin City Golf and Aviation Club, the "Little Italy" district, and the House of David Amusement Park with its remarkable semi-professional baseball team. The religious commune had established itself in Benton Harbor in 1903, and members followed a strict vegetarian diet, celibacy, no alcohol or tobacco use, and, most notably, uncut hair and unshaven faces. The miniature train at the park was a favorite of Capone, as was the baseball team with the players' signature attire of long hair and beards. Capone referred to the players as "the men that look like girls."

Reportedly, Capone attended a practice session but was disappointed that the players had tucked their hair into their baseball caps. He yelled to the players, "Show me your hair, I wanna see your hair." They ignored the gang chieftain's request.

Capone and his playmates took pleasure in the fare of Benton Harbor's "Little Italy" district as well as visiting various homes. Feeling little resistance from residents, Capone felt welcome to a certain extent. Even the most conservative rural farmer could look past certain inexcusable behavior because of Capone's generous cash tips and purchases. With new roads to access the southern and eastern edges of Lake Michigan, the amenities and offerings were the reasons why members of Chicago's South Side Outfit kept coming back. As the nine-foot dirt paths of 1913 morphed into the 20-foot concrete highways of 1928, Benton Harbor's Hotel Vincent attracted the "Who's Who," and eventually Capone received an invitation directly from management. The Hotel Vincent would become Capone's headquarters in his new playground.

William Bastar, a well-respected entrepreneur from Benton Harbor and a former business associate, called upon Daniel J. O'Connor of Chicago, Illinois, to invest in a luxury hotel project, which he agreed to, relocating to Benton Harbor in 1925. The Hotel Vincent celebrated its grand opening on June 1, 1925, with O'Connor as proprietor and stockholder. The hotel was an extravagance of the day, with eight floors, 151 guest rooms, and lavish banquet halls, all located in the heart of the city. The most modern of kitchens for the time employed 30 people, led by manager Leon Joseph Du Breuile and chef Henry Aberlie. They utilized Garland gas ranges and a Hubbard stove, with promises to bring the finest in meal preparation to the area. Two electric signs planted high above the sidewalk spelled out HOTEL VINCENT, one sign facing east and the other facing west, which could be seen in all directions.

Attracting not only the visiting tourist, the hotel was equally suited for the working-minded who were in town for business. On July 9, 1926, the Benton Harbor Exchange Club sponsored a gubernatorial debate within the Hotel Vincent. General Fred W. Green was going up against current Michigan governor Alex J. Groesbeck for the Republican nomination, while Democratic candidate W. A. Comstock faced no opposition in the race. Ultimately, the voters elected Fred Green: He would serve from 1927 to 1930. Aside from the campaign trail, the Hotel Vincent was a star on the map of the Michigan State Judge's Association. On September 9, 1926, two Michigan Supreme Court justices decided to make the Hotel Vincent their choice of accommodations while in town for the association gathering at the Berrien County Courthouse.

Daniel J. O'Connor might have had other reasons to leave Chicago and start up a new business venture. In May 1924, he was one of several people arrested during a raid at the Sieben Brewery, owned by South Side Gang leader Johnny Torrio and North Side Gang leader Dean O'Banion, at a time when the two men were peaceful business partners. The brewery had just received 13 truckloads of beer when authorities swooped in and arrested the rumrunners, including Torrio and O'Banion. O'Connor originally identified himself as James Casey when arrested; nonetheless, a little black book found at the scene revealed his true name and affiliations. Besides his association with gang leaders, O'Connor mixed with some notable political figures including Illinois governor Edward F. Dunne and Cook County treasurer William L. O'Connell, for whom he acted as a confidential advisor. O'Connor's arrest brought to light the extent of political involvement within gangland. On May 27, 1924, Torrio, O'Banion, O'Connor, and 34 others were indicted for Prohibition violations; however, four months later, District Attorney Edward A. Olson dismissed the case against O'Connor.[68]

With O'Connor's latest trouble in Chicago behind him, he reached out to his syndicate friends to further the success of the Hotel Vincent and his own interests. Al Capone, the newly crowned leader of the South Side Gang, stayed in his special suites on the eighth floor while his highest-ranking members would stay in rooms overlooking Main Street. Guards stood watch over the stairway and elevators. Capone always personally placed $100 in the hands of the elevator attendant to ensure that no one took the elevator to the eighth floor during his stay. Accomplishment of this task meant that Capone would give another $100 to the attendant when he checked out.[69] Surrounded by bodyguards at all times, Capone remained cautious and alert, but always had a smile on his face. Even though he never offered his hand in a greeting, he exhibited the utmost courtesy and friendliness whenever he was in the Twin Cities.

Fred Sims, a young bellhop at the Hotel Vincent, regularly encountered Capone, Guzik, McGurn, D'Andrea, and Campagna, who he knew were gangsters. Sims, known to Capone's group as "Bellhop Number Four," was entrusted to drive Capone's car when it needed fuel and service and even drove the "Big Fella" himself to the golf course on several occasions. Capone would wear his white fedora hat cocked to the left side. Sims and the rest of the hotel staff loved Capone because he was such a big tipper. Even a small errand like running to the drug store would earn a $5 tip. When his entourage packed up to leave the hotel, Capone would give a $500 tip to the bellhops and chambermaids to divide among themselves.

Rosalie Suwarsky frequently waited on Capone at the Vincent Café, and his generous tips came in handy as she continued her education. Dora Kuhlman, a beautician at the Vincent Hotel Beauty Shop, often worked on Thursdays when the shop would close to the public in order to accommodate Capone, his bodyguards, and the molls, or rather, women, accompanying them. The ladies would get a haircut or wave, while Capone and his men had haircuts, manicures, and their eyebrows arched. Kuhlman thought they were very nice, polite, well mannered, and big tippers.[70]

Although frightened of Capone, one local barber shaved him in his room at the Hotel Vincent for a $5 tip. One day, he positioned Capone in a chair near the bed and started shaving him. He reached over to the bed to get a towel and, by accident, picked up a pillow. There on the bed were several guns. He was so scared that his hand shook like a leaf. Capone noticed and just laughed, saying, "Ah, forget it."

The frightened barber calmed down and completed the job, but said he was glad to get out of that room.[71]

Herbert Brant, a gunsmith running a business called The Little Repair Shop on Sixth Street in Benton Harbor, was called directly to the Hotel Vincent one day. Unaware of whom he was meeting, Brant was suddenly surrounded by a slew of bodyguards. Capone made his way through his bodyguards to hand over his pistol, which needed the trigger pull fixed. Brant repaired the pistol, though hesitatingly, knowing Capone's ruthless business practices. However, when Capone then asked him to fix his Thompson submachine gun, Brant politely refused the request. He believed that by leaving the weapon in a state of disrepair, he may have saved several lives in Chicago.[72]

Capone's stay at the Hotel Vincent always included a day on the greens. He frequented the Twin City Golf and Aviation Club, located on Territorial Road, as well as the Berrien Hills Country Club, overlooking the St. Joseph River on Napier Avenue. Each course offered nine holes, but the "tenth hole" was Capone's watering hole, where he and his men drank homemade brew. Caddies clamored for the job because Capone always tipped generously and bought them each an ice cream cone. In fact, most of the caddies would put off the regular locals until they found out if Capone or any members of his crew had chosen them. Times were tough and the young caddies, such as Ed Schalon, took advantage of a good thing, even though some of Capone's golf bags were heavier than normal. Schalon noticed that "Machine Gun" Jack McGurn's golf bag had a lock on a zippered compartment, while a few caddies actually saw Thompson submachine guns tucked away with the clubs in other bags.

Don Dumpere, the head pro at the Twin City Golf and Aviation Club, thought that Capone was a mediocre golfer. He usually scored in the 90s; however, he showed interest in learning and improving his game, and he treated his fellow golfers and the employees with respect. Dumpere never experienced any trouble from Capone's group and never saw a gun, although there was a noticeable amount of tension among the staff and other golfers when Capone was around. Dumpere always had the feeling that something bad would or could happen.[73]

Even the tailor shops benefited when Capone came into town. Numerous suit coats worn by his associates required stitching in the inner pockets, ripped apart by the quick draw of handguns carried there. Capone's own specially tailored suits included reinforced inner pockets for this very reason. Tailors never complained and looked forward to the business.[74]

Leon Howorth, a masseur at the local Saltzman Mineral Bath House and Hotel, often personally provided service to Capone and his group when they were in town. Business would increase for Howorth because often when Capone and his boys got their rubdowns, many of the Chicago police officers tailing them would want to partake in the same.[75]

Similar to the Vincent, the Whitcomb Hotel in St. Joseph featured some of the finest offerings and was a popular place to stay. The hotel had 225 rooms, a dance floor, a bathhouse with 60 tubs for soaking in sulfur springs, thought to cure many ailments, and a dining hall that could seat 800 people. Restaurant server Elsa Rhodes received her biggest tips from the Capone crowd when they came into the Whitcomb Hotel restaurant. Her sister, who also worked as a server there, received $100 from Capone on one occasion.[76]

The appearance of big black sedans in front of the Hotel Vincent alerted residents and guests that Capone and his men were in town. Daniel J. O'Connor always greeted the party at the front door. Those who happened to see the action observed O'Connor bowing and rubbing his hands as the gang leader entered the lobby with a fanfare equal to that reserved for royalty. Once the day turned to dusk, workers noticed numerous trucks with Canadian license plates parked along the street behind the hotel, trucks that were always gone by dawn the next day. Hotel staff knew the vehicles were loaded with Canadian whiskey and beer, on their way to Chicago. So, too, did the police, but officers took the position that "if you don't cause problems for us, we won't cause problems for you."

While on routine patrol one evening, Deputy William Barry met Capone at the Hotel Vincent as he was conversing with some of his associates. Barry overheard Capone say, "A load will be in tonight." Then Capone turned to one of the men standing next to him and instructed, "You got a suitcase full of beer, give it to the kid," pointing toward Barry. "You can get more tonight," he then told the others.[77] Barry carefully concealed the suitcase of beer in his squad car and took it home to save for a special occasion.

As gangland's illegal business flourished, prosperity, it seemed, was the promise for everyone in the following year, 1929. Skelly and Barry would soon reap the benefits of the anticipated banner year for the nation. In a National Editorial Association article that appeared nationwide on January 1, 1929, famous Boston statistician Roger W. Babson predicted "scientific magic" would occur in the upcoming year, as well as increased payrolls, encouraging sales outlooks, and positive employment figures. Babson did warn, however: "The stock market is the only major phase of activity which is inflated. A sharp tumble at any time would not be surprising."[78]

Al Capone. *Author's collection.*

Johnny Torrio. *Author's collection.*

Philip D'Andrea's home in St. Joseph, Michigan, 1933. *Author's collection.*

Louis Campagna's 80-acre estate in Berrien Springs, Michigan. *Author's collection.*

"Machine Gun" Jack McGurn. *Author's collection.*

Philip D'Andrea, bodyguard for Al Capone. *Author's collection.*

Louis Campagna, bodyguard for Al Capone. *Author's collection.*

Fred Goetz. *Author's collection.*

St. Valentine's Day Massacre

ST. **VALENTINE'S DAY FELL ON A THURSDAY IN 1929 AS** Chicago was earning its "Windy City" designation, meteorologically and politically. It is probably safe to say that the Patron Saint of Love never spent a winter in Chicago. While the holiday had no bearing on the working public, the snow, ice, and 18-degree temperature that day did. The Beaver Paper Company driver, Elmer Lewis, did not look forward to the many deliveries he had to make that morning in the poor weather, but he loaded up his truck with his paper products and set out into the frigid air. At 10:00 a.m., he maneuvered through the morning traffic, driving north on North Clark Street and keeping watch for the address of his next delivery. Without any warning, a black Cadillac touring car heading west on Webster Street darted out in front of him while making a left turn. Desperately trying to stop, Lewis stood on the brakes of his truck but slid into the Cadillac's rear left fender. Seeing the siren gong on the driver's side and curtains in the side window, but no writing on the doors, Lewis figured that he had just hit an undercover detective's car. He began envisioning a stiff fine, being locked up in jail, losing his job, and endless other possibilities. Then, the Cadillac slowly pulled over to the curb on North Clark Street, and the driver got out to look over the damage to the rear fender. Lewis cautiously stepped out of his truck, within 50 feet of the damaged Cadillac. He caught a glimpse of three people inside the Cadillac, in uniform, all wearing police caps, just as the driver quickly waved him along and then returned to the driver's seat. Shocked that the officer had allowed him to go, Lewis could not have been any more relieved. Leaning forward in his truck, he waved at the officer, who he noted wore a dark chinchilla coat, blue suit, and gray fedora hat, rather than a uniform. He figured the man must have been a detective.

Lewis then realized that he had accidentally passed by the delivery address he was looking for, so he parked his truck about a half a block north of the location of the accident and walked back to his destination, 2129 North Clark Street. Just as he reached the building, he heard popping noises from the S. M. C. Cartage Company, located almost directly across the street at 2122 North Clark. Lewis assumed the noise was engine backfires and continued the last few steps toward the door, when he noticed that the black Cadillac he had hit was parked right outside the cartage company. After delivering his package, he saw the Cadillac pulling away but could not see the people inside the car. Not wanting to draw any further attention from the officers, Lewis hurriedly walked back to his truck and continued on his delivery route.

Jeanette Landesman, a 34-year-old housewife who lived at 2124 North Clark Street also heard the muffled popping noises. Fearing that the sounds were gunshots, she peered out her front window and noticed a man sporting a black overcoat and dark gray fedora getting into the rear of a black police car that quickly sped off heading south. Becoming quite concerned, Landesman sent one of her roomers, 35-year-old Clair L. McAllister, to see what was going on. He returned a few minutes later with his mouth gaping open and face ashen. "Mrs. Landesman, the place is full of dead men!"[79]

She immediately telephoned the police.

Josephine Morin, a third-floor resident of 2125 North Clark Street, directly across from the S. M. C. Cartage Company, had witnessed the event from a different perspective. From her upstairs window, she saw the large touring car with side curtains parked in front of the building facing south. She noticed one or two men wearing civilian clothes exit the garage with their hands above their heads, followed by two police officers in blue uniforms pointing shotguns at the civilians. She noticed that as the men got into the car, one of the civilians got behind the wheel and then drove off. Assuming that she had just witnessed a police raid, Morin kept watch out the window until she noticed two more police cars pull up. Then she went downstairs to get closer to the action. She watched as one of the officers went inside the cartage company but did not see anything more from her vantage point.

Sergeant Thomas J. Loftus of Chicago Police Department's 36th District Hudson Avenue Station was the first law enforcement officer on scene, after Jeanette Landesman's phone call had alerted him. Since there had not been an available police car at the station, an electrician performing some work at the Hudson Avenue Station offered him a ride. As Sergeant Loftus cautiously opened the door to the S. M. C. Cartage Company, the stench of death bowled him over. He maneuvered past several trucks in the cramped garage and saw a whimpering dog chained to the bumper of a truck. Then he saw the bloody carnage. The air was heavy with the acrid smell of burned gunpowder mixed with the metallic odor of ripened blood. Six bodies lay slaughtered upon the oil- and blood-soaked garage floor, surrounded by spent shells. Brain matter seeped out of one skull. Loftus saw the brick wall peppered with indentations. Then, two more officers joined him. They all heard a moan and turned toward one of the victims, who had started crawling. Recognizing the bullet-riddled form as North Side Gang member Frank Gusenberg, Loftus bent down. "Do you know me, Frank?'"

"Yes, you are Tom Loftus," he muttered.

"Who did it or what happened?"

"I won't talk."

"You're in bad shape," Loftus gently informed him, looking at his blood-ied body.

"For God's sake, get me to a hospital."

"Pete here, too?" inquired Loftus.

Gusenberg painfully whispered, "Yes," confirming that his brother Pete Gusenberg, also a North Side Gang member, was one of the six other victims.

"Were you lined up against the wall?" Loftus pressed, trying to get an explanation.

"I won't talk," Gusenberg answered again.

The lone survivor clung to life long enough to be transported to the Alexian Brothers Hospital at 1200 West Belden Avenue. There, with little left in him, Gusenberg continued to remain evasive: "You're wasting your time because I'm not talking," he told Loftus, who had followed him there.

Later, at the hospital, Loftus pressed him again, after information from witnesses began trickling in, "Frank, is that right, that three of the men wore police uniforms?"

"Yes," was all he would mutter before taking his last breath at 1:30 p.m.[80]

Sergeant Loftus initially estimated that there were about 100 empty .45-caliber shells and a couple of empty shotgun shells scattered around the floor.[81] He also discovered a .38-caliber blue steel Colt revolver lying on the floor. The serial numbers had been ground off and the hammer was cut down but it was still loaded with six bullets. In a search of the office area of the garage, officers found a uniform cap adorned with a gold band and brass buttons. It appeared to belong to a police sergeant, but upon further research authorities realized that it was only a doorman's cap, like ones used at hotels and cabarets throughout Chicago.

Chicago police commissioner William Russell arrived at the scene along with Cook County coroner Herman Bundesen. While detectives picked up the shell casings from the garage floor, the coroner sent the bodies to Braithwaite Mortuary at 2221 North Lincoln Avenue. In addition to the Gusenberg brothers, the other victims were later identified as Dr. Reinhart H. Schwimmer, Albert R. Weinshank, Adam Heyer, John May, and James Clark. Detectives collected, logged, and stored the evidence from the garage in marked envelopes, where they counted 70 .45-caliber shells, two shotgun shells, and about 25 bullet fragments. At the mortuary, the victims' bodies produced another 40 .45-caliber bullets and seven buckshot pellets. The evidence was taken back to the station.

Meanwhile, newspapers ran the story of a bloody killing, printing special editions that more than speculated about the crime. While Chicago authorities attempted to investigate the crime scene and interview witnesses, reporters began doing the same. They flocked to the garage, taking statements from anyone willing to talk. Sounds of hasty pecking and percussive tapping of Underwood typewriters filled newsrooms across the country. Rumors that the victims were part of "Bugs" Moran's North Side Gang fueled the frenzy, which then drew Al Capone, Moran's archrival, as the purported mastermind. There was even scuttlebutt that Moran may have been kidnapped during the massacre, since no one knew of his whereabouts. It was later confirmed that he was in Evanston, Illinois, a near northern suburb of Chicago. The Newspaper Enterprise Association immediately referred to the carnage as a massacre and on February 15 coined it as the St. Valentine's Day Massacre, a moniker that would be associated with the most infamous crime of the twentieth century.

Because witnesses had described seeing a detective car and men wearing uniforms, newspaper reporters logically assumed that police officers perpetrated the mass slayings, as reported in the *New York Daily Mirror* on February 15: "MURDER COPS HUNTED IN MASSACRE." "CALLS CHICAGO POLICE KILLERS OF GANGMEN," accused the *Wisconsin News*.

In an attempt to determine if this was true, the police commissioner and other police administrators investigated the whereabouts of each officer of the Chicago Police Department on February 14. While officers ran down leads and sought out additional witnesses, newspapers reported that Illinois state's attorney John A. Swanson called all ranking Chicago police officials before him on February 15 and offered a stern warning. "It is easier to send a policeman to jail than it is to send a gangster there," he said, assuring them that he would not hesitate to prosecute those responsible, no matter who they were.[82] Swanson's speech was deliberate, measured, and delivered in a tone of robust domination. His presence was equally as powerful, with broad shoulders and chest, rough fists, and wide-open blue eyes. One of Swanson's aides clarified his harsh position, "It isn't that Swanson believes the gang killers were led by city detectives, it is because he is not absolutely sure that they were not."[83]

Public criticism toward the police department was overwhelming, prompting Chief Detective John Stege to take a defensive stance. Speaking with reporters, Stege remarked, "Since those gang murders, the public has been willing to accept any rumor involving the police department in the crime. Not one real clue has developed justifying this attitude," he continued. "The public mind, nevertheless, is convinced that the police were somehow involved."[84]

After reading about what had transpired the morning of February 14, H. Wallace Caldwell came forward to give his account to police. Caldwell, president of the Chicago Board of Education, said that he and his chauffeur saw a dark Cadillac run a red light as it was heading west and making a left turn; it was then was struck by a truck, less than a block north of the scene of the massacre. Like other witnesses, Caldwell also assumed that it was a detective car and thought nothing more of it. Unlike many other witnesses, Caldwell remembered seeing a detail that would be of critical importance later: One of the occupants of the Cadillac was missing an upper front tooth.

Police later conducted a second round of interviews with others who had been in proximity to the garage. Both Jeanette Landesman and Josephine Morin reported receiving threatening letters from someone claiming to have been responsible for the massacre. Each letter warned the woman to keep her mouth shut if she knew what was best. Terrified, Mrs. Morin left town with her two children soon after the interview.

The country reacted with stunned outrage. Charles Skelly would have first learned about the massacre from the February 14 edition of the *News-Palladium*. The brutal headline read, "CHICAGO GANGSTERS KILL 7." Printed alongside were photographs not from the massacre, but from the scene of three baby killings in rural Eau Claire, Michigan. Skelly probably thought about the violent world he lived in. The real Saint Valentine, after whom the holiday had been named, represented love, although on February 14, in 269 A.D., he was clubbed to death and beheaded. It was actually a day rooted in death, and the massacre would forever tie it to that, 1,660 years later.

In a repeat of the day before, the *News-Palladium* headlines on February 15 screamed, "CHICAGO POLICE BAFFLED BY SEVEN GANG KILLINGS," and "FROM MURDER TO MASSACRE, IS GANGLAND'S PROGRESS IN CHICAGO, CRIME-RIDDEN CITY." Responding to the public outrage of the St. Valentine's Day Massacre, an editorial that day expressed what Middle America felt:

"'Chicago Gangsters Graduated from Murder to Massacre,' reads one Chicago morning paper today. That one cryptic sentence tells the whole story of gangland's latest defiance of the law in America's second largest city yesterday when seven gangsters were lined up against a wall by a rival gangland and shot down with machine gun fire. Six died in their tracks; the seventh mortally wounded, lived but a few hours.

"Chicago's gangland warfare, inspired by bootlegging activities and protected by corrupt politics, is a disgrace to American civilization. In the big city by the lake, they kill as they please and nobody cares.

"The decent element of Chicago's citizenship has comforted itself with the thought that as so long as gang warfare confines itself to gangsters it should not worry. Let the gangsters kill themselves off, say Chicago's respectable citizens. A dead gangster may be the best gangster but that isn't the end of the trouble; one killing inspires another and soon single and double murders multiply into massacres–as witness yesterday's shambles.

"Law is a mockery under such auspices and sooner or later, such a condition spreads its poison until law enforcement is just a joke. Crime of all kinds flourishes, public morals are degraded, and law and order generally are openly flouted.

"Chicago's crime situation is something more than local. The state of Illinois shares in the degradation. But that isn't all. The whole country is disgraced by it. It is a reflection of the American system of politics and law enforcement. It is an affront–a challenging affront–to everything that is decent in our ideals of government, local and national. If Chicago can't clean its own house, if the crime situation is bigger than the city and the state, then the federal law enforcement agencies should be called upon to meet this organized defiance of law.

"No nation can eventually survive and permit crime, as it is organized, protected, and developed in Chicago, to continue in operation. Sooner or later, under such conditions, the entire fabric of government becomes infected with the poison and the whole structure goes down."[85]

WITH VERY FEW MEMBERS of the underworld talking after the St. Valentine's Day Massacre, solving it proved problematic. Public cynicism called for an ending of Chicago's bloody beer wars, while Chicago business leaders worried about references to gangsters, corruption, and murder damaging their city's reputation. This led to a coroner's jury made up of leaders who had a stake in cleaning up Chicago. They would subsequently expose the dark underworld running rampant throughout the city and beyond.

CHARLES SKELLY HAD OTHER THINGS on his mind besides massacres and beer wars. For one, Skelly had many responsibilities as the assistant chief of the fire department. From keeping the fire truck running in tip-top condition to daily training and maintaining accurate logs, Skelly prepared himself and his crew of firefighters for every emergency; including one on February 25, 1929. Fire broke out in the furnace at the occupied farmhouse of Bernard M. Neumann on rural Cleveland Avenue, about three-and-a-half miles south of the city of St. Joseph. Skelly and two firefighters raced to the scene in their newest fire apparatus, which was outfitted with a 40-gallon chemical tank filled with bicarbonate soda that they pumped onto the fire. The fire had quickly spread to the roof, but the efficient actions of the firefighters saved the house with no injury or loss of life. Skelly was hailed for his triumph over the red devil and he must have felt destined for much bigger things; and bigger things were on the horizon.

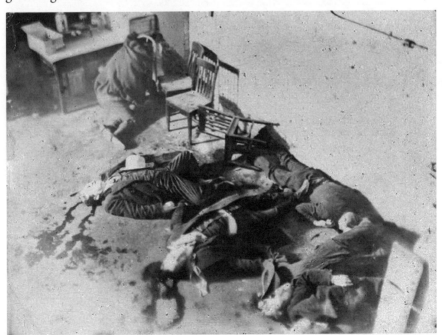

Crime scene photo from the St. Valentine's Day Massacre. *Courtesy of William J. Helmer.*

Chicago Police Department Captain William Russell. *Author's collection.*

Scene of the St. Valentine's Day Massacre at 2122 N. Clark Street, Chicago, Illinois, February 14, 1929. *Author's collection.*

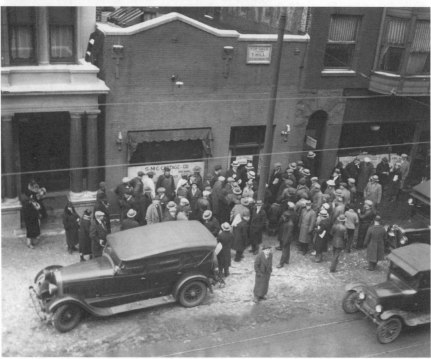

SUSPECTS AND SCIENCE ON THE STAND

THE ST. VALENTINE'S DAY MASSACRE HAD NOT BEEN the first massacre in Chicago. On August 15, 1812, before the city had been platted, soldiers and residents of Fort Dearborn battled Pottawattamie Indians in what became known as the Fort Dearborn Massacre. The Indians emerged as victors when they burned the fort to the ground, leaving 26 Americans for dead. Now, more than a century later, another massacre would be added to the history books. Since the onset of Prohibition, the country had witnessed the emergence of gangsters. There were turf wars over boundaries between gangs, political payoffs, corruption within all levels of government, and minimal efforts by police that allowed the bloody violence to occur. The reign of terror had reached new proportions on Valentine's Day, 1929, and citizens became outraged over the bloodiest day in modern American criminal history. A day normally known for love, youthful innocence, and the prick of Cupid's arrow would now forever be associated with brutality, silhouettes on a brick wall, and the piercing .45-caliber rounds through seven hearts.

When *Chicago Daily News* reporter James O'Donnell Bennett wrote his series, *"Chicago Gangland: The True Story of Its Murders, Its Vices, and Its Reprisals,"* the newspaper could not have picked a more fitting time to release it. Bennett's 10-part weekly series began on Sunday, February 3, 1929. Each Sunday, the paper printed another installment of the series. Its appearance immediately following the bloody massacre caught more attention due to the public's quest for a better understanding on the bloodshed that had occurred in Chicago. The series ran in the newspapers until April 7, 1929. To promote it, the *Chicago Daily News* featured half-page advertisements in smaller local papers, including Benton Harbor's *News-Palladium*.[86] Charles Skelly would have followed the series as he tried to understand how gangland operated and who the major players were. While people all over the country were learning about developments in the massacre investigation, some would become part of the investigation.

Immediately following the St. Valentine's Day Massacre, Cook County coroner Dr. Herman Bundesen gathered a group of the most prominent professional men in Chicago to be a part of the coroner's jury that would study the evidence obtained from the crime scene and subsequent investigation. Members of Bundesen's jury included Bert A. Massee, vice president of the Colgate-Palmolive-Peet Company; Walter E. Olson, president of the Olson Rug Company; Major Felix J. Streychmans, attorney for the Belgian Consul; Fred Bernstein, Superior Court Master in the Chancery; Walter L. Meyer, Master in Chancery; and Dr. John V. McCormick, dean of Loyola University Law School. Alternates were Colonel Albert A. Sprague, Chicago commissioner of public works, and Cyrus H. McCormick, vice president of the International Harvester Company.[87]

Dr. Bundesen had graduated from Northwestern University Medical School in 1909 and the Army Medical School in 1911. He then served in Chicago's Health Department beginning in 1914, until he was elected as Cook County coroner in 1929.[88] Bert Massee served as chairperson for the jury. Unlike most inquests, the jury did not conduct any public sessions for several months, as they reviewed the evidence brought before them.

A few days after the inquest began, Massee approached Bundesen with a request. "We are getting nowhere. For God's sake, why don't you get a gun expert out here?"

"We have no money to pay a gun expert," replied Bundesen in his distinctly Swedish accent.

"I will pay him if you will authorize him to go to work," offered Massee.

Bundesen conceded. Massee knew the right man for the job from reading an article several years before about the Sacco and Vanzetti murder trial of 1921, which utilized Colonel Calvin Hooker Goddard and the science of ballistics for the first time. With additional financial support from juror Walter Olson, Massee hired Goddard, the developer of ballistic testing, and brought him to Chicago to work on the massacre case.

The 37-year-old Maryland native received his medical degree from Johns Hopkins University in 1915 and graduated with honors in 1917 from the Army Medical School in Washington, DC. Goddard had taken an interest in firearms from an early age. Even during his stints practicing medicine, he collected weapons. His curiosity about the unique marks left on fired bullets had fueled his quest to pursue the study full time. In 1924, he set upon a new venture in New York City, and the following year he had collaborated with

Charles E. Waite, Philip O. Gravelle, and John H. Fisher to form the Bureau of Forensic Ballistics, a non-governmental laboratory. Goddard's fascination with ballistics inspired Gravelle to develop the split-image comparison microscope, allowing the viewer to see two images through the same eyepiece. Previously, scientists had to rely on their memory of the first image when comparing it to the second. Fisher had developed the helixometer, a device used to examine the interior of a gun barrel, providing clues to its caliber, rifling direction, and any powder residue. Goddard readily accepted work on the high-profile massacre investigation because it would serve as the perfect vehicle to promote his work in the mainstream.

The day after the St. Valentine's Day Massacre, Chicago police commissioner William Russell pleaded for city, county, and state agencies to work together in solving what he called a wholesale killing. Russell received word that United States attorney George Johnston's office had offered aid. Illinois assistant state's attorney David Stansbury initially blamed the massacre on rivalries and revenge motives between Capone and Moran for control over Chicago's liquor business, a scenario that seemed logical. Scrambling to get more information, newspaper reporters reached Capone via telephone just days after the massacre.

Relaxing at his posh Palm Island estate in Miami, Capone told reporters, "That fellow Moran isn't called 'Bugs' for nothing. He's crazy if he thinks I had anything to do with that killing. I don't know anything about that shooting and I don't care. Every time anything happens in that town, I did it. But I've got a good alibi this time. I was lying on the beach when it happened, getting sunburned."

On February 26, Chief Detective John Stege announced that 17 men were being sought in connection with the St. Valentine's Day Massacre. Those named were Claude "Screwy" Maddox, Tony "Tough Tony" Capezia, "Machine Gun" Jack McGurn, Joseph Lolordo, Ray "Shocker" Schulte, Danny Vallo, Rocco Fanelli, Tony Barone, Rocco "Crazy Rocky" Belcastro, Frank "Diamond" Maritote, Rocco Griffo, Samuel Aiello, Joseph Aiello, William "Boxcar" Rhode, Charles Kakel, Frank Milici, and George King. Detective Stege believed that these known criminals in the area were either directly involved or knew something about the killing, but he had no actual evidence fingering any of them.

Capone's right-hand man and chief gunner, "Machine Gun" Jack McGurn, obviously became a top suspect among the 17 named. At the time of the massacre, McGurn was staying at Chicago's Stevens Hotel with his girlfriend, Louise Rolfe. Unbeknownst to the police, the lovebirds coyly enjoyed their privacy, ordering room service and using the back stairway so as not to be spotted. Humiliation and embarrassment came to the authorities when they received information that McGurn and Rolfe had been right under their noses—just three floors separated the love nest from the police substation. Upon learning of this, Chief Detective Stege, Lieutenant William Cusack, and Sergeant John Mangan immediately conducted a raid the evening of February 27. Officers stormed in and quickly placed the couple under arrest.[89] Reporters covering the event noted that Louise was modish, sophisticated, slender, and bejeweled, wearing a black crepe dress with a squirrel coat at the time of her arrest. Other officers arrested Capone gunman Rocco Fanelli on the street at about the same time. At the station, both men were placed in a 20-person lineup. At least two witnesses who had seen something at the time of the massacre positively identified McGurn and Fanelli as being at the massacre, and accused them of being the killers.[90]

On February 28, the ever-confident Illinois assistant state's attorney Stansbury told newspaper reporters, "The crime has been solved. There is no question about it. Two witnesses have positively identified the prisoner [McGurn] as being one of the killers. The motive for the killing is also known," he said, referring to his belief that gangland rivalry was to blame. "We know the names of the five other slayers, and we will have them in custody soon."[91]

On March 5, 1929, Stansbury named two additional suspects in the St. Valentine's Day Massacre: Fred Burke and Gus Winkeler. Police had already suspected Burke and Winkeler, formerly of the Egan's Rats Gang in St. Louis, Missouri, as being two of Capone's "guns for hire" in the 1928 slaying of Frankie Uale (aka Yale) in New York, after Uale was said to have double-crossed Capone. Investigators pieced the case together and theorized that Burke and Winkeler had worn the police uniforms during the St. Valentine's Day Massacre, and that Jack McGurn had paid each of the killers $10,000. One witness specifically identified Burke for his missing tooth. On March 13, Chicago authorities set out to question Detroit gambling racketeer Al Wertheimer regarding his prior associations with Burke and Winkeler. Once he was located, police asked him if he knew the whereabouts of the two gangsters, who supposedly worked for him in several Detroit gambling houses in the past. Wertheimer said very little and was released.

Police then zeroed in on another three of Capone's guns for hire: John Scalise, Albert Anselmi, and Joseph Guinta. All were taken into custody for questioning, but Guinta was freed shortly thereafter for lack of evidence. Scalise and Anselmi posted bond and were released. Smug from previous acquittals, the men believed they had nothing to fear. When Capone finally returned to Chicago from Miami on May 7, 1929, he invited Scalise, Anselmi, and Guinta out for a celebratory dinner at the Plantation, a roadhouse in Hammond, Indiana. After a nice meal and plenty of alcohol, Capone, strongly suspecting the three men of betrayal and plotting against him, had them tied up and then produced a baseball bat and began bludgeoning them to death. The next day, their car was found alongside Douglass Park in Hammond, Indiana, in a ditch—the bodies of Anselmi and Guinta were in the back seat, and Scalise was found about 40 feet away from the car. Speculation arose that revenge for the St. Valentine's Day Massacre had been the motive for the triple killing; however, insiders told Capone of a plan by the three to have him assassinated so they could take over the gang, which was the more likely motive for their brutal deaths.

NOT LONG AFTER COLONEL CALVIN GODDARD began working with the coroner's jury, several private benefactors established a workspace for him, through the Northwestern University Law School, which became the Scientific Crime Detection Laboratory.[92] In order to utilize the newest science of forensics and ballistics, Bert Massee even sent Goddard to Europe for three months during the summer of 1929 so he could study the much-advanced systems used in England, France, Spain, Switzerland, Italy, Romania, Hungary, Austria, Germany, Denmark, and Belgium.[93] When Goddard returned, he submitted a 75-page report highlighting what he had learned. He declared, "Europe is two generations ahead of the United States in scientific police work, and when I say two generations, I mean at least sixty years."[94] With Goddard's newfound knowledge, criminal investigation in the United States was about to change.

The evidence from the massacre was the largest collection Goddard had ever studied. He knew that a shotgun had been used, based on the buckshot and shell evidence, but the identification of spent bullets and fragments would be more challenging. Goddard tackled the work using a process of elimination. First, he determined whether the bullets had been fired from a revolver or from an automatic gun. Then he narrowed down the make of the gun. Based on his examinations, he determined that all of the bullets had been fired from a Thompson submachine gun.

The Thompson submachine gun had become the weapon of choice for gangsters. The "Tommy Gun" was originally intended for use by the military, but gangsters adopted it around 1925. In 1929, a Thompson submachine gun Model 1921 with Cutts compensator and a 20-round stick magazine cost $200 from any gun dealer.[95]

Brigadier General John Taliaferro Thompson, Kentucky-born 1882 graduate of the U.S. Military Academy in West Point, developed what would become his namesake weapon. The Thompson submachine gun was first manufactured in 1916 during the Spanish-American War.[96] Thompson coined the term "submachine gun," because it used .45-caliber Automatic Colt Pistol (ACP) cartridges rather than rifle ammunition in a fully automatic operation, firing at a rate of about 700 per minute, in either a 20-round straight stick magazine, or circular drums holding 50 to 100 rounds.

A card provided with each weapon read: "Thompson guns are sold with the understanding that you will be responsible for their resale only to those on the side of law and order. Auto-Ordnance Company, 302 Broadway, New York." The cards held little value to their primary consumer and were ignored.

The last thing Goddard needed to do was determine if more than one Thompson submachine gun had been used in the massacre. In an effort to assist the police investigation and possibly salvage some of the negative publicity of its products, a representative from the gun manufacturer at Auto-Ordnance Company approached Chief Detective John Stege, hoping for a testimonial on the gun's practical use by law enforcement. "The only help you can give me is to go back and close the gun factory," replied Stege. "The weapons are of absolutely no value to police, banks, guards, messengers, or anyone other than criminals."

Goddard remained objective, and after studying all the evidence he revealed his process and findings in a report to the coroner's jury, "*The Valentine Day Massacre: A Study in Ammunition Tracing.*"

> "All of the bullets removed from the bodies were of .45 automatic pistol type, U.S. make, cannelured, in other words, identical in caliber, type, make, and vintage with those found on the floor of the garage. The buckshot found in the corpse of Schwemmer [sic] were identical in type with those used by U.S. Cartridge Company in Climax brand shells. All complete bullets from the seven bodies and all bullet fragments on which rifling marks appeared, showed evidence of having passed through the barrel having six grooves inclined to the right, the grooves being the width and angle, which tallied with the Thompson rifling specifications."[97]

In an effort to prove or disprove that police-issued Thompsons were used in the massacre, Goddard asked that police departments in the area bring their weapons to him for ballistics testing, subsequently performed in the basement of jurist Massee's home, before the laboratory facility had been completed. Goddard further explained in his report:

"I examined altogether some eight Thompson guns, five in the hands of the Chicago Police, one at Melrose Park police headquarters, and two from the Cook County Highway Police.

"I fired a number of rounds of ammunition of the same caliber, type, make, and vintage as used in the murder, through each of these. The bullets were recovered, undeformed, from a receptacle of cotton waste into which they were fired, and each bullet and empty shell was numbered with the number of the gun from which it had been issued. The bullets and shells so recovered were carefully compared with specimens of the fatal bullets and shells. In no instance did I find a duplication of markings to indicate that any of the police weapons had been employed in the killings.

"Since shotgun shells had been found in the garage, it became desirable to study the shotguns used by the various police authorities in and around Chicago. Consequently, a number of such weapons were tested. These included two Marlin riot guns of the Chicago Police, four Remington automatics, and one Remington hammerless repeater from Cicero Police headquarters; three more Remington's, one Winchester, and one Revenoc (Marlin) from the Melrose Park Police, and four Winchester repeating hammerless guns used by the Cook County Police. U.S. Climax shells were fired in all of these and the marks left upon them by the extractor, ejector, firing pin, and breech face, were compared with those on the two shells recovered at the scene of the murders. In no instance were similar markings found.

"I returned to New York, to my office in which city various Thompson machine guns were forwarded from time to time by Coroner Bundesen for testing. These were all carefully studied, but in no instance did any bullet or shell fired from them show markings identical with the fatal bullets or shells from the garage. We seemed to have reached the end of a blind alley."[98]

GODDARD'S REPORT SUGGESTED that police were not involved. While authorities continued to hunt down the massacre suspects, the coroner's jury convened to study how it had occurred. They focused on weapon sales, underworld crime, and corruption. The inquest began with jurors visiting the undertakers to see the bodies for themselves. Then they traveled to the scene of the crime where authorities performed a reenactment of the event. Thereafter, the jurors met in a closed session. On April 12, Bundesen revealed to the public that the weapons used in the St. Valentine's Day Massacre were two Thompson submachine guns and a 12-gauge shotgun, as proven through Goddard's ballistic tests.

The first public hearing of the investigation began on April 19, 1929, where a number of subpoenaed witnesses appeared. Facts emerged early on, including the realization that gangsters had gotten around the policy set forth by the Auto-Ordnance Company that only law enforcement officers, bank guards, and others with an expressed need for the firearm could purchase them. They learned that many of these purchases had been made via mail order through firearms dealers using fictitious company letterheads and addresses.

Edward Widener, manager of the gun department of Von Lengerke and Antoine, a favorite of gangland, appeared before the jury on the first day. The sporting goods store had been in business before the turn of the century and operated out of 33 South Wabash Avenue in Chicago.[99] Widener testified that a Vincent A. Daniels had purchased nine machine guns in seven separate sales between October 11, 1927 and February 7, 1928. Two of these guns wound up in the homes of massacre suspect Jack McGurn and victim Frank Gusenberg.[100] Two other machine guns, traced back to Daniels, turned up in the residence of Charles "Limpy" Cleaver, who had been found guilty in February 1928 of the Evergreen Park mail train robbery.[101]

Daniels' lawyer indicated that his client, a member of the Internal Revenue Department in California, had purchased machine guns to supply to Mexican rebels, who were fighting an uprising to the government's anti-Catholicism position, called the Cristero War. Although the lawyer could not explain how the guns ended up in the hands of known criminals, he did not allow Daniels to testify because of ongoing federal charges. However, Daniels did speak to reporters. "It was no trouble to buy machine guns," remarked Daniels. "All I had to do was send to New York for them and they were shipped to me."[102]

Police discovered that he purchased the guns for $106 each and then resold them illegally to gangsters for between $375 and $500. Daniels pleaded no contest on federal mail fraud charges, and officers hastily arrested him on illegal sales of weapons.

Peter Von Frantzius, owner and operator of yet another gun dealer, the Von Frantzius Sporting Goods Shop at 608 Diversey Parkway in Chicago, would be a key witness at the inquest. An alumnus of Northwestern University Law School, Von Frantzius had become successful when he started a mail order business, eventually opening his own shop. The lure of quick cash and notoriety, however, led Von Franztius down the wrong path.

Von Frantzius testified that a man calling himself Russell Thompson had come to his shop on at least four separate occasions. Von Frantzius had also sold and shipped 10 machine guns to a Frank Thompson's home in Kirkland, Illinois, for $55 each. As it turned out, Russell Thompson and Frank Thompson were one and the same. Apparently, Thompson told Von Franztius that he would in turn sell the guns to the Mexican consul general to control revolutionaries.

Jury members pressed Von Frantzius to provide dates when Russell Thompson had visited the shop to order the guns. He recalled four separate visits, the first on October 17, 1928. Records shown to the jury, in fact, corroborated that on October 19, 1928, gun manufacturer Auto-Ordnance Company of New Haven, Connecticut, had shipped three Thompson submachine guns, serial numbers 6926, 7580, and 7699, to Von Frantzius Sporting Goods. The shipment also included three "L" type 50-round drum magazines. Thompson had asked that the serial numbers be removed. Von Frantzius had his gunsmith, Valentine Juch, file them off for an additional $2 each.[103] He testified that Thompson had paid cash and took the three guns over the counter on October 23, 1928. Jurors further learned that Thompson had purchased six machine guns days before the massacre and ordered four more guns the day of the massacre.

When grilled about selling weapons to members of law enforcement, Von Frantzius admitted that he had sold guns to men representing themselves as members of the Evanston, Illinois, Police Department, and a William McCarthy of the Indiana State Highway Police, whose only identification had been a "star." Von Frantzius shipped the weapon to an address in Hammond, Indiana, which the jury later learned was an empty lot. When investigators checked with the Hammond Police Department and the Indiana State Highway Police, no one had ever heard of a William McCarthy. That particular machine gun was later found in the residence of Steve Oswald, a member of Spike O'Donnell's Gang. The 20-year-old Oswald had been acquitted of murder in 1926, but was accused of another murder on March 23, 1929. When authorities raided his mother's house, they found a .38-caliber revolver and a loaded Thompson submachine gun, matching the serial number of the weapon sold by Von Frantzius.

After Von Frantzius' testimony, Coroner Bundesen and the jury subpoenaed Russell Thompson, who had purchased 10 guns. When Thompson heard that police wanted to speak to him, he fled to Windsor, Ontario. This did not stop the jury from questioning his wife, Vera. On April 20, 1929, she told them that her husband's job involved soliciting students for a university so he was seldom home except on occasional weekends. Her statement carried little weight when she could not name the university. The jury learned that his elderly parents in Chicago were under the belief that their son sold cemetery plots. Under pressure, Vera finally admitted that Thompson had purchased six machine guns, which she delivered to him in Chicago. As the heat increased, Russell Thompson eventually returned to Chicago and met with authorities. While being grilled by Detective Stege, Thompson provided numerous names of his alleged clients; however, these names were fictitious. Stege updated Coroner Bundesen on the status of their interrogation, telling him, "We're going to pump Thompson until he runs out of fake names."

When Russell Thompson took the stand on April 30, 1929, he testified that he had sold the guns, with serial numbers removed, to William Jackson, a Schiller Park speakeasy owner, and Thomas McElligott, a West Side gangster. James "Bozo" Shupe, a Chicago bootlegger, purchased the gun with serial number 7580. Authorities arrested Shupe and Jackson on May 2, but when confronted, Shupe refused to make a statement and Jackson posted bond and was released.

While Thompson testified in the inquest, his wife, Vera, drove to the county seat of DeKalb County, Sycamore, Illinois, in order to file charges against her husband. She told the judge that Thompson had threatened to kill her and asked the judge for protection. She also described a confrontation that had occurred in mid-1927 after her husband had come home in the middle of the night in a soused rage, demanding to see her. When she refused to let him in, he fired his revolver through the windows of the house. At the conclusion of her plea, the judge issued five warrants for Thompson.

On April 30, 1929, jurors heard James Reynolds, secretary of a Chicago area firearms dealer. He testified that both the Hawthorne Kennel Club, once owned by Capone, and the Harbor Tool Machine Company owned by Forty-third Ward alderman Titus A. Haffa, who had since been sentenced to Leavenworth Prison on federal liquor conspiracy charges, had purchased machine guns. Reynolds also indicated that he had sold machine guns to the Sunshine Mining Company, Detective Publishing Company, and Gopher State Mines in Minnesota, a company that, as it turned out, existed only on letterhead.

Former St. Louis attorney Eddie J. O'Hare,[104] who had served as the president of the Hawthorne Kennel Club, was available to testify. He claimed that the club needed the machine guns for protection. During his testimony, jurors learned about the relationship of Burnham, Illinois, mayor Johnny Patton, and Jake Guzik, Capone's moneyman, to the Hawthorne Kennel Club.

Another witness, gun dealer and inventor Louis Wisbrod of Chicago, testified that he had sold 12 machine guns, several of which he claimed went to police departments. Wisbrod had a reputation as a "human target," for staging a publicity stunt designed to sell his bulletproof vests. In late January 1928, Wisbrod had donned one of his vests and allowed members of the Chicago Heights police department to fire six bullets into his abdomen from two feet away. Without as much as a flinch, he picked out the bullets with a knife, proving the worthiness of his vests.

As the inquest continued, police received a lead in early May 1929 that they believed could be connected to the massacre. Boys playing along the banks of the Rock River in Rockford, Illinois, discovered seven boxes hidden underneath a bridge, each containing 20 .45-caliber shells. The boys took the police to the bridge that led to a small island, directly across from Camp Grant, a United States Army facility. Then a Rockford farmer came forward who recalled hearing machine-gun fire on the island in early February 1929. He crossed the bridge to the island to investigate the source of the noise. There he encountered an expensive sedan with five men seated inside, one of whom had told him they were National Guardsmen from Chicago and were using the island as a practice range. Since that seemed plausible, the farmer gave it no further thought until he read about the massacre. When shown photos of several suspects, the man picked out the one of Fred Burke, indicating that he was the man with whom he had spoken.[105]

Shortly after Thomas McElligot and James "Bozo" Shupe were named in the inquest as machine-gun buyers, the two men were murdered. The inquest carried on, casting its net over widespread criminal elements, exposing corruption and the ease of obtaining the tools of murder. It was clear that the mission of the massacre failed because "Bugs" Moran, the supposed target, was not one of the seven victims; however, an unexpected outcome was the nationwide attention that alerted the public to an already monumental problem. Unfortunately, it did not bring authorities any closer to solving the St. Valentine's Day Massacre.

Having no physical evidence to hold Jack McGurn, and with his girlfriend, Louise Rolfe, swearing that the two were together at the Stevens Hotel during the massacre, authorities dropped the murder charges against him the first week of December 1929.[106] The press quickly dubbed Rolfe as "the blonde alibi." Three possible massacre suspects were already dead, two machine-gun buyers had been killed, and numerous witnesses had refused to talk. Although police tried to locate suspects Fred Burke and Gus Winkeler, they were not successful. Soon an event would take place in the Twin Cities of St. Joseph and Benton Harbor, Michigan, that would bring "Bloody Chicago" to their doorsteps.

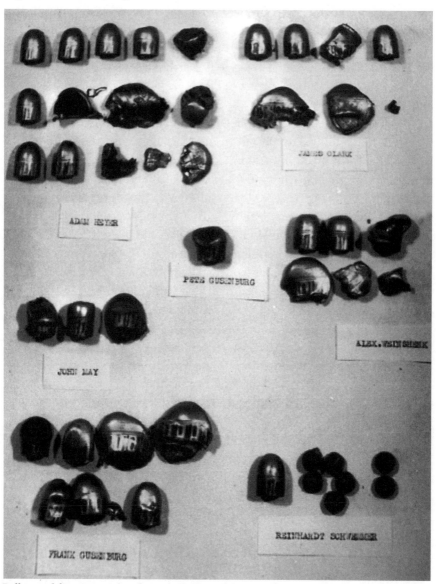

Bullets and fragments taken from the bodies of the St. Valentine's Day Massacre victims. *Courtesy of Bill Sherlock.*

Ballistics pioneer Colonel Calvin H. Goddard (seated left) and Cook County, Illinois Coroner Dr. Herman Bundesen (seated second from left) with members of the St. Valentine's Day Massacre inquest jury. *Courtesy of Chuck Schauer.*

Colonel Calvin H. Goddard at work in his laboratory. *Courtesy of Neal Trickle.*

Reenactment of the St. Valentine's Day Massacre conducted by law enforcement for the media and coroner's inquest. *Courtesy of Chuck Schauer.*

Joseph Lolordo. *Author's collection.*

William Jackson, Schiller Park, Illinois,
speakeasy owner who was called to
testify in the St. Valentine's Day Massacre
coroner's inquest. *Author's collection.*

Close-up of unique "s" stamped .45
caliber bullet found at both the St.
Valentine's Day Massacre scene and at
the Stevensville residence of Fred Burke.
Courtesy of Bill Sherlock.

Shotgun shells and five .45 caliber shells recovered from the garage floor where the St. Valentine's Day Massacre occurred. *Courtesy of Neal Trickle.*

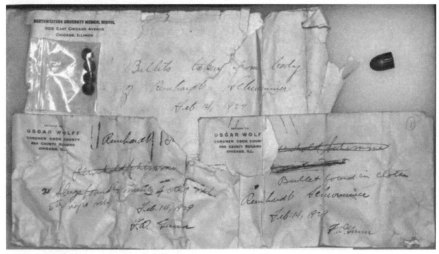

Evidence related to St. Valentine's Day Massacre victim, Dr. Reinhart Schwimmer and (below) some of the bullet evidence recovered from the garage floor where the St. Valentine's Day Massacre occurred. *Courtesy of Neal Trickle.*

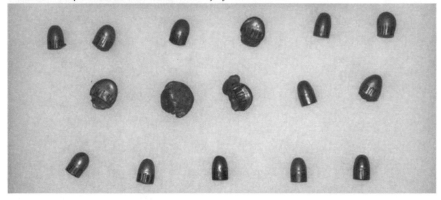

TWIN CITIES, TWIN ISSUES

THE CITIES OF ST. JOSEPH AND BENTON HARBOR, Michigan, were on the heels of transformation in 1929. The prosperous outlook inspired leaders on both sides of the river to make positive changes in the coming year. In St. Joseph, city officials were very aware of the police department understaffing issues and one of the goals of the first-ever city manager, Herman G. Crow, when he was sworn in on New Year's Day 1929, was to modernize the police department to meet much higher demands. As new mayor Theron G. Yeomans also assumed his duties on that day, he expressed the same sentiments. The commission-run government of Benton Harbor had come into existence in 1921 and now St. Joseph was following suit. Having worked as a railroad construction engineer based in Milwaukee, Wisconsin, since 1912, City Manager Crow brought optimism and natural ability to the job, setting the highest of standards for those who would follow. Mayor Yeomans, as well, represented St. Joseph, but his bloodline was far reaching: He was the nephew of two-term former United States president Grover Cleveland. Never one to ride on anyone's coattails, Yeomans had built his own career in the medical field, becoming one of the top surgeons in the profession, before seeking government office.

Law enforcement at this time was steeped in politics and quite basic in execution. Political strongholds running the police department granted authority, often resulting in self-serving outcomes. Officers would often perform duties outside of their enforcement roles, such as acting as crossing guards, aiding the homeless, working in soup kitchens, and lobbying residents to vote, usually for a specific candidate. Officers patrolled on foot, handling crime as it arose in their beat. They ruled by their nightsticks and had few investigative techniques. The bumbling and incompetent "Keystone Kops" films made from 1912 to 1917, though fictional and overdramatized, portrayed public opinion regarding the police. Communication systems for the officers and public consisted of call boxes placed on various street corners. If an officer wanted to check in at the department, he would dial a special code and speak to a dispatcher. A citizen who wanted to report a crime could also pick up the phone and speak to a dispatcher. Although the officers were more accessible and visible in the local neighborhoods, corruption, brutality, abuse, and political favors ran rampant.[107] Under City Manager Crow, things were about to change.

His plan recommended increasing the police force from three to seven officers, the equivalent of one officer for every 500 citizens, the same ratio used in Detroit. Officers would work day and night shifts, with beats covering both business and residential areas. They would also be required to check in by callbox at preestablished times for safety purposes and a squad car would be available for use during emergencies. The state of Michigan had already implemented a specific band of radio frequencies for public safety, with the Radio Broadcasting Stations Act 152 of 1929,[108] and the Michigan State Police were now patrolling in marked vehicles, instead of just motorcycles. Crow presented his new plan in April, but not all of the city commissioners were convinced of its merits. However, on April 30, 1929, the board of commissioners passed his plan by a 3 to 2 vote, with Mayor Yeomans casting the deciding vote.

Durphy D. Merrill, who voted against the plan, told reporters, "It should be understood, that I am not against improving the efficiency of the police department, but I was not in favor and I am not now in favor of tackling the problem to the extent Mr. Crow suggests."[109]

CHANGE WAS AFOOT in the city of Benton Harbor as well. When Benton Harbor city attorney John J. Sterling tossed his hat in the mayoral election against the then-current mayor, Merwyn G. Stouck, in March 1929, people heralded him as the "anti-commissioner" candidate. Already known for his tough stance as a defense attorney—representing Alex Goldbaum in the county's first murder case involving outlawed spirits that resulted in an acquittal—Sterling vowed to clean up the administration, including the police department. The *News-Palladium* later described him as "… aggressive, the star in many tempestuous political battles, fought like a tiger for his clients, loved the limelight and never was on the fence in any public issue."[110]

In 1912, Sterling had publicly predicted that the women's suffrage movement would end successfully within a few years, saying, "If an intelligent woman desires to vote, why should she be deprived of that privilege? And if an ignorant man is allowed to vote, why should an intelligent woman be denied that prerogative?"[111] On August 26, 1920, the Nineteenth Amendment to the United States Constitution indeed became law, giving women the right to vote.

During the mayoral debates in 1929, both Stouck and Sterling fired criticisms back and forth, coined as the "Stouck-Sterling Shrapnel" by the *News-Palladium*. In one such statement, Sterling asserted that Stouck supported illegal activity and had been "purchased" by men who ran gambling and prostitution houses in the city. "Ask Merwyn Stouck whether he knows that Peter Friedman, who is ardently supporting him, runs a gambling den just above the Pfister Pool Hall; he ought to know it and his police ought to have raided that place long ago."

Stouck balked at the accusations. He was a part owner of the Lockway-Stouck Paper Company that had serviced the community since 1916, and he organized the "Clean Up and Paint Up Week" from April 23-30, 1928, asking citizens to help beautify the city. His own words, nonetheless, would come back to haunt him with regard to Al Capone. "He's a perfect gentleman," Stouck told a reporter regarding his knowledge of Capone, the most renowned gangster, who was spending time in Benton Harbor. "I've met him and talked with him. He and his men are peaceful and quiet, and I know our citizens have no objections to his presence."[112] Stouck later remarked that he was speaking off the record at the time, although he did not recant the statement.

Nevertheless, the citizens of Benton Harbor saw through his polished persona and on April 1, 1929, they voted in John J. Sterling as their new mayor. The city seemed optimistic about its future.

As open-minded as Sterling was over women's rights, he was not yet ready to embrace the issue of race. Eight days after the election, he asked Dove J. Bruce, the city's first African-American police officer, who had been appointed by the city manager several weeks before the election, to turn in his badge. Mayor Sterling had other plans for the Benton Harbor Police Department.

One of Sterling's plans involved a personal meeting with Deputy William Barry, pal of Charles Skelly, inquiring if Barry was interested in working as a captain with the Benton Harbor Police Department. It was an offer Barry could not refuse; however, he would need to wait until the position opened up. Even though Skelly had hung up his blue coat to become St. Joseph's assistant fire chief in April 1928, he never let his interest in law enforcement wane. Skelly got a taste of his former profession when Berrien County prosecutor Wilbur Cunningham called him into court to testify against two men who, the year before, had allegedly stolen a generator out of the back of a Ford Flivver belonging to firefighter Lewis Mohn, while it was parked at the fire station. Appearing in front of Judge Charles E. White, Skelly took the stand to testify for the prosecution. In the end, the men pleaded guilty to theft.

Afterward, Skelly and St. Joseph police chief Fred Alden sat down to catch up on things. Alden must have missed having Skelly on his force and both men knew that big changes were coming for the department. Skelly wanted to make a difference and began to feel excitement about the possibilities that could present themselves under the city's new leadership.

Benton Harbor mayor John Sterling immediately began focusing on police department issues, including alcohol violations, corruption, and inappropriate conduct. On May 6, the Benton Harbor city commissioners asked for the resignations of all but three police officers, including Chief Charles Kocher, who had been with the department since 1923. When Kocher refused to resign, the commissioners voted 6 to 2 to oust him. The other officers resigned on the spot. Then the commissioners unanimously selected a new police chief, 41-year-old Thure O. Linde. Born in Sweden, Linde had served as a sergeant at the Oak Park, Illinois, Police Department, and had previously been a sergeant in the United States Marine Corps. William Barry was then named as captain of the department, joining Chief Linde, after serving three years with the Berrien County Sheriff's Department.

Mayor Sterling then addressed the new police department. The *News-Palladium* reported his statement: "Mr. Linde is your chief. You will take orders from him and no one else. The people have confidence in you. You must do your duty without favor to friend or foe. One thing we are going to insist on is absolute courtesy. Profanity and ungentlemanly conduct will not be tolerated."[113]

He asked each officer to pledge to abstain from alcohol consumption, on and off duty. Violations meant termination from the department. The fresh, clean, and dry Benton Harbor Police Department was ready for duty.

The push for modernization brought on in 1929 was the first wave of new police strategies that became known as the "Reform Era." The struggles for control and morality within the organizations brought out fresh views from reformists. They believed that political involvement was the problem with law enforcement. J. Edgar Hoover, director of the Bureau of Identification, took the lead as a prominent reformist and insisted that police departments become law enforcement agencies, ridding themselves of corruption and abusive tactics and remaining neutral and objective toward citizens. A widely used colloquialism of "The Thin Blue Line" came to capture this period, symbolizing the separation between citizens and police officers, between order and anarchy, and between good and evil, but the line of separation was indeed very thin.

Alcohol crime statistics for Berrien County in 1929 showed the arrests of 90 persons for violation of liquor laws, which resulted in over $14,000 in fines and costs. In addition, drunken driving put 61 persons behind bars, two of whom were the first in the county sent to prison. Although only two people had died as the result of drunken drivers, arrests for drunkenness totaled 340 persons.[114] Newfound prosperity did not curb crime, just as Prohibition certainly had not curbed drinking.

As winter transformed into spring, the new political agendas being introduced brought about fresh outlooks and growth in the Twin Cities. Coincidentally, the seventh annual Blossomtime Festival began on May 4, a weeklong celebration of Southwest Michigan's thriving fruit industry, which Reverend W. J. Cady of Benton Harbor's First Congregational Church called the "symbols of life renewed."[115] The week's highlight was the Grand Floral Parade on May 11. Since Skelly was on duty as the St. Joseph assistant fire chief, he was sure to have the best view from atop the fire truck, but he opted to stand beside the most beautiful girl in town, Mildred Thar. The two watched the lively parade down State Street, filled with marching bands, decorated floats, and Blossom Queens from each community.

Having had a remarkable experience serving the fire department, Skelly faced the prospect of returning to the newly expanded police department. When Chief Alden made him the offer, he decided to don his "blue coat" once again. On June 17, 1929, Skelly and fellow firefighter Ed Rohl were hired as motorcycle officers, fulfilling Crow and Yeoman's modernization plan. Chief Alden was extremely pleased to have Skelly back on his roster. Skelly chose to celebrate his return to the police department by entering the Class B Motorboat Races on June 23, hosted by the St. Joseph River Yacht Club. The adventuresome Skelly throttled down and felt the spray in his face as he bounced over the chop, running at maximum speed. However, in trying to turn on the crest of a wave, he lost control of the boat and it overturned. The other racers came to his aid, finding a soaked, but smiling, Skelly ready to try his luck again.

Taking on his new position in the busy summer months suited Skelly just fine because he knew there was plenty of excitement in St. Joseph. A pleasant afternoon on August 19 was marred only temporarily when a Lake Boulevard sandwich stand operator became belligerent. Skelly arrested him for drunk and disorderly conduct, but the man was released a short time later after paying a $1 fine. A few hours later, Skelly's cohort, Officer Ed Rohl, received a call out to the same man's home where he was tossing pieces of furniture around as if they were toys. After a second arrest for being drunk and disorderly, twice in one day, the judge ordered him to pay a $5 fine.

After the sand castles washed away and the beach bathers headed home, the colorful foliage began to drop along the brick streets of St. Joseph. The brutality that had occurred across the lake more than a half year earlier was hardly mentioned, as if, perhaps, it was a matter isolated to bloody Chicago. Regardless, Skelly, like so many others in the community, was disturbed by the St. Valentine's Day Massacre. This tragic event undoubtedly motivated him. He expressed an interest in taking on an even more purposeful role in the investigation and resolving of cases, just as the scientific methods for this were being developed and introduced. As the school year progressed, Skelly took an active role in teaching safety practices to children in a world that seemed to be turning more violent. His rapport with children made him the perfect school safety officer. From the grade schooler to those at the high school, Skelly knew each student by name. Aside from the school day, he appeared at most St. Joseph High School sporting events to root for the home team. Skelly was a friend to all and a popular police officer. He learned from an early age to treat everyone with respect, but soon Skelly would encounter a stranger who had learned a very different lesson.

Benton Harbor, Michigan, Police Department in 1929. Chief Thure O. Linde (seated left), Captain William Barry (seated right). *Author's collection.*

THE BIG OILMAN

ON SEPTEMBER 27, 1929, FREDERICK R. DANE AND HIS wife, Viola, became the newest residents of Lincoln Township, just north of the small village of Stevensville, Michigan. They moved into a bungalow on Lake Shore Drive, a newly developed section along U.S. Highway 12. The Craftsman bungalow was a popular housing style adopted by Sears, Roebuck and Company as a pre-cut model, featuring a porch with a roof supported by tapered square columns, and a centralized fireplace.[116] Dane bought the five-room home on a land contract from Ferdinand Wiese,[117] who originally purchased the 10-acre plot of land in 1919.[118] Dane paid $1,000 cash for the $12,785 home and would pay $100 a month for the mortgage.

Dane appeared to be doing well financially and told his neighbors that he owned a series of gas stations in Indiana. His 34-year-old wife, Viola, was an attractive, petite blonde who had been working in a Hammond beauty shop before meeting Dane. Being new to the area, Dane ventured out to acquaint himself with his neighbors and the local merchants since he planned to remodel the house and would need to acquire supplies and laborers to complete the renovations. In downtown Stevensville, Dane quickly located the Frank P. Cupp Lumber Company, which had been in business since 1900. The 69-year-old owner, Frank Cupp, and his son, Hiram "Nod" Cupp, were pleased to accommodate him. Dane ordered wood and supplies, which the Cupps personally delivered. He then enlisted the help of his neighbor, Steve Kunay,[119] and a local carpenter by the name of Paul C. Hoge, to do the work.[120] Dane wanted to finish his house with the best of everything. Kunay learned firsthand of Dane's finances when he saw him carrying a large roll of bills. Dane bragged that he made $3,000 a month from his gas stations, an exorbitant figure considering the average salary in 1929 was just over $100 monthly. Dane planned to make his home into a showplace, spending large sums on landscaping and interior furnishings. He even wanted to turn the entire second floor into a billiards room and a den.

While Dane hired the laborers and purchased the supplies and expensive furnishings, Viola added special touches to the interior. She made a trip to Chicago in late September to buy lamps and rugs for the house. Dane hired painters through the Twin City Decorating Company of Benton Harbor. Owners Ferdinand Ratz and John W. Martz were pleased to take on the project and the men became friends with Dane as well.

On one of his venturing trips, Dane met a local landscaper, Julius Burandt, and hired him to work at the bungalow.[121] Then he found the perfect shrubbery at the Cutler and Downing Nursery in Benton Harbor. Former Benton Harbor mayor Fred Cutler owned the nursery and the two men became quite chummy. Dane learned that in addition to running his business, Cutler had been approached about running for Berrien County sheriff in the upcoming election. Intrigued, to say the least, Dane kept in contact with Cutler.

It did not take him long to get a feel for the small town. Dane made friends and even comforted sick neighbors. The well-to-do entrepreneur now needed a safe place to keep his money, and he found just the location not far from his bungalow at the Stevensville Bank. There, he met Fred Jung,[122] a career banker, who opened an account for him. Dane always liked a man who knew his money. Jung greeted Dane with a smile and the two would chat on a regular basis.[123] Another frequent stop was the Stevensville Auto Shop. Ray Mongreig and his young mechanic, Theodore Fiedler, were always eager to check out Dane's shiny car.

The seemingly wealthy oilman, a term used to describe gas station owners, impressed everyone he met as he spread his dollars beyond Stevensville. St. Joseph became another regular stop for him. Dane spotted the exquisite window display of the Troost Brothers Furniture Store along State Street and walked in. Store manager John L. Swigert served Dane on several occasions, including when Dane ordered carpeting for his bungalow. Swigert appreciated a man with good taste and only the best would do. Dane then hired carpet installer Emil Frost of St. Joseph. In all, Dane spent about $5,000 to remodel and decorate his now-lavish bungalow, an amount almost unheard of at the time.

Dane took a liking to the Carlton & Walter Cigar Store located in the Rice Block at 322 State Street in St. Joseph, where owner Robert Carlton stocked Dane's favorite cigars.[124] He also scanned the news racks at the cigar store for the most recent editions of popular magazines and newspapers; Dane enjoyed reading immensely, and he was especially fond of Chicago newspapers as well as Benton Harbor's *News-Palladium*. Once he had his reading material and box of cigars, he would stop at the American Dry Cleaners at 418 State Street, just a block from the cigar store. As a first-rate dresser, he regularly had his expensive suits cleaned. The seemingly mild-mannered Dane rarely expressed discord; however, one day that fall he became irate with store clerk Elmer Smith.

All appeared normal that day when the American Dry Cleaner's clerk greeted his customer as he walked up to the counter. Smith retrieved several newly pressed suits from the back of the store and presented them to Dane. Looking over the suits, Dane noticed something that made him fly into a rage. He threw the items on the counter and leaned in toward the puzzled Smith. "I asked you specifically to not put my name and number on these," he blasted.

He continued to bawl out Smith, who repeatedly apologized for the oversight. Dane finally grabbed his suits from the counter and stomped out the door. Smith could not understand why his customer overreacted to such a minor mistake, unless for some reason there was a purposeful intent to conceal his identity.

A much less dramatic meeting occurred when Dane met Ensign A. S. Bower, the head of the Salvation Army. Highly impressed with Dane's presence, Bower recruited him for an active role in the upcoming fundraising campaign. The Salvation Army advisory board agreed with Bower's assessment and scheduled Dane to work on the kickoff campaign beginning on Monday, December 16. The wealthy oilman, it seemed, was a true philanthropist.

When his prized German shepherd became pregnant, Dane took her to Dr. James M. Miller, a well-respected veterinary surgeon, at 212 Main Street in St. Joseph.[125] As Miller examined the dog, Dane indicated that he wanted the best care possible for her. "I paid several thousand dollars for this dog and the puppies will sell for a thousand dollars each," he boasted.[126]

Those who encountered Fred Dane described him as a nice person, but some people sensed something strange about him. Many just assumed he was a bootlegger, which was not unheard of at the time. Others noticed odd behaviors, such as seeing him in the back yard teaching his German shepherd to become vicious and that he would never answer the door even though a radio could be heard playing in the house. When his neighbors, the Kunays, first met Dane, Suzanna Kunay felt very uneasy about him, and she let her husband know her concerns. However, money was tight and Dane had offered her husband work, which supplemented his fruit and vegetable sales. Neither "Nod" Cupp, Barney Yasdick, nor their friends seemed bothered by the town gossip because they asked Dane to join them in an afternoon of small-game hunting. Dane went along, wearing his long overcoat, not typical for traipsing through the brush in search of woodland creatures. The hunters thought it odd that he apparently did not know how to load a shotgun. The boys gave him a quick lesson. Soon, Dane spotted a rabbit. He drew the shotgun forward, aimed, and squeezed the trigger, but nothing happened. It seemed that he had forgotten to take the safety off.[127] The boys all laughed, suspecting that Dane had spent too much time in the city and needed more lessons in rural living.

The residents of Southwestern Michigan welcomed Fred Dane into their community, despite his peculiarities. Neighbors and business owners continued to learn more about him, but nothing could prepare them for what they were about to find out, something that Dane kept hidden, a secret to die for.

Lake Shore Drive Bungalow belonging to Fred "Killer" Burke, located just north of the village of Stevensville, Michigan, in 1929. *Author's collection.*

BEFORE THE CRASH

CHARLES SKELLY'S MARKSMANSHIP, ALONG WITH HIS witty his character and charm, presented itself on the night of October 11 when he and his partner, Officer Ed Rohl,[128] responded to a call at the Zion Evangelical Church at the corner of Niles Avenue and Harrison Street. An uninvited visitor happened in that night and made a cozy place to sleep among the hymnals and pews. The visitor was none other than a skunk, but Skelly and Rohl had a duty to protect the house of the Lord, so they proceeded to move stealthily through the sanctuary with shotguns at their sides.

"Psst, psst, don't fire until you see the whites of his eyes, I mean his tail," Skelly comically whispered.

"Oh, man, I hope I'm not nearsighted," Rohl chuckled.

Finally, the visitor showed his face. One loud boom echoed throughout the church when two beady eyes met the barrels of a shotgun. As the smoke cleared, so did the officers, while the ladies auxiliary arranged for a mop and soap brigade in the morning. The event became the topic of many conversations all over town. Skelly and Rohl gained the title of "The Skunk Squad," an obvious word play on the Prohibition enforcers, "Sponge Squad," and they received numerous requests from citizens to handle various nuisance animal complaints. In one instance, a large raccoon, with its head stuck inside a tomato can, frightened a woman on Langley Avenue. Her fear diminished once "The Skunk Squad" arrived on scene and eradicated the problem.

Skelly and Rohl savored the opportunity to have a little fun, since the majority of calls for police service in St. Joseph involved drunk and disorderly conduct. However, there was little time for that. During the October meeting of the Michigan Crime Commission held in Marquette, attendees concluded that, "... petting parties, drinking, automobiles, crime movies, and the stressing of crime by newspapers" had all contributed to the lawlessness in the state.[129]

IN MID-OCTOBER 1929, Chicago detectives received a 24-page handwritten statement from the wife of a purported Capone hitman, Frank Perry, alias Biege, that may have connected him to the case of the unidentified body found on Mizpah Beach in Benton Harbor, Michigan, the previous year. Anna Perry revealed details of high-profile homicides, and a trip to Benton Harbor. "I didn't know what his work was; with the exception that he told me he was a bootlegger," wrote Anna Perry. "Frank was offered a job in Benton Harbor around August 27, 1928.[130] The job was to execute a man. We did make a trip to Benton Harbor where we stopped for a time at the summer home of Stanley Martin in-laws.[131] I don't remember anything about any killing until he told me then that he was supposed to kill this man. I don't know who the man was and he didn't know himself, but Tony Lombardo, Capone's top lieutenant, was going to send a man to shoot him."

She claimed that she begged Frank to leave his line of work. They drove to Winnipeg, Manitoba, where she penned a letter to Capone telling him that she wanted $10,000 to ensure her husband's safe exit from Chicago's underworld, or she would squawk. At the time, Capone was serving time in a Philadelphia prison for a weapons offense. Berrien County authorities looked into her statement and the possible connection to the Mizpah Beach body, but once again the case went cold when nothing could be substantiated. However, by October 15, 1929, authorities arrested Frank Perry for extortion. He referred to his wife, from whom by then he had separated, as a "woman of great imagination."[132] John E. Northrup, Illinois assistant state's attorney, and Chief Investigator Patrick Roche were frustrated over the entire case, explaining that early publicity had made their investigation difficult.

"Frank Perry, alias Biege, may be of importance in recent gangland crimes and he may not be," announced Northrup.[133] No one really knew.

FOR THE SECOND HALF of October in Southwestern Michigan, there was less talk of gangsters and more of Mother Nature and Wall Street. On October 22, a furious Nor'easter violently tossed Lake Michigan upon the shores for three days, causing considerable damage. The lake claimed the 338-foot train car ferry S.S. Milwaukee and her crew of 52 men in the storm, considered the worst on the lake since 1894. The howling winds eventually turned calm, but devastation of another form blanketed the country when, just a week later, the stock market crashed, ending the period of wealth and prosperity referred to as "The Roaring Twenties." A new era had dawned, known later as the Great Depression, and would remain for a decade.

As winter descended upon the country, the financial crisis initially appeared as a ripple, rather than a wave, in Southwestern Michigan. Few newspaper headlines featured the dismal economic conditions, but rather a more optimistic assessment. Residents went about their daily lives and Christmas continued to be a time for spirited giving and rejoicing as the new decade approached. Merchants reported that despite the stock market fears, people were still spending their money; in fact, the number of shoppers in downtown St. Joseph actually increased compared to past years. The cheery smiles and signs of appreciation must have inspired Skelly as he walked his Christmas patrol beat. He could not have known that a simple encounter with a stranger and a split-second decision would christen a new realm of science, one that would change criminal investigations forever, and aid in the downfall of an empire.

An Accidental Encounter

SHORTLY BEFORE 8:00 P.M. ON DECEMBER 14, 1929, THE traffic light turned green at the intersection of Broad and Main Streets; however, the Hudson coupe, with Officer Charles Skelly standing on its running board, sat idling. Skelly motioned to the driver to pull forward toward the St. Joseph Police Department on the corner. Instead, the driver pulled a gun out of the door pocket and aimed it at the officer. As Skelly stared down the barrel of a pistol, he slowly raised his eyes until he met those of the man behind the trigger. He froze as his heart began pumping harder, his sight acutely focused on the danger in front of him. Although Skelly did not know it, the driver of the Hudson had at least seven reasons to avoid being taken back to the police station.

Unaware of what was taking place on the roadway just steps away, John J. Theisen, president of the Commercial National Bank, was filling his tires with air at the Dixie Filling Station on the northeast corner of the intersection, while station attendants Lowell Brunke and Victor Kolberg awaited their next customer from the warmth of the building. William Struever, a Benton Harbor house painter, and his wife, Hilda, had just left Steinke's Meat Market near the filling station. Albert Petruschke had ended his work day at the Whitcomb Service Station and was driving his Ford south when he stopped for the traffic light at the intersection of Main and Broad Streets. Harry R. Ohls of St. Joseph also stopped for the traffic light in the opposite direction, as did Charles E. Gage, the Hagar Township supervisor.

Each driver waited patiently for the light to turn green. In an instant, they all heard a blast, and another, and another, in quick succession. A few instinctively crouched in their vehicles. On the street, some ran in the opposite direction to get out of harm's way, but others turned toward the intersection to see Officer Skelly doubled over; he had just been shot.

The force of the first bullet hit Skelly at close range in his chest, just below the ribs, knocking him backwards and off the running board. He had begun to turn when a second blast pierced his right side. Feeling the burning of the hot projectiles, he gulped and inhaled, but his body could not function normally. Skelly grappled for his gun while holding his abdomen, but a third blast struck him in the left collarbone.[134] He stumbled in a semi-circle formation while doubled over in what appeared to be an adrenaline-fueled frenzy. He cried out, "Oh, my!" as the Hudson roared past him with tires screeching. Even with three bullets in him, Skelly still fumbled for his gun, but it was too late. He struggled just to remain on his feet.

Gas station attendant Victor Kolberg noticed the police officer crouched over in pain, stumbling west toward the Standard Oil Filling Station across the street. He then heard Skelly say, "My God. Take me to the hospital quick."[135]

Bill and Hilda Struever recognized the voice of the injured man as Hilda's cousin, Charles Skelly. Bill Struever bolted toward him, extending his arms to prevent the stunned officer from falling.

Just then, Albert Petruschke heard the officer holler, "I'm shot. They got me. They shot me three times."

While Skelly was swaying back and forth, Petruschke whipped his car up alongside the curb just as Skelly collapsed in Struever's arms.[136] The weakened officer struggled to catch his breath, "Help me, Bill, I'm shot," he pleaded.

Dozens of people had witnessed the shooting firsthand while hundreds had heard the shots, including officers inside the St. Joseph Police Department. From across the street, they rushed out to the intersection.

Forrest Kool, in the car that the shooter had crashed into earlier that night, immediately tried to pursue the Hudson, but his wife, Laverne, screamed, "No, no, you just saw him shoot a man." She grabbed hold of the steering wheel, while still holding her infant daughter tightly.[137] Taking heed of her warning, Kool turned into the Standard Oil Filling Station at the northwest corner of the intersection in order to notify authorities. He rushed toward the door, pushing into the attendant, who was on his way out to see what was going on. Kool urged him, "Hurry, call the police," not realizing that officers were already running to the scene.

The attendant hustled to the phone and dialed but could not get a connection, possibly due to the volume of other calls being made at the same time. While it was fresh in his memory, Kool grabbed a piece of paper and pencil from the counter and hastily jotted down the license plate number of the Hudson: 657-106, noting that it was an Indiana plate.

Just a few seconds later, a large crowd started to gather around, just as Skelly's partner, Officer Ed Rohl, arrived at the scene. Rohl had been on duty at the corner of Pleasant and State, only a block away, when he heard the shots. He had summoned the closest driver, a Mr. Stover, to carry him to the scene courtesy of his running board.[138] Stover had been directly in front of the Hudson but managed to make a turn before the light turned red. Out of breath and visibly shaken, Kool bolted out of the gas station to tell Rohl all he knew and pointed out the direction that the driver had fled. He handed Rohl the slip of paper with the license plate number on it, and Deputy Charles Inholz and Officer Ben Phairas immediately began to pursue the Hudson.

Meanwhile, Theisen ran toward Struever, who was holding onto Skelly with all his strength. The men carefully placed the weakened Skelly in Petruschke's Ford and instructed him to drive to the hospital.[139]

Gustav Getz ran from State Street just in time to see Skelly being placed in the car. Horrified at what had occurred just moments before, he stood stunned on the corner. The crowd gathered around him, and the only person he recognized was Officer Rohl.[140]

Petruschke sped toward the St. Joseph Sanitarium at 1817 Niles Avenue, just under a mile away, hoping to help save the life of the dying police officer. The sanitarium, founded in 1915 in a residential home, had been remodeled into six individual rooms. A 1928 addition created a fully equipped operating room, and Skelly would need that attention now.

Struever rode in the rear seat along with the badly injured Skelly, who seemed to know that he was fading away. Cradling his wife's cousin as best as he could, Struever asked, "Do you know who shot you?"

"I know the fellow that did it; he lives on the Lake Shore."[141] In obvious pain, Skelly continued, "Forrest Kool knows all about it. Bill, I'm not going to live long." Struggling to speak between breaths, he muttered, "The man who shot me was driving an automobile with an Indiana license, Forrest knows him."[142]

Struever could see the agony in Skelly's face when he tensed up and took another breath. "The man in the Hudson argued with me and I thought he was going to drive south on Main Street instead of the police station," he said, as he tried to clear his throat. "So I reached in for the keys and that is when the first shot hit me."[143]

Moments later, they arrived at the sanitarium. Skelly remained conscious but was in extreme pain. Petruschke rushed inside to get some help and was met by both Dr. Theron G. Yeomans and Dr. Clayton S. Emery. Besides being the city's mayor, Yeomans was a University of Michigan Medical School graduate who had moved to St. Joseph in January 1910. When he established the sanitarium, the original staff consisted of just himself and a nurse, but as business began to thrive, staff and space increased. He had asked Dr. Emery, who graduated from the University of Michigan Medical School in 1918, to join him in May 1929 as a surgeon and obstetrician.[144]

Struever, Petruschke, and several others helped carry Skelly from the car and into the care of the area's best doctors. Once inside, Skelly was transferred from a cot to a hospital bed. As the doctors lifted him, they noticed a spent bullet where he had been lying. Then, as they removed Skelly's coat, another spent bullet fell out of the left front pocket. Dr. Emery kept one bullet[145] and gave the other to Chief Alden when he arrived.[146] Struever looked over Skelly's clothes and could see a small powder burn on one wound, but the other two entry wounds appeared clean.

Nurses wheeled Skelly into the operating room. As they activated the massive surgical lamp, a bright glow illuminated him as well as the green and gray colored walls and new foam rubber floors. While Dr. Yeomans and his staff began to work to save Skelly's life, word of the shooting and his grievous injuries reached his family.

A nurse telephoned Skelly's older sister, Olga Moulds, who indicated she would leave her home in Benton Harbor immediately. St. Joseph firefighters Charles Wahl and R. Keane Evans, who had worked with Skelly, also rushed to the sanitarium. When the doctors determined that Skelly was losing blood at an alarming rate, they solicited volunteers to donate theirs. Although blood-typing had been around since the turn of the century, the newly discovered Rh system had given medical professionals a stronger match capability for blood transfusions. Having a compatible blood type, Wahl pulled up his sleeve and lay down on a cot next to Skelly. Dr. Emery inserted an intravenous line into the firefighter's arm and connected the line directly into Skelly's arm.[147] Time was critical. Wahl prayed that this would save Skelly. Evans and Struever stood by, ready to donate their blood as well.[148]

As the doctors worked on Skelly, scores of bystanders gathered in front of the St. Joseph Police Department in disbelief of the tragedy that had occurred. The clouds from exhaled cigar smoke were visible in the masses of headlights. Screams and cries drowned out the Christmas bells, while tire screeching and engine revving replaced the prominent sounds of this once pleasant winter evening. As curious onlookers joined the stunned witnesses, those who saw the event unfold stood silent as they flashed back to those critical images and sounds.

"Mr. Kool, we need you to come down to the station," prompted a sheriff's deputy, who had just arrived on scene.

The deputy escorted Kool, the leading witness, to the Sheriff's Department, just two blocks from the scene of the crime, while his family returned home. Kool sat down with hands trembling and recounted what he saw to Chief Deputy Thomas Carpenter. At the same time, Sheriff Fred Bryant began putting all of his resources to use. He called Benton Harbor horse dealer and special deputy Harry Litowich to assist with the search for the gunman. "Harry, get a gun and get right down to the corner of Fair and Territorial. If you see a Hudson car come through, hold the driver there and we'll come get him."[149]

Word reached Skelly's brother, Richard, while he was at work for Mammina Brothers Moving and Storage Company at 399 Territorial Road in downtown Benton Harbor. One of the men told him, "Hey, you better get up to town. Your brother's been shot."[150] Without any hesitation, Richard began running toward St. Joseph, probably barely noticing the chilly air and darkness as he focused on the well-being of his older brother, Charles.

TWO MILES SOUTH OF THE SANITARIUM, where Skelly lay in critical condition, a whistle sounded as the train coasted to a stop at the Pere Marquette Train Depot, directly below the bluff in St. Joseph. Viola Dane, wife of oilman Fred Dane, descended the stairs, stepping down onto the platform from the normally late 7:49 p.m. train arriving from Chicago. She held several bags brimming with brightly colored wrapping paper while she glanced over the parking lot looking for her husband, whom she had expected to pick her up.

Harry Lewis, a Bainbridge Township farmer and wintertime driver for McCracken Taxi Service, sat parked at the depot awaiting his next passenger. Noticing the woman's fervent looks, he rolled down his window and asked if she needed a ride. Scanning the area again, Viola told him she needed to make a call first. She spotted a telephone booth, inserted some coins, and called home, but her husband did not answer. Just then, the whistle sounded again as the train slowly chugged northbound toward the next stop. Realizing the taxi was her only option, she strode back over to the driver. "I guess my husband forgot to pick me up, so would you take me to my home on the South Shore?[151] It's near the Stewart school house, the fourth house on the left-hand side."

Lewis knew she was actually referring to Lake Shore so, without hesitation, he got out of the car and began loading her shopping bags into the back. Then, he opened the door to the taxi and motioned for her to get in.

He drove up the hill around the corner and headed south down Lake Boulevard, then got on U.S. Highway 12 and continued south for a few miles.

The demure woman made small talk, leaning forward and letting out a raspy cough, "I feel like I'm coming down with the flu or something. I've been Christmas shopping in Chicago the last two days and, you know, I thought I'd better get home before it gets worse."

The taxi headlights illuminated the blackened, wet roadway a few feet at a time, but Lewis could see that he was nearing the address. The passenger pointed out the house and Lewis turned left into the driveway.

AT ABOUT 8:10 P.M., Harry Sauerbier, the son of former St. Joseph police chief Charles Sauerbier, heard a loud crash outside his home at 1417 Lake Boulevard. He ran to the front door, looked out, and saw a Hudson in the street with two wheels broken off. Just as Sauerbier ran out to help, he saw the occupant of the vehicle, a rather large man wearing a cap but no overcoat, climb out and start running south down Lake Boulevard, crouching low as he ran.

He tried to get the man's attention, but he just kept running. As Sauerbier approached the car, he saw it had an Indiana license plate. The engine was still running and the headlights were on. He realized that something was terribly wrong. Just then, a police car pulled up next to him. The officer, Berrien County sheriff's deputy John Lay, jumped out. "This guy just shot Officer Skelly!" he shouted, pointing at the car.

Shocked by the statement, Sauerbier explained that the driver had fled on foot and offered to help the deputy look for him. Both men got into the squad car and Lay drove south. Sauerbier pointed him in the direction he had seen the man running, from Lake Boulevard to Winchester. Without seeing a trace of him, they drove down State Street, over to LaSalle and back toward Lakeview to Lake Boulevard, to where the abandoned Hudson sat. Both of them got out of the car, discouraged at not having found the driver. Lay started to nose through the Hudson to see if he could find any evidence of its owner, and instead found a gun on the rear seat. It was loaded and still cocked. He also found one spent shell on the floor of the car. Lay pointed out the items to Sauerbier and laid out his plans: "I'll go down to the jail and get some more men. You stay with the car, okay?" he asked.

AT THAT SAME TIME, taxi driver Harry Lewis drove onto the dirt driveway of the house on Lake Shore, and stopped near the front door. His watch indicated that the time was 8:20 p.m. As she exited the taxi, Viola Dane asked the driver, "Can you wait for a minute? Let me check if I can get in."

Expecting her husband to pick her up, she did not carry any house keys.

She tried the front door but found it locked, so she climbed back into the taxi. Lewis pulled forward to the rear of the house, and turned the taxi around so that its headlights were shining on the back door. Figuring there might be a key hidden somewhere, Lewis helped the woman search around the exterior of the house, but they could not find one.

Looking up, Viola Dane noticed that a second-floor window was open and asked Lewis to retrieve a ladder from the garage. Lewis did so and then offered to climb up, but Viola insisted she do it herself. "We've got a dog with puppies and she's quite vicious. I don't think she'll let you in."

Lewis guided her as she grabbed the first rung. He held onto the ladder and watched her make it through the window. Then he saw the room light pop on. Viola leaned out the window and told him to go around to the front door. Lewis returned to the taxi and repositioned it facing the roadway. He pulled forward a few feet, and then turned off the headlights.

MEANWHILE, ANOTHER SQUAD CAR arrived at the scene of the crashed Hudson. Deputy Erwin Kubath, a seven-year veteran of the department, got out, acknowledged Sauerbier, and began circling the Hudson. "Son of a gun, I think Skelly is dead," exclaimed the 31-year-old deputy, repeating a rumor he heard in the crowd that gathered around the injured officer, just blocks away.

"Well, it's too bad," remarked Sauerbier, as he held his head.

Focusing on the task, Kubath waved him over, "Let's look this bus over."

As Kubath and Sauerbier began going through the car, Nelson Foulkes from the *Herald-Press* arrived and offered to assist, actually hoping for a few exclusive details for a story he was writing. The exterior of the car exhibited surface marks, as if Skelly's overcoat had rubbed against it. Scratches and smears in the dirt that clung to the car resembled a handprint, probably left by Skelly when he was shot. Kubath made note of what he saw.

UNBEKNOWNST TO THE OFFICERS, the shooter had made it from Lake Boulevard to Winchester and was now running past State Street. That residential area of St. Joseph had seen little to no crime and certainly never an escaping gunman. The man crouched low and dodged from tree to tree, scoping out the area. He stopped about 50 feet away from a Model A Ford parked on Winchester near the St. Joseph High School. He noticed a lone man with long hair and a beard sitting behind the wheel. Unaware that a gunman was watching him, the 37-year-old occupant, Monroe Carl Wulff, a member of the House of David religious colony, sat waiting patiently for his wife, Elna, who had gone into the McMullen house at 1520 Forres to sell some linen.

Wulff had had his own brush with the law during his forced service in the Great War, when he disobeyed direct orders that he felt violated his religious principles. He had spent one year in Leavenworth Prison, labeled a "conscientious objector."[152] A decade later, though, he played for a time on the House of David infamous baseball team and enjoyed a simple existence in Southwest Michigan. However, the evening of December 14, 1929, would be anything but simple.

In the illumination of a streetlight, Wulff suddenly noticed a large man hurriedly approaching his car alongside the passenger window. Wulff rolled it down. "Do you need something?" he asked incredulously, leaning away from the man, who smelled strongly of alcohol.

The man jerked the door open and pulled a gun out of his right pants pocket. "Start this thing up and drive," he commanded, pointing the gun at Wulff as he jumped in the passenger seat and began directing Wulff to drive down certain streets. Frightened, but with no idea how to resist, Wulff realized he had been unwillingly forced to be a getaway driver.

"Turn here," the man ordered as they drove south, just as Wulff passed a sign on Lake Boulevard pointing toward Silver Beach. Wulff was surprised that the man ordered him down a series of streets that seemed more like a scenic tour of downtown St. Joseph. "Where do you want me to take you?" inquired Wulff, realizing that the man had no clear plan.

"I'll tell you where to drive," ordered the man.

Continuing south, Wulff saw a wrecked Hudson along Lake Boulevard. In his peripheral vision, he saw his passenger duck down as they passed the wrecked vehicle, even though no one was around. "Turn onto U.S. Highway 12 and go south."

They passed the St. Joseph Auto Camp and then Cleveland Avenue. Once they passed Glenlord Road, just over four miles from where the man commandeered Wulff's car, he pointed out a bungalow to the left. "Turn into that driveway," he demanded.

"But this here's a private drive," Wulff pointed out.

"Go in anyway," he said.

Wulff slowly turned into the driveway.

THE TAXI DRIVER, HARRY LEWIS, had just gotten back into his vehicle parked at the rear of the bungalow. He wanted to move closer to the front door, so he started to drive forward a few feet. Suddenly, another car pulled into the driveway. Not knowing if that driver would be able to see the taxi sitting in the dark, Lewis flipped on his headlights.

As Monroe Wulff pulled into the driveway, he saw the glare of a car's headlights pop on a few feet ahead of him, and immediately slammed on the brakes.

Excitedly, the gunman hollered, "Back up, back up. Hurry, let's go."

Lewis watched as the driver of the other car suddenly screeched to a halt, hurriedly backed out into the road, and quickly accelerated south. He simply reasoned the driver must have turned into the wrong driveway.

Seconds later, Viola Dane walked out of the front door, unaware of the vehicle that had come and gone so quickly. She was able to secure the dog in the cellar, so Lewis hopped out of his taxi and helped her carry her packages to the door. "That'll be a dollar fifty, ma'am," he told her.

Viola gave him an extra dollar for his help. Lewis got back in his taxi and headed north towards St. Joseph.[153] It was now just after 8:30 p.m.

AT THE MAN'S COMMAND, Wulff drove south on U.S. Highway 12 but noticed his passenger nervously looking back, with beads of sweat trailing down his face. Attempting to develop a strategy for escape, Wulff tried to engage the man in conversation. "So, do you know any of the boys in the House of David?" he asked.

"I don't know anybody, well, except for a short fellow by the name of John, who's a painter," replied the man, still looking back.

"John Martz?"

"Yep," he answered, "that's him."

As Wulff saw that they were approaching the Stevensville Cemetery and the road leading toward the small village, the man ordered him: "Turn back around."

Now headed north, Wulff passed the driveway he had just turned into a few minutes before. Trying a different strategy to get away from the goon, Wulff began driving as slowly as he could in high gear. This only irritated his passenger, who kept telling him to speed up. At one point Wulff felt the sharp cold steel of a gun pressing against his temple as the passenger declared, "You must wanna get shot?"

Wulff certainly did not, so he promptly sped up. As they neared Stewart School at the intersection of Glenlord Road and U.S. Highway 12, the man directed, "Go toward Cleveland Avenue." Then, after a short distance, he said, "Turn back around."

Wulff made another U-turn and headed back toward Stewart School again. "Get on U.S. Highway 12. Go south," the man commanded.

Frustrated, but still frightened, Wulff noticed his unwelcome passenger holding his stomach, and saw that he was sweating even more. They passed the driveway once again and when they had gone about two-and-a-half miles south, past Stevensville, the man said, "Pull over, pull over," as his stomach gurgled quite noticeably.

Wulff followed his order, hoping he could finally get free of this hoodlum before he decided to do something crazy, like firing his gun.

The man staggered out of the vehicle, still pointing the gun at Wulff, while demanding, "Don't you run away."

Wulff watched as the man placed his free hand on the trunk of a tree, bent over, and began to vomit, while trying to keep the gun aimed at the taxi. At that moment, Wulff saw his chance. When the man bent over for a second round of hurls, Wulff gripped the wheel tightly and slammed his foot all the way down on the accelerator. The Model A Ford spewed a trail of mud and rocks on the man and his pile of vomit.

Wulff headed south toward Bridgman, cut over on the next road heading east to get to Cleveland Avenue and from there drove straight to the Berrien County Sheriff's Department in downtown St. Joseph.

DEPUTY ERWIN KUBATH, with the help of others, was still searching through the wrecked Hudson on Lake Boulevard when he glanced up and noticed a taxi that had just pulled up alongside them. It was Harry Lewis on his way back to town, hoping to catch another fare, but the sight of a squad car and people milling around had caught his attention. He immediately recognized Kubath and newspaperman Nelson Foulkes. Lewis asked the men what had happened. Kubath filled him in on the Skelly shooting,[154] while Sauerbier and Foulkes continued to rummage through the car. On the floor, they found a small piece of white paper; it was a receipt from the Frank P. Cupp Lumber Company in Stevensville for material purchased on December 8 and delivered on December 9. It was signed by Fred Dane.[155]

Sauerbier brought the receipt to Kubath's attention, just as Lewis pulled away. Kubath honed in on Dane's address on Lake Shore Drive. Recognizing this as a significant lead, he motioned to Sauerbier, "Get in my car and we'll pick this fellow up on the Lake Shore."

Kubath instructed Foulkes to wait for Deputy Lay and to let him know where they were headed. Foulkes agreed. While on the way, Kubath thought it might be more prudent to get an idea who they were dealing with. He decided to stop by the Cupps' house to see what the lumber company owner could tell him about Dane. They found Cupp at home with his son, "Nod," and they were more than willing to share what they knew. "Sure, I know the fella I sold that lumber to," the senior Cupp said to Kubath. "It was Fred Dane, a big oilman. He's having his bungalow done over."[156]

"I think he was building a garage, too," "Nod" chimed in.

After quizzing the Cupps for a few more minutes, Kubath and Sauerbier left to first scout around Dane's neighborhood. They spotted Dane's house, but cautiously pulled into the driveway of a nearby neighbor's house. Sauerbier waited in the car while Kubath went up to the house and knocked on the door. Ross Bookwalter, a 71-year-old fruit farmer, answered and, in fact, confirmed that Fred Dane lived next door. While Kubath spoke with Bookwalter, Sauerbier peered through the car window in the direction of the Dane bungalow and noticed a light flash off and on. A minute later, Kubath got back in the squad car, backed out of that driveway, and drove into the driveway of Dane's house, which they felt certain belonged to the man who had just shot Officer Charles Skelly. "I guess this is the bird's house," announced Sauerbier, "because his coupe could fit in that garage, and I can see tracks where the car had been backed out."

Kubath gathered his thoughts and checked his gun as he prepared to approach the front door.

HAVING LOST BOTH his ride and the contents of his stomach on a rural road south of Stevensville, the gunman was making his way on foot over the old M-11 Highway in the darkness, just when he spotted a car turning into the property of Wishart's fruit farm.

Occupants 55-year-old Albert M. Wishart; his wife, Mary Buckley Wishart; and their 28-year-old daughter, Lillian, who were returning home from shopping when they spotted the man, were surprised to see anybody walking along the road in the dark. Their farm was along a deserted stretch of the rural road to Bridgman, so Wishart was cautious as he slowed down to assess the situation. As the man neared him, Wishart realized it was the new businessman in town, Fred Dane. He let down his guard, continued to pull the car into the driveway, rolled down his window, and greeted him. "Say, what are ya doing out here, Fred?"

"Look Al, I need a ride to the highway," Dane said, keeping his right hand in his pocket and appearing very uncomfortable and disheveled. "I need to get outta town."

"Well, uh, it's...," uttered Wishart, just as he saw Dane remove his hand from his pocket and reveal a revolver. As a farmer and secretary for the Stevensville Board of Education, Wishart had never dealt with a gunman. However, he kept a cool head for his family's sake. Already forming a plan, he told

Dane, "This isn't my car, so let me get my family into the house and we'll go get my car in Stevensville and I'll take you where you need to go."

Wishart escorted his wife and daughter, who had not seen the gun, inside the house and the two men got into the borrowed car. With the gun pointed at his side, Wishart started driving to where Dane directed him, namely, to a dirt road just east of them. "Can't do that, Fred," Wishart said with insistence. "The car will get stuck in the mud."

Instead, Wishart continued north toward Stevensville, all the while continuing to form his escape plan. Dane seemed to be getting antsy, grumbling. "Say, let's hurry this up."

Wishart hit a street curb quite hard as he pulled into the Stevensville Drug Store parking lot and stopped. With no explanation, he simply got out of the car and hurried inside.[157] The aggressive maneuver must have startled Dane. However, it did not take him very long before he realized he had been duped. Dane jumped out of the car and dashed behind the Stevensville Post Office.[158] Wishart remained inside the store trying to summon a deputy, while Dane took off north on foot.

AS KUBATH AND CRASH WITNESS Sauerbier exited the squad car and prepared to make contact with the occupants of the Lake Shore Drive bungalow, they took note of their surroundings. The two-story, shingled home sat on a large lot and included a grape vineyard, an attached garage, and a detached garage. "I'll go in through the back way," instructed Kubath, "and you go in the front."

"Listen, before you go too far, how many guns do you have?" asked the unarmed civilian.

"I've got one gun, and it's my own," responded Kubath.

Realizing this was a difficult predicament for a civilian, Kubath asked Sauerbier to stay back and just watch the front door. Sauerbier found a pine tree in the front where he took cover and kept his eyes on the door.

From the rear of the house, Kubath pounded on the door and shouted, "Police. I want to get in."

A few seconds later, a woman replied from inside the house, in a meek voice, "You can't come in this house, I don't know you."

"I am an officer and here to see your husband, Fred Dane."

After a few moments, the woman opened the back door and allowed Kubath in.

Sauerbier remained behind the tree but was startled when another squad car drove up to the residence at a very high rate of speed and stopped on the street. St. Joseph police chief Fred Alden, Benton Harbor police captain William Barry, and Deputies John Lay and Charles Andrews[159] all got out of the car, conferred with each other in what appeared to be a football huddle, and then proceeded to walk up the driveway to the back door. Relieved to have police reinforcements, Sauerbier followed them as they hustled to the back door.

Seeing the door was open, the group entered the house and found Kubath speaking with a woman. She took a seat in the living room while Kubath explained to the other officers what he had learned from the Cupps and Bookwalter and then found the telephone to call Sheriff Bryant at the department.

The group of officers discussed their plans while Sauerbier went into the living room and sat next to the woman, who had buried her face in her hands. Chief Alden joined him. "Ma'am, we're here because we found your husband's car demolished and we need to know what happened," Alden remarked, avoiding mention of the shooting and trying to reassure her.

She sat up, and then told him that she knew nothing about that, but wondered if her husband was all right.

Moments later, Kubath returned from the dining room where he had made his phone call and remarked, "Sheriff Bryant doesn't really know where this house is so I told him we'd wait outside for him."

After checking to make sure Dane was not in the house and locking the back door, the men walked out the front door while Sauerbier stayed inside with Mrs. Dane and talked with her alone. "Here, let me get a fire going," offered Sauerbier, as he walked over to the fireplace.

"I'm not cold," replied Viola Dane, as she crossed her arms over her chest, acting somewhat standoffish. Sauerbier looked around the room and noticed all the fine décor, including thick rugs, oil paintings, ornate furniture, and fixtures. Viola Dane just watched him as he bent down to start the fire.

"Something terrible happened, someone got killed," she sharply blurted out.

That's strange. How did she know this? thought Sauerbier. *No one mentioned the shooting, just the crash.*

He just stoked the fire as the orange glow filled the room. "One thing, young lady, you are very brave," remarked Sauerbier. "I don't think anyone is killed or anyone hurt, all they want your husband for is that he wrecked his car."

"You're trying to humor me," she said defiantly, as she blew her congested nose with her handkerchief.

WHILE THE BUNGALOW filled with warmth, Fred Dane trekked through the woods to stay hidden from passing motorists and their headlights. Cold, wet, and covered with mud, he made his way to the point where he could see his bungalow. The lights were on inside. He crouched down and approached the rear of the house through the grape vineyard. He tried opening the back door, but it was locked.

Suddenly, Sauerbier heard a noise at the back door, then the door handle shaking. "Did you just hear that?" asked Sauerbier, as he stood up from the fireplace.

"No, I didn't hear anything," she replied, followed by a rattling cough.

"Must be Kubath and Sheriff Bryant," Sauerbier muttered to himself.

UNABLE TO GET IN, Dane peeked around the back corner of the house and saw a squad car in the driveway and a gathering of men approaching the front of the house from the road.

SAUERBIER WENT TO THE FRONT window and noticed Kubath walking up the driveway from the street. He wondered who could have been at the back door. He stepped out the front door and approached Kubath. "Were you just at the back door?"

"No," replied Kubath, looking puzzled that he would ask such a question.

"You trying to kid me?" Sauerbier responded.

"No, I wasn't there," emphasized Kubath.

Out of the corner of his eye, Kubath saw a figure bolting through the field bordering the railroad tracks behind the house. He drew his weapon from the holster, aimed in that direction, and paused for his peripheral vision to pick up movement in the darkness. He squeezed the trigger to the point of firing. *Plug him*, he thought. Kubath suddenly remembered that Chief Alden was on the perimeter of the house and worried that it might be him, so he did not shoot. Then the figure disappeared.[160]

AFTER THE HARROWING experience of being carjacked at gunpoint, Monroe Wulff arrived at the Berrien County Sheriff's Department at 9:20 p.m.[161] Out of breath and shaking, he ran into the building where he saw a group of officers gathered. "Say, I've been held up. I got here as soon as I could," he said, trying to catch his breath. "A man got into the car and forced me to drive him south of Stevensville."

Certain that this had something to do with the earlier shooting, the officers jumped out of their chairs and surrounded Wulff, peppering him with questions. "What did he look like?" asked one of the officers.

"He was a big man, about 40 or 45 years old," the harried man recounted as best he could. "He was heavy, weighed 180 or more. He'd been drinking and had a mustache." Wulff then tried to describe the gun, which officers concluded was an automatic pistol smaller than a Colt .45.

After Wulff relaxed a bit and retold his story many times, he took a deep breath. "Guess I'd better get back downtown," he said, thinking of his wife whom he had left to sell her linens. "My wife's been waiting for me all this time."[162]

FRED DANE, having just narrowly escaped being shot when he had tried to sneak into his house, obviously needed a new plan since the police had already surrounded his bungalow. He crept up the side of another neighbor's house a safe distance away, and rapped on the window.[163] Suzanna Kunay heard the noise. She looked out and saw a man standing in her driveway. Afraid, she called her husband. At first, Steve Kunay thought it might be a chicken thief, but after looking out the window, Kunay recognized the man and assured his wife that it was just their neighbor, Fred Dane. He went out the side door and found Dane pacing. In his distinct Hungarian accent without a hint of concern, he asked Dane what he needed.

"I need a ride to Coloma. I've got to see a friend there and my car broke down."

Noticing how filthy Dane was, Kunay thought the request seemed legitimate. He agreed to help so he walked out back to the garage to get his Ford truck and told his wife he would be back in a while. Suzanna Kunay, on the other hand, was very suspicious of the request. She never liked Dane because he often bragged about his money.

Dane did not say much, but once they got going, he instructed Kunay to cut over to Niles Avenue and then go over the Napier Avenue Bridge. Realizing that this was a much longer route to Coloma, Kunay looked over at his neighbor and only then noticed the revolver in Dane's hand. "Fred, what's wrong with you?" he asked.

"I'm in great trouble, Steve," Dane replied, sounding nervous, "but it's not your business."

Unsure if he should probe any further, Kunay nonetheless continued, "Well, where do you go from Coloma?"

"I need someone to drive me to Paw Paw," he replied, referring to the county seat of Van Buren, about 20 miles east of Coloma.

Now fearfully concerned about the nature of Dane's trouble, Kunay began pondering a plan to get away. He drove to Territorial Road on the eastern outskirts of Benton Harbor, as directed, and north onto Red Arrow Highway toward Coloma. Once they arrived in the popular resort area of Paw Paw Lake, Dane told Kunay to stop at a small park along the road, close to Fairview Beach.

"I'm just about out of gas, Fred," announced Kunay, hoping that this would convince Dane that he could not keep driving.

Dane began to reach into his pocket, as Kunay nervously watched out of one eye, not wanting to make direct eye contact with him. Dane, much to his surprise, slapped a five-dollar bill in his hand and exited the truck. Relieved, Kunay watched as he walked out into the darkness and disappeared. Rather than turning around and potentially coming in contact with whoever or whatever Dane was running from, Kunay decided to take a different route home, heading west on Riverside Road and eventually back to Stevensville.[164]

ONCE SHERIFF BRYANT ARRIVED at the Stevensville bungalow, Kubath informed him that some officers had already performed a cursory search of the premises, but found no sign of Dane. He had sent a few officers to scope out the surrounding area for the mysterious figure that had been spotted running toward the railroad tracks, and the others decided to check out the last unchecked part of the house, namely the cellar.

As the men began to open the cellar door, Viola Dane warned them, "No one is in the cellar but the dog and six puppies and she's liable to bite you." However, she did offer to hold onto the dog when they descended the stairs.[165]

As the officers maneuvered through building materials and moved various boxes around, it became clear that Dane was not hiding there, but they found something equally incriminating. One officer came across dozens of boxes of .45-caliber bullets, two sacks full of pistol and shotgun cartridges, and 20 one-gallon jugs of wine, all stacked on a shelf. He alerted the others.

In a dark corner of the basement, they also found three Dunrite vests, — thin, flexible steel bulletproof vests—designed specifically to fit, undetected, underneath formal attire. Glancing over the contents found in the basement, Sheriff Bryant ordered a detailed search of the whole bungalow.

Everyone dispersed through the house. Sheriff Bryant arranged for one of the officers to drop Harry Sauerbier off at his residence and then led Viola Dane to a quieter part of the house while the search ensued. Kubath and Andrews headed for the master bedroom on the main floor toward the rear of the house. They began opening up dresser drawers and found men's dress shirts neatly folded with initials embroidered onto them. Some shirts had the initials F. W. D., while others had the initials F. R. B. In the bedroom closet, they found at least 25 custom-made suits, several tuxedos, and dozens of dress shirts. Kubath then checked a small box on the nightstand. Inside he found an upper and lower dental plate. Examining them closely, Kubath noticed that the lower plate had two teeth, one on each side and the upper plate had one tooth in the front. Surprised that Dane would leave them behind, he probably envisioned him as having a very distinctive smile.

Next, they began searching the living and dining rooms. In a drawer, Andrews discovered several loaded revolvers, as well as a business card bearing the name of Willie Harrison with an address of 403 West State Street in Calumet City, Illinois. More revolvers were tucked away in every conceivable place: inside a Victrola phonograph, underneath the piano cover, one beneath a pillow, one in a silverware drawer, and others near the windows.

Meanwhile, Alden and Barry were busy on the second floor. They uncovered dozens of disguises inside a closet. Noticing a slight depression on the carpet, Alden lifted it up and found a trap door that led to a room between the main and second floor. Barry, who was the thinnest of the group, climbed through the narrow opening and discovered that the room, less than five-and-a-half-feet in height, had a flap that opened up to the roof. Barry theorized that it was an escape passage because a person could easily slide or climb down the side of the house from there.

After finding the collection of loaded guns in the living room, Kubath and Andrews noticed a shelf stocked with hundreds of books and magazines. The titles ranged from detective mysteries to textbooks on chemistry and metallurgy. The collection appeared to be well worn. Opening up a few books, they noticed that some included underlined text and highlighted passages, with notations referring to blunders made by the criminals.[166]

As Kubath and Andrews pointed out various excerpts to each other, a loud pounding upstairs interrupted them. Curious as to what was going on, they climbed the steps and found Barry and Alden breaking a padlock off a closet in the hallway. The lock gave way after a few hits with a hammer. Barry opened the door and saw a small trunk, and Kubath and Barry stooped to pull it out. They kneeled down beside it, unlatched the clasps, and lifted up the top. Inside, they found neatly bundled bond certificates from the Farmers and Merchants Bank of Jefferson, Wisconsin. Each bundle included a list of denominations written in what appeared to be a feminine hand. A later count revealed that the bonds totaled $319,950.

The men yelled downstairs for Sheriff Bryant, who was still questioning Viola Dane. When he set his eyes on the trunk and its contents, he remembered reading about a bank robbery in Jefferson, Wisconsin, the previous month, and presumed that the bonds could be from that robbery. While the sheriff thumbed through the certificates, the others pulled more items out of the closet. Tucked behind a wall joist near the closet door they found a Thompson submachine gun, fully assembled, and loaded with a 50-round drum. They opened a black leather suitcase located behind the trunk and found another Thompson. The second submachine gun was stored unassembled, presumably for easier transportation. The men continued to drag boxes out of the closet. Once they laid out everything, they sat back in disbelief. When the arsenal was later itemized, the contents included:

> Two Thompson submachine guns
> One Winchester .350 automatic high-powered rifle
> One Savage .303 high-powered rifle
> One 20-gauge sawed-off shotgun with pistol grip
> Seven automatic pistols
> Five 100-round drums loaded with .45-caliber ammunition
> Many 50-round drums
> Three 20-round stick magazines
> Nine hundred rounds of .45-caliber ammunition
> Two bags estimated at 5,000 shells of miscellaneous ammunition
> Half a dozen fruit jars and tin cans filled with miscellaneous
>   ammunition including smokeless shotgun shells, shells
>   loaded with iron slugs, and small shot
> Eleven tear gas bombs
> Several bottles of nitroglycerin
> Three Dunrite bulletproof vests
> Detectographs (audio recording device used in wiretaps)
> Acetylene torches

AT ABOUT 10:30 P.M., Chief Alden left the bungalow to check on Skelly at the sanitarium while Sheriff Bryant headed back to his department with Viola Dane, whom he placed under arrest while the investigation continued. Deputies loaded all of the guns, ammunition, and other criminal accessories into the sheriff's car. As they drove north on U. S. Highway 12, they passed a pickup truck with a sole occupant, but had no idea it was Dane's neighbor, Steve Kunay, who had just driven their most wanted suspect to Coloma. By the time he later pulled in his driveway, Kunay saw several squad cars and many people milling about, making it very clear to him that something horrible had occurred. No sooner had Kunay parked his truck than officers quickly approached him and asked him to come down to the sheriff's department. Officers had already questioned his wife, who told them that her husband had driven Fred Dane to Coloma.[167] At the station, deputies escorted Kunay into a room with Sheriff Bryant, who suspected that he might be an accomplice. Bryant had located Chief Deputy Carpenter in the building and arranged to send officers to Coloma and Paw Paw Lake to conduct a thorough search for Fred Dane. The sheriff then questioned Kunay, probing him for the next two hours about everything he could remember about his neighbor, Fred Dane.

Kunay nervously told Sheriff Bryant how Dane had bought the house early in the fall and had paid him to help with remodeling and odd jobs, but that he had not seen much of Viola Dane. He recounted that he had been inside the house only a few times and never saw anything suspicious. He described his drive with Dane, who never said anything about the shooting, but Kunay thought it was odd that Dane directed him the long way out of town, avoiding the downtown area.

After the interrogation, Sheriff Bryant became convinced that Kunay was an unwilling participant in the gunman's escape and promptly released him. The next act was to call the Berrien County lead prosecutor, Wilbur M. Cunningham, to bring him up-to-date on what had transpired.

As word spread among residents in the search areas, fear kept most people inside their homes with lights burning all night. One man found himself in a bad predicament when his car tire blew out and he had to return home on foot. As he passed by a squad car, he remarked, "I'm not him."

Van Buren County sheriff's deputies checked the area surrounding Paw Paw and learned from a few youths at the Paw Paw Dance Hall that a man fitting Dane's description had gotten a ride out of town. The trail went cold from there.

One Berrien County deputy took the Colt pistol that had been used to shoot Skelly and placed it in the safety deposit vault at the Farmers and Merchants Bank in downtown Benton Harbor, separating it from the other evidence collected at the bungalow. Detectives processed the wrecked 1928 Hudson for evidence, then had it towed to a service station where it remained impounded for the time being.

While at the sanitarium, Chief Alden met up with City Manager Herman Crow and handed him the Cupp Lumber receipt found in Dane's Hudson. Crow, like the others who gathered there, waited for word on Skelly's condition.

Back at the bungalow, officers were surprised when they heard the telephone ring at 11:00 p.m. Thinking that it might be Dane himself calling, one of the officers answered the phone with a brief greeting.

"Doc?" asked a deadpan voice.

The officer began to question the caller's identity, but the line immediately disconnected. The call was later determined to have originated from one of three pay phones in South Bend, Indiana, but the caller remained unidentified.

While authorities worked diligently on the case, Skelly clung to life, even after some thought he had died. Firefighter Charles Wahl stood vigil by Skelly's side ready to give more blood. Chief Alden tried to remain strong as he comforted Skelly's older sister, Olga Moulds.

At one point, Skelly whispered to those around him, "I'll never get out of here, they finally got me."

Wahl encouraged him to keep fighting. Dr. Yeomans and Dr. Emery readied Skelly for an operation to try to remove the bullet still lodged in his body. Olga tearfully pleaded to the doctors to do whatever they could to save him. Yeomans now had to perform the most important surgery of his career, while as mayor he also had to lead the city through this devastating event. As the anesthetic was prepared, Skelly raised his head from the table and begged his sister to come to his side.

"You had better kiss me goodbye now; I'll never pull out."[168]

With tears running down her face, Olga leaned over him and closed her eyes as tightly as she could to keep from breaking down. She gently kissed him on the cheek, leaving her tears on his ashen face. Skelly grabbed her hand and squeezed with every bit of strength he had. Olga thought she was going to scream from the pain. Suddenly his grip loosened, his skin drained of color. He cried out, "Get that guy,"[169] closed his eyes, and died. It was 11:10 p.m.

Olga draped herself over her brother's body, unable to control her emotions.

Dr. Yeomans pulled down his surgical mask and made the walk from the operating room to the lobby where his look alone spoke thousands of words. Tears of utter sorrow, cries of disbelief, and prayers filled the sanitarium. Skelly's younger brother, Richard, despite running the distance to the sanitarium as soon as he heard of the shooting, arrived too late.

A nurse pulled the white linen sheet over Charles Skelly's face and wheeled the gurney carrying his body into the back room.

A short time later, Dr. Emery delivered Skelly's uniform to Alden. He could not help but touch the buttons and the fabric. Seeing the tiny region of frayed woolen fibers where a bullet pierced through brought a quiver to

Chief Alden's bottom lip. He had thought of Skelly as a son, and now he was gone. Folding up the uniform, Alden handed it to Officer Oliver Slater and instructed him to take it to Sanitary Cleaners. He planned to have it cleaned and pressed, and then delivered to Olga Moulds.[170]

Olga and her siblings wept as they gathered together with their father at home. Minnie felt lost without her Chuck. Little Mary Emma had never experienced a death, and at seven years old, could not comprehend that she would never see Uncle Chuck again.

Charles Skelly's law enforcement career had spanned two years and six months, during which time he was credited with making 96 arrests. Skelly never completed his 97th arrest; however, in the name of justice, others would see Skelly's final act through to the end.

St. Joseph Police Department Officer Charles Skelly circa 1926.
Courtesy of the Berrien County Sheriff's Department.

124

This photograph of the St. Joseph, Michigan, police force, taken just a few days before Charles Skelly's murder, appeared on the front page of *The News-Palladium* (as pictured on this book cover) on December 16, 1929. This is the last image captured of Charles Skelly, who is pictured second from the right. The other officers (from left to right) are Ed Rohl, Dave Hunter, Chief Alden, Ben Phairis, and Raymond Slanker to the right of Skelly. Vowing vengeance on the slayer of their comrade, Chief Alden was quoted as saying, "If I ever meet him, we'll shoot it out to the death."

"THEY CALL WOMEN DUMB..."

AS TEARS FLOWED ACROSS SOUTHWESTERN MICHIGAN for the senseless loss of Charles Skelly, Viola Dane wept as Deputy Charles Andrews booked her in at the Berrien County Jail, just before midnight.[171] Arrested for a felony charge of receiving stolen property, Viola was most likely alone in her sadness. Once news of Skelly's death reached those still collecting evidence at the bungalow, the sheriff's department, and elsewhere, sadness quickly turned to vigilance. City Manager Crow took command of the police department phones, calling other departments all over the Midwest looking for information about Dane. Detectives and troopers from the Michigan State Police deployed to the area. Sheriff Bryant was keenly aware of the importance of the arsenal recovered, which led him to seek out the assistance of the Chicago Police Department. He knew that ballistics expert Colonel Calvin Goddard was working with them in an attempt to solve the St. Valentine's Day Massacre case. Bryant hoped that he could enlist their aid in this case. Once he arrived back at the office, the sheriff made a phone call to Chicago authorities, who took an immediate interest in the arsenal. Chicago Police Department chief detective John Stege and several officers made the trip to the Stevensville bungalow early the next morning. Together with the Michigan State Police, they processed evidence in the home that morning. Stege and his fingerprint expert dusted every possible surface, hoping to link Fred Dane to other open cases. While that was going on, other officers boxed up all the clothing, shoes, and hats found in the residence so the items could be thoroughly cataloged. A few Chicago detectives returned to the station with deputies so they could get an up-close view of the arsenal recovered in the bungalow.

Meanwhile, Berrien County prosecutor Wilbur Cunningham prepared for the most challenging case of his career. A 1907 graduate of Benton Harbor High School, Cunningham completed his education with a law degree from the University of Michigan. He then went on to serve as a lieutenant commander in the Great War. Now, as lead prosecutor for Berrien County since 1928, he was ready to put the screws on Viola Dane, who he believed was covering for her husband.

Deputies led Viola to a private section of the jail, which served as Sheriff Bryant's living quarters. Viola took a seat in a rocking chair in the living room. A canary, caged in the corner, sang filling the silence. She dabbed her eyes and nose with a yellow-trimmed lace handkerchief, her legs crossed underneath a thick mink coat that she said was a Christmas gift from her husband. She wore a brown skirt adorned with pale yellow silk at the waist. The raucous lifestyle she chose was beginning to show on her attractive face. Her big blue eyes appeared puffy and red. Cunningham carried a large file folder, which he purposely smacked down on the table for effect.

Her eyes filled with tears and with a tremor in her voice, she said, "They call women dumb, and I guess they are! I can see it all now but it's too late. If my husband shot the officer, I hope officers arrest him."

Clearly not interested in her tears, Cunningham leafed through some of the papers recovered in the search and asked her how she met her husband.

Viola sat for a moment, rubbing her fingers in the moistened handkerchief.

"I first met Fred Dane at a party in Chicago during the summer of 1927," she began. "He told me that he worked for the Columbia Commercial Feed Company at the Wrigley Building in Chicago. At the time, I was running my own beauty salon on the south side. I used to work at another salon in Hammond, Indiana."

Listening attentively and rubbing his chin, Cunningham asked when they got married.

"We married on November 11, 1927, Armistice Day, at one of his friend's homes. I don't remember the address, but then we moved to 14015 Green Bay Avenue in Burnham, Illinois, just outside of Hammond."

"Who is Herbert Church?" asked Cunningham.

She responded with a puzzled look on her face, "I don't know him."

He then presented her a business card, recovered from the bungalow, of the Columbia Commercial Feed Company that had the name of Herbert Church in the lower right-hand corner.

"I believe a man named Church worked with my husband."

Reaching for the stack of papers again, he showed her the 1928 Hudson vehicle title, noting that it had been purchased in August 1928 from Bergl Auto Sales in Cicero, Illinois. "Then why should the title to his auto be made out to Herbert Church?"

"I don't know, maybe it's his car," Viola suggested.

"But your husband has been driving it since early this year, hasn't he?"

"Oh, yes," she replied.

Cunningham tossed the title onto his pile, and then, pointing his finger close to her face, he demanded, "You're shielding him, aren't you?"

"Do you think I'd shield him now that I know what he is, a murderer? Anything but that."

Cunningham returned to his chair and picked up another piece of paper from the stack.

"Have you ever stayed at the Savoy Hotel in Hammond?"

"I was there once in the fall of 1928, I think," she responded.

"And didn't you register there as Mr. and Mrs. Herbert Church?"

"He did the registering. I went on up to the room."

Cunningham reminded her of another stay, "You were there in May, 1929, also."

She dabbed her eyes and nose, appearing more and more frail as the questioning continued.

Cunningham then placed a photo of a rather large, clean-shaven man in front of her. "This is a photo of your husband, isn't it?"

Viola picked up the photo. "Oh, no," she said, recognizing the man, "don't get him mixed in this. He's an innocent man."

"If he is innocent, nothing will happen," assured Cunningham.

"He just got married, I heard. I don't know where he is."

"Yes, but who is he?"

"His name is William Krusch (a friend of hers from school), but don't get him mixed in this. You can do what you want with me," offered Viola. "I'm the one who's going to suffer."

"Haven't you any photos of your husband?" the prosecutor pressed.

"No, he would never have any taken. He didn't like them."

"He wouldn't? I suppose that never impressed you as peculiar? Didn't that arouse your suspicions?"

"No, I didn't think anything of that."

"You knew he always carried a gun?"

"No, I never saw him with a gun."

"Well, you know his hobby was holding up banks?"

"I should say not. The biggest surprise I ever got in my life was when that officer carried all that stuff out of the clothes closet. It's got me, oh, oh …" Viola began sobbing uncontrollably, burying her face in her hands.

After several minutes, she wiped her eyes and blew her nose in her handkerchief. Believing that she had regained her composure, Cunningham continued with his questioning.

"What do you think all those guns were in the closet for?"

Viola swallowed and looked directly at Cunningham. "I tell you, I never saw them before. Fred always kept the door locked. We were finishing the house and there were workmen around all the time. I told him once or twice to unlock it so I could clean it, but he always said it didn't need cleaning."

"What do you think all those bonds were doing in there?"

"Bonds? I know nothing of any bonds."

"But you know now that they were there."

"I saw them when they were carried out."

"But you don't know how they got there?"

"No, I don't."

"There were shells found in every corner of your house; in the radio, in the drawer where you kept your silverware. You certainly knew about those?"

"No, I didn't."

Viola crossed her arms in front of her, crouching backward in her chair. She sat there appearing to be in deep thought. Cunningham gazed at her, reading her body language.

"Did you accompany your husband often?"

"I was not allowed to go anywhere around town without him. One time he did take me to the movies in St. Joseph."

"Ever been to Stevensville?"

"No, he never took me up town."

"Did your husband ever discuss his business with you?"

"Men don't tell their women everything. They just get you in deeper and deeper. I can see a lot of things now that I didn't see then."

"What, for instance?"

"Why, all that stuff in the closet, why he kept it locked."

When asked about whether her husband would stay away from home, she said, "He seldom was away but when he was, it was for business."

"Did you ever discuss bank robberies with your husband?"

"We talked about them," Viola sighed. "He always said what fools men were to rob banks."

"How did you happen to be talking about that?"

"Why, when we read about them in the newspapers."

Viola Dane then suddenly took a different approach, trying to soften the man she seemed to know little about.

"Fred never cursed or swore. He even objected to me using slang. He did drink wine, sometimes a little too much and he would become grouchy. He would take little things up with me. But when he was sober, he was a wonderful husband. A woman never had a better one. Always spoke kindly of everyone. Always willing to help anyone." Beginning to break down again, Viola cried, "Oh, I don't believe it. It all seems like a dream."

Cunningham was unmoved by her story and directed her to go back over the trip to Chicago. She blubbered and sniffled as she spoke.

"I left St. Joseph on Friday morning, December 13, and took the cash Fred had given me a few days before. I had a fifty-dollar bill, twenty-dollar bill, and quite a few one-dollar bills. I spent all but the fifty, and decided to have change made at the train station in Chicago before boarding."

Cunningham inquired, "What was the idea of changing the bill if you had your ticket?"

"Well, I hadn't any change to pay the taxi driver on the other end, and they never have any change."

Pointing out her glaring inconsistency, Cunningham persisted, "But you have said you expected your husband to meet you. That he never failed you before?"

"I always have change for an emergency."

Cunningham could see she was growing weary and frustrated, but her statements lacked vital information and contained too many pauses. He kept grilling her, making her repeat stories over again, looking for discrepancies and a chance to break her. It would not happen, though. Finally, at 5:00 a.m., after five hours of intense interrogation, deputies led Viola Dane back to her cell.[172]

After going home for a few hours of hardly restful sleep, Prosecutor Cunningham, Sheriff Bryant, and the others were back at the investigation table later that morning with their Illinois comrades: Harry S. Ditchburne, assistant Illinois state's attorney; John Stege, chief detective for the Chicago Police Department; and Patrick Roche, chief investigator for the Illinois state's attorney. They were prepared to look over the evidence and take part in additional questioning of Viola Dane.

Deputies had worked through the night contacting personnel from the Farmers and Merchants Bank in Jefferson, Wisconsin, in an attempt to match up the recovered bonds with any that had been reported stolen. By Sunday morning, the bank's president, Lynn H. Smith, confirmed that the serial numbers on the bonds recovered in Dane's bungalow matched those stolen on November 7, in what had been the largest bank heist in Wisconsin history. Authorities in Wisconsin theorized that in early November 1929, suspected bank robber, or "yegg" as they were referred to, Harvey Bailey and four of his

pals scoped out the Farmers and Merchants Bank on South M
Jefferson, learning all the "ins and outs" that they could. Luck h
realized the bank was equipped with an audible alarm that sounded
day just before noon, and residents had become accustomed to it as always
being a false alarm. When their plan was put into action on November 7,
just before noon, the alarm did not seem to bother anyone much. A lookout
reportedly stood in the drug store opposite the bank while the holdup was in
progress. They gagged the teller while the robbers stole over $352,000 in cash
and bonds. When another teller tried to pull a secondary alarm, one of the
robbers fired a shot, but the bullet passed by the employee's ear and landed on
the floor. The entire venture only took three minutes. Their driver had waited
in a stolen Buick and once the group got in, they headed west on Highway
18. Machine-gun barrels displayed out the rear window discouraged anyone
from trying to follow. That night they ditched the car in Richland Center,
Wisconsin, where authorities found spent shells and Minnesota plates from
another stolen vehicle as well. A third stolen vehicle, reported taken in the
town of Viola, Wisconsin, 25 miles from Richland Center, might have been
the source of their ride out of the area. Leads had all but dried up until the
call came in from Berrien County.

Chief Fred Alden began contacting merchants in St. Joseph while two
detectives from the Michigan State Police, Lyle Hutson and George Waterman, joined in questioning the neighbors and associates of Fred Dane, including lumberyard owner Frank Cupp.

"I remember Dane had left town on November 1. Said he had some business to tend to," recalled Cupp. "I don't know where he went, but I saw him
next on November 7 at the bungalow, after I brought over materials. He was
with another man and they were carrying two suitcases. I just assumed he
returned home then."

On Sunday, detectives tracked down Ferdinand Ratz, of the Twin City
Decorating Company, to ask him about his experience with Dane. He willingly
told the detectives that he was at Dane's bungalow on Saturday and even drank
wine with Dane and another man named Robert Conroy, but that Dane and
Conroy had left to go buy a fan belt for Conroy's Studebaker. Hutson asked if
he knew where they went and Ratz told them he thought it was Warner Motor
Sales at 267 Territorial Road in downtown Benton Harbor.[173]

Two men hired for the remodeling job came forward, giving their firsthand account of what they had seen several days earlier. Reinhold Mischke
and John Zilke said they saw a man they did not know give a large amount of
cash to Fred Dane just days before the shooting.[174]

Just as the questioning of Viola Dane was about to resume, Sheriff Bryant received a phone call from Chief Detective Stege, who was at the bungalow. He reported that officers had been able to lift two clean latent prints from the saltshaker above the stove.

They rushed the fingerprint evidence to Chicago where identification experts immediately classified the prints and then isolated potential matches that were already on file. After meticulous comparisons, experts found an exact match. Fred Dane was none other than Fred "Killer" Burke, a ruthless killer and lead suspect in the Valentine's Day Massacre.

Michigan State Police detectives bringing Viola Brenneman to the sheriff's department for questioning. *Courtesy of Milt Agay.*

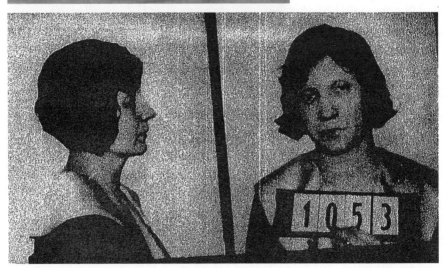

Mugshot of Viola Brenneman at the Berrien County Jail, 1929. *Courtesy of the State of Michigan Archives.*

THE SALTSHAKER DID HIM IN

ONCE THE FINGERPRINTS ON THE SALTSHAKER confirmed the identity of Fred "Killer" Burke, it was time to confront Viola Dane, who they now assumed was actually Viola Burke, with the facts. Deputies led her back into the sheriff's living room Sunday afternoon to face Prosecutor Cunningham, Illinois state's attorney Ditchburne, Chicago chief detective Stege, and Illinois state's attorney chief investigator Roche. They had already determined that the man seen with Burke the day before, known as Robert Conroy, was actually 34-year-old Robert "Gimpy" Carey, a close associate of Burke and fellow massacre suspect Gus Winkeler. Tracing the bill of sale for the 1928 Hudson revealed that the purchase was made by a fellow named Van Clark, an alias name for Fred Goetz, another member of Capone's forces.

More defiant and less tearful now, Burke's wife took a seat, folding her arms tightly across her small frame. Cunningham walked over to her and presented her with an affidavit from the Berrien County Circuit Court, charging her with felony possession of stolen property. He carefully explained to her that the bonds found in the upstairs closet were stolen from a Wisconsin bank robbery and all the weaponry and ammunition belonged to her husband, who they knew was really Fred Burke.

Interrupting the prosecutor, Viola blasted, "What difference does it make about me? I haven't done anything. It's him you want."

"Well, if you have nothing to hide, what difference does it make?"

Viola quieted down, but she did not appear cooperative. Cunningham then began questioning her about her personal life.

"What is your maiden name?"

"Viola Burke," she replied, obviously lying.

He then asked about her parents.

"They're both dead. They died when I was just a girl."

He asked about any brothers or sisters.

Viola paused and then answered, "No, I have no relatives."

Cunningham saw through her impudence and leaned in toward her, "You're lying about that. You want to shield them from publicity."

"Am I?"

"Where did you go to school?" quizzed Cunningham.

"At Bradley, Illinois. It's just a little place. I only went through the grades."

"After your parents died, whom did you live with?"

She sat silently again and then began sobbing, "Why must you ask me those questions? It has nothing to do with this case. You can do what you want with me now. But why drag in those of my childhood days?" She wiped her eyes and regained composure. "I won't answer now. Later, if you have to know, I will tell you. I'm not trying to hold back anything about him. I tell you the God's truth when I say I don't know anything about those machine guns, bonds, or anything."

"We can easily determine whether you have a criminal record or not." Cunningham opened up his file folder and showed the woman a few cancelled checks found in the bungalow. "Now, isn't this your handwriting?"

"No, here, I'll write for you." Viola took a pencil and paper and began writing the words dictated by Cunningham.

He then showed her the handwritten list of bonds, pulled from the same folder.

"Now, isn't that the same handwriting as yours?"

"Oh, no. I never saw those," she quickly replied.

Cunningham and the others realized that she was still not cooperating and asked that deputies take her back to her cell. Before leaving the room, Cunningham confidently remarked to her that the Illinois authorities might even find enough evidence to charge her as an accessory to murder, for the seven men killed at the Clark Street massacre. Not giving her a chance to respond, he closed the door.

Finally, on Monday evening, in her weakened emotional state and realizing what deep trouble she was in, she asked to speak to Prosecutor Cunningham again. Her once striking blue eyes, now surrounded by puffy dark circles, were almost unrecognizable. She admitted to him that she was not really married to Fred Burke and was ready to tell the truth.

With her voice raspier than the day before, she began, "My real name is Viola Brenneman. I married John Brenneman on November 7, 1914, in Kankakee, Illinois, and my daughter, Juanita, was born the same month. John worked as a brakeman on the Illinois Central Railroad at the time, but the marriage did not work out. I obtained a divorce on March 3, 1917, on the grounds of desertion and was given custody of Juanita. My maiden name is Viola Ostrowski and my mother still lives in Kankakee. My father died several years ago. I am 34 years of age and have a common school education."

Now that she was opening up, Cunningham exhaled with some amount of relief and prompted her to describe how she met Burke, while the others listened intently. She cleared her throat and then continued.

"I met Fred Dane…I mean Burke, about a year and a half ago. When I was living at 6214 Evans Avenue in Chicago, my friend, Gladys Davidson, phoned me and invited me to her home in Hammond. I accepted her invitation and while I was there, I met Fred for the first time. The three of us went to a roadhouse that evening and I stayed all night with Gladys. The next day was Sunday and we ate dinner at a roadhouse run by Phil Smith. That night I returned to my home in Chicago. After that, I visited Gladys almost every week and met Fred there. Gladys then got married to Fred Hartman, who runs the Coney Island Cabaret."[175]

Stege leaned over and whispered to Cunningham, informing him that former syndicate leader Johnny Torrio owned the Coney Island Cabaret, in Burnham, Illinois. Cunningham nodded in understanding.

"When I met Fred in Hammond, he lived in a wooden cottage in Burnham, Illinois. I went to that cottage with him on different occasions. This continued until I took my first trip with Fred in the summer of 1928, when I went to Wisconsin with him. We stayed in a log cabin near Ladysmith and this is where I started living with him as Mrs. Dane."

Cunningham asked her when they returned to Hammond.

"In the fall. Then we went to the Cordova apartments in Hammond. While we were living there, I took a trip to New York and stayed five days. Later, Fred met me at the railroad station in New York and we stayed at the Almac Hotel. After we returned from New York, we again lived at the Cordova apartments. This time we went by the name of Reed."

Curious as to the series of aliases used, Cunningham inquired as to any other names and why.

"Fred always told me he would marry me as soon as he was free from his wife. I have gone by the name of Callahan. The reason he gave me for going under so many names was to protect me because he knew I had no right to live with him as his wife as long as we were not married. We lived two months at the Dalton apartments on Fifth Avenue, east of Broadway in Gary, under the name of Church. We were going under the name of Church when Fred was a salesman for the Columbia Commercial Feed Company."

He then asked if they had taken any other trips.

"The later part of May or the early part of June 1929, we went to Johnson Lake, Minnesota, which was southeast of International Falls. Mr. Brown was the name of the proprietor of the resort. Johnson Lake was about fifteen miles from Grand Rapids, Minnesota. I stayed there until the last of August. I returned before Fred did and he later telephoned me to come to Hammond, where I stayed with him at the Hotel Lyndore."

Cunningham asked her where she went after that.

"Fred told me to go to my sister Helen's house in Maywood and wait for him to contact me."

Attorney Ditchburne remarked to Cunningham that Al Capone had used the alias Al Brown, and then he asked Viola if she had ever met Capone.

Viola shook her head, no.

Cunningham continued by asking if they ever had any visitors.

"A man I know by the name of Bullard stayed with us. Mr. Bullard was tall and slender. Mrs. Bullard's name was Georgia and she had red hair and blue eyes, was about five-feet-five inches, weight about 120 pounds. They brought me back from Minnesota but I have never seen them since. When we lived at the Dalton apartments, Mr. and Mrs. Bullard visited for about one and a half hours. She later came alone but acted secretive."

Attorney Ditchburne took the opportunity to grill Viola about any associations with Capone or McGurn.

"Fred talked about the arrest of Jack McGurn and Louise Rolfe but I got the impression that he did not know Jack personally. However, Fred was always talking about Al Capone."[176]

Ditchburne next asked where she and her husband were on February 14, 1929.

"On St. Valentine Day, 1929, we were living in Hammond. Fred sent me some chrysanthemums that day."

He asked if Burke was home all day.

"No, he left at 7 a.m. and did not return until 11 a.m. I remember this because he came home and I asked him about dinner and he suggested that I go to the delicatessen store down stairs and buy something for dinner. I persuaded him to go out and buy some groceries, which I then cooked." Viola began to smile, and said, "I think he ordered the flowers for me when he was after the groceries."

"Did he stay at home the rest of the day?"

"That afternoon he went and got some magazines and was gone a couple of hours."

Ditchburne raised his voice and asked if she was aware that Fred Burke had masterminded the St. Valentine's Day Massacre.

Astonished at the accusation, Viola sat up on the edge of her seat. "Oh, Fred wasn't in that terrible thing. I know he wasn't," she asserted while beginning to sob. "Why, he couldn't have been in Chicago and got back to Hammond." She quivered nervously as Cunningham segued with questions about how she arrived in Stevensville.

"Well, we moved to Michigan, near Stevensville, on September 27, 1929," she said, dabbing her eyes and nose. "We bought the house furnished and paid about $1,000 cash down. Before we came to Stevensville to live, Fred told me he thought he would buy an oil station in either Stevensville or St. Joseph. He just got a Hudson coupe, 1928 model. I think he used to drive a Chevrolet. After we moved here, we had no visitors, well, except a few local people and two men who came to our place on two or three different occasions. On one occasion, one of those men brought a woman and they ate a turkey dinner with us."

"Do you know who they were?"

"The only names I heard this man called was 'Prince' and the girl was 'Hon.' The girl weighed about 120 pounds, and about five-feet-five inches tall with dark bobbed hair. The men were about 30 years of age. Both of them were short, wore hats and light gray overcoats, weighed about 150 pounds each. The last time they were there, they stayed about an hour. The two men had a large dark car, which I think was a Buick, but I am not sure. I thought it had a light yellow license on it."

Cunningham knew that only Kansas and New York license plates used a yellow background color in 1929. He then asked what Burke talked about when the visitors came over.

"Oh, I always went to the bedroom whenever Fred would have men come over to the house. I do remember meeting a man named Willie Heeney." Heeney was a powerful member of Capone's Cicero operation of gambling houses and speakeasies, and he often acted as a liaison between the St. Louis hoodlums and those in Chicago.

Cunningham then asked how often she and Burke left the house.

"During the time we lived at Stevensville, Fred was not away for over two or three hours at a time and I was only away three times. The first time I went to Chicago to purchase some drapes and lace curtains was in November and I was gone two or three days. The second time I went was on Thursday, December 12, when I went to Chicago to do some Christmas shopping. The first time I went to Chicago after we were living in Stevensville, he gave me about $600 in cash with which to buy furnishings for the house. The money was mostly in hundred dollar bills, although there were some fifty-dollar bills and some one-dollar bills. Every time he gave me money, it was in large denominations."

He then asked her to describe Burke and divulge what she knew of his background. She paused for a moment, probably figuring out how to describe him, then began.

"Fred is six feet tall, weighs about 220 pounds, he's had a dark moustache ever since I have known him, dark brown hair, plenty of it, which he plastered back. He has no scars, moles, or tattoos. He used to wear glasses but does not any more."

"Did the officers at the house show you the dental plates they found?"

"Yes, they did. Fred was missing two teeth on each side of his lower jaw and one tooth from the upper."

She then shared what she knew of his early years. "Fred is of German parentage although he does not speak German. He was in the Army during the World War and from what he told me, he had seen service in France. I have heard him talking to the other boys about it."[177]

Finding it incomprehensible that she never saw the guns or stolen bonds, Cunningham pressed her on why she never opened the closet door.

"This closet had been kept locked by Fred for the past several weeks. His reason for this was that the decorators were working there and he thought things should be locked up. There was another clothes closet. I kept my clothing there and Fred kept part of his there that he wore every day." Beginning to tear up once again, Viola continued, "I had no knowledge that all that stuff was in the house and I do not know how it got there because none of the visitors who came to see us brought anything with them while I was there."

Viola maintained her innocence throughout the questioning. Despite her unwillingness to cooperate at first, her insight into Burke's associations pleased Cunningham and the other investigators. Her statements would later verify specific connections to Al Capone's syndicate.

NEWS OF SKELLY'S SHOOTING and the arsenal recovered in Burke's bungalow hit the front page of newspapers all across the country. Local reporters took the lead in portraying the scene. The *News-Palladium* described the abode as "The House with the Mask," saying, "Behind its bland and trim exterior lay the machinery of crime and bloodshed. But there are no concealing clumps of trees, no lanes and twisting by-ways, no tunnels and no secret chambers so dear to the heart of fiction writers."[178]

Newspaper reporters from the national news services flocked to the area and camped outside the jail, looking for the latest scoop. Efforts by newsmen to delve into the virtually obscure Burke led to their discovery of an extensive list of alleged crimes. In its December 30, 1929, issue, *Time Magazine* deemed Fred "Killer" Burke "The Most Dangerous Man Alive." The expression stuck, and soon newspapers all across the country were referring to him as such.

Inside the Lake Shore Drive Bungalow belonging to Fred "Killer" Burke on December 16, 1929. Michigan State Police Inspectors Fred Armstrong (left) and A. M. Devon (right). *Author's collection.*

Arsenal found on December 15, 1929 at the Stevensville, Michigan, bungalow owned by Fred "Killer" Burke, as displayed before taken to the Berrien County Sheriff's Department. *Courtesy of the Berrien County Sheriff's Department.*

Berrien County Sheriff's Department, 1929. Front row: Sheriff Fred G. Bryant (center), Second row: Charles Andrews (left) Third row: Erwin Kubath (left) Fourth row: Bill Hedrick (left), William Barry, John Lay, and Charles Davis. *Courtesy of David Agens.*

Arsenal recovered from the Stevensville, Michigan, bungalow owned by Fred "Killer" Burke, December 15, 1929 as displayed on the front steps of the Berrien County Sheriff's Department. *Courtesy of the Berrien County Sheriff's Department.*

Berrien County Sheriff Fred G. Bryant and Deputy Charles Andrews displaying two weapons and bulletproof vests recovered in the Stevensville, Michigan, bungalow owned by Fred "Killer" Burke, December 15, 1929. *Courtesy of the Berrien County Sheriff's Department.*

MOURNING

WHEN ST. JOSEPH RESIDENT JOSEPH KIJAK OPENED the *Herald-Press* on Monday, December 16, 1929, he realized how lucky he was to be alive. The detailed account of how Fred Dane, now known as Fred Burke, eluded the law by hitching rides convinced him that he, too, had picked up Fred Burke.

On December 14, in the evening hours, the 37-year-old Kijak was returning home from downtown St. Joseph. He turned onto Cleveland Avenue heading south from U.S. Highway 12 toward his farm. A few miles before his home, he saw a figure standing alongside the road. As the car headlights illuminated him, the man signaled Kijak to stop. He pulled over and asked the man if he needed a lift. The man got into the vehicle and asked Kijak to take him up the road a little ways. Not feeling the least bit apprehensive, Kijak complied.

They did not travel far before the man blurted, "Let me out."

Kijak stopped the vehicle and the man got out. Watching out the passenger window, Kijak could see the man briskly walking across a farmer's field as he headed west toward U.S. Highway 12. Once the man was out of sight, Kijak turned back around and headed home.

After reading about the fate of Skelly and the evil deeds attributed to Burke, Kijak pointed out the front page of the newspaper to his wife, Ella. "This is the man I gave a ride to on Saturday night," he announced as his hands trembled.

Both sat for a moment in stunned disbelief.[179]

As others read their newspapers on Monday, a bewildered audience wanted answers and a few came forward who might have those answers. William Hutchinson of New Buffalo, Michigan, alerted authorities that he had seen Burke in Chicago the previous day. While having breakfast at the cafeteria in the Victoria Hotel, at the corner of Illinois and Halsted Streets,

Hutchinson had spotted Burke and another man eating there, too.

"I could not have been mistaken," he said. "I know him well. We used to play cards together at the Jefferson Poolroom in St. Joseph, Michigan." Hutchinson described his encounter with the wanted man. "His eyes lighted on me and I knew in a flash that he recognized me. I got the impression that he held a weapon and was prepared to shoot me if I tried to have him arrested."

Illinois state's attorney chief investigator Patrick Roche did not believe that Hutchinson had seen Burke, telling a reporter with the *Chicago Daily Tribune*, "If the killer is in a downtown hotel, he would take his meals to his room."

Back in the Paw Paw Lake area of Coloma, Burke's last known whereabouts, Captain Fred Armstrong of the Michigan State Police, a Benton Harbor native, followed up another lead.

"We have been reliably informed that Burke is still hiding in this district," Armstrong told newspaper reporters. "It was in this vicinity where the last trace of him was had, when he fled following the murder Saturday night. This same informant tells us that Burke was seriously injured when his car crashed following the shooting."[180]

Troopers within a 100-mile radius responded to help with the search. Armed with machine guns, high-powered rifles, and other arms, they searched every vehicle leaving the area. Benton Harbor police, led by Captain William Barry, looked through every idle train car, while St. Joseph police chief Fred Alden traveled to Hammond and Gary, Indiana, to work with authorities there. St. Joseph fire chief William Hudson Mitchell and the firefighters, all armed with their own .45-caliber revolvers, set up roadblocks. Hundreds of people flocked to the Berrien County Jail seeking the latest information and offering aid.

Front-page articles across the nation described the horrendous details of Burke's deeds, so the *News-Palladium* went with a different approach, featuring a poignant editorial about Charles Skelly's death that personalized the community's pent-up feelings of anger and resentment toward Chicago's corruption, lawlessness within their own system, and the lackadaisical efforts of law enforcement.

> "Gangland snarled and showed us its teeth on the busy, peaceful, and Yule-lighted streets of St. Joseph Saturday night. It made a mockery of the Christmas spirit of 'peace on earth, good will toward men' and without warning, without reason, without a single spark of human decency.
>
> "It took the life of young Charles Skelly, member of the St. Jo-

seph's police department. Skelly's savage murder by Fred Dane (who was really Fred Burke), whose house on the Lake Shore Drive afterward proved a veritable desperado's cache of stolen gold and armament is a sensational chapter in local crime history, but in the day's run of the nation's criminal news it is just an incident.

"And that, behind the brutality and wantonness of the slaying, is the shocking condition that confronts the nation's forces of law and order. 'Bandit Kills Cop' has become a familiar headline to all newspaper readers in the 48 states; it is only when such drama is enacted on our own streets that we give it more than passing attention or consideration.

"As we say, it is shocking, but not so surprising that Skelly was killed as he was. Chicago, politically corrupt and crime beset, spills its underworld denizens and terror into adjacent areas. These shores are but a two-hour auto drive from the fountainhead of lawlessness.

"It is only natural that we would get some of the backwash and that on our streets and in our peaceful neighborhoods that we should, all unknowingly, brush elbows with men who are all set to kill at almost the provocation of a scowl.

"The community's heartfelt sympathy goes out to the family of this young policeman who met such a violent, sudden, and heartless death. If there can be any consolation for his kinfolk in the tragedy of his ruthless murder, it lies in the fact that he died in the line of duty; that he made the supreme sacrifice, as the soldier makes it, that life and property might be more safe and more secure for those who live on.

"The public owes one solemn duty to this boy who gave his life to the common cause. And that is that it sees no efforts be spared to get the slayer. Nothing short of a herculean effort by the constituted authorities to bring this deadly enemy of society to the bar of justice to atone for this foul deed. Unless prison doors close for all time upon Charles Skelly's slayer, the star he so worthily wore, the duties he so faithfully performed, the supreme price gangland made him pay will all have been made in vain, while law in these parts will only be a plaything.

"Mr. Sheriff, GET YOUR MAN!"[181]

THE FLAGS IN ST. JOSEPH and all across Southwestern Michigan were lowered to half-staff, and whipped in the northeast wind on Tuesday, December 17, 1929. The intersection of Main and Broad Street was now revered as a site of tragedy, the place where Officer Charles Skelly counted down his final hours. However, hope kept watch from the opposite corner, a sacred building that welcomed all. The First Methodist Church would offer a dignified celebration of his life. Although not the Skalay family's church, it was the biggest church in town, necessary for what officials expected to be one of the largest funerals.

The casket holding the body of Charles Skelly was first revealed to mourners in the small chapel of Esalhorst Funeral Parlor at 235 High Street in Benton Harbor. Five hundred citizens shared their presence and heartfelt sadness there. Then, at 11:00 a.m., a hearse transported the body to the church, where it would lie in repose for three hours. Honor guard members standing at his bier were 23-year-old officer Raymond Slanker and 25-year-old firefighter Charles Wahl. Slanker and Wahl represented Skelly's youth and the two professions for which he had proudly worn the uniforms. The Skalay family sat nearby, along with Charles Skelly's girlfriend, Mildred Thar, and tearfully watched the scores of mourners pass by the body.

The golden casket sat open, lined with gold baronet silk and displayed atop a bronze bier beneath the pulpit, flanked by floral arrangements. Undertaker Harry Esalhorst had dressed the body in a dark suit and folded Skelly's hands across his chest. He looked peaceful, as if he were sleeping. Pinned to his suit was the emblem of the Fraternal Order of Police, an organization that had established a Berrien County chapter only a month before, with Skelly as a charter member. To the right of the choir pews, the American flag hung proudly.

Hundreds of floral bouquets and wreaths honoring the dead officer filled the room with a sweet fragrance. The St. Joseph Fire Department had sent a large arrangement of roses and the St. Joseph Police Department had sent a wreath made up of roses and carnations. Another large wreath from the students in St. Joseph schools, who considered Officer Skelly their hero, adorned the church. All of the schools in St. Joseph let out at noon, so students and teachers could attend the funeral. They remembered Skelly as the big strong police officer who had a smile and a kind word as he protected the children walking to and from school. His humbleness, humor, and kindness made him a friend to everyone, especially to the city's youngest. As the children lined up to see their hero for the last time, one youngster said, "Gosh, I hope they find the guy that done it."[182]

His words resonated to all.

By noon, scores of mourners began filing in to get seats for the service while floral arrangements continued to arrive even after 1:00 p.m. A special section reserved for police officers and firefighters quickly filled with representatives from the Berrien County Sheriff's Department and the United States Coast Guard, and police officers from Benton Harbor, Niles, South Haven, Kalamazoo, Dowagiac, and Buchanan, Michigan, and South Bend, Indiana, all in uniform. Extra chairs set up beneath the pulpit were also filled. Local clubs and businesses were represented: Fraternal Order of Police, Benevolent and Protective Order of Elks, Fraternal Order of Eagles, St. Joseph Chamber of Commerce and Retail Merchants Association, St. Joseph Post Office, Auto Specialties Manufacturing Company, Southties Manufacturing Company, and the South Haven Metropolitan Club. Men, women, and children crowded the aisles, crammed the stairways, and stood elbow-to-elbow in the hallway; still others packed the streets outside, braving the 34-degree temperature. Altogether, 4,000 mourners gathered in hushed tribute for Officer Charles Skelly, the biggest funeral the city had ever hosted.

At 2:00 p.m., First Methodist Church Reverend W. F. Ledford cued the organist to begin, drenching the room with dramatic melody as the choir joined with an opening hymn. Ledford had known Skelly personally, when he was a firefighter. He and his family lived across from the fire department and his sons would watch the firefighters sliding down the brass pole. Allowing them to experience the thrill, Skelly once had welcomed the Ledford boys to take a slide for themselves. Right before the service began, one of the young Ledford boys approached his father, "Don't forget to say the boys loved him, Dad."

A vocal quartet from the Church of God represented the Skalay family's denomination. People listened with bowed heads and moistened eyes. Reverend Ledford began the service with a reading of scriptures while First Church of God Reverend Gustav Butgereit gave an address in German, the elder Skalay's mother tongue. Saron Lutheran Church Reverend Victor J. Tengwald delivered a prayer, as all religions and denominations in the area bonded as one. After the prayer, people lifted their heads and Reverend Ledford stepped back up to the pulpit to begin his eulogy:

> "We, as citizens of St. Joseph, join his loved ones in mourning the tragic death of Officer Skelly. We are here to pay tribute to his memory. Truly, he was one of the best of public servants. He was a clean lad—what the soldiers during the war would have called a 'white man.' He did nothing to soil his character or his uniform. He was an honor to his comrades and an honor to St. Joseph.

"Police officer Skelly had the reckless daring of youth. He belonged to the youth of today—the youth that is not afraid to risk all in a worthy purpose. Youth is fearless, and it is dauntless. It leads to flights across the Atlantic and over the icy wilderness of the Antarctic. It keeps fresh the essence of life. Officer Skelly was a fighter, and so with Browning could say: 'I was ever a fighter, so one fight more, the best, and the last!'

"The tragic going of this brave lad should be a reminder to us of several things, of our dependence on each other in community life. When one suffers, we all suffer. If we are to make progress against social outcasts and law violators, we must stand together for the higher things of civilization.

"This sad event reminds us of our duty to maintain the highest regard for the law and for those whose duty it is to enforce it. We criticize all too easily those who must endanger their lives on our behalf. There is all too much sympathy for the men who use desperate and criminal means to further their own selfish purposes, and not enough appreciation of those who serve us.

"Too often, the attitude of our best citizens—of us all—unwittingly encourages the criminal. We should teach our children reverence for law and order and respect for the rules of society. How much are we, as a community, responsible for the making of criminals? I do not know but God help us to do our best to make this a good community, firm in our support of officers of the law.

"The innocent die for the guilty. Christ was sacrificed for the guilty. St. Joseph has laid upon the altar one of its finest young men. It seems to be a rule of life that the innocent shall give their lives— yet perhaps their sacrifice keeps a continual inspiration of nobility before humanity and lifts it ever upward toward the ultimate in right living. Death in such a cause is not in vain."[183]

Reverend Ledford then asked the mourners to bow their heads in prayer.

Upon the close of the service, pallbearers David Hunter and Ben Phairas of the St. Joseph Police Department, Thomas Schillinger and R. Keane Evans of the St. Joseph Fire Department, and Chief Thure O. Linde and Captain William Barry of the Benton Harbor Police Department lifted the casket off its base. All the uniformed police officers and firefighters in attendance formed a double line, through which the pallbearers carried the casket down the aisle of the packed church. The empty looks and streaming tears of those in uniform were hard to ignore. Once the lingering lines of heartbroken mourners cleared a path, the casket was loaded into the hearse and a somber processional of cars proceeded toward Crystal Springs Cemetery.

A six-man motorcycle team from the sheriff's department led the processional. The Skalay family rode behind the hearse, while cars of other mourners crept slowly behind. Two vehicles filled entirely with hundreds of deep red roses, lilies, sweet peas, carnations, and chrysanthemums rounded out the processional. From Main Street the vehicles traveled to Wayne Street, then across the St. Joseph River and through downtown Benton Harbor. The five-mile drive to the cemetery was slow moving. Traffic stopped and large crowds watched as the processional passed. There was no doubt that this emotional memorial touched even those who did not attend the service. From a tipped hat, to the words of condolences mouthed to the passing processional, everyone acknowledged the loss of Officer Skelly.

At the cemetery, an enormous display of floral arrangements graced the open hollow that would be Skelly's final resting place. The pallbearers carried the casket to the draped base and his family followed behind.

Once the mourners had gathered around, Reverend Ledford raised his arms to hush the crowd. In a booming voice to reach even those distant, he began his closing words.

> "This tragic death reminds us of our dependence on God, for in our grief we are brought into closer communion with Him. His family has the memory of a brave boy, who served his community well and died in that service. We commit his spirit unto God in the sure hope and trust that nothing of good is lost and that all who have faithfully performed their duty shall receive due recompense."

Then, in a perfectly choreographed maneuver, everyone looked up as a wreath gently floated down from the grey skies and landed on the wilted grass, just a few feet away from the grave. They watched as the airplane that dropped it banked sharply before vanishing into the distance, the roaring engines fading to a murmur. A final hymn by the First Church of God vocal quartet filled the chill-dampened air as the casket descended into the earth.

As if Mother Nature were orchestrating her own somber closing, flakes of snow began to fall as the mourners retreated to their cars. For several days, cold temperatures and heavy snow blanketed the entire Midwest.[184] In the days, weeks, and months that followed, the community slowly returned to a semblance of normalcy. However, Chief Alden and Captain Barry would remain haunted by Skelly's death. Alden, especially, felt the despondency of another loss and would soon face blame from city officials for Burke's escape. The Skalay family had a difficult time adjusting to the loss of their loved one. The relationship between the siblings and their stepmother, Bertha, spiraled downhill. Her violent outbursts and maniacal episodes became prevalent, forcing several of the younger siblings to take up residency with other family members, putting Gustav in a tough situation. He chose to stand by his wife. Gustav also had difficulty collecting on Skelly's life insurance policy from the Hartford Accident and Indemnity Company and eventually had to hire attorney Arthur Leckner. His main concern, though, was getting justice for his son. "I am always for law and order like Chuck was," he remarked to a reporter. "Every citizen should rise up against these gangsters who shoot down people in cold blood. If the people helped the authorities, there wouldn't be so many victims like my boy."

Indeed, Charles Skelly's death served as a call to action.

Charles Skelly's coffin carried by pallbearers on December 17, 1929. Officer David Hunter front left. *Courtesy of the Berrien County Sheriff's Department.*

Endnotes

1 *News-Palladium*. Benton Harbor, MI. December 13, 1929. 1.
2 ---December 14, 1929. 9, 11, 14.
3 ---December 14, 1929, 1, 2.
4 *Herald-Palladium*. St. Joseph, MI. "St. Joe Tie to Valentine Massacre Recalled." February 13, 1982.
5 Nineteen Hundred Thirty United States Federal Census. St. Joseph, Berrien County, Michigan. Roll 977, Page 10B, Enumeration District 49, Image 197. http://www.ancestry.com. (Accessed September 6, 2011).
6 *News-Palladium*. December 10, 1929. 5.
7 State of Michigan Department of Public Safety. *Fred Burke*. "Transcript William Lorf/Lohraff interview given to Phillip Hutson and George Waterman." List of Witnesses. No date. Case #2208, December 14, 1929 – July 10, 1940. Michigan State Police. Lansing, MI.
8 Joyce Kool Ender. Interview by author. St. Joseph, MI. September 6, 2011.
9 State of Michigan Department of Public Safety. *Fred Burke*. "Transcript Lawrence Terry interview given to Phillip Hutson and George Waterman." List of Witnesses. No date. Case #2208, December 14, 1929 – July 10, 1940. Michigan State Police. Lansing, MI.
10 State of Michigan Department of Public Safety. *Fred Burke*. "Transcript Arthur Truhn interview given to Phillip Hutson and George Waterman." Special Report. April 8, 1931. Case #2208, December 14, 1929 – July 10, 1940. Michigan State Police. Lansing, MI.
11 State of Michigan Department of Public Safety. *Fred Burke*. "Transcript Phil Daly and Ted Lucker interview given to Phillip Hutson and George Waterman." Special Report. April 8, 1931. Case #2208, December 14, 1929 – July 10, 1940. Michigan State Police. Lansing, MI.
12 State of Michigan Department of Public Safety. *Fred Burke*. "Transcript Gustav Getz interview given to Phillip Hutson and George Waterman." No date. Case #2208, December 14, 1929 – July 10, 1940. Michigan State Police. Lansing, MI.
13 Berrien County Archives. Berrien County Death Records. "Chas. H. Skallay." Book E, Page 294. Benton Harbor, MI. - Mothers name listed as Mary Schultz.
14 Judge Orville W. Coolidge. *A Twentieth Century History of Berrien County, Michigan*. The Lewis Publishing Company, 1906.
15 Nineteen Hundred Ten United States Federal Census. Benton Harbor Ward 1, Berrien County, Michigan. Roll T624_638, Page 8B, Enumeration District 60, Image 168. http://www.ancestry.com. (Accessed June 30, 2010).
16 Sharon Skelly. Interview.
17 State of Michigan. Department of State, Division of Vital Statistics. Death Certificate for Anna Skalay. Registered #22. Lansing, MI. March 23, 1913.
18 --- Death Certificate for Freda Skalay. Registered #58. May 8, 1918.
19 --- Death Certificate for Mary Skalay. Registered #21. Page 36. November 21, 1919.
20 --- Death Certificate for Helen Skalay. Registered #63. Page 649. December 6, 1919.
21 *New York Times*. New York, NY. August 14, 1920.
22 ---http://chroniclingamerica.loc.gov/lccn/sn85058393/1920-08-31/ed-1/seq-8/. (Accessed September 21, 2011).
23 *Daily Globe*. Ironwood, MI. September 3, 1920.
24 *New York Times*. July 28, 1920.
25 Ken Murphy. *Waterloo Courier*. Waterloo, IA. "Pugilists of the Past." Nov. 4, 1975. 2.

26   Roger Kahn. *A Flame of Pure Fire: Jack Dempsey and The Roaring '20's.* "Preliminaries." Houghton Mifflin Harcourt, 1999. 208.

27   *New York Tribune.* New York, NY. September 6, 1920.

28   *Detroit Free Press.* Detroit, MI. September 6, 1920. 10.

29   *Daily Globe.* September 7, 1920. 1.

30   *New York Times.* September 7, 1920. 1, 13.

31   *Daily Globe.* September 26, 1921. 1.

32   *New York Times.* September 26, 1921.

33   Berrien County Archives. Berrien County Marriage Record. Book M, Page 336. Benton Harbor, MI. Gus Skelley.

34   Name also spelled "Schanert."

35   Berrien County Archives. Berrien County Marriage Records. Book N, Page 236. Benton Harbor, MI. Gus Skaly – Bertha's age listed as 32 years, living in Benton Harbor, father's first name is August, and her mother's maiden name is Lippert. Gustav's mother's maiden name shows Schaleen and Gustav lives in Sodus.

36   Nineteen Hundred Thirty United States Federal Census. Benton Harbor, Berrien County, Michigan. Roll 976, Page 14A, Enumeration District 13, Image 429. http://www.ancestry.com. (Accessed July 16, 2010).

37   David Agens. Interview by author. Benton Harbor, MI. January 24, 2011.

38   ---August 20, 1923. 1, 8.

39   Edward Butts. *Outlaws of the Lakes: Bootlegging & Smuggling from Colonial Times to Prohibition, a Prohibition Primer.* Toronto: Lynx Images, 2004. 227.

40   ---January 1, 1930. 16.

41   Benjamin L. Reber. *History of St. Joseph.* St. Joseph, MI: St. Joseph Chamber of Commerce. 1925. 131.

42   Berrien County Archives. Berrien County Death Record. Book E, Page 113, Record # 872. Benton Harbor, Michigan. March 15, 1926.

43   Berrien County Historical Association. Fede, Famiglia, e Amici: The Italian Experience in Berrien County 1900-2004. "Death." 2004. 12.

44   *News-Palladium.* March 17, 1927. 1

45   David Critchley. "Goodfellas: Berrien County and Prohibition Era Gangsters." *Historical Society of Michigan Chronicle.* April 2008. 19-23.

46   Variations of surname include Vireigilo and Vereigilo, which appear in various newspapers.

47   *News-Palladium.* August 30, 1929. 1, 16.

48   Berrien County Jail Ledger Book. "Tony and Charles Domingo." October 22, 1927. Berrien County Historical Association. Berrien Springs, MI.

49   *Time Magazine.* "Crime: Glum Gorilla." December 19, 1927. http://www.time.com/time/magazine/article/0,9171,731283,00.html. (Accessed February 21, 2013).

50   *Herald-Press.* September 12, 1962. Section 2. 1.

51   *Coloma Courier.* Coloma, MI. September 14, 1928.

52   *Chicago Daily Tribune.* September 14, 1928, 2.

53   Eric Hess. "Facial Recognition: A Valuable Tool for Law Enforcement." *Forensic Magazine*, Vicon Publishing, Inc., October/November 2010.

54   *Herald-Press.* September 12, 1928.

55   *News-Palladium.* October 12, 1928, 1.

56   *Herald-Press.* May 10, 1955. 10.

57   Jack Lait and Lee Mortimer. *Chicago Confidential.* "The Brave Bulls." New York, NY: Crown Publishers, 1950.

58   Federal Bureau of Investigations. "John (Handsome Johnny) Roselli Part 1 of 12." Chicago File #58-194. http://vault.fbi.gov/John%20%28Handsome%20 Johnny%29%20Roselli. (Accessed November 12, 2011).

59   Berrien County Register of Deeds. Liber 245, page 339. St. Joseph, MI.

60   Michael Moore. Interview by author. Benton Harbor, MI. August 26, 2011.

61   http://www.harborcountry.org/Union-Pier-84/. (Accessed February 15, 2012).

62   http://www.lakesideinns.com/history.htm. (Accessed February 15, 2012).

63   Barbra Stodola. *The Beacher*. "Sands of Time." Michigan City, IN. July 17, 2003.

64   June Sawyers. "It's 1924, And to 'Big Al', Cicero is His Kind of Town." *Chicago Tribune*. November 15, 1987.

65   Federal Bureau of Investigation. *John (Handsome Johnny) Roselli*. Chicago File #58-194. Part 1. http://vault.fbi.gov/John%20%28Handsome%20Johnny%29%20Roselli. (Accessed November 12, 2011).

66   Investigation of Organized Crime in Interstate Commerce. "Hearings Before a Special Committee to Investigate Organized Crime in Interstate Commerce." United States Senate. Eighty-first Congress. Second session. Volume 5. Illinois. http:// www.archive.org/search.php?query=organized%20crime%20in%20interstate%20 commerce%20AND%20mediatype%3Atexts. (Accessed October 9, 2011).

67   Barbara Stodola. *Michigan City Beach Communities*. "Long Beach." Charleston, SC: Arcadia Publishing, 2003.

68   *Illinois Crime Survey 1929 Part III Organized Crime in Chicago*. "Torrio as Overlord." Chapter XX. 909-919.

69   William Kruck. Interview by author. Benton Harbor, MI. February 8, 2012.

70   *Tri-City Record*. Watervliet, MI. April 7, 1993.

71   *News-Palladium*. February 1, 1947. 3.

72   ---September 8, 1964. 11.

73   *Seattle Daily Times*. Seattle, WA. April 17, 1960. 60.

74   William Kruck, interview.

75   *Herald-Press*. March 15, 1961. 20.

76   *Herald-Palladium*. May 19, 1977. 13.

77   *Herald-Palladium*. August 1990, 4, 5, 9.

78   *News-Palladium*. "Babson Forecasts for 1929-1954." January 1, 1929.

79   Jay Robert Nash. *Bloodletters and Badmen: The Definitive Book of American Crime*. "St. Valentine's Day Massacre." Book 2, Warner Paperback Library. 1973. 363-367.

80   City of Chicago Department of Police. Report of Murder of Seven Men at Garage at 2122 N. Clark St. February 14, 1929. 36th District Report #3378. Chicago, IL.

81   ---Report of Murder of Seven Men at Garage at 2122 N. Clark St., Feb. 14, 1929."

82   *Dunkirk Evening Observer*. Dunkirk, NY. February 16, 1929. 1.

83   *Ludington Daily News*. Ludington, MI. February 19, 1929. 1, 8.

84   *Chicago Daily Tribune*. February 24, 1929. 5.

85   *News-Palladium*. February 15, 1929. 2.

86   ---February 2, 1929. 3.

87   *Chicago Daily Tribune*. December 24, 1929. 3.

88   Elmer L. Williams. *That Man Bundesen*. Volume 1. 1931.

89   Jeffery Gusfield. *Deadly Valentines – The Story of Capone's Henchman "Machine Gun" Jack McGurn and Louise Rolfe, his Blond Alibi*. Chicago, IL: Chicago Review Press, 2012.

90   ---*Deadly Valentines – The Story of Capone's Henchman "Machine Gun" Jack McGurn and Louise Rolfe, his Blond Alibi*.

91   William J. Helmer and Art Bilek. *The St. Valentine's Day Massacre.* "Chronology." Nashville, TN: Cumberland House Publishing, 2004.
92   William J. Helmer. The First American 'Crime Lab'. http://www. gangstersandoutlaws.com/CrimeLab.html, (Accessed August 1, 2010).
93   Calvin H. Goddard. A History of Firearm Identification. "Police 13-13." *Chicago Police Journal.* 1936.
94   *Chicago Tribune/*Northwestern University Alumni News. January 1930. 20.
95   P. Von Frantzius Sport Manual. 1928.
96   http://www.nramuseum.com/the-museum/the-galleries/ever-vigilant/case-64-world-war-ii-us/us-auto-ordnance-thompson-m1a1-submachine-gun.aspx. (Accessed April 21, 2011).
97   Calvin H. Goddard. "The Valentine Day Massacre: A Study in Ammunition-Tracing." *A Crime and its Clues.* 1929.
98   --- The Valentine Day Massacre: A Study in Ammunition-Tracing.
99   Mario Gomes. *My Al Capone Museum.* "Von Lengerke and Antoine: Gangland Armorer." http://www.myalcaponemuseum.com/id83.htm. (Accessed May 20, 2011).
100 Chicago Crime Commission. Inquest on the Bodies of Albert Kachellek, Et Al. April 19, 1929. Fourth A.M. Session. Chicago, IL. 21-26.
101 *Kokomo Tribune.* Kokomo, IN. April 20, 1929. 1.
102 *Chicago Tribune.* May 13, 1929. 8.
103 Mario Gomes. *My Al Capone Museum.* "Peter Von Frantzius: Gangland Armorer." http://www.myalcaponemuseum.com/id83.htm. (Accessed August 1, 2010).
104 Before getting into the dog racing business, O'Hare was an attorney in St. Louis. His son, Edward Butch O'Hare was the first Naval Ace Pilot in World War II, eventually earning him a tribute when Chicago's Orchard Airport was renamed O'Hare International Airport in 1949.
105 *Rockford Morning Star.* Rockford, IL. December 18, 1929. 1, 2.
106 *Logansport-Pharos Tribune.* Logansport, IN. December 3, 1929. 2.
107 Larry K. Gaines and Roger LeRoy Miller. *Criminal Justice In Action.* "Law Enforcement Today." Thompson Wadsworth, 2009. 137-138.
108 Michigan Legislature. Section 28.282. Radio Broadcasting Stations Act 152. Aug. 28, 1929.
109 *News-Palladium.* May 1, 1929. 6.
110 ---April 29, 1959. 2.
111 ---February 15, 1912. 1.
112 *Telegraph-Herald and Times-Journal.* Dubuque, IA. July 19, 1931. 2.
113 ---May 7, 1929. 1, 6.
114 ---January 17, 1930. 1.
115 http://www.blossomtimefestival.org/?page_id=66. (Accessed January 21, 2013).
116 Amy L. Arnold. *Southwest Michigan RoadMap: The West Michigan Pike, Volume 1: Historic Context Narrative,* "Architecture – Architectural Styles." State Historic Preservation Office. September 2010. 38.
117 Various newspapers listed original owner of house as Edward Weise, John Weise, Freeman Weise, and Fred Wiesel.
118 *Herald-Press.* September 6, 1946. 6.
119 State of Michigan Department of Public Safety. *Fred Burke.* "Transcript John Swigert and Emil Frost interview given to Phillip Hutson and George Waterman." List of Witnesses. No date. Case #2208, December 14, 1929 – July 10, 1940. Michigan State Police. Lansing, MI.

120 State of Michigan Department of Public Safety. *Fred Burke*. "Transcript Paul Hoge interview given to Phillip Hutson and George Waterman." List of Witnesses. No date. Case #2208, December 14, 1929 – July 10, 1940. Michigan State Police. Lansing, MI. – Witness list shows Pete Hoge while Special Report shows Peter Hodge.

121 State of Michigan Department of Public Safety. *Fred Burke*. "Transcript Julius Burandt interview given to Phillip Hutson and George Waterman." List of Witnesses. No date. Case #2208, December 14, 1929 – July 10, 1940. Michigan State Police. Lansing, MI.

122 State of Michigan Department of Public Safety. *Fred Burke*. "Transcript Fred Jung interview given to Phillip Hutson and George Waterman." List of Witnesses. No date. Case #2208, December 14, 1929 – July 10, 1940. Michigan State Police. Lansing, MI. – Surname also spelled Yung.

123 Chicago Crime Commission. Inquest on the Bodies of Albert Kachellek, Et Al. December 23, 1929. 10:15 o'clock a.m. Chicago, IL.

124 State of Michigan Department of Public Safety. *Fred Burke*. "Transcript Robert Carlton interview given to Phillip Hutson and George Waterman." List of Witnesses. No date. Case #2208, December 14, 1929 – July 10, 1940. Michigan State Police. Lansing, MI.

125 State of Michigan Department of Public Safety. *Fred Burke*. "Transcript James Miller interview given to Phillip Hutson and George Waterman." List of Witnesses. No date. Case #2208, December 14, 1929 – July 10, 1940. Michigan State Police. Lansing, MI.

126 *News-Palladium*. March 30, 1931. 9.

127 Karen Gobert. *Stevensville & Area, Stevensville, Michigan 1884-1984*. "Fred "Killer" Burke Alias Fred Dane." Stevensville Village Council. 1984. 85-86.

128 One article states that Officer Ed Rohl was Skelly's partner while another lists Officer Ben Phairas.

129 *Ironwood Daily Globe*. October 31, 1929. 4.

130 *Chicago Daily Tribune*. October 16, 1929. 1.

131 *News-Palladium*. October 16, 1929. 1, 15.

132 ---October 16, 1929. 1, 15.

133 *Sterling Daily Gazette*. Sterling, IL. October 15, 1929. 1.

134 Berrien County Circuit Court. State of Michigan v Fred Dane. April 27, 1931. Berrien County Clerk, St. Joseph, MI.

135 State of Michigan Department of Public Safety. *Fred Burke*. "Transcript Victor Kolberg interview given to Phillip Hutson and George Waterman." January 9, 1930. Case #2208, December 14, 1929 – July 10, 1940. Michigan State Police. Lansing, MI.

136 State of Michigan Department of Public Safety. *Fred Burke*. "Transcript Albert Petruschke interview given to Phillip Hutson and George Waterman." No date. Case #2208, December 14, 1929 – July 10, 1940. Michigan State Police. Lansing, MI.

137 Joyce Kool Ender. Interview by author. St. Joseph, MI. September 6, 2011.

138 State of Michigan Department of Public Safety. *Fred Burke*. "Transcript Ed Rohl and Mr. Stover interview given to Phillip Hutson and George Waterman." List of Witnesses. No date. Case #2208, December 14, 1929 – July 10, 1940. Michigan State Police. Lansing, MI.

139 State of Michigan Department of Public Safety. *Fred Burke*. "Transcript William Struever interview given to Phillip Hutson and George Waterman." No date. Case #2208, December 14, 1929 – July 10, 1940. Michigan State Police. Lansing, MI.

140   State of Michigan Department of Public Safety. *Fred Burke.* "Transcript Gustav Getz interview given to Phillip Hutson and George Waterman." No date. Case #2208, December 14, 1929 – July 10, 1940. Michigan State Police. Lansing, MI.

141   State of Michigan Department of Public Safety. *Fred Burke.* "Transcript Charles Wahl interview given to Phillip Hutson and George Waterman." Special Report. April 8, 1931. Case #2208, December 14, 1929 – July 10, 1940. Michigan State Police. Lansing, MI.

142   State of Michigan Department of Public Safety. *Fred Burke.* "Transcript Albert Petruschke interview given to Phillip Hutson and George Waterman." No date. Case #2208, December 14, 1929 – July 10, 1940. Michigan State Police. Lansing, MI.

143   State of Michigan Department of Public Safety. *Fred Burke.* "Transcript William Struever interview given to Phillip Hutson and George Waterman." No date. Case #2208, December 14, 1929 – July 10, 1940. Michigan State Police. Lansing, MI.

144   Dr. William Emery. Interview by author. September 28, 2010. St. Joseph, MI.

145   Dr. William Emery, son of Dr. Clayton Emery said that his father kept the bullet. When his father passed away, Dr. William Emery took possession of the bullet and kept it at his practice located in the Uptown Building but since his retirement, the bullet has been lost.

146   State of Michigan Department of Public Safety. *Fred Burke.* "Transcript William Struever interview given to Phillip Hutson and George Waterman." January 4, 1930. Case #2208, December 14, 1929 – July 10, 1940. Michigan State Police. Lansing, MI.

147   Peg Williamson. Interview by author. St. Joseph, Michigan. July 25, 2013.

148   State of Michigan Department of Public Safety. *Fred Burke.* "Transcript William Struever interview given to Phillip Hutson and George Waterman." January 4, 1930. Case #2208, December 14, 1929 – July 10, 1940. Michigan State Police. Lansing, MI.

149   *News-Palladium.* November 10, 1962. 11.

150   Sharon Skelly, interview.

151   Viola Dane referred to the road as on South Shore when in fact it was on Lake Shore.

152   *Jackson Citizen Patriot.* Jackson, MI. July 2, 1918. 4.

153   State of Michigan Department of Public Safety. *Fred Burke.* "Transcript Harry Lewis interview given to Phillip Hutson and George Waterman." January 10, 1930. Case #2208, December 14, 1929 – July 10, 1940. Michigan State Police. Lansing, MI.

154   State of Michigan Department of Public Safety. *Fred Burke.* "Transcript Harry Lewis interview given to Phillip Hutson and George Waterman." January 10, 1930. Case #2208, December 14, 1929 – July 10, 1940. Michigan State Police. Lansing, MI.

155   State of Michigan Department of Public Safety. *Fred Burke.* "Transcript Frank Cupp and H. K. Cupp interview given to Phillip Hutson and George Waterman." List of Witnesses. No date. Case #2208, December 14, 1929 – July 10, 1940. Michigan State Police. Lansing, MI.

156   *Chicago Daily Tribune.* December 16, 1929. 1.

157   State of Michigan Department of Public Safety. *Fred Burke.* "Transcript Albert Wishart interview given to Phillip Hutson and George Waterman." Special Report. April 8, 1931. Case #2208, December 14, 1929 – July 10, 1940. Michigan State Police. Lansing, MI.

158   Karen Gobert. *Stevensville & Area, Stevensville, Michigan 1884-1984.* "Fred "Killer" Burke Alias Fred Dane." Stevensville, MI: Stevensville Village Council, 1984. 85-86.

159   State of Michigan Department of Public Safety. *Fred Burke*. "Transcript John Lay, Charles Andrews, and Erwin Kubath interview given to Phillip Hutson and George Waterman." Special Report. April 8, 1931. Case #2208, December 14, 1929 – July 10, 1940. Michigan State Police. Lansing, MI.

160   State of Michigan Department of Public Safety. *Fred Burke*. "Transcript Harry Sauerbier interview given to Wilbur Cunningham, Phillip Hutson, and George Waterman." No date. Case #2208, December 14, 1929 – July 10, 1940. Michigan State Police. Lansing, MI.

161   State of Michigan Department of Public Safety. *Fred Burke*. "Transcript Monroe Wulff interview given to Phillip Hutson and George Waterman." No date. Case #2208, December 14, 1929 – July 10, 1940. Michigan State Police. Lansing, MI.

162   *News-Palladium*. December 16, 1929. 1-2.

163   State of Michigan Department of Public Safety. *Fred Burke*. "Transcript Steve Kunay interview given to Phillip Hutson and George Waterman." Special Report. April 8, 1931. Case #2208, December 14, 1929 – July 10, 1940. Michigan State Police. Lansing, MI.

164   While the official report made to police was that Fred Dane was dropped off in Coloma, descendants of Steve Kunay remember a much different destination all together. Kunay's great-nephew, David Ratajik, recalled the destination as Chicago, not Coloma. The revolver that Dane had kept in hand throughout the drive was then placed in Kunay's palm. Dane told him he would not need it anymore; a Smith and Wesson hammerless .38-caliber revolver Model 2.

165   State of Michigan Department of Public Safety. *Fred Burke*. "Transcript Harry Sauerbier interview given to Wilbur Cunningham, Phillip Hutson, and George Waterman." No date. Case #2208, December 14, 1929 – July 10, 1940. Michigan State Police. Lansing, MI.

166   *Time Magazine*. "Crime: The Most Dangerous Man Alive." December 30, 1929. http://www.time.com/time/magazine/article/0,9171,929144,00.html. (Accessed October 19, 2010).

167   *Chicago Daily Tribune*. December 16, 1929. 1.

168   *News-Palladium*. December 16, 1929. 1, 8.

169   ---December 16, 1929. 1.

170   State of Michigan Department of Public Safety. *Fred Burke*. "Transcript Fred Alden and Ollie Slater interview given to Phillip Hutson and George Waterman." Special Report. April 8, 1931. Case #2208, December 14, 1929 – July 10, 1940. Michigan State Police. Lansing, MI.

171   Berrien County Jail Ledger Book. "Viola Dane." December 14, 1929. Number 9, Page 54. Berrien County Historical Association. Berrien Springs, MI.

172   *News-Palladium*. December 16, 1929. 14.

173   State of Michigan Department of Public Safety. *Fred Burke*. "Transcript Ferdinand Ratz interview given to Phillip Hutson and George Waterman." List of Witnesses. No date. Case #2208, December 14, 1929 – July 10, 1940. Michigan State Police. Lansing, MI.

174   State of Michigan Department of Public Safety. *Fred Burke*. "Transcript Reinhold Mischke and John Zilke interview given to Phillip Hutson and George Waterman." List of Witnesses. No date. Case #2208, December 14, 1929 – July 10, 1940. Michigan State Police. Lansing, MI.

175   Johnny Torrio owned Coney Island Café located at 2800 E. 138th Place, Burnham, Illinois.

176   *Chicago Daily Tribune.* December 17, 1929. 2.

177   State of Michigan Department of Public Safety. *Fred Burke.* "Transcript Viola Dane aka Brenneman interview given to Wilbur Cunningham." December 17, 1929. Case #2208, December 14, 1929 – July 10, 1940. Michigan State Police. Lansing, MI.

178   *News-Palladium.* December 16, 1929. 2.

179   Cheryl Schulte. Interview with author. May 19, 2012. St. Joseph, MI.

180   *Rochester Evening Journal.* December 18, 1929. 1.

181   *News-Palladium.* December 16, 1929/ 2.

182   ---December 17, 1929. 6.

183   *News-Palladium.* December 18, 1929. 1, 11.

184   National Weather Service. http://www.crh.noaa.gov/grr/history/?m=12. (Accessed October 3, 2011).

Charles Skelly's gravesite in Crystal Springs Cemetery, Benton Harbor, Michigan, after his funeral on December 17, 1929. *Courtesy of the Berrien County Sheriff's Department.*

Gus Winkeler and Fred "Killer" Burke after being arrested in St. Louis, Missouri, 1925. *Courtesy of David Agens.* **Opposite: Mugshot of Fred Burke from 1919 at Michigan's Jackson Prison.** *Courtesy of State of Michigan Archives.*

CAPTURE

"*They tell me you are wicked and I believe them, for I have seen your painted women under the gas lamps luring the farm boys. And they tell me you are crooked and I answer: Yes, it is true I have seen the gunman kill and go free to kill again.*"

- Excerpt from Carl Sandburg poem, Chicago, 1916

THE MOST DANGEROUS MAN ALIVE

THE HUNT FOR FRED "KILLER" BURKE BECAME LOCAL law enforcement's highest priority, conducted through a cooperative investigative effort between the Michigan State Police, the Berrien County Sheriff's Department, and the St. Joseph and Benton Harbor police departments. Now that Burke was connected to the St. Valentine's Day Massacre and other high-profile crimes, the search expanded nationwide, while in the Twin Cities every police officer, firefighter, coastguardsman, railroad worker, and laborer volunteered to bring the mass murderer to justice. Berrien County sheriff Fred Bryant printed up thousands of wanted bulletins featuring four different photos of Fred Burke, his fingerprints, and other key information. Newspapers and police departments across the nation received the bulletins. St. Joseph police chief Fred Alden solicited information from downtown merchants who knew Dane/Burke. Employees at the American Dry Cleaners, the Loshbaugh Brothers Electric Company, and the Richter & Achterberg's Hardware Store all identified a photo of Burke as being the man they knew as Fred Dane. "He's head of the most desperate band of outlaws in the country," remarked Henry J. Garvin of the Detroit Crime and Bomb Squad, to a reporter who asked about Burke.

Burke immediately became the topic at every police department's roll call. Officers everywhere remained on high alert in search of "The Most Dangerous Man Alive." Chief Alden received a telegram on December 16 from the Chicago Police Department, asking officers to exercise caution if encountering Burke. The telegram provided a warning, "This man is well-known and has been arrested in Detroit, St. Louis, and Louisville. He is a very dangerous murderer and bank robber."[1]

One of the first solid clues would come from Fort Scott, Kansas, and would deliver yet another surprise. After receiving one of the wanted posters, a deputy from the Bourbon County Sheriff's Department wrote a letter to Chief Alden, indicating that the man known as Fred Burke was a former classmate of his, and his name was actually Thomas A. Camp. Members of the Camp family, he noted, were still living in Mapleton, Kansas, although he believed that Thomas Camp had not returned to the area in the last 15 years.[2]

Now authorities needed to untangle yet another alias. Reviewing his extensive case files, they surmised that Fred "Killer" Burke, Fred Dane, John Burke, Thomas Brooks, Thomas Kemper, Theo Cameron, F. A. Campbell, Jas F. Lewis, Herbert Church, Fred Stevens, Fred Dean, and Fred Campbell were all the creation of one man—and that man was Thomas Camp. Unlike his given name and the majority of aliases he used, the name Fred Burke had been the primary alias he used during the most notorious time in his life; therefore, the justice system still referred to him as Fred Burke. As the task of connecting his identities progressed, and word continued to spread over the wires about him, the number of his alleged crimes rapidly increased. Suddenly, the criminal known to the world as Fred Burke became a suspect in every unsolved bank robbery and murder in the country. On December 19, the Farmers and Merchants Bank of Jefferson, Wisconsin, filed suit against Fred Burke in the Berrien County Circuit Court for the outstanding balance of bonds and cash stolen in the November robbery. Serving as the co-plaintiff was the United States Fidelity and Guaranty Company based in Washington, DC. Judge Charles E. White ruled in favor of the plaintiffs, who were represented by Assistant Prosecutor E. A. Westin, for $33,500 in damages. The task of serving the summons to Burke would be the responsibility of Berrien County deputy Charles H. Inholz;[3] however, the man born as Thomas Camp had much harsher punishment on the horizon.

FROM ALL ACCOUNTS, Fred "Killer" Burke began life as a normal boy from a close-knit family in Middle America. What he grew into was much less typical. As authorities would eventually learn, Thomas Amos Camp entered the world on May 29, 1893, in rural Mapleton in Bourbon County, Kansas. Born to native Ohioan Warren (Wall) J. Camp, a farmer, and West Virginian Martha B. Pritchard Camp, Thomas Camp was part of a large farming family that included older siblings Early, Lola, Anson, Mortimer, and Fenton, and later the youngest two, Lovell and Mattie.[4] Camp was fortunate to have built an early relationship with his paternal grandparents, Anson and Louisa Tippie Camp. His Tippie ancestors made significant contributions to Mapleton in the early 1800s. Great-grandfather Michael Tippie served as a preacher and doctor, reportedly delivering thousands of babies, while one of his sons, Lord Mortimer, worked as a veterinarian. Thomas shared ancestral lineage with Uriah Tippie, who not only served in the Revolutionary War but also crossed the Delaware River with George Washington. However, he would probably have known little of his heritage since his grandmother, Louisa Tippie Camp, passed away in 1898, and his grandfather, Anson Camp, died the following year. Just beyond his toddler years, Thomas would have known little about death, but he would become all too familiar with it in later years.

Even though they owned almost 200 acres of land, the Camp family remained poor. However, they put a great deal of emphasis on money, maybe too much. Thomas' mother, Martha, was ashamed of their poverty and refused to associate with the wealthy, aristocratic Tippie relatives on her husband's side, probably out of fear of being perceived as inferior. If character was built by nature and nurture, her perception certainly could have contributed to the value young Thomas developed for money. Townspeople said he was brighter than average and that he possessed the attributes of reliability and driving ambition. Those close to the family believed that Thomas was his mother's favorite son. She encouraged him to become educated, not wanting him to become a mere farmer like his father. Already devoted to attending Sunday school every week, he took his mother's advice and registered at Fort Scott High School, and later enrolled at Kansas State Agricultural College in Manhattan to study veterinary medicine just as his great-uncle had done. Unfortunately, and for reasons unknown, Camp never completed the program beyond the first year and returned home.[5]

In 1910, the impressionable 17-year-old Thomas Camp encountered Texan Ed Griffin. He appeared one day at the Camp farm selling tracts of land in what Camp would later discover to be a bogus company, known as the Rio Grande Development Company. Camp took an immediate liking to Griffin and joined his door-to-door scheme, selling the worthless tracts of land in order to close his deals. Camp duped his customers into believing that his father, a respectable man of the community, had invested into the company. When his father learned how his son had conned their neighbors, he apologetically paid them back.

The swindle appealed to Thomas Camp, though, and whetted his appetite for fraud, con jobs, and lucrative schemes, so much so that he would turn his back on his father, his family, and all the residents of Mapleton.

Warren Camp must have been disappointed in his son for bringing such shame to the family. However, Thomas was not the first of his family to turn to crime. In April 1866, Warren Camp's cousins, brothers Joseph and Granville "Sam" Tippie, were accused of robbing a man in Monmouth, about 70 miles south of Mapleton, and murdering another man who intervened in the robbery. The murder, trial, and conviction all occurred on the same day, and so did their death sentences. An angry lynch mob strung up the Tippie brothers on an oak tree. An eloquently sarcastic portrayal of the mass justice appeared in the *New York Times*, "Two men… danced in the air on Lightning Creek… they immediately retired to a hole in the ground after their exercise."[6]

Thomas Camp undoubtedly could not thrive in one of the strictest and driest states in the nation: Kansas had banned alcohol since 1881. Consequently, he fled to Kansas City, Missouri, a state that had one of the most lax views on alcohol violations before and during the Prohibition Era and lived at the local Y.M.C.A. in the rough part of town. There, Camp hung out at saloons and pool halls, consuming large quantities of booze and looking for his next opportunity. At the end of 1915, he relocated to St. Louis where he met Anthony Ortell, a member of the powerful Egan's Rats Gang, who would introduce him to his fellow misfits. Either coincidentally or by plan, Camp returned to Mapleton on March 3, 1916, just as his mother, Martha, passed away at 60 years of age. He honored her by being a pallbearer at the funeral and burial in Dayton Cemetery but left as soon as the service was over. The residents of Mapleton, Kansas, never saw him again.

Then in his early twenties, Thomas Camp began building his career as a rookie member of the Egan's Rats Gang. His first brush with the law occurred in January 1917 when police arrested him for fraud, but the case was dismissed. Police arrested him again two months later, this time in Kansas City. In November, St. Louis police arrested him for forgery, in connection to a falsified deed of trust with which he attempted to get a $1,250 loan.[7] A judge found Camp guilty and sentenced him to two years in prison. However, Camp claimed that a detective in St. Louis offered to wipe his slate clean if he enlisted in the United States Army. He pondered the offer but left town immediately.

The United States needed soldiers after the country declared war on Germany in April 1917. The Selective Service Act required all males between the ages of 18 and 45 to register for the draft, regardless of their willingness to serve. Camp registered on June 5, 1917, giving his home address as 2310 Park in Kansas City, Missouri, the same address as that of his older brother, Anson. He listed his occupation as a real estate salesperson for Cramer Investment Company at 2120 East 15th Street in Kansas City. On the form, he described himself as tall in stature, medium build, with brown hair and brown eyes.[8] He checked a box to indicate that he was married; however, there are no records to verify that he was married at that time.

While on the lam for forgery, Camp returned to his familiar activities.

This led to his facing arrest in March 1918 in Kansas City on the charge of being a suspicious character, an accusation allowable by law if authorities believed a person might commit a crime. The charge was likely thrown at him as a last resort, when not enough evidence existed for one more serious. Federal authorities had the case transferred to them but released him after two days, for unknown reasons.[9] Two months later, Camp decided to enlist in the Army, believing that his active charges would be erased in St. Louis.

On September 25, 1918, he was sent to France as a member of the 302nd Battalion of the Tank Corps.[10] The Tank Corps' "Treat 'em Rough" motto was celebrated by those wearing the insignia. The American Expeditionary Forces were then involved in the Meuse-Argonne Offensive, so Thomas Camp was sure to have participated in active combat. He transferred to the 329th Battalion, where he would get his first taste of machine guns, becoming a member of the motorcycle machine-gun detachment and a prolific machine gunner. He was assigned to the two-man gunner unit with Raymond "Crane Neck" Nugent of Cincinnati, Ohio. As it turned out, their partnership would continue long after the war. On May 8, 1919, Camp was honorably discharged at the rank of sergeant at Fort Meade, Maryland, a location he may have strategically planned to avoid going back to St. Louis. From Maryland, he went to Detroit, where he began using the alias Fred Burke, one that would stick with him for the rest of his life. Clearly, he did not intend to give up a life of crime.

A veteran of the Armed Forces and the Great War, with both a new identity and newly acquired gunnery skills, Burke met a beautiful 19-year-old socialite, Nan Wright, from Saginaw, Michigan. He began romancing her in a style all his own, one built on charm, charisma, and diamonds. He would bite his lip and narrow his eyes at the sight of her. Nan fell for the war hero, but it did not take long before he slipped up. He signed the name Thomas Camp on a financial document. On August 9, 1919, Detroit police arrested him as Thomas Camp for obtaining money under false pretenses. The judge gave him a sentence of one to five years in Jackson State Prison.

Thomas Camp took to his new confines of steel and cement on September 23, 1919, and became one of the 1,033 inmates, during one of the highest inmate counts in years; 53 more convicts were expected.[11] Consequently, he served only a portion of his sentence. On October 12, 1920, Camp received parole and walked out of the facility 10 days later.[12]

At age 27, and back to using his alias of Fred Burke, he returned to St. Louis. It did not take him long to get the wrong kind of attention from the police, who still had charges on him. Burke went to prison in Jefferson City, Missouri, on February 25, 1921, charged with third-degree forgery. He insisted that the St. Louis detectives had tricked him when he enlisted in the Army, telling him that his active charges would be erased for serving his country; however, there was never a deal with the St. Louis detectives. Burke got an early release for good behavior on January 13, 1922, after serving less than a year,[13] but he had no intention of keeping on "the straight and narrow." Instead, he rejoined forces with the Egan's Rats Gang through fellow Rat Lee Turner, most noted for his use of airplanes in the business of robbery. It was also during this time when he would develop a long-term friendship with another Rat, Gus Winkeler.

AUGUST HENRY "GUS" WINKELER was born March 28, 1901, in Carondelet Township, Missouri, just outside of St. Louis. He was the youngest son of Missourian Bernard J. Winkeler and German immigrant Mary K. Wilmas Winkeler.[14] Before his birth, Mary spent time in a sanitarium, suffering from mental and physical exhaustion. Winkeler had six older siblings, but it became apparent that "Little Gus" was the favorite child. His mother adorned him in silken shirts and sent him to a parochial school through the eighth grade. All the pampering and attention gave him a sense of entitlement that would carry over into his adulthood. Winkeler and Burke were both from large families, both had older siblings, both were doted on by their mothers, and both were the favorite child. It seemed that the two had a great deal in common.

Being too young for the war draft, Winkeler volunteered by altering the year of his birth on his birth certificate. He served his country overseas as part of the 362nd Ambulance Corps, where he became proficient in high-speed driving and lifesaving medical care, skills that would be utilized in his future career. After returning from service, he loafed around in the comforts of his childhood home. On January 20, 1920, he married Pearl E. Hays, a woman who introduced him to a world of shady characters known as the Egan's Rats in St. Louis.[15] Once Winkeler became involved with the gang, his unrestrained desire for anything he wanted set him off on a course of crime. He was first arrested on March 30, 1920, for passing a forged check for $205. At the time, Winkeler listed his occupation as that of a chauffeur residing at the Model Hotel at 1507 Market Street in St. Louis. After spending the night at the Central District Headquarters lockup, Winkeler posted bond until his court date of April 3; at the hearing, the judge discharged him and the case was dropped.[16] Eventually, Winkeler parted ways with his wife, but he stayed with his new crowd. Soon, his pal Isadore Londe introduced him to the woman who would stay by his side for the rest of his life, Georgette Bence.

With her red hair and blue eyes, the well-spoken Georgette stood out. She was smart and had the ability to read people, but she never accepted Winkeler's career choice. There was no doubt, however, that they adored each other. They reportedly married in 1920 or 1921, although no official record exists.

When Winkeler and Burke became close friends, both were still novice criminals. After holding up a dice game one night, Winkeler was shot in the arm. Rather than seek medical attention, where he might encounter the police, Winkeler asked Burke to remove the bullet from his arm using a razor blade. From that point on, Winkeler gave Burke the nickname of "Doc."

On January 7, 1923, police in St. Louis arrested Burke for stealing. He was released after posting the $2,500 bond; however, he forfeited that bond later when he failed to appear for his court date.[17] Not long after that, Winkeler received some terrible news. His mother had died on March 5, 1923.[18] The attending doctor listed the cause as mental exhaustion, although some suspected she died out of despair, knowing that her golden child had become a criminal.

On April 25, 1923, Burke disguised himself as a police officer for the first time. The ruse fooled the guards at a North St. Louis liquor warehouse, allowing his Rat partners to make off with $80,000 worth of "medicinal whiskey." His next job was not as successful, though. On July 3, 1923, Burke led a group of four Rat gunmen and a getaway driver as they robbed the United Railways Office. Their prize was $38,000; however, witnesses recognized Burke, giving the police a solid suspect, because he chose to not wear a mask as the others had. Dissatisfied with the direction of Egan's Rats, Burke left and headed back to Detroit in late 1923.[19]

Burke had a different panache than most gangsters. His soft voice paired with a hardened frame made him distinguishable and striking. He took pride in his dress, usually wearing something expensive but not flashy. Notably, his speech mirrored that of a highly educated individual. Burke reportedly told others, "None of this 'dese, 'dem, and 'dose stuff for me." He preferred freelancing or being a contract man rather than affiliating with a specific gang. This distinctive approach had its advantages, but trouble was never far away.

ON SEPTEMBER 8, 1923, Burke's father, Warren Camp, passed away in Mapleton at the age of 81. His son, now calling himself Fred Burke, was hardly the Thomas Camp anyone knew back home. His siblings attempted to locate him for the settlement of their father's estate, but were unsuccessful.

Near the same time, Burke's friend Gus Winkeler may have thought he could outsmart the St. Louis police when, after crashing his Paige touring car, he attempted to report it stolen. Minutes after the crash on September 16, the police went to Winkeler's residence at 4543-A Delmar Boulevard. They immediately noticed spots of blood on his clothing; his vehicle was located nearby with bloodstains on the driver's seat. Officers charged Winkeler with leaving the scene of an accident and the careless operation of a motor vehicle. He did not stick around for his day in court and wound up joining Burke in Detroit, along with Isadore Londe and a few others, where they rubbed elbows with members of Detroit's Sugar House Gang, colorfully known as the Purple Gang.

Once back in Detroit, Burke contacted the girl he had left behind, Nan Wright; she was willing to take him back and accept his proposal of marriage. Business was on his mind and his next opportunity for cash came on March 10, 1924, when the group held up John Kay's Jewelry Store in the Book-Cadillac Hotel using his fiancée's car. Though the gang made off with $7,000 worth of jewels, Burke's taste for spirits would get him into trouble when a disturbance broke out at a restaurant on the corner of Joseph Campau and Sherwood Streets. A very inebriated Burke staggered out to Nan's car as the police were cruising up. Rather than acting cool, Burke drew attention to himself, causing the police to search the car. They found a number of loose jewels in the side-pockets of the vehicle. In a weak attempt at hiding his identity, he gave his name as Thomas Kemp and denied any knowledge of the jewels. A check of fingerprint records, however, returned a state of Michigan record for Thomas Camp. Still tied to his given name, Burke wound up back at the Jackson prison on March 12, 1924, for parole violation. His cohorts in the crime, Isadore Londe, Robert "Gimpy" Carey, and James Callahan, also were caught, but only Londe was pegged for the robbery. Nan Wright moved on without Burke.

After spending less than a year in prison, Burke was discharged on January 27, 1925. However, he was then turned over to St. Louis authorities to face charges for the rail office robbery. He was allowed to post bond in St. Louis, and then hightailed it to Louisville, Kentucky. Sticking with what he knew best, Burke held up the Portland Bank in Louisville on April 2, 1925. Nevertheless, the aftermath was just as predictable: another arrest and another getaway while on bond, as Burke quickly fled out of Kentucky. While still out on bond in St. Louis, Burke met up with his pals Gus Winkeler and Ezra Milford Jones, a 24-year-old fellow robber. On June 5, the men were travelling in Winkeler's Chrysler touring car when an attention-getting turn into an alley between Main and Second Streets aroused the suspicions of officers patrolling the area. They pursued the vehicle while dodging bullets being fired upon them from the Chrysler. The fleeing gangsters abruptly turned east, slamming into a large black truck. Burke, Winkeler, and Jones leaped out of the car and began running, tossing their weapons into the street. The police caught up with the men, placed them all under arrest, and confiscated the wrecked Chrysler. Inside they found the bill of sale showing that Winkeler had paid $1,150 for it on May 19, 1925, not even a month before.[20]

The weapons recovered at the scene included a Smith & Wesson .38-caliber revolver, a Colt .45-caliber model 1911 semi-automatic pistol marked "U.S. Army," and a Colt .45-caliber model 1911 semi-automatic pistol, a commercial version manufactured after the Great War.[21] A black leather handbag found at the scene contained a Mauser-Waffenfabrik model 1896 semi-automatic pistol, sometimes known as a "machine pistol,"[22] and two loaded magazines.[23]

Still having to face the jury on the United Railways robbery, Burke appeared in court, represented by St. Louis attorneys Sigmund Bass and Thomas Rowe. Burke produced an alibi as his defense, and despite witness testimony the jury found him not guilty on November 22, 1925. Sickened by the verdict, Judge Mix lashed out at the jurors. "You have released one of the most infamous ex-convicts in the United States," he scolded. "It is an insult to the intelligence of the people of St. Louis for an apparently intelligent jury to acquit a man on the evidence presented in this case."[24]

As the jury filed out after being dismissed, Judge Mix continued his lecture in an angry but sarcastic tone, "If any of you gentlemen see that good-looking young man, Burke, in the hall, look out. He is 'Dint' Colbeck's first assistant in crime," referring to Egan's Rats leader William Colbeck, who was serving time in the Atlanta Penitentiary for murder. "Colbeck planned the jobs at Maxwelton Inn, and this man Burke, with the assistance of other gangsters, executed them."

Even after his incredible acquittal in the United Railways robbery, Burke remained in St. Louis and met a woman who would remain a constant in his life. After his first pinch in St. Louis, Burke said, "A man in the rackets is a fool to be encumbered with either a cripple or a woman." However, women fascinated him, maybe as much as the rackets did. His new gal, Theo Marjorie Gephart, who was 33 years old and from Columbus, Ohio,[25] had just been granted a divorce, ironically at the same time and in the same court Burke had just left. She stood five-foot-five-inches tall and weighed around 180 pounds, with baby-blue eyes and blonde hair. Theo fell hard for Burke. As Burke courted the new divorcée, she began to divulge her life. She told him that she had married William Franklin Gephart, held a degree from Ohio

State University, and was doing post-graduate work at Columbia University in New York. She had studied economics and sociology with a yearlong stint at the University of Chicago, even teaching at Hull House in Chicago. In July 1921, the Gepharts had set sail from New York to the British Isles, Belgium, Holland, Switzerland, and Gibraltar, giving Theo experiences most Midwestern women would never have.[26]

The idea of falling in love with Burke was a case study in how opposites attract, as the relationship heated up. Theo stood by his side as authorities picked him up on the forgotten court case from October 1923. Even though he had forfeited his bond money, on February 18, 1926, the jury, once again, acquitted him of the charges. Burke quickly proposed to Theo and the two were married on February 26 in St. Charles, Missouri, before Justice of the Peace Max Joseph Frey.[27] Frey was known as the "marrying justice" of St. Charles, averaging almost 15 weddings a day. He even advertised by placing placards on the sides of St. Louis taxicabs that read, "If you want to get married on the Q. T., come to St. Charles."[28]

The new Mr. and Mrs. Burke settled down for a short time in St. Louis, which proved to be not such a good choice. He was arrested by the St. Louis Police Department for a federal detainer on April 30, 1926, but they released him the next day.[29] The acquittals, releases, and dropped charges made it appear that Burke was making a mockery out of the justice system.

The couple returned to Detroit where Fred had an idea for a profitable new venture. While acting as a bodyguard for a few big-shot gamblers, he convinced fellow convicts Johnny Reid, Harry Hallisay, and Joseph O'Riordan to go in on a kidnapping scheme with him, dubbed the "snatch racket." They would kidnap the gamblers, take them to Burke's suburban home, lock them up in the windowless attic, and wait for the families to pay big dollars for their safe return. This racket worked and was quite profitable for Burke and the others. Since the kidnapped men were criminals, their families would not call the police. Purple Gang member and gambling racketeer Mert Wertheimer was one such kidnapping victim. After Burke received the $50,000 ransom, Wertheimer was released unharmed.[30] When another gambler they held refused to pay the ransom, they took him to a barn and tied him up. In what became a gang custom, Burke fired several rounds from his submachine gun within inches of the man's head, "just to get [him] thinking it over."[31] It did not take long for the $20,000 ransom to be paid.

Greed got the better of them and eventually the kidnapping scheme began to include law-abiding citizens, which brought on the attention of the police. When police arrested members of his crew, Burke knew that he had to leave town once again. Hallisay maintained control of the group in Burke's absence.

Egan's Rats members enticed Burke back to St. Louis. There, he participated in a robbery at the North St. Louis Trust Company, taking $30,000 in May 1926. Later in August, though, Burke, Winkeler, and a few others were summoned to Detroit to avenge the honor of a friend. Burke and four other gunmen raided a restaurant, killing several people and injuring many more. The intended target of the hit got the message, but battles between factions of the gang would continue back and forth, ultimately leading to the killing of his pal Johnny Reid, allegedly by Frank Wright, on Christmas Day 1926.

The Burkes decided to move to Pittsburgh, Pennsylvania, in early 1927, and they ended up at the Lorraine Hotel on North Highland Avenue where it did not take long for Burke to lose several thousand dollars in one of his bad business ventures. Then the couple returned to Detroit once again. Theo Burke managed to get to know some of her husband's friends. Among those visiting the couple were Gus and Georgette Winkeler; Joseph "Red" O'Riordan and his wife, Doris Kidd O'Riordan;[32] and James Callahan, with his wife and baby.[33] In 1927, a mix of Egan's Rats and Purple Gang members represented by O'Riordan, Burke, Ezra Milford Jones, Abe Axler, Eddie Fletcher, and Raymond Bernstein kidnapped a Detroit bootlegger, Abe Fein, and held him on a $14,200 ransom. Eventually, O'Riordan took the heat for the kidnapping and was sent to Marquette Prison in Michigan's Upper Peninsula.[34]

One of Burke's prized possessions was his Thompson submachine gun, one with the serial number 2347. He had acquired the gun in December 1926 from Lester Farmer, a sheriff's deputy from Williamson County, Illinois, who originally purchased the weapon on November 12, 1924, and was an alleged member of the Egan's Rats.[35] On March 28, 1927, this weapon made history when Burke sprayed a room full of bullets, an incident dubbed the Miraflores Apartment Massacre, likely a retaliation effort for the murder of Johnny Reid. Burke did not know it at the time, but this was the first use of a Thompson submachine gun in Detroit. Dead were Frank Wright, Joseph Bloom, and Ruben Cohen. Police had already suspected Burke, so when he was located and his fingerprint file checked, police learned that authorities in Louisville, Kentucky, also wanted him for the Portland Bank holdup in April 1925.[36] Without having established any solid evidence on Burke for the Miraflores killings, Detroit surrendered him to authorities in Louisville. Once he was arraigned there on the bank robbery charge, he posted bond for $10,000. In his predictable *modus operandi*, he jumped his bond and headed back to Detroit. During this time, Theo's mother became very ill so Theo made a trip home to Williamsport, Ohio, to be with her. She succumbed in mid-June.

Fred Burke's relationship with the Purple Gang splintered after they accused him of killing one of their members outside the Exchange Café on July 21, 1927. It was, once again, time for a change of scenery. The Burkes and the Winkelers relocated to Chicago that September to begin a new alliance with the big man himself, Al Capone. Initially, the Burkes moved into an apartment near Sheridan Road but shortly thereafter they found a different apartment only one block away from the Winkelers' residence.

Burke lay low for a few months, but reemerged nine months later on April 16, 1928, as one of five men who robbed an armored truck in Toledo, Ohio. Gus Winkeler, Robert "Gimpy" Carey, Fred Goetz, and his machine-gunner cohort during the war, Raymond "Crane Neck" Nugent, assisted him. After watching an American Railway Express truck leave Union Station, the bandits forced the driver to pull over; they disarmed the guards and forced the driver to an out-of-the-way location near the University of Toledo. A student who witnessed the men transferring the safes between the mail truck and their vehicle alerted authorities. Just as the bound and gagged guards loosened themselves from their binds, a squad car approached the scene. Burke and his partners seized the moment, fleeing with what cash they could grab from the two safes. They made it to their designated hideout in the 2300 block of Upton Avenue, although Toledo police officers George Zientara and John Biskupski tailed them there. As Zientara approached the house from the front, Biskupski covered the rear. Before either of them was in position, a one-sided gun battle ensued. A bullet from a Thompson submachine gun passed through Zientara's skull, dropping him to the ground. Biskupski crawled to the rear of the garage and set his plan in motion. He feigned as though wounded, falling to the ground. Burke and the others emerged from their retreat, thinking that a clean escape was possible. Seeing an opening for a clear shot, Biskupski opened fire. The five bandits scrambled into the squad car and fled the scene, leaving their getaway car and part of the stolen loot behind.[37] A search of the hideout revealed all the tools for bank robbery including explosives and a cache of weapons. Officer George Zientara died in the line of duty, leaving a wife and three children.

The botched robbery attempt in Ohio prompted Burke to rethink his strategy. However, his appearance on the front cover of the June 1928 edition of *The Detective*, published monthly and touted as the official journal of police authorities and sheriffs across the country, meant Burke needed to watch his back. The notice offered a $1,000 reward for his arrest and conviction for his participation in the Portland Bank robbery in April 1925 in Louisville.[38]

His new alliance with Al Capone brought him to a city where he was little known. On July 1, 1928, Burke, Winkeler, and Goetz went to Brooklyn, New York, along with Capone lieutenant Louis Campagna. They climbed into a black Nash with revolvers, sawed-off shotguns, and Burke's personal Thompson submachine gun. In broad daylight, they pulled alongside a new Lincoln on 44th Street driven by 35-year-old racketeer, Frankie Uale,[39] a former Capone comrade who had double-crossed the boss. The men delivered Capone's message in the form of simultaneous gunfire from the rear of the Nash; two of the bullets struck Uale's head. His Lincoln then plowed through several trees and brush, hitting a house at 923 44th Street. Uale died at the wheel.[40]

SEVERAL MONTHS LATER, Gus Winkeler's father was unable to handle the reality of his son's lifestyle. On November 23, 1928, Bernard J. Winkeler walked out to the barn at the family residence and hanged himself.[41] As heartrending as it was for each of the wives of these ruthless gangsters, Theo Burke was one person who took it especially hard. She loved and trusted her husband, but his dangerous lifestyle was something she very much despised. She pleaded with him to stop affiliating with criminals. He had promised to go straight many times, but she learned from some of his close associates that he had been deceiving her. Theo became furious at the end of 1928 and decided to leave Burke and Chicago and return to Detroit. Love was not enough to convince Burke to give up his dangerous associates, but with them he would find companionship again.

The next time Theo Burke heard of her husband was on the front page of a December 16, 1929, newspaper, when Burke was sought for the killing of Officer Charles Skelly in St. Joseph, Michigan. The national news coverage about Fred Burke had residents in Williamsport, Ohio, talking quite a bit because one of their own, Theo Walston, had married him. Most thought the couple had divorced earlier in 1929.[42] When Theo saw the references to herself in the newspaper, she panicked. Burke may have had plenty of clandestine activities to hide, but Theo had secrets of her own that could destroy her, if they were ever revealed. She, too, went on the run.

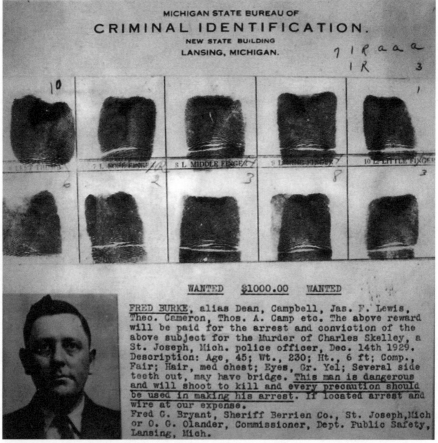

Fred Burke's Wanted Poster for the murder of Charles Skelly in December 1929. *Courtesy of the Berrien County Sheriff's Department.*

BURKE AGAINST BALLISTICS

ON **DECEMBER 16, WHILE THE SEARCH FOR FRED BURKE** continued, Berrien County deputies Erwin Kubath and Charles Andrews were sent to hand-deliver the two Thompson submachine guns and other weapons found at Burke's bungalow to the Chicago authorities, who would try to determine if they had been used in any other crimes, including the St. Valentine's Day Massacre. Traveling from St. Joseph by train with such critical evidence became a daunting task, as several suspicious-looking characters boarded the train at various stops along the route. Deputies Kubath and Andrews remained alert and arrived safely at their final destination, just before the weather rapidly changed. In the next 24 hours, a combination of rain, sleet, and snow began to fall, burying St. Joseph, Benton Harbor, and the Chicago area under 10-foot snowdrifts. However, gale force winds in the "Blizzard of 1929" did not stop the important scientific investigations or the search for Burke.

Deputies Kubath and Andrews met Chicago Police chief detective John Stege at the Cook County Coroner's Office, where they logged in the evidence. One submachine gun, they noted, carried a serial number of 2347, while the second gun appeared to have had its serial number professionally removed. In an effort to raise the ground-off serial number, Detective Stege asked Lieutenant William Cox from the Automobile Bureau to assist. The technique used to raise numbers from an engine chassis proved just as successful for obtaining the serial numbers of the gun. Number 7580 appeared.

Colonel Calvin Goddard then ran ballistics tests on Burke's 20-gauge sawed-off shotgun. He ruled out the gun immediately because the two shells found at the St. Valentine's Day Massacre scene were 12-gauge. Next, he turned to the two Thompsons, and on December 19 Berrien County prosecutor Wilbur Cunningham joined the men in Chicago, waiting for Goddard to reveal his findings. Then, on December 23, the coroner's jury reconvened and Goddard was called to testify about his conclusions of the ballistics tests.

Evidence presented to the jury consisted of Thompson submachine gun 7580 with a Cutts compensator, marked as "Exhibit A," and Thompson submachine gun 2347, marked as "Exhibit B." Goddard explained how he used a microscopic identification procedure on the test bullets fired from each of the guns. In addition, he took note of the ejector piece from the Thompson 7580, Exhibit A, and of the irregular firing pin from Thompson 2347, Exhibit B, in order to identify each gun as having a unique fingerprint. Features that isolated the Thompsons were the six-groove barrel, the 10½-inch barrel length, the one turn in 16-inch rifling (1:16 inches), and their "right-hand" twists. This applied to the twist rate of the projectile and only two .45-caliber automatic guns at the time had a "right-hand" twist: the Thompson submachine gun and the Model 1917 Smith & Wesson revolver.[43] The Cutts compensator found on the Thompson 7580 consisted of a 2½-inch-long muzzle brake threaded onto the front of the barrel, which would redirect some of the muzzle blast upward, reducing recoil and "climbing" during full-automatic fire.

After examining all of the evidence found at the St. Valentine's Day Massacre scene, Goddard testified that Exhibit A had fired a 20-round stick magazine at the massacre scene while Exhibit B fired a 50-round drum magazine. This accounted for the 70 .45-caliber shells found on the garage floor. Goddard pointed out the significant fact that the ammunition confiscated in the Burke bungalow was identical in make, caliber, and vintage to the fatal ammunition. The jacketed bullets were an alloy of copper and 5 percent zinc, and given a nickel wash. They appeared shiny, sometimes mistaken for steel.

"An interesting feature of these bullets," testified Goddard, "and one which will be seen later to have considerable significance, was the fact that they were cannelured, or encircled at the base by a ring of knurling marks. Above the cannelure was stamped a small letter 's' (which stood for smokeless), an identifying mark used only on U.S. Cartridge Company bullets in this caliber and type." He went on to say, "Those which I purchased were uncannelured. Accordingly, I wrote to Mr. Merton A. Robinson, ballistic engineer of the Winchester Repeating Arms Company, at New Haven, Connecticut, where the U.S. Cartridge Company line has been made for some time past, and learned from him that this particular vintage of U.S. ammunition had been produced for a relatively short period only, July 1927 to July 1928."[44]

It was clear that Goddard's ballistics tests had proved that both Thompson submachine guns had been used in the St. Valentine's Day Massacre.

Previous testimony by gun dealer Peter Von Frantzius at the inquest indicated that Thompson 7580 Exhibit A was shipped to his sporting goods store on October 19, 1928, as part of an order placed by Russell Thompson. A Von Frantzius employee then removed the serial number, and Thompson picked up the gun on October 23, 1928. Further testimony from Russell Thompson revealed that he then sold this particular gun to Chicago bootlegger James "Bozo" Shupe, who was killed in May 1929. Police assumed that Fred Burke acquired that particular Thompson prior to February 14, 1929, and it had remained in his possession until December 14, 1929.

Chicago chief detective John Stege was recalled to the witness stand following Goddard. Jurors asked him if photographs or other forms of identification contributed to Burke's identity.

"Yes," testified Stege. "The banker in Stevensville, where he had an account, identified him. We had photographs taken, and have them in our possession... We have a sample of his handwriting that jibes with the handwriting on the back of the cancelled checks that were given at Stevensville." Stege further noted that about a half a dozen of his neighbors in the immediate vicinity of the cottage had identified Fred Dane as Fred Burke.[45]

New York City police commissioner Grover Whalen became highly impressed with the vast amount of information introduced by Calvin Goddard at the inquest. He asked Goddard to perform the same process on the bullet retrieved from Frankie Uale's body. New York City detectives Stanley Gorman and Harry Butts were dispatched to Chicago, bringing with them the .45-caliber bullet from the July 1, 1928, Uale killing. Responding to reporters, Commissioner Whalen remarked, "The check up of the Uale bullet was complete in every way, I was told." He also clarified that the second fatal bullet found in Uale's body was from a revolver. Goddard was able to match the markings on the .45-caliber bullet with Burke's Thompson submachine gun 2347. This proved to be the first machine-gun killing in the state of New York.

WHILE THE INVESTIGATION CONTINUED, Forrest Kool pursued restitution from Burke for damage to his car. He sought the advice of an attorney, who then began the process of garnisheeing Burke's bank account in Stevensville. Attorney John Rody drafted the papers and served them upon the Stevensville Bank officials. Kool was granted the $25 he originally asked Burke for to cover the damaged fender.

Even gangland leaders sought restitution. Members of gangs from the east coast to the Midwest were abuzz with the news of Burke's recklessness. He had broken the gangland code by the ruthless, useless killing of a police officer, something that no one, even in the underworld, tolerated. The added attention to illegal activities was bad for business; gangland business, that is.

Chief Detective John Stege explained to reporters, "Without a doubt, Burke, alive, has the power to throw an unknown number of men within the shadow of the electric chair. We will take him alive, if possible, but he is a dead man if the gangsters find him first, or if he attempts to fight us."

Gangsters began to worry that law enforcement officials were now going to concentrate on mopping up Prohibition violators and their outlawed businesses, all due to Burke's booze-fueled, heat-of-the-moment action. They were right.

After the arrest of Viola Brenneman, known at first as Viola Dane, investigators found a letter addressed to a Mrs. D. Rosewall of Maywood, Illinois, among her belongings. Learning that Helen Rosewall was Viola's sister, police began round-the-clock surveillance on her house, believing that Fred Burke might seek refuge there.[46] Another sister, Mrs. Rose Scott, of Kankakee, Illinois, spent Christmas visiting with Viola in jail and pushed prosecutors to release her. Family members retained James T. Burns, a Kankakee attorney, to work on Viola's behalf. However, through intermediaries, Fred Burke had already hired a St. Joseph attorney, Charles W. Stratton, to represent her.[47]

On January 1, 1930, Stratton began a letter-writing campaign to free Viola Brenneman, on the basis that she was still in custody 10 days after the justifiable arrest holding time had expired. Stratton's letter to prosecutors declared, "Further detention is a violation of her legal rights."

Stratton scoffed at prosecution theories with his observation, "Anyone who thinks Viola is so smart and intelligent as to withstand these attacks pays her a compliment her intelligence does not warrant. Not one person believes she has brains enough to fool the police authorities of the entire United States."

He further mentioned that she was without funds, did not have a criminal background, and had no known contact with Fred Burke; therefore, there was no reason to hold her any longer.[48]

On January 4, 1930, Viola waived her right to a preliminary examination. She was then arraigned by Justice Joseph R. Collier. After being bound over to circuit court, she was released on her own recognizance without having to post bond, and returned to her mother's home in Kankakee. Viola Brenneman never spoke of Fred Burke again.

THE IRREFUTABLE EVIDENCE presented during the coroner's jury led members to conclude that Burke was responsible for the St. Valentine's Day Massacre. On January 3, 1930, National Editorial Association writer Bruce Catton gave his take on Fred "Killer" Burke in an *Olean Times* editorial:

"We have a fiction in this country that our really big gangsters–the aristocrats, so to speak, of our underworld–are very clever, brilliant men. That man, we say of an Al Capone or an Arnold Rothstein 'could have made a great success if he had gone into some legitimate business or profession.' That's one of our favorite myths. But once in a while, something happens that makes one wonder if these lawless big shots aren't pretty dumb.

"There is, for instance, Fred Burke, or Fred Dane, the Chicago gangster who lived in a mansion in St. Joseph, Michigan, as a millionaire businessman. Burke is called the greatest gangster in America. Robberies totaling one million dollars and the deaths of a dozen men are charged to his account. Evidentially the man was the best specimen our underworld has yet produced. According to our traditions, he must be a highly gifted and brainy chap.

"But here is what Burke did. First get the picture, Burke was sitting pretty. He was a respected citizen of St. Joseph. No one there dreamed of suspecting him. He had 300,000 dollars in cold cash at his disposal. Whether he wanted to retire from crime and live in peace and quiet, or continue with his various rackets, the situation was perfect; indeed, that it sounds more like fiction than fact. All right.

"Here was Burke, with all of this, driving along a street in his automobile. A traffic officer stopped him for some minor traffic law violation. And what did Burke, the 'brainy' gangster do, but draw his gun and shoot the policeman to death!

"It wasn't, remember, as if he had been arrested for some serious crime. It was just a traffic charge. It might have meant a fine of 25 dollars–not more. It could not possibly have harmed Burke. But instead of submitting and paying up, he murdered the policeman. Then, of course, everything came out. He had to flee. The police went to his house and the whole story became known. He lost that super-perfect position of his, lost that 300,000 dollars, lost his headquarters–lost, in fact, lost everything he had. And simply because he didn't have sense enough to take a traffic ticket quietly. Smart?

"This gang leader was the dumbest specimen we have ever heard of. Our underworld kings aren't the brainy chaps we suppose. They are subnormal in intelligence. Burke's dizzy fiasco proves it."[49]

THE SEARCH FOR BURKE continued at full force. St. Joseph officer Ben Phairas was assigned to follow up on the business card found in Burke's dining room. He went to the address listed on the card, 403 West State in Calumet City, Illinois, looking for Willie Harrison. The address happened to be the location of Harrison's Tavern, then a speakeasy. Officer Phairas found the five-foot-six-inch Harrison, and with reassurance that the policeman was only interested in asking a few questions about Burke, Harrison invited him to sit down. Phairas learned that Harrison was originally from St. Louis and knew Burke casually from a few rounds of golf, but said he was not well acquainted.[50] Harrison himself was at the level of being a professional golfer and was often seen on the greens with Capone and others. Without any solid information about Burke's whereabouts, the officer returned to St. Joseph.

Tips and information about Burke flowed in from every conceivable place. Dora Kuhlman from the Hotel Vincent Beauty Shop identified him as "Mr. Berkie," who would come into the shop for haircuts, eyebrow waxing, and manicures, often along with Capone. Alleged sightings placed Burke in a New Buffalo, Michigan, hotel; hiding out in Coloma, Michigan; driving a Hudson Coach in Kalamazoo, Michigan; bumming a ride in Spring Green, Wisconsin; dining in a Mansfield, Ohio, eatery; and even making a break for the Canadian border. Outside of the Midwest, possible sightings were made in Centralia, Washington, and Nogales, Arizona (an entry point to Mexico), and in a London, England, tavern, where alcohol consumption was legal. Authorities followed up on all of these tips, but not one ever panned out.

In the midst of the intense and widespread investigation, Benton Harbor Police Chief Thure O. Linde announced his resignation from the department effective February 1, 1930. Linde cited the low pay of $150 a month as his reason for leaving. Mayor Sterling attempted to remedy the situation, but instead, the commissioners named Charles L. Peapples, a former Berrien County sheriff's deputy, as their new chief.

Even with these internal changes occurring, investigators kept on task. They theorized that Burke's partner, Gus Winkeler, who remained free, might try to aid him via airplane. Winkeler had a pilot's license and authorities believed that he could easily swoop in and whisk Burke off to somewhere far away. Investigators then decided to seek out the help of other state and federal agencies. On January 24, 1930, the Wisconsin Bankers' Association Protective Department manager, Andrew M. Devoursney, sent a memo to Michigan State Police captain Fred Armstrong, to inform him that Winkeler's airplane was a Stearman C-3B, with a tail number of NC9063 and a cockpit number of 199,[51] stored at the Ford Airport in Lansing, Illinois. Agents believed the plane had been freshly painted because the lower portion of the fuselage was black, and the upper portion and the wings were bright yellow. After a thorough search of records, the Aeronautics Branch of the Department of Commerce confirmed that Gus Winkeler possessed a pilot's license; however, the license was issued under the name of M. L. Bullard and was valid until November 30, 1930. Efforts were being coordinated through the Michigan State Police to have the license revoked.[52]

The investigation on the airplane proceeded with the assistance of the Illinois State's Attorney's Office and its chief investigator, Patrick Roche. The Michigan State Police Secret Service Division discovered that a man under the name of Bullard had purchased the plane, and then resold it to Joe Bergl in Cicero, Illinois.[53] Roche was familiar with Bergl, a gangster affiliate through his company, Bergl Auto Sales, located next door to Ralph Capone's Cotton Club. Authorities in Washington, DC, traced the plane's original owner to Bob King of Los Angeles, who had purchased it on March 27, 1929, and then resold it on October 9, 1929, to Winkeler. King admitted that Winkeler was using the alias M. L. Bullard at the time. Winkeler had given his address as 403 West State Street, Calumet City, Illinois.[54] The Pinkerton National Detective Agency determined the address to be that of a speakeasy and gambling house;[55] coincidentally, this was the same address used by Willie Harrison that Officer Phairas had previously checked out.

Chief Detective Fred Montgomery of the Peoria, Illinois, Police Department sent a memo to authorities in St. Joseph, New York, Chicago, and St. Louis on April 16, 1930, regarding a possible sighting of Burke in Springfield, Illinois, while he was driving a new Studebaker President model. Supposedly with him was Earl Reed, who was wanted for the killing of a St. Louis police officer in 1929, and Leo V. Brothers, also wanted for murder in St. Louis. The continued emphasis on watching the movements of former Burke associates led investigators into the heart of gangland's more infamous characters. One such associate was Johnny Patton, known as "The Boy Mayor" of Burnham, Illinois. Elected as village president in 1908, Patton would keep this title for the next 40 years. Starting out as a bartender at the age of 14, he met syndicate leader Johnny Torrio and began working for his organization. Patton later befriended Capone and continued his reign within Burnham. "The Boy Mayor" laid out the welcome mat at the Coney Island Cabaret, where the clientele included many underworld characters. Cottages nestled away off the main roads were ideal hideouts and used frequently. Capone spent quite a bit of time at the Burnham Woods golf course along with his henchmen. Caddying for the boss beginning in 1927 was 12-year-old Walter (Bud) McCay. He met not only Capone but also Jake Guzik and Fred Burke. "One day a fellow named Fred Burke came out and I caddied for him," explained McCay. "He was with a blonde woman. He just about ruined the three holes he played. He kept swinging at the ball, missing it, and tearing up the turf. Every time he did, I would just laugh. It was so funny I just could not help myself."[56]

Timmy Sullivan had a similar experience caddying for Capone, Guzik, Burke, and McGurn, who would bet $500 on each of the nine holes. Sullivan learned that carrying a few extra balls in his pocket earned him points with Capone when he sliced the ball into the woods. Sullivan quietly dropped another ball down for Capone, who told him, "You're O.K., kid."[57]

AS CAPONE AND BURKE'S GOLFING habits were discovered, Chicago detectives worked a lead in Charleston, West Virginia, with a man claiming to have been involved with the St. Valentine's Day Massacre. Assistant Chief Detective John Egan left Chicago by train, arriving in Charleston on January 13, 1930, to meet with the tipster. He immediately reported the results of this worthless interview over the phone to Chief Detective Stege: "Well, Chief, I got here. I'll be in the office tomorrow night. I'm taking the first train home."

"Bringing the prisoner back with you?" asked Stege.

"He ought to be brought back and charged with perjury and contempt of the Chicago Police Department. There was a bald-headed fellow about 40 years old in the cell. Said his name was Robert Ray and that he used to live at 319 North Clark Street, Chicago," explained Egan.

"Lived on Clark Street, hey? Go on."

"The fellow tells me that he and two other fellows did the massacre with a machine gun they found out in Cicero while they were hoisting beer."

"Could he describe the garage?" inquired Stege.

"It wasn't a garage, he said, but a stable. At least, he claimed they kept horses there. He described the place about three blocks north of the river."

"But the massacre was at 2122 North Clark Street. That's at least 20 blocks north of the river. And there are no horses kept there; it's a garage for motor trucks."

"Don't I know it? Listen, Chief, I'm catching the first train to Chicago. If I stay here another day I'll lose my temper and there's liable to be a massacre right here in Charleston."

Despite the bogus tip, there would be more witnesses coming forward, some much closer to home.

Berrien County Sheriff's deputies Erwin Kubath and Charles Andrews meeting with Cook County coroner Herman Bundesen and Illinois State's attorney Patrick Roche. *Author's collection.*

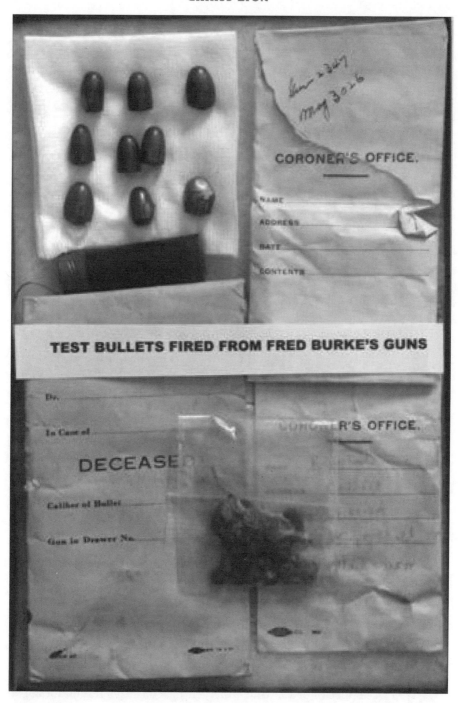

Evidence envelopes containing test bullets fired through Fred Burke's Thompson submachine guns. *Courtesy of Neal Trickle.*

THE CHAMBERMAID

ON **JANUARY 25, 1930, A WOMAN ASKED TO SEE** detectives at the Berrien County Jail, anxious to tell them about her month-long adventure with Fred Burke. The 35-year-old, Florence Faurote, born in Missouri, was a mere five-foot-two-inches tall, weighing 143 pounds. Her brown locks, however, went against Burke's trademark preference for blondes.[58] Although suspicious of her motives, investigators were willing to hear about her alleged ordeal with "The Most Dangerous Man Alive."

The detectives wanted to know a little bit more about the woman first, so they started the interview with a series of questions about her past. From that, they learned that her name was Florence Geneve Dow and she had been born in March 1895 to Charles and Clara Dow; up to the age of five, she lived in Missouri, Minnesota, and Wisconsin.[59] In 1905, the Dow family moved to Battleford, Saskatchewan, but in 1912, at the age of 17, she was married in Michigan to Ernest Calvin Faurote, a divorced man from South Haven, Michigan. They moved back to Battleford, and in 1915, Florence Faurote gave birth to her first daughter.[60] Two more daughters eventually followed, and shortly afterward, the family moved back to Michigan, where Florence set up a residence on Highland Avenue in Benton Harbor.

Investigators asked her to explain how she met up with Burke. Faurote began by telling them that she arrived in Detroit on November 14, 1929, having previously been in New Era, Muskegon, Grand Rapids, and Lansing, Michigan, while working in different restaurants for a few days at a time. The investigators appeared to be puzzled as to why she was not home with her husband, rather than seeking short-term employment throughout the state, but they let her continue.

"On December 14 or 15, while I was getting a meal at a restaurant in Detroit, a few young men stole $15.15 from me," explained Florence. "I needed money, so two girls I met told me they could get me a job at the Manhattan

Hotel at 126 East First Street in Detroit. I started right away, working on the second floor as a chambermaid."

"Then on that next Friday, December 20, after about a week on the job, the proprietor introduced me to Fred Burke, who was going by the name of Jess Denison from Pontiac." She described him as not having a moustache, his hair was black with no gray, he weighed about 220 pounds or more, very good shape, dark eyes, scars on his right hip from pulling knives, and a scar on his right wrist from a knife wound. Then she continued, "Burke and the proprietor told me he had been staying at the hotel since two weeks before Christmas."

The investigators did the math and figured the date to be around December 11, a few days before Officer Skelly's shooting, but they continued to listen to her story, already forming a not-so-credible impression of her. The vagabond Florence seemed to have taken an interest in this man she thought was Burke and the investigators felt she was naïve, gullible, and easily charmed. She said that once Burke felt that he could trust her, he began to divulge more about himself. Curious as to what he said, they asked her to continue.

"He said that police wanted him in St. Joseph for bumping off a police officer. He described how he got away by getting into a relief car, then another, then driving to Detroit. Burke told me that he stopped twice to telephone back to St. Joseph to see how close the officers were to him. One stop was in Coldwater and the other was outside of Detroit. He knew there was a lot of money offered in St. Joseph for him. He mentioned losing two of his best machine guns but had more in a Studebaker car. He left many papers in the house that he wished he had not left there. He seemed to miss the sweet blonde-haired woman he left behind and did not know what happened to her."

The investigators glanced at each other, acknowledging that this dame might have the goods on Burke.

"Then he went on about various jobs his gang had pulled. He reached for a piece of paper tied around his ankle in the sock that listed these jobs, like at the Statler Hotel, Tuller Hotel, and Book-Cadillac. The note listed the amount of jewelry and money obtained. Then he told me about his gang. There was Bob, Jack, Clem, Gene, Joe, and some other foreign names. He described Bob as short and fat while a man named Phin was tall and had a long face, small mustache, and sideburns. I also remember him talking about Winkeler and the bank robbery in St. Joseph about a year before."

Her detailed memory of crimes Burke allegedly committed needed verification. The investigators were not aware of any bank robberies in St. Joseph within the past year. They took notes and let her continue with her story.

"One night, I passed by him while he was using the desk telephone at the hotel and I overheard him calling a woman in Pontiac. I really couldn't hear the conversation because I was sitting across the hall in the parlor, but I did hear him ask her for some papers.

"After he told me all of this, I felt uncomfortable. I got the impression that he wasn't going to let me walk away from him. We took a walk down the street so he could show me his car. It was parked in front of another hotel and was a Studebaker 8 that fit seven people. I remember it was dark colored, had a spare tire on the back end, and a 1929 Michigan license plate. He told me to get in the driver's seat, but I drove so terribly that he had to take over. We drove back to the Manhattan Hotel. I got out of the car and walked up to the second floor.

"He talked about five men and a robbery. I was scared because I think he wanted me to drive the car on his next robbery. I needed to get away, so I ran for the door. Suddenly he was right there, and he asked me where I was going. I told him that I was hungry and was going to get something to eat. Well, he insisted on taking me. We waited for a few minutes to see if any of his friends wanted to come along. He told me that he wasn't armed, and he wanted to have someone guarding him."

The investigators probably thought that Burke would never go anywhere without being armed, but they asked where Burke took her. Faurote said the two ended up going to what he deemed a "coffee house," although it lacked coffee and a food menu. Men, liquor, and dancing girls, however, were served in abundance. They opted for the small restaurant next door. She ate while Burke studied the newspaper intently. Afterward, they drove to the Victory Hotel where Burke registered them under the names of Mr. and Mrs. Jesse James, most certainly paying homage to the famous outlaw. He paid for the room with a crisp 10-dollar bill. She noticed that all the bills in his wallet looked brand new.

The investigators leaned forward in their seats, as if interested in the anticipated details she was about to reveal. Sensing this, Florence Faurote blurted out, "I did not sleep with Fred Burke. While we were in the room, he read a newspaper article about a witness who spotted him in Indianapolis. He chuckled about it."

Still trying to work her way out of this situation, Faurote said she woke up Burke at 8:00 a.m. and told him that she would be going out. She told him she would meet him at 4:00 p.m. back at the Victory Hotel. The Victory was conveniently on the same road as the Detroit Police Headquarters, so she hurried down the street to report her encounter to detectives.

"They recommended that I leave town, so I left the station at 1 p.m. and began walking down the street. Two men came up along the sidewalk, either Fifth or Sixth Street near Jefferson. They were rough looking, either Italian or Greek. Then one man put his hand over my mouth while the other pushed my hat down over my eyes and forced me into a Nash touring car. They told me to keep my mouth shut."

Faurote said that the men took her to Cleveland, Ohio, and checked into a rooming house at 1545 East Superior. Their room was right next to the front door on the left as they walked in. Two of the men stayed in the room with Faurote and guzzled booze. She noticed the street name and address, 1545 East Superior, when she looked out of the window. She also noticed all the streetcars going by. At about 1:00 a.m., she awoke and the two men guarding her perked up. She told them that she had to use the bathroom. The men allowed her to use the bathroom down the hall, and there she met another woman. Faurote told her the story of how she was kidnapped, so the woman helped her escape out the back door, unnoticed by her captors.

Relieved but frightened, Faurote kept walking until she found a ride to Sandusky, Ohio, and then back to Toledo. Once there, she overheard a police officer talking about Fred Burke. Instead of informing the officer of her encounter and kidnapping, she began to make a joke about Burke. She said the officer failed to see her humor and she quickly found herself under arrest and lodged at the Toledo jail for the next three weeks, charged with a felony in Berrien County. Florence Faurote was accused of bigamy and extradited there.[61]

Apparently, Florence had married three men but never divorced any of them. She was wed the first time to Ernest Faurote, in 1912. Then on January 5, 1929, she married Lewis Allen, but he eventually moved to Montague, Michigan, without her. Florence took another trip down the aisle on October 8, 1929 with 53-year-old widower Charles F. Steedley, just six months after his first wife passed away. Steedley claimed that she had married him for his money and began signing checks without his knowledge.[62] He reported that Florence left to care for her sick child shortly after they were married, but he later found out that she instead went to visit her second husband, Lewis Allen, in Montague. Steedley was granted an annulment in November 1929 through the Berrien County Circuit Court.

After listening to her colorful tale, investigators tried to verify her statements. Regarding any prior holdups Burke allegedly committed, they found that on July 14, 1923, a jeweler reported to police that he had been robbed at the Statler Hotel in Detroit. His stolen jewels were valued at $200,000.

He told authorities that two men forced their way into his room where they placed a sack over his head and grabbed the jewels. Since no reports of a disturbance or robbery came in, police believed that the thieves had casually walked out of the hotel.[63] Then, there had been a reported jewelry robbery at the Tuller Hotel in Detroit on July 8, 1929, where a diamond merchant had his $45,000 collection stolen.[64] In both cases, Burke could very well have been in Detroit, but no evidence ever linked him to those thefts.

Florence Faurote pled guilty to the charge of bigamy on February 27, 1930, in front of Berrien County circuit court judge Charles E. White. She was sentenced to three to five years at Detroit's Women Prison in Northville Township, later called the Robert Scott Correctional Facility, where she resided as Florence Faurote,[65] her first and only legitimate married name, as it turned out.

Authorities ultimately discounted her claims of being involved with Burke, probably believing that she had been seeking a reduced sentence. Florence Faurote never spoke publicly of this again.

THE AMATEUR DETECTIVE

ON THE FIRST DAY OF THE NEW DECADE IN 1930, A tall stranger calling himself Richard F. White arrived at the Bailey Farm in rural Sullivan County, just outside of Green City, Missouri, looking for work as a farmhand. The 200-acre farm was situated in the rolling hills of northern Missouri and had been home to Civil War veteran John Hannibal Bailey and his wife, Amanda Ellen Burnside Bailey, until John's death in 1907. The couple had raised Aberdeen-Angus cows, geese, and hens, and grew colorful country flowers. Seventy-six-year-old Amanda Bailey was able to keep the farm by receiving her husband's Civil War pension.[66] Their 45-year-old widowed daughter, Lucretia E. Bailey Gum, worked with her mother on the family farm, which also served as a retreat for her son, Harvey Bailey, a bank robber of note.

Unbeknownst to both the mother and daughter, the tall stranger was actually Fred Burke, using an alias, who had traded his elegant suit for a set of overalls, and his lavish tastes in top-line hotel luxury for dusty soil and a newfound life of simplicity. In an effort to lie low after the Skelly slaying, Burke sought out the help of his pal, Harvey Bailey, who arranged for him to live with Bailey's mother and sister at the family farm. Amanda Bailey welcomed Burke, as any mother would do for a friend of her son, but she was quite naive as to the true nature of their careers. Green City's 1.4-square-mile area hardly compared to that of Chicago, St. Louis, or Detroit. Nevertheless, Burke was grateful for the slower pace and the general naïveté of the farming community, as well as the help of Harvey Bailey.

Bailey's quick speech and leadership made him stand out among the criminally noteworthy, but his clever intelligence distinguished him as of the most successful yeggs of the time. He owned several airplanes, which he used for running liquor, but bank robbery was more lucrative. Unlike the big-city gangs with established turfs, Bailey kept mobile most of the time and would show up at the Green City farm on occasion, driving his Cadillac sedan with several men inside and staying there a week or two at a time.

The Baileys treated Burke like a member of the family and anything he requested was readily available. Bailey even provided large bundles of Chicago newspapers for Burke to read.[67] When dental services were needed, a Bailey family friend, Dr. Andrew Wayne Herington of nearby Milan, took Burke on as his newest patient. Bailey usually paid for Dr. Herington's services by giving him all the whiskey he wanted.[68] To the Green City townspeople, Burke was Richard F. White, a farmhand. Only one observant resident eventually saw through the masquerade, which would end up being the undoing of Fred "Killer" Burke.

Twenty-nine-year-old gas station attendant Joseph Hunsaker, Jr. was a professed crime buff who cherished his collection of *True Detective Mysteries,* the monthly true crime magazine published by Bernarr MacFadden. He convinced the proprietor of the Green City General Store to carry the magazine, even though Hunsaker was the sole buyer in a town of almost 800 residents. He loyally bought three copies each month and relished stories of the St. Valentine's Day Massacre, the slaying of Officer Charles Skelly, and the naming of Fred "Killer" Burke as a suspect for both. What he lacked in education and eloquence, Hunsaker made up for as he developed a keen sense of observation, like any good detective, and he took notice of the town's newest resident, Richard White.

The two first met when White drove the farm truck into the Green City Shell gas station. He had torn out the differential gears while trying to plow through mud. Hunsaker considered it odd for an experienced farmhand to try this, but not totally out of the question, so Hunsaker made the repair without mention. White thereafter stopped by the gas station about once a month, which guaranteed Hunsaker a tip of between $0.50 and $1.00, each visit. The married father of one appreciated the extra money during the rough times.

Hunsaker's curiosity was piqued when he learned that someone else had started buying *True Detective Mysteries* from the general store. Hunsaker saw Lucretia Bailey Gum walk out with the magazine and several Chicago newspapers and return to her farm, where Hunsaker knew White worked. From that point, Hunsaker became extremely suspicious of White. The next time White appeared in town, Hunsaker observed his hands. They were softened and unblemished, certainly not the hands of a farm laborer.

Neighbors also took note of White. One day, 20-year-old schoolteacher Ramah McNabb watched White pull something out of his automobile that looked like a machine gun. When he saw her, he quickly shoved it back in the car. McNabb knew Bailey and his friends were gangsters, but she thought they were just involved in bootlegging activities.[69] Talk about White began to increase among residents, and Hunsaker heard that every time a vehicle would pass by the Bailey farm, White would hide behind the barn. Friends spoke of White's card-playing ability and his uncanny sense of awareness of his surroundings. Townspeople noticed his suspicious appearance at an estate sale. As the crowd filed into the kitchen for some homemade delicacies, one woman remarked that she did not like the way White looked, comparing him to a hoodlum. Another commented on how black his eyes were, and how he was always looking around at the crowd.[70]

White started sending some of the local boys out to get gas and cigarettes for him, giving them a $100 dollar bill each, figuring that they were safer with it than he was. The sudden appearance of large bills in the heart of rural Missouri roused more than a little suspicion. Some had taken notice of White's way with youths in the community, especially babies and small children, insisting on holding them in his lap whenever the opportunity arose.[71] Hunsaker was not fooled, though. He believed the man's actions had little to do with any form of perverse sexual desire but that White's association with children was a way to avoid anyone taking aim at him with an innocent child in the way; even the most ruthless gangster would not sacrifice a young child in an attempt to seek revenge. The amateur detective began building his case.

ON THE ONE-YEAR ANNIVERSARY of the St. Valentine's Day Massacre, Cook County coroner Herman Bundesen touted the victory of science over crime, telling reporters, "The story of the massacre itself, and its solution, best illustrates the practical use that can be made of the microscope and the laboratory in the investigation of murders. It marks the turning point in police methods in the United States."[72]

In the eyes of Bundesen and ranking Chicago officials, they had solved the massacre, even though Burke and Winkeler were still on the lam. Likewise, Burke faced accusations of many other crimes, as well. The Farmers and Merchants Bank in Jefferson, Wisconsin, and the United States Fidelity and Guaranty Company lawsuit was still active. The following appeared in the legal section of the *News-Palladium* on February 8, 1930, and ran each day through March 15, 1930:

> "Notice of Attachment
> State of Michigan
> In the Circuit Court of the County of Berrien

The Farmers and Merchants Bank in Jefferson, Wisconsin and the United States Fidelity and Guarantee Company, plaintiffs vs. Fred Dane, alias Herbert Church, defendant.

Notice is hereby given that on the 19th day of December, A. D. 1929, a writ of attachment was issued out of said court in favor of the Farmers and Merchants Bank in Jefferson, Wisconsin, and the United States Fidelity and Guarantee Company, as plaintiffs, and against the lands, tenements, goods, chattels, moneys, and effects of Fred Dane, alias Herbert Church as defendant for the sum of thirty three thousand five hundred and no .100 dollars, which said writ was returnable on the 18th day of January, A. D., 1930.

Dated January 29, 1930
E. A. Westin
Attorney for Plaintiffs
Business Address,
Benton Harbor, Michigan
Feb. 8th–Mar. 15th"[73]

BACK IN GREEN CITY, MISSOURI, in mid-February 1930, Barney Lee Porter, whose 80-acre farm butted up to the Baileys' property, invited some of the fellas over for a game of cards. Taking Porter up on the offer, Richard White joined in the card game, but he seemed slightly distracted by Porter's beautiful daughter. Bonnie Gwendolyn Porter had just returned home for a visit from nursing school in Kansas City, where she had been studying for the past year. The 20-year-old, golden-haired, blue-eyed miss was a sight for a poor gangster-turned-farmhand's eyes. Some townspeople saw Bonnie as a tart, an attractive woman who acted promiscuous. She would often hang around the men at the garage in town, but now a much older man caught her attention.[74] It was not long before the Burke charm and charisma, under the guise of Richard F. White, took over the unwary Miss Porter and her family. Once Bonnie returned to Kansas City, the two kept up a regular correspondence until she came back to the farm in June. They were smitten with each other and a long-distance relationship ensued. White, in the meantime, kept busy.

One snowy night, White set off in his car for the town of Kirksville, Missouri, about 25 miles east of Green City. He drove a new Chrysler; however, the depth of the snow proved too much for a light vehicle and it became stuck. Seeing a farmhouse not far away, he trudged to the front door.

Hearing a knock, John Tomich stood up, walked to the door, opened it, and noticed the well-dressed man standing before him who explained his predicament. Tomich called for his teenaged son to harness up a team of horses to pull the car out and into town. Johnnie Tomich took the stranded man back to his car on Highway 63. After Tomich hooked up the rigging to the horses, they began pulling the expensive car along the road. The boy knew exactly how to handle the team of horses, but he had never seen a car like this. Once he managed to pull the car into town, Johnnie unhooked the ropes and prepared to head back home.

"Don't run off," hollered the man as he walked to the back of car and opened the trunk. "Johnnie, does your father like nice shirts?"

"He likes even old shirts," responded Johnnie.

The man handed him three boxes of shirts.

"Would your father drink whiskey?" the man inquired as he poked through the trunk.

"Yes, he probably would and if he didn't, the neighbors would."

The man then reached into the trunk, grabbed a fifth, and handed the bottle to the boy, whose mouth was gaping open by then.

"Okay, now hold your hand out," the man instructed Johnnie. He reached into his pocket and placed a bill in Johnnie's hand, "Now this is just for you. Just put it in your pocket."

The man drove off and Johnnie returned home. Each of the three boxes contained two silk shirts, and when Johnnie pulled the bill out of his pocket, he was shocked to see it was $50.[75]

Unbeknownst to the young man, the stranger was interested in later making a large withdrawal from the Bank of Kirksville, long after its closing time.

ON FEBRUARY 24, 1930, days after White/Burke's visit to Kirksville, the chief of the Secret Service Division contacted Andrew M. Devoursney at the Wisconsin Bankers' Association, sharing the results of their surveillance. They believed that the entire mob was in Miami, Florida, together with some well-known racketeers from Detroit. They had gathered photographs and fingerprints of Gus Winkeler, Raymond Nugent, Ted Newberry, Claude Maddox, and Fred Goetz, although their primary target, Fred Burke, had not been seen there.[76]

Another person noticeably missing from Miami was Al Capone, who had been locked up in the Eastern State Penitentiary in Philadelphia, Pennsylvania, since May 18, 1929, serving time on his concealed weapons charge. On March 17, 1930, Capone was released. In a controversial move, *Time Magazine* put Capone on the cover of its March 24, 1930, issue. Publicizing Capone irritated President Herbert Hoover, who was said to have told his

Secretary of the Treasury, "I want that man Capone in jail."

Capone had some competition for front-page news around Southwestern Michigan. At the same time, former Benton Harbor mayor and business owner Fred Cutler announced his candidacy for Berrien County sheriff on the Democratic ticket. Charles Skelly's old pal, William Barry, now Benton Harbor police captain, did the same on the Republican ticket. Soon others threw their hats in the race for outgoing sheriff Fred Bryant's former position.

When attempts to locate Burke proved futile and legal notices were ignored, Judge Charles White ordered the acquisition of Burke's property and possessions to be used toward fulfillment of his judgment. On May 5 in Jefferson County Court, Wisconsin, Farmers and Merchants Bank President Lynn H. Smith was deposed in the matter. Notary Public Lawrence J. Mistele asked Smith to explain what had been taken in the November 7, 1929, robbery.

"Cash and bonds of the approximate value of $352,000," testified Smith.

"Has any part of that been recovered, and if so, how and where?" continued Mistele.

"Yes," replied Smith. "Bonds to the extent of $319,950 were recovered from the residence of Fred Dane, located near St. Joseph, Michigan, on December 14, 1929."

"What has not been recovered?"

"Cash amounting to more than $9,000 and liberty bonds of the approximate value of $26,500," declared Smith.[77]

After a thorough inventory and appraisal was completed, deputies prepared to auction off property and belongings left by Burke in his Stevensville bungalow. William McFaul of St. Joseph purchased the damaged 1928 Hudson Coupe, valued at $200. Items from within the home included a console table valued at $4.50, new carpeting with ozite cushioning valued at $200, a 27-inch Gulistan rug valued at $8, and a 9-by-12-foot Sahara rug valued at $100.

As the bank attempted to recoup its losses, Gustav Skalay, the father of Charles Skelly, revealed that the funeral expenses were still unpaid. In April 1930, the court granted a settlement of $2 per week for 300 weeks, but the insurance company appealed to the State Industrial Board, arguing that Charles Skelly had been single and without dependents; therefore, his father was not entitled to compensation. Then, on April 28, 1930, the State Insurance Commission reduced the award to a lump sum of $500, in addition to the costs already paid for the hospital and funeral.[78] The insurance company had been paying Gustav Skalay $50 a month to cover the $600 funeral cost, so the family hired a lawyer.

NESTLED IN WITH HIS FRIENDS and using his latest persona, the reinvented Burke managed to slip away from Missouri occasionally. In one adventure in early April 1930, Gus Winkeler joined him in a jaunt to Los Angeles, where they robbed at least four people of their jewelry. All four victims positively identified the thief as Fred Burke by his photograph, but the photograph of Winkeler stumped them.[79] Realizing that they were too easily recognizable, Burke and Winkeler planned to see a doctor in Chicago.

Dr. David Vermont Omens was a Russian-born physician who had been providing medical services for members of the syndicate. He would register them under assumed names if they were being treated in the hospital; if they were too easily recognizable, he would treat them at their home. Omens referred Burke and Winkeler to plastic surgeon Dr. Edward Otto von Borries, a 50-year-old Kentuckian who probably was known more for his court appearances and police reports than his medical expertise. Dr. von Borries' high-profile reputation did not hinder either Burke or Winkeler from seeking his services.

When Georgette Winkeler saw her husband for the first time after his surgery, she screamed, not recognizing him underneath the gauze and bandages. Her reaction had him laughing so hard that tears streamed down his face, probably from the pain. He then proceeded to pull off part of the bandage for her to see.

"How do you like it?" he asked, pointing at his nose. "Pretty doggie, eh?" Georgette cringed at the sight.

"I admit my nose looks as if I smelled something rotten in Denmark, but it sure does change me," chuckled Gus. "Hell, honey, if you think I look funny you ought to see Fred Burke. The sawbones did him up in great style. He looks like a Boston terrier, and has a peach of a harelip. He looks like the very devil, but even you wouldn't recognize him."[80]

Indeed, Burke's procedure involved reworking his normally concave nose into one that was convex, nostrils slightly upturned, and left him with a permanent scar above his lip. He eventually returned and stayed in hiding at the Winkelers' apartment for the month of May while he healed, before heading back to the Bailey farm in June 1930.

While Winkeler and Burke recuperated in Chicago, gangland attempted to silence one of their own in the small town of New Milford, Illinois, west of Chicago in Winnebago County. This time the victim was Russell Thompson, a key supplier of guns to gangsters, whose testimony at the St. Valentine's Day Massacre inquest made him a marked man. On June 8, 1930, a single bullet pierced his chest and, although conscious and still able to speak, Thompson refused to identify his shooter, telling police, "I've seen everything, I've done everything, and got everything, and you're smart enough to know I won't talk. Go to hell." Upon learning of Thompson's fate, Chicago chief detective John Stege remarked to reporters, "Thompson seems to have gotten his desserts." Although he had been given no hope of survival, Thompson surprised everyone by making a full recovery six weeks later; even prompting a change of heart about keeping his would-be killer's name a secret.

AFTER A MONTH OF HIDING OUT, the slick Richard F. White, with his new refined look, returned to Green City, Missouri, and asked Bonnie Porter, the farmer's sweet daughter, for her hand in marriage. She accepted, never questioning his time away or his new look, likely explained away by the master charmer. Just a few days later, Richard and Bonnie drove north to the town of Keokuk, Iowa, in southeastern Iowa, where Bonnie bought herself a wedding dress. The following day, June 17, 1930, the couple motored to Centerville, Iowa, to get married. Posing as a wealthy broker, Burke confidently walked into the Appanoose County clerk's office to obtain a marriage license. Little did he expect to see his own likeness staring back at him from a wanted poster for the murder of police officer Charles Skelly.[81] However, Appanoose County clerk Ed Hanson did not recognize him. Burke filled out the marriage application as 34-year-old Richard F. White, born in Kansas City to parents Warren White and Mattie White, and currently residing in DeKalb, Illinois. He listed no previous marriages. Upon securing the license, he escorted Bonnie to the home of Reverend W. O. Bloom of the Swedish Lutheran Church. Reverend Bloom did not like the man's appearance and thought that he was too old to marry the girl, and so he questioned the two as to whether the bride's parents knew of the wedding. White, 16 years her senior, managed a slick enough response to end Bloom's doubt.[82] There, along with the reverend's wife, Arleen Bloom, and two of Bonnie Porter's relatives, Eliza Porter Stuckey and Ethel Swanson, serving as witnesses, the pair became husband and wife.

Coincidentally, while the couple were exchanging vows in Centerville, Iowa, a public auction was taking place in St. Joseph, Michigan. The exquisite carpeting that graced Burke's bungalow was being auctioned off at the very place he had purchased it: Troost Brothers Furniture. The highest bidder, at $200, was the Farmers and Merchants Bank in Jefferson, Wisconsin. This purchase was a way to try to recoup some of the missing funds.[83]

After the wedding, the new Mr. and Mrs. White set off on their honeymoon, taking Bonnie's father and mother along on their three-week adventure to Colorado Springs, Denver, Salt Lake City, San Francisco, Seattle, and Yellowstone Park.[84] They then drove into Brownsville, Texas, and crossed the border into Matamoros, Mexico.[85] White appeared the epitome of a sensitive and caring gentleman. After seeing the dead bodies of poor Mexicans who had been dug up because their relatives could not pay the rent owed for the gravesites, he expressed shock and grief for the undignified treatment of the dead.

When they returned to Green City, Richard White transformed himself from a measly farmhand into a wealthy Kansas City real estate developer. He began spending money freely, even more than before, usually $100 at a time. He bought the most expensive cuts of meat at the Baldridge Butcher Shop and regularly patronized Bob Ash Furnishings in Milan. Fred Bertschman's tailor shop in Milan made him two suits, five pairs of golf trousers, and a top coat. Bertschman was surprised to receive a $100 bill for an order that totaled only $3.50. "We don't see hundred-dollar bills in Milan, except at a bank," Bertschman explained to White. "I don't have any idea where I could take it to get it changed."

"Oh, never mind about that," said White. "Just keep the change and I'll trade it out."[86]

Mr. and Mrs. White would spend days and weeks on the road traveling, with occasional visits back to the Porter farm. On one trip, the newlyweds took along Bonnie's younger sister, Pansy. They returned in time for Pansy to start school. Richard White's new life appeared carefree, but at the core he still was "The Most Dangerous Man Alive," and Joseph Hunsaker, the amateur detective, was about to make that connection.

Bonnie Porter. *Author's collection.*

Joseph Hunsaker. *Author's collection.*

Allen D. Morrison of Green City, Missouri. *Author's collection.*

Barney Porter of Green City, Missouri. *Author's collection.*

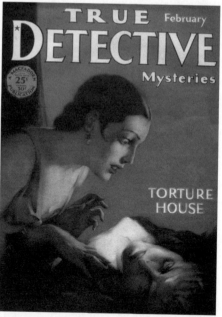

True Detective Mysteries magazine, February 1930 issue. *Author's collection.*

SILENCING THE SPY

AS FRED "KILLER" BURKE'S CRIME COUNT INCREASED, so did the reward money for his capture: now up to $90,000. The enticement of money motivated many average citizens. Anyone appearing suspicious or remotely resembling "The Most Dangerous Man Alive" was duly reported, keeping authorities very busy. Thomas Hendricks Bonner, a 43-year-old Chicago auto salesman/manager who dabbled in petty rackets, liquor trades, and confidence games, knew Burke and pursued the idea that he could double-cross Burke and collect the money. Bonner first met Burke at the speakeasy he owned on 97th Street and Vincennes in Chicago. Burke told him he was a brakeman on the Chicago Panhandle Division of the Pennsylvania Railroad. The two men spoke frequently and Burke became his best customer.[87] Bonner enlisted the help of 44-year-old Chicago pharmacist Philip Rodger McDonnell after he learned that Burke regularly made stops at McDonnell's drug store at 501 West 79th Street in Chicago and at a West Randolph Street shop for his "home brew" supplies.[88] Bonner saw this as a viable lead and in the spring of 1930, he managed to work his way into McDonnell's inner circle and focused on the movements of Burke. Bonner certainly knew enough to finger Burke and the financial incentive was his reason for doing so.

As Bonner planned how to carry out his plan, he approached Captain John Norton at the Chicago Police Department and suggested that they watch McDonnell's drug store. Detectives began their surveillance of the store but through a leak the information that Bonner provided to Norton made it into the Chicago newspapers.

When Burke did not show up at the drug store as McDonnell and Bonner had hoped, McDonnell made contact with William A. Smith from Grand Rapids, Michigan, who he had heard offered his country cottage in Western Michigan as a hideout for Burke. McDonnell managed to get an invitation to the cottage on the pretense of a vacation getaway, and on Sunday, July 6, 1930, he invited Bonner to accompany him. Bonner informed detectives of the trip and they asked him to report back when he returned. Bonner took the wheel of McDonnell's Cadillac while McDonnell and his wife, Bessie, rode in the backseat for the long journey to Newaygo, Michigan. Several hours later, they arrived at the fenced-in cottage retreat, nestled in the woods between Hess Lake and Bigelow Creek. Unfortunately, Smith's houseguest and his blonde companion were not present at the time. McDonnell handed over the stack of Chicago newspapers that Smith had requested. Unbeknownst to Bonner, one of the newspapers featured the information about the West 79th Street surveillance, which would be his undoing.[89]

Both Bonner and McDonnell got right down to their business of snooping around. Bonner spoke to neighbors about the new guest staying at the cottage. Some of the neighbors accused him of being a Chicago bootlegger. Bonner also took a good look around the cottage when he thought no one was watching to see if he could find any clues to prove that Burke was there. After staying overnight, Bonner and the McDonnells prepared to leave the morning of Tuesday, July 8. However, for some reason, their car would not start, so Smith offered them the use of his Buick. He gave them instructions on where to park it in Chicago so he could exchange cars later. Unfortunately for Bonner, Smith had noticed that he was snooping. Once they were back in Chicago, Bonner immediately drove to the Chicago Police Department to report to Captain Norton that he believed Burke was hiding at the cottage and was supposed to return to Chicago on Wednesday, July 9, or Saturday, July 12, after he made a trip to Flint and Detroit. Bonner dropped off Smith's Buick on 79th Street at Parnell, though he suspected the car actually belonged to Burke. After revealing what he knew to Captain Norton, Bonner expressed his growing concern. "I think this whole thing was a mistake, a big mistake." He felt that someone was watching him. In fact, someone most certainly was.

The next evening, July 9, Bonner and his family were home in their Chicago apartment at 7353 South Yale Avenue. Moments before midnight, they heard a knock at the door. Bonner's wife, Mary, held their five-month-old son, Bobbie, in her arms as she watched her husband answer the door. Whether it was from a sense of foreboding or having a photographic memory, Mary paid close attention. She saw two men illuminated in the porch light, one of whom she had seen before: Fred Burke. Then she heard her husband cry out, "Wait, fellows, you've got me wrong." Those would be his last words. A single .45-caliber bullet pierced his skull. His 250-pound body fell backward into the living room while the two assailants disappeared into the darkness. Mary ran to the window just as the men drove off in a Ford. She even had the presence of mind to take note of the license plate before calling for help. Bonner remained alive but unconscious for several hours. However, on July 10, 1930, at 4 a.m., the spy was forever silenced.[90] He was gangland's 47th victim of the year.

On Friday afternoon, July 11, Philip and Bessie McDonnell arrived at the garage on 79th Street where Bonner had left the Buick, but instead of them picking up the car, Chicago police picked up them. Placing a watch on the car since learning of its origin, Captain Norton had ordered officers to bring in anyone who showed up for it. After a few hours of questioning, police released both of the McDonnells, but Philip McDonnell was not off the hook just yet.

Bonner's wife identified Fred Burke as one of the two men who had shot her husband. Believing that Burke had returned to Hess Lake, authorities in Chicago acted quickly. On Sunday, July 13, Lieutenant John McGinnis, head of the homicide division at the Chicago Police Department, set off for Newaygo with three squads of officers. The convoy stopped at noon in Grand Rapids, Michigan, where they enlisted the help of two detectives and one sergeant from that city's force. They continued driving to White Cloud, the Newaygo County seat, situated north of Hess Lake. Additional forces from the Newaygo County Sheriff's Department met the group. McGinnis went over plans for a raid of the cottage, describing the layout and possible escape routes, just as Bonner had previously described to him. After their briefing, the primed officers loaded their machine guns and prepared to meet "The Most Dangerous Man Alive" and the most wanted man in the nation.

As the convoy split up and drove in from different directions in the wooded area surrounding Hess Lake, deputies on other assignments learned of the raid. Shortly before 4:00 p.m., one Newaygo deputy stopped at the Crossroads Store, near the cottage, and used the telephone to inform another deputy about what would be taking place. Little did that foolhardy deputy know that Smith, the cottage owner, happened to be in the store and overheard the entire conversation. In a flash, he bolted out of the store.

Thirty minutes later, the officers arrived at the cottage and staked out the four corners of the property, ready for a possible gun battle. Then a small team of officers approached the front door. Mrs. Smith opened the door and indicated that she was alone at the cottage. Believing that Burke might be out for the afternoon, officers repositioned themselves. Some stationed themselves inside the cottage, while others hunkered down in the woods that surrounded the property.

Minutes later, the sound of an approaching vehicle caught everyone's attention. It was a Cadillac bearing Illinois plates. As it slowed to turn into the driveway of the cottage, officers formed a takedown position. In one sudden movement, they surrounded the car, reached in through the open windows, and pulled out the driver. Police took the man into secure custody and those stationed on the perimeter cleared the area. Unfortunately, the officers had seized William Smith. He explained that he just purchased a load of ice in Newaygo and was bringing it to the cottage.

Officers demanded to know the whereabouts of Fred Burke.

"Burke? Never heard of him," Smith coyly replied.

The officers had little tolerance for the man they knew was lying. They searched his vehicle and, not surprisingly, found two high-powered rifles hidden in the trunk, in addition to the ice.[91] He explained away the guns with a ridiculous story, saying that a stranger had arrived at the cottage on Tuesday, July 8, and asked to borrow a car to drive north to tend to an ailing relative, indicating that his Cadillac was too nice to drive on the rough rural roads. According to Smith, he allowed the stranger to take his vehicle, if he could use the Cadillac in the meantime. Officers took note of a fresh set of tire tracks from another vehicle. Smith suggested they were from the car he loaned to the stranger. Realizing that they were not getting much information out of Smith, they conducted a thorough search of the cottage and found a sawed-off shotgun, a rifle, and 20 gallons of whiskey and beer, enough evidence to hold Smith for further questioning. The officers would later take him back to Chicago.

Meanwhile, after having found no signs of Burke at the cottage, Lieutenant McGinnis and another team of officers questioned area residents. They learned from the clerk at the Crossroads Store that around 4:30 p.m. that afternoon a man who resembled Burke and a blonde female companion had sped by the store in a Ford. Unfortunately, that man had just over a 30-minute head start on the police. McGinnis alerted authorities in West Michigan to be on the lookout for Burke driving a Ford. One report that came in put him at the Oxbow Dam on the Muskegon River at about 7:00 p.m., so the search effort turned to that direction. Officers in Muskegon, about 40 miles northeast of the Hess Lake cottage, donned bulletproof vests and began searching every boat and train leaving the city. State troopers from the Grand Haven Post, at the request of Muskegon police chief Peter F. Hansen, began to assist by searching Muskegon-area hotels. Unfortunately, most officers did not reach the area until after 11:00 p.m. and by then, the trail was cold. Consequently, from Battle Creek to New Buffalo, the patrol coverage area increased,[92] paying special attention to U.S. Highway 12, a main thoroughfare between Chicago and Detroit.

As the hunt progressed, McGinnis sent three members of his squad back to Chicago with Smith and the Cadillac. It had already been an exhausting day that crept into a late night for the investigators. In Chicago, Captain John Norton put Smith in a holding cell. One of their top priorities was to determine whether Smith was one of the men who had gunned down Bonner. On July 14, officers took Smith over to the Bonner home in the Cadillac so that Mrs. Bonner could view him and the car.

After seeing the suspect, she told officers, "That's not the man. I'd know Tom's murderer anywhere. It was Fred Burke and a sandy-haired fella with him who shot Tommy."[93]

She noted that the man with Burke was drunk and held the gun in his left hand. Officers asked if she was certain that Smith was not the killer. "I know it was Fred Burke who killed my husband," sobbed Mrs. Bonner. "My husband knew Burke for many years. I saw Burke many times and recognized him the night he came to our house and killed my husband."[94]

In addition to naming Burke, Mrs. Bonner confirmed that the license plate on the Cadillac was the same one she saw on the Ford driven by the killers of her husband. Authorities believed that Burke left Hess Lake after transferring the license plates on McDonnell's Cadillac to his own car. Once he executed Bonner, Burke returned to the cottage and reattached the plates to the Cadillac.

On July 14, Michigan newspapers broke the story of the hunt for Fred "Killer" Burke, including his photograph. Local police sifted through numerous calls reporting sightings of him, but all led to dead ends. James Ogilvie of Fountain, in Mason County, reported a man resembling Burke at a cottage on Bass Lake in Lake County. Once troopers met with Ogilvie, they found the man in question was just a regular summer resort visitor from Fort Wayne, Indiana.[95]

On the afternoon of July 14, two Owosso, Michigan, men, Louis E. Johnson and John Thuma, reported a run-in with a man who resembled Burke, who was upset about having to pay a $2 storage fee for the Buick he had left on Thursday and never picked up. Johnson became concerned that the man might be carrying a gun because he never took his hand out of his right pocket. Not wanting the argument to escalate, Johnson refunded the money to the man he believed was Burke, who went on his way.

Newspaperman Chad Wallin of Grand Rapids alerted authorities after he approached a man in the small village of Casnovia, between Kent and Muskegon Counties, who reacted by leaping out of a parked car and disappearing into the darkness. By the time officers made it to the area, the car and man were gone.[96]

Almost at the same time, several suspicious-looking Italians had reportedly rented a cottage located just off M-55 on Lake Cadillac. Troopers from the Reed City Post and the sheriff of Wexford County acted on the information. On July 13, a citizen reported seeing a Buick sedan driving around the city of Cadillac and spotted it at the cottage as well. Upon investigation, police learned that no one had occupied the cottage for the season and no one had seen anyone resembling Fred Burke in the area.[97]

A local bank teller in the eastern Michigan town of Bad Axe reported that a man he thought to be Burke had asked to make change for two $100 bills and left in a Ford Tudor sedan with a blonde woman. Another tip came in saying that Burke had rented a cottage in Port Hope, near Bad Axe,[98] but police found no evidence of Burke in the area.

The police did not discount any leads in the hunt for "The Most Dangerous Man Alive." Even a man of the cloth became a suspect. In the city of Marquette, in Michigan's Upper Peninsula, the proprietor of a Washington Street business told troopers that a new preacher appeared to be Burke in disguise.[99] Upon investigation, troopers learned that the preacher was legitimate and only minimally resembled the killer.[100] They even investigated a former Copemish Township, Michigan, supervisor, Frank E. Burke, under the presumption that he might be Fred's brother. However, it soon became obvious that he had no connection to Fred "Killer" Burke.

Although the Chicago police had not been able to connect pharmacist Philip McDonnell to the murder of Thomas Bonner, they did charge him with the theft of the Cadillac that he and Bonner had driven to the Hess Lake cottage. It belonged to a Samuel Wagner, who had reported it stolen on July 1.[101] Police released the owner of the cottage, William Smith, and he returned to his primary residence in Grand Rapids, Michigan.

As evidenced by Burke's killing of Officer Skelly, criminals were evolving, and becoming more brutal. In fact, by the close of 1930, 293 police officers would die in the line of duty, making it the deadliest single year in law enforcement history.[102] Despite all the efforts made by authorities across the nation, Burke remained at large.

THE WATCH

JOSEPH HUNSAKER, THE AMATEUR DETECTIVE LIVING IN Green City, Missouri, had been keeping notes on all the suspicious activities of Richard White. He noticed that White almost never removed his right hand from his pocket, except on one occasion while picking up some coins in order to purchase a bag of peanuts, and then he immediately put his right hand back into his pocket. Hunsaker also noted that White always used his left hand to open doors, and he suspected that White was concealing a weapon in his right-hand pocket. In addition, during these trying economic times when most people were barely scraping by, White was spending money freely. He even purchased a new set of tires for his vehicle from the gas station where Hunsaker worked. Hunsaker often wondered about White's rather odd habit of always remaining in the vehicle with the engine running when filling up his gas tank, and insisting the tank be filled to overflowing, as if that was his only way of knowing that it was actually full.

That was clear on one particular occasion when he pulled up to the pump and Hunsaker greeted him. "Fill 'er up," the dapper White ordered.

When Hunsaker inserted the nozzle, he realized that the tank was nearly full already.

"You're pretty near full up already."

"I *said* fill 'er up," White replied sternly.

His demeanor that time really scared Hunsaker, who carefully washed the windshield while trying to avoid eye contact with the man he believed could be a killer.[103]

GEORGETTE WINKELER became startled when, alone in her Berwyn, Illinois, home in late August 1930, she heard a knock at the door. Opening it a crack, she saw a man with a turned-up nose and bristly mustache. "Georgette, invite me in," said the man, whom she now recognized as her husband's friend, Fred Burke. He charged in and made a beeline for the lounge chair. Georgette saw that Burke was pale and lacked vitality. He shivered occasionally, despite the summer heat. "Where have you been?" she asked.

"Hiding out with Harvey Bailey's relatives near Green City, Missouri," he replied.

Sometime later Gus Winkeler arrived home and, although he was glad to see his old friend, he was concerned that Burke's presence could bring trouble for the couple. It became clear that Burke did not intend to leave until he got a car, and he was too recognizable to go out to try to deal for one himself. Winkeler offered to get him in contact with someone from the syndicate, but that would take time since most of the men wanted nothing to do with Burke now.

As they waited, Georgette noticed that Burke began drinking large quantities of whiskey day and night. He would set a pitcher next to him while listening to the radio. Hearing news reports only seemed to excite him more as he began pacing the floor. He would glance out the windows, peering behind the blinds at vehicles and pedestrians that passed in front. His nervousness and agitation frightened Georgette, who begged her husband to make him leave. Although Gus was certainly anxious to get rid of him, he could not do that out of loyalty to his friend. One night while Winkeler was out, Burke freaked at the sight of a police cruiser passing slowly by the house. "Cops," he slurred in a hushed voice that Georgette overheard. "They've found me and they've probably got Gus and found an address on him. Sure, that's the reason he isn't home yet. I got to get out of here quick."

The clearly intoxicated Burke threw off his slippers and began searching frantically for his shoes. "I won't get you killed, Georgette. I'll get out right now. Where the hell is my coat, where's my hat? They'll shoot us both; we haven't got a Chinaman's chance. Oh, God, Georgette, get my hat, can't you hurry?" he implored.

He managed to grab his gun and house slippers, but remained shoeless as he ran for the back door. Just then, Winkeler met him at the door and pushed him back inside. "Get inside, you crazy fool! What in the hell is the matter with you?"

Burke felt like a sitting duck and could not take the stress any longer, so the next day he managed to get a ride and left.[104] However, he did not go far because at the end of August that year, he allegedly kidnapped Brighton Park, Illinois, beer hustler Harold Cusack outside of a Hoyne Avenue saloon. Cusack paid a $10,000 ransom and was released unharmed in early September. Shortly after that, Richard White showed up back in Green City, Missouri.

White's return to the farm in Green City coincided with Joseph Hunsaker's finding himself out of work after a stint with the Missouri Highway Department. He decided to focus his free time on watching Richard White again. His suspicions that White was a criminal would be confirmed a few weeks later when he received his copy of the October 1930 edition of *True Detective Mysteries*. A story on the Egan's Rats Gang included a photograph of Fred "Killer" Burke and it brought chills to Hunsaker's spine. He studied the photos of Burke, noting every detail: yellow-brown eyes, chestnut hair, mustache, and a distinct scar on his upper lip. Staring from the pages was the face of none other than Richard F. White! Hunsaker just then realized how deep he had burrowed into the case, and it left him cold and weak.

Needing someone else to recognize White as Burke, he took the magazine downtown and showed it to several of his friends. None of them saw the resemblance. Knowing that his boss at the filling station had seen Richard White before, Hunsaker hustled over to show him the magazine. Barely glancing at it, his boss said, "You're up to something, Joe."

That casual comment alone unnerved Hunsaker. Realizing that he could have compromised himself by letting so many people know that he had matched the identity of Richard White with that of Fred "Killer" Burke, Hunsaker clutched the magazine and left. His excitement now turned to fear and paranoia, but he remained convinced he was on the trail to catch "The Most Dangerous Man Alive."

Hunsaker decided to write a letter to the Department of Justice in hopes of receiving a more current photograph and other pertinent details about Burke. He did not have an address but figured that the postmaster would direct it to the right place. Hunsaker used a two-cent pre-stamped envelope and wrote his return address as "Box 96, Green City, Missouri," specifically not identifying himself. Recognizing that in a small town, his actions could become fodder for the next day's gossip mills, he took the letter directly to the railroad station rather than to the Green City Post Office. He handed it to agent J. W. Ferguson and explained the importance of getting the letter directly into the mailbags on the train. Ferguson promised Hunsaker that he would see to it personally.

When the train arrived, Ferguson handed the letter to one of the young postal helpers, who looked at the address. "This letter won't go," he said. "It doesn't have any city on it." The helper thought it looked like a child's letter to Santa Claus. Ferguson snapped at the young man, "You're working for Uncle Sam and that's part of your job." Seemingly intimidated, the young man put the letter on the train anyway.

Hunsaker waited patiently for a response from the Department of Justice, but a week passed and he had heard nothing. A few days later while walking on a downtown street, he spotted local independent banker Allen D. Morrison, who shouted to him from across the street. "When did you get to be a detective?"

The 44-year-old Morrison worked in the banking business in Green City, dabbled in legal matters, and had been a member of the Missouri legislature in 1922, but now made private loans from his farming interests.

"Oh, I don't know," Hunsaker responded. Confused by the detective reference, "What do you mean?" he asked while crossing the street.

"You don't understand? I got your letter from the Department of Justice," Morrison replied loudly, while reaching into his pocket.

"Wait a minute, what's going on here?" Hunsaker demanded, running toward Morrison. "And for Pete's sake, don't talk so loud."

Hunsaker did not understand why Morrison received the response, but he knew he would now have to confide in him. Morrison gently explained to Hunsaker that the letter he sent to the Department of Justice was illegible and rather incoherent. In an attempt to determine what it was all about, an agent contacted Morrison, knowing of his previous service in state government.

"Look, Morrison," Hunsaker began, while looking over his shoulder, "White bought a car overnight-like," he said, referring to the man he believed might be Fred Burke, "and there is nothing to show where he got the money. He doesn't work on his father-in-law's farm where he is staying, but he always seems to have money."[105] Morrison stood assured but remained quiet, letting Hunsaker continue.

Hunsaker went on, fidgeting and nervous, "Now then, Morrison, you keep your trap shut, because I'm into this thing now and I've got something started that I hardly know what to do with. If you say anything now, it will spoil everything. Understand?"

Hunsaker had no idea that Morrison actually knew quite a bit about the hunt for Fred Burke. "You know, there's a reward of $90,000 being offered for Burke's capture," Morrison piped up as they slowly walked along the sidewalk.

Hunsaker was shocked. He had heard mention of a reward, but did not know how much. This reward was more money than he had ever known. He thought to himself, *Joe, this is your one big chance. All your life, ever since you were a little tyke, you've waited for something like this. And here it is, opportunity, with a great big capital "O," knocking right at your very door.*

After some more discussion and reassurance, the two men decided to team up. Morrison certainly had the professional background and connections while Hunsaker had the means to get close to Burke. As the men schemed about how to capture Burke and collect the reward money, they understood that they were the only ones who realized Burke was hiding in Green City.

WHILE THE FUTILE HUNT FOR BURKE continued in Michigan, St. Joseph city commissioners expressed their displeasure with Chief Fred Alden for failing to bring Burke to justice. In November 1930, just before the one-year anniversary of Skelly's brutal death, Alden was pressured to step down. The humble 63-year-old was not ready to retire, but he resigned to avoid being fired. Officer Ben Phairas, one of Alden's early trainees, became the new St. Joseph police chief. The Berrien County Sheriff's Department then re-hired Alden as a deputy. At the same time, voters in Berrien County chose Benton Harbor businessman Fred Cutler as their newest sheriff, effective January 1, 1931. Having lost his bid for the coveted position, William Barry resigned from the Benton Harbor Police Department and returned to work as a deputy along with his uncle, Fred Alden.

ON DECEMBER 23, 1930, Richard White and his new bride visited relatives in Bloomfield, Iowa, for Christmas. Lon Warner, a professional photographer and a second cousin to Bonnie Porter White, played host to the couple. After dinner, Warner suggested they go to his photo studio downtown and have their portraits taken. Everyone participated except Richard White, who explained how self-conscious he was about the scar on his lip. At the end of the day, the couple bid their farewells and headed on their way.[106]

The dutiful husband drove his wife back to the Porters' farm so that she could spend Christmas with her family before having to return to school in Kansas City. White did not stay with her, explaining that he needed to take care of some business in Kirksville, Missouri. He arrived on Christmas Eve, checked into the Traveler's Hotel, and headed over to the Bee-Hive Restaurant for a meal. Johnnie Tomich, the teenaged son of a Kirksville farmer, had taken a job at the restaurant and noticed White as soon as he sat down. The customer looked familiar; however, Tomich could not immediately place him. White must have seen the teenager staring, because he called him over. Suddenly, Tomich recognized him as the generous stranger whose car he had pulled out of the snow with his team of horses, a year earlier. They exchanged pleasantries, and then White made him an offer.

"Listen, I'm staying at the Traveler's Hotel and I need you to bring me a meal from here every day. I want it by noon, here's my room number."

"Sure," the eager Tomich replied, remembering the last time he helped and was compensated generously.

"Don't tell anyone about it and come by yourself."

For the next couple of weeks, Tomich delivered the meals and received $5 a day for his efforts. On January 13, he spotted his new employer sitting in his car just outside of the Citizens National Bank of Kirksville. Tomich watched for a few minutes, curious about his seemingly wealthy benefactor, but the man never exited the vehicle. Then the next day, January 14, 1931, Tomich learned that the bank had been robbed of $5,700 cash, gold, silver, and $60,000 worth of bonds.[107] The newspapers reported that five men escaped in a large black sedan while firing submachine guns out the window. Tomich did not connect the two incidents until he showed up the following day at the Traveler's Hotel with the daily meal delivery, only to find out that the generous stranger had already checked out. That coincidence piqued his suspicions, but since he did not know the man's name, Tomich never reported him to the police.

AT THAT POINT, only Joseph Hunsaker and Allen Morrison knew Richard White's real identity and they were treading carefully because they did not want the murderer to slip away. At the end of February 1931, Morrison received a reply via wire from the Department of Justice, suggesting that he communicate directly with either the Chicago or the St. Joseph, Missouri, Police Department. While Hunsaker continued to keep an eye on Burke and his movements, Morrison was ready to schedule a face-to-face meeting with authorities. He asked Hunsaker if he would rather meet with the police in Chicago or St. Joseph.

"St. Joseph, by all means," Hunsaker replied. "I'm a Missouri boy and Missouri is my home. I want to see Missouri get all the breaks she can on this thing."

Handling all the correspondence to and from authorities, Morrison then wrote a letter to St. Joseph police chief Earl Mathews, requesting more information on Fred Burke and expressing his belief that he knew the fugitive's whereabouts. Hunsaker showed up at Morrison's office on a regular basis, hoping for new developments. "The Government's awfully slow, Joe," declared Morrison.

A few days later, Morrison received a letter at the post office from Mathews, who provided a photo of Burke and offered assistance in locating him, but did not seem to take Morrison seriously. Disappointed by the lack of interest, Morrison decided to send a letter to the Chicago Police Department. Captain John Norton received the letter from Morrison, but replied instead to the Sullivan County sheriff, L. C. Hoover, in Milan, requesting he get the "dope" on Morrison, Hunsaker, and the alleged Burke sightings. Sheriff Hoover dialed up Morrison and asked to see him immediately. Upon hearing of the letter being forwarded, Morrison became even more fearful of their plan leaking out, but convinced Sheriff Hoover that he was certain about his information. It was now early March and they needed to act fast. Morrison went ahead and scheduled a meeting with Hunsaker and two St. Joseph, Missouri, detectives, who suggested meeting halfway, in the city of Chillicothe.

Hunsaker counted off the days in his mind, and then seemed to become agitated. "I think we're sunk," he said. "We're going to Chillicothe next week on the thirteenth."

"Why you say?"

"Because that's Friday the thirteenth."

Morrison laughed, "I hadn't given that a thought."

On that Friday, Morrison and the superstitious Hunsaker drove the 70 miles to the town of Chillicothe, Missouri, which in 1928 had earned the title, "The Home of Sliced Bread." They waited at the designated spot near the Federal Building to meet with the detectives. When an unmarked squad car pulled up next to them, they joined Missouri detectives Melvin Sweptson and E. Ray Kelly in their car and drove to a secluded spot where they could talk privately. The detectives showed the men a photo of Burke. "That's your man," Hunsaker remarked, pointing his index finger at the photo. "There is absolutely no question about it." He and Morrison explained that Burke was living in Green City under the alias of Richard White.

"You've got some pretty good dope," Detective Sweptson mentioned, while taking notes. "Do you know when he will be back in Green City?"

"It might be a week or it might be a month or two," Hunsaker replied. "We'll wire you when he shows up. Be sure of that."

Hunsaker and Morrison returned to Green City and prepared for the big moment. Morrison rented office space on the second floor of a building facing east from the Green City square; Hunsaker got a temporary job at the Pfeiffer Restaurant, which was on the ground floor of the same building but on the opposite side. From those two vantage points, they could watch the entire square, hoping to spot Richard White, or rather Fred "Killer" Burke, the moment he returned to Green City.[108]

True Detective Mysteries magazine, October 1930 issue that featured an article about Fred "Killer" Burke. *Author's collection.*

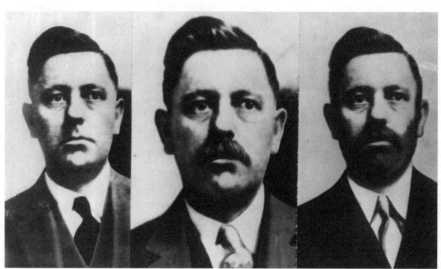

Newspaper articles enhanced a photograph of a clean-shaven Fred "Killer" Burke, adding facial hair, to aid in recognition of the wanted man. *Author's collection.*

This illustration appeared in an issue of *True Detective Mysteries* depicting the physical changes of Fred "Killer" Burke' as he aged and after his facial surgery. *Author's collection.*

"TONIGHT'S THE NIGHT"

ALTHOUGH NEW DEVELOPMENTS IN THE SEARCH FOR Burke were taking place in Missouri, on March 19 Chief Detective John Stege of the Chicago Police Department remained tightlipped, but remarked to reporters, "Burke will be turned up yet. Too many in it to keep quiet. Somebody will squawk."

Indeed, somebody had.

On the alert Saturday evening, March 21, as he had been every day since realizing Richard White was, in reality, Fred Burke, Hunsaker stopped out at the gas station in Green City, where he continued to work during the day. There, a few of the local townsfolk gathered around the stove to chat, among them Barney Porter, White's father-in-law. Hunsaker listened intently as Porter and the others talked about the snow falling up north in Chicago, hoping to hear something about White's plans.

"I got a card from Dick and Bonnie at Kirksville," Porter mentioned to the others. "They're saying they couldn't get through on account of snow and mud in the road. They said they'd gone on to Kansas City."

Hunsaker wondered if, after their wait in Kansas City, the Whites would head back to Green City and his big opportunity to capture Burke would be at hand. He continued listening to Porter, trying to be inconspicuous.

"Likely I'll spend Sunday at the foot of the lane with the mules to pull their car through the mire," Porter continued, chuckling, while the others joined in.

So, Sunday's the big day, Hunsaker thought.

After the chat session wound up, he shared the news with his partner, Morrison, who contacted the St. Joseph detectives. They set up a stakeout; however, the killer and his wife did not show up that night.

The stress was beginning to take its toll on Hunsaker. He was on edge, anxious, and beginning to question the loyalty of those he had entrusted with his secret. Even a night out at the movie theater with his wife was anything but enjoyable, especially considering the subject matter of the film. They saw "Dance, Fools, Dance," starring Joan Crawford and Clark Gable. The movie was based on the 1930 murder of Chicago newspaper reporter Jake Lingle, who had befriended both gangsters and police, working one against the other, often tipping off the bad guys prior to police raids in exchange for favors. One double-cross was all it took before Lingle became a marked man, eventually being cut down in broad daylight on his way to the Illinois Central train in downtown Chicago.

As Hunsaker watched in the darkened theater, he felt himself become part of the film. He thought *this job is just too big for a chap like me to handle.* He was ready to give up, but a couple of days later, another good opportunity to catch Burke presented itself.

On March 25, while working behind the counter at the Pfeiffer Restaurant, Hunsaker could barely contain his excitement when, at around 8:00 p.m., he saw the man who had consumed his every thought. Richard White and his father-in-law, Barney Porter, pulled up in a brand-new Studebaker President 8 coupe. The Studebaker glistened as Porter exited the vehicle, but White remained in the car. Unbeknownst to Hunsaker, White had just returned from Kansas City where he and Bonnie had put $300 down to purchase a $9,200 home across from the Ivanhoe Country Club. The killer had actually been planning to settle back into his hobby of gardening and wanted a place where he could grow trees and flowers.[109] He obviously thought he could elude authorities. However, other plans were blooming.

Hunsaker casually made his way to the restaurant window and peered out at the man he now knew to be "The Most Dangerous Man Alive." He watched as Porter bought a can of his favorite chewing tobacco and walked back to the Studebaker, got in, and drove off. Hunsaker immediately untied his apron, tossed it on a chair, and told the manager that he was going to take a break. He ran a block over to the town hall to summon help from Green City constable A. L. Pickett, who knew of the plan.

"You'd better go home and oil up your guns," Hunsaker boldly instructed, visibly keyed up at being so close to the capture he had been dreaming of. "You're going somewhere tonight and you may never come back."

Hunsaker then called Allen Morrison at his home. "Our man's here," he whispered.

"Okay, my car is up on the north end of town," Morrison directed. "You get Pickett and you fellows can get in my car on the dark street and we'll all go to Milan."

Morrison met up with Hunsaker and Pickett shortly thereafter, and then drove 12 miles southwest to Milan to enlist the help of Sullivan County sheriff L. C. Hoover. At the sheriff's office, Hunsaker set off to locate Hoover, who he had learned was at home, while Morrison called the St. Joseph police.

Captain John Lard answered the phone at the station.

"This is Morrison, Green City. Do you understand?" he asked, speaking in a clipped code, in case anyone was listening on the line.

"Yes," replied Lard.

"Where's Kelly and Sweptson?" he asked, referring to the two detectives who had been working the case.

"On duty."

"Can I get in touch with them as soon as they report in?"

"Affirmative."

"Tell either one of them to call Number Eight, Milan," instructed Morrison, and then he hung up.

Morrison waited about 30 minutes, but when he did not get a return call, he impatiently called back. Captain Lard answered again.

"Morrison ...."

"I just now have Kelly on the phone," Lard interrupted. "Do you wish to talk to him?"

"Yes."

There was a short pause as Lard transferred the call.

"Kelly? This is Morrison, Green City," he said anxiously, still talking nondescriptly. "It's now ten o'clock, how would two o'clock do?" he asked, knowing that the drive from St. Joseph would take them about three-and-a-half hours.

"Fine," responded Kelly, who had been waiting for the call.

"The place is designated," Morrison said, referring to the sheriff's office at Milan. Then he quickly hung up and went to find Hunsaker and Pickett.

The gathering men wisely used the wait in Sheriff Hoover's office to plan their next move. Deputy Ralph Clubine joined them. They studied maps of the Porter farm and outbuildings and discussed how best to attempt to capture Burke. Shortly after 12:30 a.m., St. Joseph police detectives Marvin Swepston and E. Ray Kelly arrived ahead of schedule, and the two others, Captain John Lard and Deputy Arend Thedinga, showed up soon after. They shared their plans and elicited additional input from the four seasoned officers. By 4:00 a.m., the group was ready. They hoped to find the entire household asleep in the early morning hours. Sheriff Hoover took Clubine and Hunsaker along to do an initial drive past the Porter farm in one car, so as not to draw any unnecessary attention. They spotted the new Studebaker parked very close to the house near a window. Sheriff Hoover drove up the road about a half mile to a designated spot and met with the others. Hunsaker held his knee as it bounced with anticipation.

"Well, boys, if it's Freddie Burke, we're going to have a gun battle," remarked Captain Lard. "That's all there is to it."

Hunsaker gulped, realizing the danger of what he was about to witness.

"Are there any woods around here?" asked Kelly, worried about a possible escape attempt by Burke.

"Not for some distance," Hunsaker replied. "But what would you do if he tries to make a break for it?"

"We'll give him a couple of high ones," Kelly said as he racked a shotgun. "And then bring him down if he won't stop."

Sheriff Hoover asked Hunsaker what he thought about the plan.

"Well, you're the sheriff of Sullivan County," he replied, clearly unable to comprehend the scope of their tactical operation.

"All right," said Hoover to his own men. "Now listen. We'll have to map this out. Those fellows from St. Joe have more experience than I have."

They all decided to wait until morning because of Burke's known use of guns. If he were going to start shooting, they wanted the advantage of daylight. Hunsaker's nervousness intensified as the clock ticked. They sat restlessly in their cold vehicles until 6:00 a.m.

As the sky lightened, Detective Swepston gathered the team for a final briefing. "Sheriff Hoover, Pickett, Kelly, and myself will go inside the house," he directed. "Captain Lard will wait at the corner of the house with a submachine gun. Deputy Clubine will stay at the northwest corner of the house and watch the windows on that side of the house."

"Well, if it is Freddie Burke, what do you want me to do?" Hunsaker asked nervously.

"We want you to come to St. Joe," replied Swepston, "and if this egg don't have a mighty good alibi, that's where he's going."

Morrison and Hunsaker stayed back a safe distance to view the action, while the two unmarked squad cars maneuvered into the driveway with planned precision. The officers quietly exited the vehicles and took their assigned positions. Detectives Kelly and Swepston rapped on the door with hearts pounding, as they braced for whatever might take place. A man who matched the description of Barney Porter, as relayed to them by Hunsaker, slowly cracked open the door. His eyes squinted as he adjusted to the dawn's light and the sight of the officers. Before he could say anything, Kelly and Swepston pushed in the door and rushed past him. Lard and Thedinga followed, wielding submachine guns. The four officers headed directly for the bedroom.

The ruckus outside the door had awakened Burke, but did not give him enough time to react. He was trying to free himself from the rumpled bed coverings and leaning over toward a bedside chair, when four men barged into the room. "Hold up your hands where we can see them, and don't try anything," Lard shouted, pointing a submachine gun within inches of Burke's face.

One of the other officers quickly grabbed the .38-caliber revolver that Burke had been reaching for on the chair.[110] "What are you going to do, take me for a ride?" Burke asked, sitting upright in bed,[111] as if he thought they were other gangsters who had caught up with him.

Once Sheriff Hoover identified himself and said they would be taking him to St. Joseph, Missouri, Burke grunted. He did not seem convinced that these were real police officers, recalling his own attempts to fool his victims with a police badge and uniform.

Having caught Burke wearing only his pajamas, officers allowed him to change clothes, maintaining their aim on him with their submachine guns. As they escorted him to the door, Burke turned to his stunned father-in-law, "They say they're taking me to St. Joe, but I don't believe that's where they mean."

When he saw the squad cars outside, it seemed he finally understood that the law had caught up with him. At that point, he sighed in what seemed relief and actually smiled. Before they shackled him, Burke pulled a large wad of cash out of his pocket, thumbed off two $100 bills, and handed them directly to Barney Porter. "Employ the best legal talent you can find,"[112] Burke instructed.

Sheriff Hoover led Burke out to the squad car and secured him in the backseat; Kelly and Swepston climbed in on either side of him, while Lard took control of the wheel. The other officers returned to their squad car. Hoover then traveled the short distance down the road to inform the amateur detective and his partner of Burke's capture. Hunsaker and Morrison were beyond ecstatic, believing that they would soon reap the rewards.

As Burke tried to get comfortable sitting in between the two large detectives, he inquired, "What's the charge, boys?"

"Investigation and you are going to St. Joseph," Lard replied, glancing back at Burke but not offering any details.

"Well, why not investigate me here?"

"Nothing doing," Lard said, keeping an eye on Burke in the backseat.[113]

During the 90-mile ride, Swepston made small talk with Burke. At some point, he learned that both he and Burke had fought in the Battle of Argonne in France in 1918, although in different units.[114] They had been brothers in arms during the Great War, but now things were quite different. Hoping that the shared coincidence might cause Burke to open up, Swepston asked if he had had anything to do with the St. Valentine's Day Massacre. Clearly, Burke was not going to confess to anything. "Put me in the cell, boys," he replied. "I'm not going to talk to anyone about anything."[115]

Once they arrived at the Buchanan County Jail in St. Joseph, Missouri, that is just what the officers did. "The Most Dangerous Man Alive" was finally in custody.

On Thursday, March 26, while Fred "Killer" Burke was being booked, Joseph Hunsaker and Allen Morrison served verbal notice to Sheriff Hoover of their claim to the reward money for capturing Burke. They learned that the reward money was a compilation from several agencies for the capture of the perpetrator of individual crimes. Cook County, Illinois, had offered a total of $41,000—$20,000 from State's Attorney John Swanson and $21,000 from other Cook County officials—specified for the arrest and conviction of those who took part in the St. Valentine's Day Massacre. Additionally, about 30 municipalities, bankers' associations, banks, and counties offered another $34,000 for various robberies. The state of Wisconsin offered a reward of $3,000 for the Farmers and Merchants Bank robbery in Jefferson, and St. Joseph, Michigan, offered $1,000 for the capture of Officer Skelly's killer. Lexington and Louisville, Kentucky, as well as Cincinnati and Hamilton County, Ohio, added to the pot for the capture of the perpetrator for various bank robberies in those locales. Even the federal government offered a reward for the capture of Burke for his role in the Toledo mail truck robbery and murder of Officer Zientara on April 16, 1928. In all, the amount exceeded $120,000.

Hunsaker had big plans for the reward money. He wanted to give his wife, Mary, a shopping trip to Chicago, and his daughter, Ruth, a formal education. He planned to open a plumbing shop and move his family into a fine home in Kansas City.

In the weeks that followed, he received letters in the mail almost every day, some congratulating him on his detective work, others asking for a handout from the reward they expected him to receive. Salesmen found their way to his home to offer him the finest products and services. In fact, a delivery of a brand-new, 8-cylinder automobile and a radio came with instructions for Hunsaker to accept now and pay once he obtained the reward money. However, the modest man refused both products, explaining that he only intended to spend the reward money once he had it, and not a minute before.

Since Morrison had played a key role in the capture, as did other officers, Hunsaker and Morrison came up with a plan on how to split the money. They agreed that Hunsaker should receive the first $100,000, Morrison $20,000, and the seven officers who had a role in the arrest would divide what remained. The officers were not allowed to receive any money personally and would have to place it in their department coffers. However, the acquisition of the reward money would prove even more difficult a task than Burke's capture.

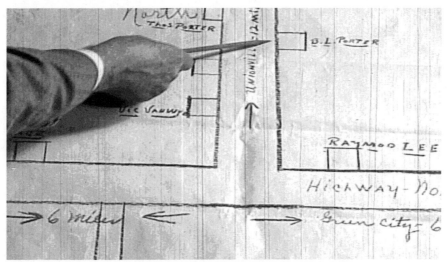

Map of Porter farm used during the planning of Fred "Killer" Burke's capture. *Author's collection.*

The Green City, Missouri, farmhouse owned by Barney Porter, where Fred "Killer" Burke was captured on March 26, 1931. *Author's collection.*

223

CAPTURED

ST. JOSEPH, MISSOURI, ALREADY HAD UNWELCOME notoriety for being the stomping grounds of many noteworthy criminals. The most famous outlaw in American history, Jesse James, took his last breath there on April 3, 1882, essentially closing the door on the era of the Wild West, only to open up for the Prohibition Era. Flashes of light now filled the Buchanan County Jail. Shuffling feet and doors slamming shut echoed throughout the building. During the booking procedure, Fred Burke gave his address as 86th and Park Streets in Kansas City, even though the deputies knew that the area was just a cornfield. Once he was securely in custody at the jail, Burke demanded to see a lawyer.

Dozens of reporters and officers hounded the newest inmate. Unlike any other prisoner, Fred Burke was allowed to have a mattress, a chair, and a cushion, in hopes that if he felt comfortable he might open up and talk freely. After Deputy B. T. Andrews fingerprinted the well-mannered convict (the only official identification required by the police at the time), he matter-of-factly announced, "The prints show this man is Fred Burke."

Burke congratulated the deputy, saying, "You've got me nailed down."[116]

However, beyond that, Burke was not forthcoming. When a guard asked if he killed Officer Skelly, Burke coldly cracked, "None of your goddamn business."[117]

Other officers received the same reaction when they quizzed him about whether he killed Frankie Uale or had been involved with the St. Valentine's Day Massacre. "Don't make me laugh, cops," Burke snarled. "I've got nothing to say, nothing."[118]

The questions never let up.

He did agree to speak for a few seconds to Chicago police captain John Norton over long-distance telephone, saying, "I am not a damn bit afraid to come back to Chicago."[119] Burke then hung up angrily.

Detective Ed Tyrrell arrived from Chicago the next day and immediately noticed a change in Burke's appearance from the last time he had seen him. He thought that either Burke had suffered a direct blow to his face or possibly received dental work on his lower jaw. Burke's face was much fuller, with a noticeably receding chin and upturned nose.

"So, have you seen the beauty doctor?" Tyrrell chuckled.

Burke sat silent but cracked a smile.

When asked about whether he participated in the bank robbery in Lincoln, Nebraska, Burke snapped, "Anyone who accused me of that job is a liar."

Pacing back and forth in his cell, Burke drank several cups of coffee. Once the out-of-town officers had left, guards allowed the newspaper reporters to question him. One reporter asked him the same question asked by every officer and reporter since Burke arrived at the jail, "Were you in on the St. Valentine Day's Massacre in Chicago?"

When he failed to respond, the reporter pushed, "You refuse to answer the question?"

"I'm not saying a word about that. I'm in bad enough trouble as it is."

When the questioning turned to the killing of Officer Skelly, Burke responded, "I haven't the faintest idea of what that's all about."[120]

When a group of photographers turned their cameras toward him, he said, "You very likely are a nice bunch of fellows, but I don't see why I should pose for you. You never did anything for me."[121]

However, he did finally agree to sit for a few photographs and had special instructions for Max P. Habecker of the St. Joseph, Missouri, *News-Press*. "No feet. I don't like feet in a picture."[122]

The questioning did not let up. When asked again about the massacre in Chicago, Burke sidestepped the real question. "Chicago is a nice town. I've been there several times. I was in Chicago last week and while there I purchased a motor car."[123]

Investigators traced Burke's new Studebaker to the Capone syndicate. Bergl Motor Sales Company in Cicero, the car dealership to the syndicate, sold the vehicle on March 5, 1931. A salesman recalled that a short, neatly dressed man had come in on March 3, wanting to buy a new Studebaker in trade for a 1930 coupe. They told the man it would take them several days to get one delivered. He returned two days later to pick it up, paying $1,358 cash in addition to the coupe. A clerk notarized the permit to purchase out-of-state license plates and titled it in the name of Richard F. White. Authorities felt the description of the man purchasing the car resembled a Capone gang member and Burke friend, Ted Newberry.

As the investigation continued, Burke remained in the spotlight at the

Buchanan County Jail. A phone interview with the *World Herald* of Omaha on March 26 exposed some of Burke's personality.

"Are you Fred Burke?" asked the reporter.

"That's what they call me."

"But are you really Fred Burke?"

"Well, why don't you ask the chief here?"

"I did and he said you were Burke."

"Well, I guess that settles it then. I am Fred Burke."

"Where you been hiding?"

"Oh, here and there," Burke casually remarked.

"Where have you been for the past several months?"

"At my father-in-law's place."

"It must have been hard to lie low when every copper in the country was looking for you."

"It wasn't a tough job. And did you say every copper in the country was on the lookout for me? Now isn't that funny. I didn't know that."

The reporter then asked about whether he was involved in the 1930 Lincoln, Nebraska, bank robbery, which at the time was the largest heist in history, with a $2.5 million take.

Burke quickly changed his tone, "I was not, and anyone who says I was, is a damn liar."

Pushing for an exclusive scoop, the reporter asked him what so many others had already asked, "Were you involved in the St. Valentine's Day Massacre in Chicago?"

"Get a spiritualist and go into a dark room and hold hands. Maybe you'll find out. I'm not saying a word about that, buddy."[124]

Burke returned to his cell where he lay down on his cot, covering himself with a blanket to keep the curious from peering in.

Burke received a house call on March 28 from William E. Pentz, a St. Joseph, Missouri, physician, and Dr. Charles Byrd, head of the local sanitarium. Seeing the two physicians enter the cell, Burke asked, "What are you here for? To examine me mentally?"

After brief interviews with the infamous killer, both doctors classified Burke as having high intelligence. Later that day, his wife, Bonnie, dressed in a blue tailored suit and red fox fur coat, was finally allowed to see her husband, having had been thoroughly interrogated by officers. She repeatedly told investigators that she had no knowledge of any crimes he may have committed. She explained that her husband received registered mail often from his real estate firm in Chicago. Since she did not have a bank account, he regularly supplied her with cash. Bonnie kept her composure in the officers' presence. "He never told me he had been in jail. He always seemed to have plenty of money. My folks didn't dream he was a criminal."[125]

Officers explained to her that they suspected her husband as being involved in the St. Valentine's Day Massacre. "It couldn't have been Richard who shot those men in Chicago," she responded. "He couldn't be a killer. He is not that kind of man. There never has been an indication of a cruel disposition in his nature."[126]

When she was finally taken to her husband's cell, Fred Burke reached through the bars to hug her, and pulled her as close as he could to himself. He kissed her repeatedly.

However, Bonnie was dry-eyed and unemotional as she looked at him, maybe from the intense grilling by authorities. "I want some money," she said to her husband. "I need it."

"Will $300 be enough?" he asked, not flinching. He then signed an order to release the money as "Fred Burke," apparently dropping the White alias.[127] Bonnie asked if he needed anything. "Socks, a shirt, and little things like that, but no suit. I don't want another suit."

"What about the car?" she asked.

"It's paid for," he replied. "Go ahead and drive it."

Burke had no idea that a mere amateur detective was the person responsible for his undoing, as he now began to focus on his next destination. He knew that Illinois had capital punishment, but even the electric chair was a more lenient terminus than what he could have received from gangland, had certain members gotten to him first.

The St. Joseph, Missouri, police officers who captured Fred "Killer" Burke. *Author's collection.*

Fred "Killer" Burke in custody at the Buchanan County Jail, St. Joseph, Missouri, March 26, 1931. *Author's collection.*

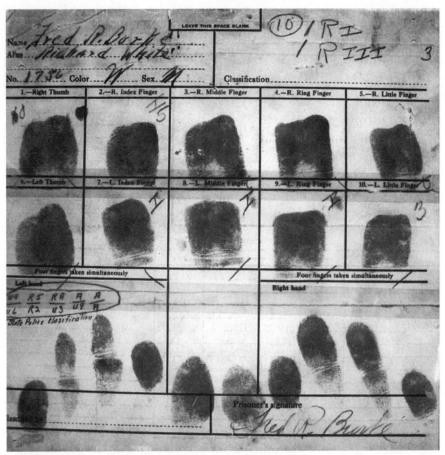

Fred Burke's fingerprint card and classification from Berrien County Jail. *Courtesy of the Berrien County Sheriff's Department.*

RACE FOR JUSTICE

"HE'S CAUGHT, OH, I CAN'T BELIEVE IT," WEPT Olga Moulds to her neighbors after hearing the newsies on the street singing out the latest headline. "Now that he's caught, I hope that he pays the limit."[128]

Headlines all across the nation reported the capture of Fred Burke. People felt certain that Burke would finally face justice but in which state and for what crime? Legal methods of capital punishment included hangings, electrocutions, and firing squads in all 48 states except Kansas, Maine, Michigan, Minnesota, North Dakota, Rhode Island, South Dakota, and Wisconsin. Authorities in Michigan wanted him extradited to their state, but the decision of where to send Burke was the sole responsibility of Missouri governor Henry S. Caulfield. Burke soon learned that Illinois, Indiana, Ohio, Wisconsin, Michigan, and the federal government were all eager to take custody of him.

On March 27, 1931, Governor Caulfield announced that he would not make a decision on extradition for 48 hours so that all states had enough time to complete the proper paperwork. Berrien County, Michigan, prosecutor Wilbur Cunningham, Sheriff Fred Cutler, and Undersheriff Bryan Wise drove to Lansing where Michigan governor Wilbur Brucker issued and signed the extradition papers for Burke. The men then set off for Jefferson City, Missouri, to meet with Governor Caulfield. Brucker sent a telegram to Caulfield regarding the papers, saying, "I shall thank you to show these men all possible courtesy and consideration."

Caulfield wired a reply back assuring him that he would not make a decision until the Michigan authorities arrived. Brucker followed up with a phone call to Caulfield. "We have an excellent case against Burke," argued Brucker in favor of his state, "whereas Chicago's charges of participation in the St. Valentine's Day Massacre may not be so clear-cut and definite because they involve so many other gangsters. But at St. Joseph, Michigan, he killed a policeman."

"You don't have capital punishment in Michigan, do you?" Caulfield asked.

"No," answered Brucker, "but would that make any difference?"

"Not necessarily," Caulfield replied.

Illinois assistant state's attorney Harry Ditchburne and his crew arrived in Missouri ahead of the Michigan authorities, but their extradition papers were still in the hands of Governor Emerson in Springfield. Chicago police captain John Norton told waiting reporters, "We haven't a leg to stand on," and recommended that Illinois defer its right to Michigan. He knew that the basis of Chicago's case against Burke was from evidence collected in Berrien County.

Chicago's acting police commissioner, John Alcock, admitted that Ditchburne's visit was principally to quiz Burke on the massacre and to promise him immunity from the electric chair if he provided information. Ditchburne's attempt failed; Burke admitted nothing.

The chief postal inspector decided not to pursue Burke in connection with the mail truck robbery in Toledo, Ohio, since the other suspects in it had already been sent to the penitentiary.[129] Sheriff John Gruel from Jefferson County, Wisconsin, hoped that they could get Burke for the Farmers and Merchants Bank robbery, telling reporters, "We have the goods on Burke in this bank job, and now that he's captured, our charges will be filed promptly."

A reporter from the *Milwaukee Sentinel* spoke to Burke over long-distance telephone, while St. Joseph, Missouri, police chief Earl M. Mathews listened in. "I can think of a lot worse places than Wisconsin in which to stand trial," the affable Burke remarked, remaining noncommittal when the questioning turned to his other alleged crimes.

Later that day, reporter Dan Kelliher from the *Kansas City Journal-Post* sat down and spoke to Burke in his cell while five guards watched over them. Kelliher noted that Burke's white teeth flashed in a smile while he sat on his chair smoking a cigarette. His black hair was slicked back in a pompadour while his face was smooth except for the mustache that covered his rather broad, scarred lip. He wore a blue shirt, opened several buttons down from the throat, with the sleeves rolled up at the elbows, and he had on a light-colored, unbuttoned vest. Before Kelliher asked any questions, Burke interjected, "I am not saying anything. I have met reporters before."

"Now, Fred," Kelliher tried to reason, "you know that you're going someplace from here. Michigan wants you. Chicago wants you. Toledo wants you. A half dozen other places have asked that you be sent there. Where would you rather go to answer the charges against you?"

"Oh, I don't know," Burke yawned. "I'm pretty well satisfied right here. These coppers have treated me O.K. and anyway, my wife lives near here, you know."

"The rap in Chicago isn't as strong as was at first believed," pointed out Kelliher. "Would you rather be taken to Chicago to stand trial?"

"There are other persons who have that matter in hand," Burke replied. "They know more about it than I do."

"Were you glad to see Mrs. Burke last night?"

"Yes, she is a 100 per cent girl," Burke smiled, "the finest I ever met."

"Did you know that your wife said yesterday that her parents presented you with a Bible last Christmas? Did you read that Bible, Fred?"

The smile on Burke's face suddenly widened. He grabbed another cigarette from his pocket, struck a match to light it, and then tossed the match across the cell floor. But he did not answer.

"That scar on your nose," Kelliher inquired, "is that the result of an automobile accident you had in Chicago? Your wife said you were driving your car shortly after you visited a plastic surgeon to have the hump taken out of your nose. She said a woman riding a bicycle suddenly appeared in front your car and you were hurt when you tried to avoid hitting her. Is that correct?"

Still grinning broadly and ignoring the question, he repeated, "My wife's 100 per cent girl, the finest I ever met."

"You're permitted to read the papers, aren't you?"

"No," Burke lied, probably hoping to end the questioning.

"How about magazines? If it will help you any, I'd be glad to bring you several magazines. You'd be permitted to read them, wouldn't you?"

"No," replied Burke, although two magazines were clearly visible on his cot. "It's not permitted. I don't get much time to read, buddy. I've got good company here. This is the finest police department I've ever met. They treat a fellow fine."

"You haven't any complaints, then?" prompted Kelliher.

"I've just told you, haven't I, that it's the finest police department I've ever met."

Now that Burke had turned from evasive to hostile in his responses, Kelliher tried something a little simpler. "How about the food? Do the police furnish the meals you eat or do you send out for your food?"

"They furnish it," Burke snapped. "Listen, buddy. I haven't anything more to say."

Burke got up from his chair, turned it around, and sat down with his back to the reporter. Then, with a choreographed look over his shoulder, Burke grinned, showing his white teeth.[130]

BY NOON THE NEXT DAY, Michigan had officially filed extradition papers. Because Michigan cited an airtight case with the Skelly murder, Illinois conceded. On Saturday, March 28, 1931, during a 15-minute hearing, the governor of Missouri announced to the Michigan authorities present, "If your papers are in order, you can have the prisoner."

Illinois assistant state's attorney Ditchburne indicated that his office would work with officials in Michigan to ensure a conviction, but did let his dissatisfaction with the decision show, "We will have to be satisfied with Governor Caulfield's decision. We were here first, but Michigan filed its requisition first."

When officers told Burke that he would be returning to Michigan, his only response was, "Is that so? Well, when do we start?" Beneath his smug response, he must have been relieved, knowing that Michigan did not have capital punishment.

The authorities did not waste any time. The next morning, Sunday, March 29, at 4:00 a.m., an officer awakened Burke in his jail cell, provided him with a hearty breakfast, and then led him to the armored car—outfitted with mountings for machine guns, and accompanied by an army of security officers—to start the journey back to St. Joseph, Michigan. Before being shackled and placed in the car, Burke called out to a familiar face in the crowd, "Hello, Cutler." Burke had known him as the shrubbery salesman in Benton Harbor, but Fred Cutler was now the sheriff of Berrien County. "Hello, Burke," remarked Cutler, as the two men shook hands like old school chums.

Before they motored off, Burke had a small token of appreciation for his captors. He gave each of the four officers an expensive fountain pen,[131] something he probably asked one of his guards to purchase on his behalf.

"I may plead guilty. It looks like they've got the goods on me and I guess I'll take a rap this time," Burke remarked to St. Joseph, Missouri, police chief Earl M. Mathews, as officers helped the prisoner into the vehicle.

Detectives from St. Joseph, Missouri, rode with Burke during the first leg of the trip. Sheriff Fred Cutler, Undersheriff Bryan Wise, and Prosecutor Wilbur Cunningham followed behind in another car. Michigan State Police detectives George Waterman and Lyle Hutson; St. Joseph, Michigan, police chief Ben Phairas; and Berrien County deputy Fred Taylor occupied the third vehicle of the convoy.

Burke did not talk much during the trip, but he did admit that he had lived in a luxury home out on the lakeshore, where he was known to the neighbors as Dane. He declined to talk about the Skelly murder or any of his other crimes. Twice, when the convoy stopped for sandwiches, Burke refused to get out of the car. "I don't want these yokels staring at me," he said. This did not stop the curious villagers from pressing their noses against the windows of the armored car, hoping to get a glimpse of him.

At one point during the trip, Chief Phairas asked Burke, "You must have lost heavily when the officers confiscated the bonds stolen from the Jefferson, Wisconsin, bank?"

"Only a small amount," replied Burke, implying that he had plenty of money left.

They kept the route a secret to all but those in the party, in order to avoid any potential ambushes. From St. Joseph, Missouri, they drove to Hannibal, Missouri, via U.S. Highway 36; then north to Springfield, Illinois; then they took Route 4 to Joliet, and Chicago Heights, Illinois; then to LaPorte and New Carlisle, Indiana. They crossed into Michigan on Cleveland Avenue in Galien Township and continued on that road north toward the city of St. Joseph.

Wire and radio communications with Lansing alerted troopers at the Paw Paw Post around 7:30 p.m. that Burke was due in St. Joseph soon. Troopers Peters, Krietlow, Seim, and Ruhl headed to the detail in one vehicle, while Lieutenant Babcock and Corporal Katke followed behind in another.[132] They arrived at the jail, ahead of Burke's caravan, where hundreds of people had gathered to watch the spectacle. Disregarding the cold winds, blinding sleet, and darkness, onlookers watched and waited, crowding the streets, sidewalks, and parking lots. The caravan arrived shortly after 8:00 p.m. that Sunday.

In all, they had made the trip, including 11 stops for meals, fuel, and to fix a blown tire, in just 15 hours, a record time because they ignored speed limits, running at 75 miles per hour.[133]

After the convoy cleared a path through the crowd by the wailing of their sirens, the officers led Burke to the steps of the Berrien County Jail. Dozens of camera flashes popped, blinding Burke as he covered his face with his shackled hands. He ran up the half-dozen steps to the door, and then was out of sight as guards rushed him down the hallway. Only a few spectators got more than a brief glimpse of him.

During the booking process, deputies commented to Burke that he looked scared.

"How many people were out there, 5,000?" Burke asked Deputy Fred Alden, who was the St. Joseph police chief when Skelly was killed.

"Oh, not that many, but plenty," replied Alden, who remained professional despite what he might have actually felt about Burke.

"Well, how long have they been waiting?"

"Most of the afternoon and evening. Why, you scared?"

"No, I'm not scared but that crowd outside made me kind of nervous," Burke admitted. "You know, you never can tell when someone might lose his head."

Burke deposited $385 into his prisoner account.[134] Then guards led him into his new confines, third cell from the front on the east side of the lower level. They completed the booking procedure by 8:26 p.m. Once he had settled in, guards allowed members of the newspaper press to photograph the caged man. Dressed in his now-rumpled gray suit, Burke flinched and tried to cover his face while camera shutters clicked and flash bulbs blinded him. One newspaper photographer barged past the others and begged Burke, "Please let me have a picture. I'm in an awful predicament."

"So am I, buddy," Burke grimaced sarcastically,[135] as the photographer snapped away.

When the last flash bulb went off, several guards escorted the photographers into the hallway. Seemingly frazzled by the attention, Burke still had two more visitors left to face: Gustav Skalay, the father of Charles Skelly, and Olga Moulds, his sister.

The meek, white-haired man showed no anger as he waited for his chance to see Burke in person. The now 53-year-old Gustav had become a widower for the second time, in September 1930, when his wife, Bertha, died at the age of 40. He remained strong, despite the loss, and his children came to his side to reconnect their family. Now working 14-hour shifts, four days a week, to make ends meet, he stayed close to the radio monitoring the bulletins and updates on Burke's capture and extradition. His oldest daughter, Olga Moulds, and sons Walter, Richard, and Erven had kept in hourly communication with the sheriff's office. Outside, reporters asked the elder Skalay what he thought about Burke's punishment.

"Life imprisonment is too easy for the man who killed my son," Skalay remarked as he clutched a photo of his son. "He is like a mad dog. His electrocution or hanging wouldn't bring my boy back, but it would keep him from killing someone else. I am going into the jail to get a good look at this man, Burke. And I'm going to tell the sheriff that if my help is needed, he can call on me. I should be there, too. Then I wouldn't have to worry about Burke getting away."[136]

Sheriff Cutler waved Gustav and Olga to come inside, where he and a deputy then escorted them through the maze of officers to the cell holding Fred Burke. Clinging to each other for support, the father and sister of Charles Skelly stood face-to-face with Burke.

"Good evening," Burke said, expressionless, not knowing who they were.

Neither of them said a word, but tears filled their eyes as they turned and walked back into the crowd of officers.

"What do you want to eat, Burke?" inquired Deputy Vincent O'Neill, after the Skalays left.

"A thick steak, and bring me some tomatoes, too."

"Give him what he wants," Sheriff Cutler said, turning to his deputy. "He's had nothing but sandwiches all day."

Thirty minutes later, Chief Deputy Phil Cutler carried in a large tray with the requested meal plus french-fried potatoes, bread and butter, and coffee. "I'm not going to eat unless you promise to keep those reporters out of here," Burke announced as he took the cigar out of his mouth.

Cutler assured him that he would not be bothered. Burke then asked about the crowd outside. Deputy O'Neill told him that they were townspeople and newspapermen.

"Are there any Chicagoans other than newspaper men?" he asked.

"Not sure, but most of the crowd is gone now."

Corporal Raymond Katke of the Michigan State Police reported to Lansing that they went inside to keep order in the crowd and among the newspapermen, but the people were very good and not a bit noisy or troublesome.[137] To ensure there would be no breakout attempts or a gangland slaying to silence Burke, troopers with machine guns positioned themselves around the building, and round-the-clock guards were stationed outside the cell of "The Most Dangerous Man Alive."

Berrien County Sheriff's Department and Jail in 1931 on the morning after Burke arrived. *Courtesy of Critical Past.*

FACING THE COPPERS

AFTER THE SENSATIONAL RIDE BACK TO MICHIGAN AND his first night at the Berrien County Jail, Fred Burke awoke in a surprisingly jovial mood. He tried to make small talk with Deputy John Schreiber. "The grape wine here is great," praised Burke.

Not interested in anything other than this matter, Schreiber asked Burke if he knew Al Capone. Burke only grinned, tired of hearing the same questions. When asked about the St. Valentine's Day Massacre yet again, all Burke said was, "Bugs Moran must be a smart guy. I wonder why they call him 'Bugs.'"

After his breakfast, Burke was given the option of a preliminary hearing. Claiming to have no money for a lawyer, or a mouthpiece as they were often called, Burke told those gathered, "My friends are going to have to help me out on this rap. And I feel sure they will. I'm about broke."[138]

His friends must have heard his plea because he met for about an hour with attorney Barrett O'Hara, a native of Benton Harbor and a former lieutenant governor of Illinois. According to O'Hara, "certain individuals in Chicago" retained his services to confer with Burke. Coincidentally, several persons reported seeing Capone on the streets of downtown St. Joseph that same morning and the *Detroit News* later reported, "CAPONE REPORTED SEEN ON TWIN CITY STREETS TODAY."[139]

Sheriff Cutler ushered Justice of the Peace Joseph Collier into the kitchen of the Berrien County Jail, the only space large enough to accommodate officials, Burke, and the press without the risk of an escape attempt. Universal Studios filmed the unconventional scene for its newsreels, which appeared each week in movie theaters. Reporters described it as the strangest arraignment ever staged in Michigan. The freshly shaven Burke, immaculately dressed in a dark gray suit, blue shirt, and tie with a matching handkerchief tucked into his lapel pocket, puffed away on a cigar, casually flicking ashes to the floor. His appearance seemed to be that of a refined gentleman, not one of a hardened killer, with his neatly combed black hair, softened hands, and manicured nails. Sitting at a small table, Burke listened as Justice Collier explained the state law to him. "You can demand a preliminary hearing or you can waive it."

Fred "Killer" Burke stared at him for a moment, and then replied, "I demand it."

Collier set the hearing for April 8, 1931. Burke indicated that he would plead not guilty. "There will be a lawyer here," he said. "I don't know who he will be or where he will be from, but there will be one. He should have been here yesterday. I'm positive he will be here this morning."[140] Burke made it clear that O'Hara was not the attorney he was expecting. Cunningham later told reporters, "I don't know who is going to pay this attorney he is expecting, but I have my suspicions. I am somewhat doubtful whether there will be a defense fund."

After the entourage of coppers, mouthpieces, and news hawks left, guards moved Burke back to his cell. Deputy Vincent O'Neill then took over watch duty. Several trunks filled with expensive suits arrived from Missouri. Burke went through them, mentioning to O'Neill, "You know, each of these suits cost between $100 and $150."

O'Neill instructed him that he could only keep two of the 15 suits.[141] After Burke made his selection, O'Neill moved the trunks to another part of the building.

That prompted Burke to ask what had become of his remaining clothing and his golf clubs, fishing tackle, and other belongings. He was told that Viola Brenneman sold or gave away all of his property that was left after police seized the arsenal during the original raid. Burke scowled at hearing this bit of news. "I guess you've got a good case against me, all right. It looks bad for me."

Taking advantage of the moment, O'Neill pressed him about George "Bugs" Moran. "What do they call him 'Bugs' for?"

"When they say a man is bugs, they usually mean he's crazy," Burke remarked. "And I always thought of Moran as being a smart fox."

Still curious, O'Neill reiterated questions about Skelly. "Where were you on the night Skelly was knocked off? You must have been out drunk. Nobody but a drunk man would have shot like that."

"Oh, drop it." The question only seemed to anger the hard-boiled Burke, "I don't want to talk about it, it's too serious. If it wasn't for the newspaper men, those news hawks, I would be just an ordinary man in this case."

THE MISSOURI POLICE OFFICERS who had escorted Burke back to Michigan experienced a bit of Southwestern Michigan hospitality before heading back to St. Joseph, Missouri. Berrien County undersheriff Bryan Wise and Deputy William Barry gave the group a tour of the Twin Cities, including Burke's bungalow. They completed their sight-seeing trip with a visit to the House of David Amusement Park, followed by a fish dinner, and a cruise on Lake Michigan in the newest vessel acquired by the U. S. Coast Guard Station in St. Joseph.

Meanwhile, the prosecutor's office became a frenzy of activity. Wilbur Cunningham contacted the Michigan State Police to begin tracking down potential witnesses, in order to bolster his case. "I don't know that I ever ran up against a more foxy criminal," explained Cunningham to the detectives.

Michigan State Police deputy commissioner Fred Armstrong and Detective Philip Lyle Hutson reviewed the statements of those who had already been interviewed, and then started to solicit other persons with information about Burke or accounts of the Skelly shooting. Key witnesses Forrest Kool and Albert Wishart made their appearances in Cunningham's office and were reassured that they would receive protection from the Secret Service Division.

Later, on Monday afternoon, two New York City police detectives, Captain Michael McVeigh and Sergeant Patrick McNamara, spent over an hour in Burke's cell to question him about the 1928 murders of Frankie Uale, Capone's former employer, and of Arnold Rothstein, known for allegedly staging the "Black Sox Scandal."

"How do you like it here?" asked McVeigh, easing into the interrogation.

"Almost as good as the Ritz," Burke flippantly replied.

When the topic turned to New York and the murders of Uale and Rothstein, Burke sarcastically answered, "Of course I'd be glad to assist you men in any way I can because I know you're here to help me." His tone quickly changed, though. "I don't know anything about it and I wouldn't tell you if I did."

Remaining defiant, Burke continued, "I haven't been in New York since the war. The only gangster I ever knew was Gus Winkeler in St. Louis. You coppers have got me all wrong. You birds will be telling me next that I kidnapped Charlie Ross," he said, referring to the four-year-old boy kidnapped in 1874 and thought to be the first person ever held for ransom.

"Who are your friends in Chicago?" asked McVeigh.

"Church people," replied Burke.

"What kind of church people?"

"I'm a Hindu," remarked Burke, sarcastically. "Mahatma Gandhi is a pal of mine."

"Yeah, well, you're short a turban, aren't you?" replied McVeigh.

Without missing a beat, Burke cleverly responded, "I gave that to a photographer to drape over his camera."[142]

At the end of the interview, the New York City detectives both concurred that he was "too hard a nut to crack."[143]

On Wednesday, April 1, the attorney that Burke had been expecting finally arrived–namely, Benton Harbor attorney Charles W. Gore, a 42-year-old, Minnesota-born, former Berrien County prosecutor, retained by Bonnie Porter White, Burke's current wife, who chose to keep the name she married Burke with. Additionally, Burke met with Thomas Rowe, a St. Louis attorney and friend, whom Burke appointed to handle his personal affairs.

"I can't say as yet whether we will go on trial," Gore remarked to a group of waiting reporters who tackled him after the meeting.[144] "It is possible that there will be no trial and Burke will plead guilty." Gore continued, "Burke is a smart man, and whatever turn his defense takes will be at his dictation and election. He has certain fundamental legal rights, which I am looking after, as any attorney would. But he knows what he wants to do and his defense will be conducted exactly as he desires."[145]

After meeting with Gore, two individuals arrived, demanding to see Burke: former Detroit Municipal Court judge Charles L. Bartlett and attorney Thomas F. Kennedy. Chief Deputy Phil Cutler contacted Prosecutor Cunningham, who indicated that the men needed to see Charles Gore first, since he was representing Burke. Enraged by the brush-off, Bartlett insisted that he had full authority to act on Burke's behalf. "This is the first time in my 30 years of practice at the bar that I've been refused to be allowed to see my client," sputtered Bartlett.

Trying to diffuse the situation, the chief deputy asked Burke if he wanted to see the Detroit men. Burke indicated that he did not, and he preferred that they first meet with Gore. When the chief deputy informed the men of Burke's decision, Bartlett lunged toward him, but guards quickly broke up the scuffle and restrained the agitated Bartlett. Finally, Gore arrived and met with Bartlett and Kennedy, and then escorted them to Burke's cell. Burke thanked the men and the efforts of his friends in Detroit to help, but told them Gore would be his only defense attorney. Bartlett and Kennedy left quietly.

Burke's apparent ties to Detroit surfaced again when Lieutenant Frank Holland of the Detroit Police Department showed up later that day as well. Holland knew Burke from his early days in Detroit over 10 years ago and Burke regarded him as "a real copper," an officer who was all about law and order. Both Holland and Fred Armstrong of the Michigan State Police probed him about his ties in Detroit, and he freely admitted his acquaintance with Harry Hallisay, the leader of Burke's kidnapping gang, who was then serving a prison term. Burke named a few other Detroit associates, including Mike Dipsa, who was killed in 1928; Charles T. "Doc" Brady; and pal Johnny Reid, who was killed in 1926. He refused to discuss the Miraflores Apartment Massacre and other killings in which he was a suspect.

Despite that, Holland told reporters that their talk "was quite satisfactory... but I did not accept the denial of the Miraflores Massacre." Holland further explained his experience with him. "Burke was known as a confidence man in Detroit ten years ago, associating with gamblers instead of racketeers. He was not regarded as dangerous then, but just as a clever forger. He was in on the kidnapping of gangsters and racketeers in the early days. Later when it became too popular, he dropped out." Holland emphasized, "His methods were always modern in whatever branch of crime he undertook."[146]

THE SENSATIONAL STORY of Burke's capture in Missouri, the fight for extradition, and his return to St. Joseph, Michigan, attracted the attention of the media throughout the country. Newspaper headlines, as well as radio broadcasts, kept readers and listeners constantly informed of the day-to-day developments. One such radio program was the weekly "March of Time" series sponsored by *Time Magazine* that originated in New York City. The program aired on the CBS Network of radio stations, including WBBM Radio in Chicago, Illinois, and WOWO Radio in Fort Wayne, Indiana. The format of each episode featured dramatic dialogue of actors retelling the story, utilizing music and sound effects. The Friday, April 3, broadcast was devoted to Burke's capture.

The day after the radio program aired, six men who resembled Fred Burke were brought to the Berrien County Jail. Michigan State Police detectives arranged a "show-up," otherwise known as a line-up, so that witnesses could positively identify Burke. The look-alikes all had mustaches and were each approximately six feet tall and weighed 200 pounds or more and included Dick Larue Lybrook, Martin Nelson Boonstra, Charles Spies, Charles Edward Kroening, Richard R. Tollas, and Charles G. Evans. Burke had the option of standing anywhere among the others in the line. Witnesses arrived, including Forrest Kool and his wife, Laverne; his mother-in-law, Hattie Carlson; his brother-in-law, Harold Carlson; Monroe Wulff, Albert Wishart, and Steve Kunay, who had all driven Burke; and others who had conducted business with him, including Ray Mongreig, Walter Wishart, and Theodore Fiedler.[147] Each witness identified Fred Burke in the "show-up" as being the third person from the left, the man each knew as Fred Dane.

At the same time witnesses were identifying the real Fred Burke, the Detroit Police Department's ballistics expert, William Cavers, arrived at the Berrien County Sheriff's Department to meet with Sheriff Cutler. Cavers brought along bullets recovered from the bodies of the three gangsters slain in the Miraflores Apartment Massacre in Detroit. In order to compare the markings, Cavers filled a wastebasket with old rags and then fired two rounds through both of the Thompson submachine guns recovered from Burke's bungalow. Using a comparison microscope, he viewed one bullet retrieved from the wastebasket next to one taken from a corpse. Cavers' efforts led him to conclude that the guns found in Burke's bungalow were not those used in the Miraflores Apartment Massacre, a conclusion that triggered much debate for years to come.

WHILE BURKE DISHED OUT plenty of sarcasm and cold-shoulder treatments, he did feel comfortable around Sheriff Fred Cutler and Deputy William Barry. Cutler recalled Burke patronizing his garden shop, Cutler and Downing, before the Skelly shooting. As a business owner, Cutler practiced a customer service attitude based on respect and honor. Even as sheriff, he treated inmates as he would a customer in his store. This characteristic also rubbed off on others. Deputy William Barry, who felt a responsibility to his pal Charles Skelly in ensuring that his killer would see justice, was now in a unique position to gather incriminating statements from Burke. He made a point of visiting with Burke frequently, treating him kindly and building up a level of trust with the prisoner, so much so that he spoke often to Barry. One such conversation led to Burke's recounting a previous encounter with the police: "I remember one time I was sitting inside one of those screened-in porches when a strange car pulled up to the house and a man got out. I thought for sure it was the cops so I crashed through the screen and ran out back to this lake. I jumped in and submerged myself underwater, just my nose sticking out. All of a sudden I felt something rubbing on my arm; it was a dead dog that just floated up."

Both Burke and Barry let out a hearty chuckle. Burke ended the story by saying that he found out the man was only a real estate agent.

On Easter Sunday, April 6, a chipper Burke received a postcard from his wife, Bonnie, sent from Kansas City. She wrote that she was sending clean clothing to him, via special delivery. A little later that day, Burke received a visit from an elderly woman. She told the gunman how she thought of him during Easter services at church, compelling her to reach out to him. "Do you ever pray?" she inquired.

"No, I've got along so far without it," Burke replied.

Guards escorted another group of visitors in to see Burke, specifically arranged by Sheriff Cutler. As a way to show her children what happens to those who commit evil deeds, Margaret B. Upton of St. Joseph, Michigan, brought her sons, nine-year-old David and six-year-old Stephen, to the jail so they could see the murderer for themselves. Terrified of the imposing man standing a few feet away, separated from them only by iron bars, the boys crept past the cell, staying close to each other and keeping their mother in sight. Burke took notice of the innocent boys and chose to give them a bit of advice. "Gentlemen," said Burke to the fearful, wide-eyed lads. "Listen to your mother. If I would've listened to my mother, I wouldn't be here. Don't end up like me." [148] The Upton boys took his words to heart, which delighted their mother.

As Burke reflected in his cell, a key witness, Forrest Kool, lived in fear. To ensure that the judge would hear his crucial testimony, Kool received full protection up until the trial. In mid-April 1931, he received a packet of information at his home from A. J. Colby of Detroit. It consisted of advertisements from the American Armor Corporation and Bovite Bullet Proof Vests, noting how impenetrable the vests were to pistol and revolver bullets. Although it seemed that Colby had sent the package to be helpful, it also appeared to imply a threat. Kool immediately turned the letter over to detectives, who forwarded it to the Michigan State Department of Public Safety. On April 15, 1931, Commissioner Olander followed up by asking Colby to refrain from sending such advertisements to important witnesses. [149]

While the attorneys hashed out their strategies, Burke continued to meet with uniformed visitors on a regular basis. One group arrived from the Miami County, Ohio, Sheriff's Department, attempting to gather information about the April 11, 1930, robbery of the Citizens National Bank and Trust, where one man was killed and others were injured. "Fred, where you ever in Piqua?" asked Miami County sheriff Charles Green.

"Piqua? I never heard of the place," Burke responded as he sat up in his cot and closed the book he was reading. "Where is it?"

"It's on the Dixie Highway and about thirty miles north of Dayton."

"That's interesting," he commented, "I know of Washington Court House, for that is where Harry Daughtery's home was," referring to the man who was United States Attorney General from 1921 to 1924 and who was charged with graft and fraud while in office.

"Are you sure you've never been to Piqua?"

"No, but how far is it from Washington Court House?"

Sheriff Green told him it was just less than 100 miles.

"Well, I've been in Circleville and Hamilton, but not Piqua." Burke lay back down on his cot and returned to his book.[150]

As the group began to leave, one of the officers from Ohio remarked, "Burke, we'll be waiting at the gates," referring to returning him to Ohio if he were ever released from prison. Burke snarled at the comment.

While Burke awaited his hearing, the country was catching a glimpse of him as part of a feature article in *Time Magazine* on April 6, 1931. Upon opening his issue, Harry B. Peters, president of the Fairfield National Bank in Lancaster, Ohio, instantly recognized Burke as the man who had slugged him.[151]

Five months earlier, on October 28, 1930, three men entered the bank during the noon hour and demanded that someone open the vault. When Peters delayed the process, the man he now recognized as Burke began to pistol-whip him. The men managed to make off with $10,000. Three others, waiting in a stolen blue sedan outside the bank, escaped. When officers showed Peters an array of photographs of known criminals, he had been unable to identify any of them. Now, thanks to *Time Magazine,* authorities could attribute another robbery to Burke.

Newsreel film featured Fred "Killer" Burke's arrival back in St. Joseph, Michigan, March 30, 1931. *Courtesy of Critical Past.*

Fred Burke's arraignment conducted in the kitchen of Berrien County Jail. Justice of the Peace Joseph R. Collier (left), Sheriff Fred Cutler (right). *Author's collection.*

A jovial Fred Burke sitting alongside Berrien County Sheriff Fred Cutler. Chief Deputy Phil Cutler (standing center), Deputy Vincent O'Neill (standing right). *Courtesy of Critical Past.*

GREEN CITY SPEAKS

THE **PEOPLE** OF **GREEN** CITY, **MISSOURI**, **REMAINED** abuzz following Burke's arrest. As more and more details emerged on the comings and goings of many noteworthy criminals in the area, residents showed their disdain, especially when they learned that the notorious bank robber, Harvey Bailey, had offered up the comforts of his Green City farm as a hideout for Burke. However, the notable arrest in the quiet rural community exposed more than townsfolk could imagine. Bailey's childhood friend and brother-in-law, Charles C. Branaman of Springfield, Missouri, was aware of some of the lesser criminal acts attributed to Bailey and his group, but upon the arrest of Burke, whom he had been introduced to as Richard F. White, he contacted Missouri authorities to tell them what he knew. St. Louis police referred him to the Department of Justice, where he became a federal informant.

Branaman arranged for a trip back to Green City during the first week of April 1931. He offered to probe into activities at the Bailey farm. Special agents and post office inspectors eagerly awaited his return. Once Branaman arrived in town, everyone he encountered wanted to talk about Burke's arrest. One person told him, "Too bad for the Porters... Burke had paid off all their debts, which amounted to about $4,800, and they had never lived better. Barney Porter was fixin' to go into business someplace."

Branaman then ran into Barney Porter, who was driving Burke's Studebaker. He was curious as to how Porter now felt knowing his son-in-law was a gangster.

"I never made any statement about being against Burke," Porter revealed, contradicting what the newspapers had printed. "I'm for him."

"You have to be careful," cautioned Branaman regarding all the attention Porter was receiving.

"There is no mail or any communication that would cause anyone any trouble," remarked Porter.

"So how does Bonnie feel?"

"Okay. She's been well provided for. She'll be home Sunday," responded Porter, referring to his daughter's studies in Kansas City. She still believed in her husband and stood by his side, despite what others were telling her.

Branaman mingled a bit more with some of the locals, learning that the amateur detective, Joseph Hunsaker, feared for his life. As to the disposition of Fred Burke's belongings while he lived in Green City, Branaman found out that at least one of his guns wound up at a second-hand store in town. A Schuyler County, Missouri, deputy sheriff residing in Queen City eventually purchased Burke's large pistol with a rifle stock. A little later, Branaman drove out to the Bailey farm and stayed for dinner. Amanda Bailey was pleasantly surprised to see a familiar face. While the two ate dinner, the topic of her son came up. Seemingly oblivious or unmoved by Harvey's criminal background, Amanda told Branaman that her son and four or five other men had stayed all night at a place about five miles north of the farm on March 26, the night Burke was apprehended. Amanda said they all went on to Texas and did not plan to come back to Green City, but rather continue on to Chicago.

"The law looked my place over, a bum search," revealed Amanda. "The law must think people are dumb. There was a box of shells on the dresser for an automatic pistol and they never found it."

Branaman asked her who had visited.

"About 20 different men in the last three years," Amanda answered as she began counting on her fingers. "There was Gus Winkeler, the dago, Joseph "Red" O'Riordan, Raymond Nugent, and Harry "Slim" Morris, also John R. Moran, who was here about three weeks ago and went to either St. Louis or Kansas City." Of course, Branaman could verify that Fred Burke stayed there, too, having first met him in 1930.

She continued, telling him that the men would drive 18 miles to Unionville, Missouri, to reach Harvey Bailey by long-distance telephone, usually once or twice a week. Since Burke's arrest, though, she said they had only gone to Unionville once.

"There will be no communications until things clear up," advised the wise woman, who knew that law enforcement was watching her house and probably intercepting her mail and phone calls. "A better boy was never born," she gloated, referring to Harvey Bailey. "He never sassed his parents. He comes from the finest families in West Virginia." Amanda never believed that her son or any of his friends did anything wrong.

"Mrs. Bailey, do you remember when Harvey told me to come to Chicago if I ever needed to make some money?"

"Yes," she responded.

"I might have to take him up on that offer," Branaman inquired, hoping to learn of Harvey Bailey's current whereabouts on behalf of the federal authorities he was now working for.

"Oh, it's a bad time now, but you could go up and wait for Harvey. He might see you soon, but you would have to go out to the farm as they have no home in Chicago at this time."[152] She explained that Harvey's wife went to live at their Wisconsin farm, but they still owned other farms in Michigan and Richmond, Illinois.

Before leaving the Bailey farm, Branaman scooped up a letter that was lying on a table and later forwarded it to the special agents. As an informer, Branaman provided valuable information in several federal investigations, which would ultimately aid in the downfall of Harvey Bailey's gang.

Amanda Bailey died three years later, in 1934, after seeing her son sent to prison.

True Detective Mysteries cover from July 1931 describing the capture of Fred "Killer" Burke. *Author's collection.*

THE TRIAL AND JUDGMENT

THE MOST ANTICIPATED MURDER TRIAL IN THE HISTORY of Berrien County was set to start on April 20, but when Judge Charles E. White fell ill with a sinus and throat infection, the trial was delayed until April 27. Charged with murder in the first degree, Burke seemed to know his fate before the trial even started. As a personal request, Burke asked Deputy William Barry if he would speak to the judge and ask to be sent to Marquette. "I'm going to be in prison a long time and I want to be with lifers."

Deputy Barry indicated that he would try.

Even though officials kept the exact start time of the trial a secret from the public in order to prevent any potential ambushes, word leaked, and the courtroom quickly filled. Ten additional Indiana state troopers from South Bend served as reinforcements to the assemblage of other officers protecting Burke. At 2:20 p.m., Burke emerged from the confines of the jail, wearing a stylish brown suit, a blue shirt, tan shoes, a fedora, and visible handcuffs locking his wrists together in front. Escorting Burke the few steps from the jail to the courthouse were Michigan State Police detective Lyle Hutson, Troopers Carl Kamhout and Edd Freeman, Sheriff Fred Cutler, and Burke's defense attorney, Charles Gore. The parties sat down at 2:27 p.m. as the crowd hushed. Then, promptly at 2:30 p.m., Judge White emerged from his chambers and took the bench.

Gore began by asking for a technical change in the wording of the warrant, from "Murdered in the first degree one Charles Skelly," to "Did kill, and murder one Charles Skelly." Judge White approved the new wording, scratching out the original wording on the form. In acting on behalf of his client, Fred Burke, Gore waived the reading of the warrant and entered a formal plea of guilty. Audible gasps from spectators echoed in the packed room. Despite that, the judge then asked to hear witnesses.

Burke appeared nonchalant as he listened to the testimony. Forrest Kool retold the story of the traffic accident, Burke's drunken state, how Burke disobeyed Officer Skelly's command to drive to the police station, and, finally, the shooting.

"You say he was intoxicated?" interrupted Judge White.

"Yes, he was drunk," replied Kool, as he looked around the courtroom.

"How drunk was he?"

"He was staggering," testified Kool. "He didn't know what he was doing because he was driving on my side of the road."

Next, Dr. Clayton Emery was called to the stand.

Emery described how three bullets fatally injured Skelly, one below the ribs, one in the right side, and the other through the left collarbone.

After the dismissal of the two witnesses, Judge White announced, "The crime was in hot anger, not premeditated." He changed the first-degree murder charge to second-degree murder, since willful intent to kill had not been proven.

Burke remained silent and unmoved. White then directed Burke to approach the railing and asked him if he had anything to say.

"Thank you," were Burke's only words.

"I sentence you to life in hard labor at Marquette Prison," declared the judge.[153] Apparently Deputy Barry had been able to convince the judge.

Burke appeared nervous for the first time. He placed his hands in his pockets, then removed them and began stroking his asymmetrical mustache.

Judge White read his decision:

> "There is no doubt but what this respondent has is a long criminal record having been engaged in many cases of robbery and burglary and a number of killings. Had it not been for the evidence taken by me after a plea of guilty in this case to the effect that respondent Burke was very much intoxicated at the time of the commission of this offense it would have been the duty of the court to have found the respondent guilty of murder in the first degree.
>
> The evidence taken, however, disclosed that respondent was so under the influence of intoxicating liquor that I had grave doubts of his being able to form a specific intent to kill by reason of his intoxication and therefore the court felt it was its duty to find the respondent guilty of murder in the second degree.
>
> There is no doubt in my mind but that the respondent killed the deceased Skelly because of his fear of being identified as Fred Burke if he were taken to the police station."[154]

THE SENSATIONAL TRIAL was over and the crowd was quickly hustled out of the courtroom, leaving Burke to face the scores of cameramen waiting to document his reaction. After several moments, guards escorted him, attorney Charles Gore, and Sheriff Cutler into Judge White's private chambers. Several photographers joined them. Burke reached into his vest pocket and took out a cigar. He began to light it when one of the photographers asked, "Glad it's over?"

Burke took a drag and blew the smoke artfully above his head, answering, "You bet."

He would leave for Marquette Prison the following morning.

WORD OF THE CONVICTION reached Allen Morrison and Joseph Hunsaker, the two who brought about the capture of Burke in Green City, Missouri. They presumed this cleared the way for the delivery of their reward money. A reporter interviewing them mentioned that if convicted on just the Skelly murder, the reward for Burke would only amount to $6,000—$5,000 from the state, and $1,000 from the city of St. Joseph, Michigan. They did not realize that the approximately $120,000 in reward money was a compilation of rewards for the specific crimes Burke allegedly took part in and was dependent on his arrest and conviction for each crime. Burke's guilty plea and life sentence in Michigan essentially guaranteed that no other state would invest its money or effort to convict him of any other crimes.

Although despondent at learning that the reward was much smaller than anticipated, Hunsaker wrote a letter addressed to the state of Michigan to inquire how to go about claiming the $6,000 reward. The response that he received weeks later broke his heart. Unfortunately, the $5,000 reward offer from the state was contingent on an arrest and conviction within six months of the Skelly slaying and, consequently, had since expired. The only reward left was the $1,000 from the city of St. Joseph.[155] Thoroughly disappointed, Hunsaker told reporters, "I expect we'll be lucky if we get a couple hundred apiece out of it."[156]

As he would later learn, even the $1,000 reward had an expiration of one year, and the conviction came more than four months after that date. The amateur detective, Joseph Hunsaker, and his associate, Allen Morrison, would receive nothing.

ONCE HE WAS TAKEN BACK to his cell for the night, Burke leaped onto his cot, exclaiming, "Back home again." He then was given a hearty dinner of spaghetti, meatballs, rolls, salad, celery, radishes, coffee, and pie, as he chatted casually with some guards. He wrapped up the conversation by pulling out a big cigar. As a last request after dinner, Burke asked the guards to summon the *News-Palladium* reporter who was in the building. The eager reporter quickly reached his cell.

"Say, I'd like to have the *News-Palladium* sent to me at Marquette," Burke requested.

"Sure, always glad to increase the circulation, in jail and out," the reporter replied. "How long shall we send it?"

"Oh, make it a year."

Before turning in, he settled some debts accrued during his stay, including a $42 tab for 42 meals provided by the Temple Café. Guards brought in the two trunks filled with suits, which had been shipped to the jail shortly after his arrival. Burke laid the suits out on his bunk.

While Sheriff Cutler and several guards stood by, the grinning Burke said, "You fellows have been pretty square." He picked out one to keep, and then presented the other 14 expensive tailor-made suits to Sheriff Cutler and his deputies as a gift.

"Going to take your fishing tackle along when we go to Marquette in the morning?" Burke asked Cutler.

"I'd like to, but the season hasn't opened yet and we might all go to jail for catching trout," replied the ever-so-professional lawman.

"That'd be too bad for you, but it wouldn't make much difference as far as I'm concerned," Burke chuckled as he waved goodnight.

Rather than sleep, Burke chose to read all night. His favorite book was *On the Up and Up*, by Bruce Fairchild Barton. Ironically, the hardened killer found Barton's writing inspirational, filled with tales of optimism and success. However, a chapter of the book entitled "Rogues" may have referred indirectly to Burke. Barton mentioned villains like Al Capone and the notorious Brooklyn gangster killed the year before, acknowledging that hardworking scholars are dull company compared to those who choose to live by their own rules. Certainly, Burke would have known Barton's reference was to Frankie Uale and probably became smug by the mere mention. Burke gave his copy to Sheriff Cutler as another token of appreciation before he set off for his new home. He signed it, "Optimistically, Fred R. Burke."

The Berrien County prosecutor's office remained busy with clerks, attorneys, and some members of the curious press, even though the criminal case against Burke was over. Assistant Prosecutor E. A. Westin spent a considerable amount of time reviewing statements and comments made by Burke while he was in custody in an attempt to provide clues to other crimes.

While preparing paperwork for Burke's trip the next morning, Westin caught a glimpse of Detective Hutson in the hallway. "Cy," Westin hollered, using Hutson's nickname.

Hutson turned around and walked up to Westin.

"Were you able to get anything out of Burke on whether or not the advertising of stolen bonds cramps his style?" inquired Westin. "Any dope at all?"[157] Investigators had uncovered an organized "bond fence," operating in conjunction with many bank robbers, as a type of money laundering scheme that kept the actual bandits away from the money trail.

"He refuses to make any statement," Hutson replied, "claiming, of course, that he knows nothing about any bank robbery."

Westin slowly shook his head as if he was not at all surprised by Burke's denial, but he still had hopes of exposing a much larger operation.

"My personal opinion," Hutson continued, "having had considerable experience with bond fences, I do not believe it stops the dealer from handling the bonds. If they continue doing so and it can be shown that they were notified the bonds were stolen, it will eventually be the means to building a strong case against them in federal court."

The case of James A. Connolly of St. Paul, Minnesota, had been one of the most notorious bond fences in the United States. Authorities learned that he deposited $5,000 worth of stolen bonds into a Minneapolis bank—bonds that were traced to the 1928 U.S. Mail truck robbery in Toledo, Ohio, in which Burke participated. Connolly had been eventually convicted in federal court and sentenced to 10 years in prison.[158]

Westin smiled after hearing the outcome. He reached out to shake Hutson's hand and the two men agreed to keep in contact.

THE NEXT MORNING, at 4:37 a.m., Sheriff Cutler escorted Fred Burke to a waiting vehicle and within moments, the armored caravan of three cars set out for Marquette, Michigan. Guarding Burke were Undersheriff Bryan Wise, Deputies William Barry and Clarence Dunbar, Troopers Carl Kamhout and Edd Freeman, and Detective Lyle Hutson. Burke had been permitted to travel in style by wearing a perfectly tailored gray suit, along with a soft gray hat and a dark overcoat, rather than the cliché striped jumpsuit. Burke knew that this long ride would be his last as he gazed out the windows onto the vast expanses of rural Michigan. The Thompson submachine guns he once wielded were never too far from his sight. He seemed to enjoy the scenery and talked openly about it on the trip.

Burke took a special interest in a bit of police radio traffic heard during the trip. A dispatcher at the Michigan State Police Headquarters in East Lansing sent out an APB (All Points Bulletin) or BOL (Be On the Lookout), alerting all officers statewide to a bank robbery that had occurred in Cement City, within Lenawee County. Although the caravan was not near the area of the bank robbery, Burke smiled and remarked, "I hope the big fellow is in on this job," likely referring to one of his many bank robber pals.

As the caravan sped along U.S. Highway 31, the men stopped for breakfast in Cadillac. The entourage filled the Northwood Hotel Coffee Shop and curious spectators positioned themselves for a look at the famous Fred Burke. He dined on a half grapefruit, cereal, toast, bacon, and eggs, and washed it down with two cups of coffee. "Look at the lions," he remarked regarding the hordes of spectators, as he gulped the last drop of coffee.

Shortly before noon, the caravan passed through Petoskey. Calling up ahead to the Cheboygan Post, a trooper requested officers to meet them in Mackinaw City. Sergeant Aldrich and Trooper Barton soon reached the Straits of Mackinac state boat dock, making sure no suspicious persons or vehicles were waiting there to cause problems.[159] The caravan arrived at 12:20 p.m. and the group ate lunch in a restaurant, amid a crowd of 200 people who wanted to see Burke for themselves. "I sure am popular with the folks," Burke remarked, seemingly irritated.

At 1:30 p.m., they boarded the ferry to St. Ignace, the only method of reaching the Upper Peninsula at the time. Crossing the Straits of Mackinac proved to be rough for the hardened killer. Over the five-mile boat ride, he displayed signs of seasickness. Resuming their road travels, they departed from St. Ignace while Deputy Barry reminded Burke that he had promised to tell him how he managed to escape after shooting Officer Skelly. Rumors circulated that he was hiding out at the Hotel Vincent or at a cottage along Paw Paw Lake. Another rumor had a Benton Harbor doctor treating Burke while in his hideout.

A poised Burke paused for a moment, and then changed his mind, saying, "I have nothing to gain by it, and I don't want to get anyone in a jam."

"Is that right?" Barry replied harshly, finally ready to confront Burke about the death of his friend. "Why in the hell did you want to kill this kid?"

Burke let out a sigh and turned to Barry, "A man on booze will do crazy things."[160]

His demeanor changed now that they were getting closer to Marquette. The caravan made a quick stop in Newberry for refueling and then continued along the two-lane road, cutting through the vast pine forests of the Upper Peninsula.

The group reached Marquette at dusk, having made the 600-mile trip in record time. The sunset would not come that day for Burke, remaining hidden behind the clouds as darkness set in. As the cars turned into the prison entrance, their headlights illuminated the iron gates that swung open at sight of the caravan. Burke looked at Sheriff Cutler.

A glimpse of a much different man appeared. Burke said, "I'm glad it's all over! I'm terribly sorry for everything, not because I have to serve my time, I-I don't mean that, but I'm sorry I killed that boy."[161] That was the first and last verbal confession of Fred "Killer" Burke.

At the steps of the Michigan State Reformatory and Branch Prison at Marquette, Warden William Newcombe greeted the party and took custody of Burke. The prison in this mining town along Lake Superior housed some of the most violent criminals. Burke would be in good company.

While prison guards led him down the hall, Burke handed his expensive overcoat to Sheriff Cutler and asked that he give it to one of the boys at the jail. "Write to me once in a while," he said, as he nodded to the sheriff and disappeared behind the iron doors. Members of the transport team could now breathe a sigh of relief and return home for a bit of normalcy.

Burke became prisoner number 5293. Going through the standard booking procedure, he answered all the basic questions. Guards asked him if he drank, to which he lied, "no." He answered "yes" when asked if he smoked and "yes" to ever having venereal disease. Guards photographed him in typical fashion using a front and a side pose, and then he was led into quarantine, where he would stay for 30 days in order to be tested and evaluated by prison staff.

SHORTLY AFTER SHERIFF CUTLER'S return to Berrien County, a surprise greeted him in the mail. The Missouri officers involved in Burke's capture had sent him a leather gun holster, inscribed as "Sheriff Fred J. Cutler from Missouri Officers." They were proud of their monumental accomplishments through their once-in-a-lifetime experience with the notorious gunman, but that was not the case with Joseph Hunsaker. The amateur detective who had quit his $16-per-week job at the gas station to help capture "The Most Dangerous Man in Alive" now wished he had minded his own business.

This photograph was captured by a reporter soon after Fred "Killer" Burke arrived at the Berrien County Jail. *Author's collection.*

Attorney Edwin Donahue, Berrien County Circuit Judge Charles E. White, Berrien County Prosecutor Wilbur Cunningham, December 18, 1931. *Author's collection.*

Fred Burke posing for photo with Deputy William Barry, while en route to Marquette Prison. *Courtesy of David Agens.*

Personal photograph of William Barry, who took great pride in being part of the team that brought Fred "Killer" Burke to justice, taken while escorting him to Marquette Prison. Berrien County Sheriff Fred Cutler (left), William Barry, Clarence Dunbar, Undersheriff Bryan Wise. *Courtesy of David Agens.*

Caravan group photo at a stopover in Newberry, Michigan. *Courtesy of David Agens.*

Endnotes

1   ---December 16, 1929. 5.

2   ---January 16, 1930. 13.

3   Berrien County Circuit Court. People v Fred Dane alias Herbert Church. December 19, 1929, Berrien County Archives. Benton Harbor, MI.

4   Nineteen Hundred United States Federal Census. Timberhill District 51. Bourbon, Kansas. Roll T623_471. Page 5A. Enumeration District 51. http://www.ancestry.com. (Accessed July 15, 2010).

5   L. A. Foster. *True Detective Mysteries.* "How Fred Burke Was Captured: High Lights of Burke's Crimson Career." July 1931.

6   *New York Times.* July 4, 1866.

7   Federal Bureau of Investigation. Criminal Record of Frederick R. Burke – FBI #43089 (Deceased) Washington, DC September 23, 1940.

8   World War I Draft Registration Cards 1917-1918. Jackson County, Missouri. Roll 1683383. Draft Board 10. United States. Selective Service System." http://www. ancestry.com Federal Bureau of Investigation. Criminal Record of Frederick R. Burke – FBI #43089 (Deceased) Washington, DC September 23, 1940.

10 *Every Week Magazine.* "Analyzing "Killer" Burke's Career." 1931.

11 *Evening Chronicle.* Marshall, MI. October 2, 1919. 2.

12 Federal Bureau of Investigation. Criminal Record of Frederick R. Burke – FBI #43089 (Deceased) Washington, DC. September 23, 1940.

13 IBID.

14 Nineteen Hundred Ten United States Federal Census. Carondelet, St Louis, Missouri. Roll T624_809. Page: 5B. Enumeration District 106. Image 991.http://www.ancestry. com. (Accessed October 3, 2010) – Surname spelled Winkler and mother's name listed as Anna M. Winkler.

15 Georgette Winkeler. *Georgette Winkeler Memoirs.* "The Seventh Child." Federal Bureau of Investigation. Washington, DC. 1934.

16 St. Louis Police Department. Secret Service Memo and Arrest Disposition of August H. Winkler. St. Louis, MO. March 30, 1920, April 3, 1920.

17 Federal Bureau of Investigation. Criminal Record of Frederick R. Burke – FBI #43089 (Deceased) Washington, DC. September 23, 1940.

18 Missouri State Board of Health. St. Louis, MO. Mary Winkler Certificate of Death. File #10675. Registered #2491.

19 Daniel Waugh. *Egan's Rats: The Untold Story of the Prohibition-Era Gang That Ruled St. Louis.* Nashville, TN: Cumberland House Publishing, 2007.

20 St. Louis Police Department. Narrative of Arrest, Fred Burke. Milford Jones, Gus Winkler. "Det. /Sergeant Edward Dowd and Det. /Sergeant P. Girard Supplemental to Arrest Report." June 5, 1925. St. Louis, MO.

21 Chuck Schauer. Email correspondence with author. September 25, 2011.

22 From Chuck Schauer, the Mauser-Waffenfabrik Model 1896 Semi-Automatic Pistol fired semi-automatic (one round for one pull of the trigger). This gun was made in .30 caliber and could be altered easily to fire fully automatic. With the detachable shoulder stock, it resembled a submachine gun and held a large magazine.

23 St. Louis Police Department. Narrative of Arrest, Fred Burke, Milford Jones, Gus Winkler. "Det. /Sergeant Edward Dowd and Det. /Sergeant P. Girard Supplemental to Arrest Report." June 5, 1925. St. Louis, MO.

24 *San Antonio Express.* San Antonio, TX. March 27, 1931. 3.

25   Marquette County Probate Court. Estate of Fred Dane alias Fred Burke, Deceased. July 11, 1941. Marquette, MI.

26   New York Passenger List 1921. Microfilm Serial T715. Microfilm Roll T715_3000. Line: 22. Page Number 211. http://.www.ancestry.com. (Accessed January 30, 2012).

27   Marquette County Probate Court. Estate of Fred Dane alias Fred Burke, Deceased. July 11, 1941. Marquette, MI.

28   *Jefferson City Post Tribune*. April 24, 1934. 1.

29   Federal Bureau of Investigation. *Criminal Record of Frederick R. Burke – FBI #43089 (Deceased)* Washington, DC. September 23, 1940 – The entry has Burke being arrested on 4/31/26, which is not a valid date.

30   Federal Bureau of Investigation. Purple Gang (aka Sugar House Gang). http://vault. fbi.gov/Purple%20Gang%20%28aka%20Sugar%20House%20Gang%29. (Accessed January 2, 2012).

31   Edward Dean Sullivan. *The Snatch Racket*. "Chapter III Killer Burke and His Imitators." New York, NY: The Vanguard Press, 1932.

32   Theo Burke refers to Doris with the surname of O'Riordan but she did not marry Joseph O'Riordan until late 1928.

33   Marquette County Probate Court. Estate of Fred Dane alias Fred Burke, Deceased. July 11, 1941. Marquette, MI.

34   O'Riordan also took part in a plot to kidnap either Edsel Ford or one of his sons in 1930; however, the plan fell through and the kidnapping attempt never took place.

35   Daniel Waugh, interview – This gun would be used in the St. Valentine's Day Massacre and most likely in Detroit's Miraflores Massacre.

36   Daniel Waugh. *Egan's Rats: The Untold Story of the Prohibition-Era Gang That Ruled St. Louis*. Nashville, TN: Cumberland House Publishing, 2007.

37   *Portsmouth Daily Times*. Portsmouth, OH. April 16, 1928. 1, 3.

38   The Detective. Edition XLIV. No. 512. Chicago, IL. June 1928. 1.

39   Surname also spelled, Yale.

40   State of New York Department of Health of the City of New York. Bureau of Records. Certificate of Death for Frank Uale. Registered #14764. July 1, 1928. New York, NY.

41   Missouri State Board of Health. St. Louis, MO. Bernard J. Winkler Certificate of Death. File #38116. Registered #396.

42   *Coshocton Tribune*. Coshocton, OH. March 29, 1931. 1, 12.

43   Chicago Crime Commission. Inquest on the Bodies of Albert Kachellek, Et Al. December 23, 1929. 10:15 o'clock A.M., Chicago, IL.

44   Calvin H. Goddard. "The Valentine Day Massacre: A Study in Ammunition-Tracing," *A Crime and it's Clues*. 1929.

45   Chicago Crime Commission. Inquest on the Bodies of Albert Kachellek, Et Al. December 23, 1929. 10:15 o'clock A.M., Chicago, IL.

46   *Sheboygan Press*. Sheboygan, WI. December 17, 1929. 23.

47   Federal Bureau of Investigation. *Barker-Karpis Gang, Bremer Kidnapping*. http:// vault.fbi.gov/barker-karpis-gang. (Accessed October 24, 2011).

48   *News-Palladium*. January 1, 1930. 115, 123.

49   Bruce Catton. *Olean Times*. "Not Brainy, Just Dumb," New York, NY. January 3, 1930. 20.

50   Federal Bureau of Investigation. *Barker-Karpis Gang, Bremer Kidnapping*. http:// vault.fbi.gov/barker-karpis-gang. (Accessed August 12, 2012).

51   State of Michigan Department of Public Safety. *Fred Burke*. Case #2208. "Wisconsin Bankers' Association Memo from A. M. DeVoursney to Capt. Fred Armstrong." January 24, 1930. Michigan State Police. Lansing, MI.

52   State of Michigan Department of Public Safety. *Fred Burke*. Case #2208. "Memo to Commissioner Oscar Olander from Department of Commerce Aeronautical Branch Assistant Chief/Inspection Service Howard F. Rough." February 20, 1930. Michigan State Police. Lansing, MI.

53   State of Michigan Department of Public Safety. *Fred Burke*. Case #2208. "Secret Service Division Memo to Patrick Roche." February 8, 1930. Michigan State Police. Lansing, MI.

54   State of Michigan Department of Public Safety. *Fred Burke*. Case #2208. "Secret Service Division Memo to Patrick Roche." February 10, 1930. Michigan State Police. Lansing, MI.

55   State of Michigan Department of Public Safety. *Fred Burke*. Case #2208. "Pinkerton's National Detective Agency Superintendent Memo to Commissioner Olander." February 26, 1930. Michigan State Police. Lansing, MI.

56   *Hammond Times*. Hammond, IN. May 15, 1963. H1.

57   Michael K. Bohn. *Money Golf: 600 Years of Bettin' on Birdies*. Dulles, VA: Potomac Books, Inc. 2007.

58   Berrien County Jail Ledger Book. Florence Dow Jail Booking Record. January 25, 1930. Book Number 8. Entry #4459. Berrien County Historical Association: Berrien Springs, MI.

59   Nineteen Hundred United Federal Census. Tainter, Dunn, Wisconsin. Roll T623_1787. Page 2A. Enumeration District 92. http://www.ancestry.com. (Accessed April 2, 2011).

60   Nineteen Hundred Sixteen Canadian Census. Saskatchewan, Battleford. Roll T-21936. Page 14. Family No 198. Library and Archives Canada, Ottawa. http://www.ancestry.com. (Accessed April 21, 2012).

61   State of Michigan Department of Public Safety. *Fred Burke*. Case #2208. "Florence Faurote aka Dow testimony transcript signed." No date. December 14, 1929 – July 10, 1940. Michigan State Police. Lansing, MI.

62   *News-Palladium*. November 13, 1929. 13.

63   ---July 16, 1923. 1.

64   *Syracuse Herald*. Syracuse, NY. July 8, 1929. 2.

65   Nineteen Hundred Thirty United States Federal Census. Northville, Wayne County, Michigan. Roll 1075. Page 9A. Enumeration District 1032. Image 465.0. http://www.ancestry.com. (Accessed April 21, 2012).

66   National Archives and Records Administration. Civil War Pension Index: General Index to Pension Files, 1861-1934. T288 546 rolls. http:://www.ancestry.com. (Accessed October 22, 2011).

67   State of Michigan Department of Public Safety. *Fred Burke*. Case #2208. "Memo from Chief Special Agent to M. F. Muldoon." April 1, 1931. December 14, 1929 – July 10, 1940. Michigan State Police. Lansing, MI.

68   Federal Bureau of Investigation. *Charles 'Pretty Boy' Floyd, Kansas City Massacre*. "Memo from Anonymous Milan, MO resident to Agent Joseph B. Keenan." August 28, 1933. http://vault.fbi.gov/Charles%20Arthur%20%28Pretty%20Boy%29%20 Floyd. (Accessed October 22, 2011).

69   Ramah Peek. Interviewed by Enfys McMurry. May 22, 2004. Green City, MO.

70   Evelyn Vance Daily. Interviewed by Enfys McMurry. July 2001. Green City, MO.

71   Ramah Peek interview.

72   *Rockford Register*. Rockford, IL. February 14, 1930. 8.

73   *News-Palladium*. February 15, 1930. 10.

74   Ramah Peek interview.
75   Ellen James. *Chariton Collector*. "Gangster Connections." Spring 1981. http://library. truman.edu/scpublications/Chariton%20Collector/Spring%201981/Gangster%20 Connections.pdf. (Accessed January 17, 2013).
76   State of Michigan Department of Public Safety. *Fred Burke*. Case #2208. "Memo from Secret Service Division to A. M. DeVoursney." February 24, 1930. December 14, 1929 – July 10, 1940. Michigan State Police. Lansing, MI.
77   Berrien County Circuit Court. *Farmers & Merchants Bank of Jefferson and the United States Fidelity and Guaranty Company v Fred Dane*. "Deposition of Lynn H. Smith." May 5, 1930, Berrien County Archives, Benton Harbor, MI.
78   *News-Palladium*. April 28, 1930. 3.
79   *Ironwood Daily Globe*. Ironwood, MI. May 2, 1930. 1.
80   Georgette Winkeler. *Georgette Winkeler Memoirs*. "Physiognomy and Fingerprints." Federal Bureau of Investigation, Washington, DC. 1934.
81   *Centerville Daily Iowegian*. Centerville, IA. March 30, 1931.
82   ---March 26, 1931.
83   Berrien County Circuit Court. *Farmers & Merchants Bank of Jefferson and the United States Fidelity and Guaranty Company v Fred Dane*. "Statement of C. H. Inholz." June 17, 1930. Berrien County Archives. Benton Harbor, MI.
84   Gladys Wells Crumpacker. *The Complete History of Sullivan County Missouri, Volume II 1900-1979*. Milan, MO: History Publications, Inc., 1980, 208.
85   *Moberly Monitor-Index*. Moberly, MO. March 27, 1931. 1.
86   Joseph Hunsaker, Jr. *True Detective Mysteries*. "How Fred Burke Was Captured Through *True Detective Mysteries*: The Amazing Story of How It Was Done By the Man Who Did It." MacFadden Publications, July 1931, reprint July 1941.
87   ---July 15, 1930. 4.
88   *Chicago Daily Tribune*. July 13, 1930. 1, 4.
89   ---July 13, 1930. 1.
90   Cook County Clerk, "Death Record for Thomas Bonner." Chicago, IL. http://www. ancestry.com. (Accessed September 19, 2010).
91   State of Michigan Department of Public Safety. *Fred Burke*. Case #2208. "Grand Haven Post Complaint #137." July 13, 1930. December 14, 1929 – July 10, 1940. Michigan State Police. Lansing, MI.
92   Ret/Lt. Kenneth White. *Remembrances*. Michigan State Archives. RG 90-240. Box 55. Folder 11. Lansing, MI.
93   *Chicago Daily Tribune*. Chicago, IL. July 15, 1930. 4.
94   *St. Petersburg Times*. St. Petersburg, FL. July 15, 1930. 2.
95   State of Michigan Department of Public Safety. *Fred Burke*. Case #2208. "Manistee Post Complaint #Man 833." July 14, 1930. December 14, 1929 – July 10, 1940. Michigan State Police. Lansing, MI.
96   *Owosso-Argus*. Owosso, MI. July 15, 1930. 1, 2.
97   State of Michigan Department of Public Safety. *Fred Burke*. Case #2208. "Manistee Post Complaint #Man 1508." July 14, 1930. December 14, 1929 – July 10, 1940. Michigan State Police. Lansing, MI.
98   State of Michigan Department of Public Safety. *Fred Burke*. Case #2208. "Bay City Post Complaint #BC 1652." July 15, 1930. December 14, 1929 – July 10, 1940. Michigan State Police. Lansing, MI.

99 The police report lists Mr. Pedlar of the Pedlar Drug Co. as the complainant; however, Marquette historians say there has never been a Pedlar Drug Company there, but instead a Pendill Pharmacy that may have been the reference. The original report, somewhat unreadable, does not indicate that officers made contact with the complainant, but tip was investigated.

100 State of Michigan Department of Public Safety. *Fred Burke*. Case #2208. "Marquette Post Complaint #Marq 192." July 21, 1930. December 14, 1929 – July 10, 1940. Michigan State Police. Lansing, MI.

101 *Chicago Daily Tribune*. Chicago, IL. July 17, 1930. 14.

102 National Law Enforcement Memorial Fund. Washington DC http://www.nleomf.org/facts/enforcement/impdates.html. (Accessed August 26, 2010).

103 *Omaha World Herald*. Omaha, NE. April 5, 1931. 50.

104 Georgette Winkeler. *Georgette Winkeler Memoirs*. "Killer Burke." Federal Bureau of Investigation, Washington, DC. 1934.

105 Gladys Wells Crumpacker. *The Complete History of Sullivan County Missouri, Volume II 1900-1979*. Milan, MO: History Publications Inc., 1980.

106 *Mouton Weekly Tribune*. Moulton, IA. April 2, 1931. 1.

107 Ellen James. *Chariton Collector*. "Gangster Connections." Spring 1981. http://library.truman.edu/scpublications/Chariton%20Collector/Spring%201981/Gangster%20Connections.pdf. (Accessed February 24, 2013).

108 Gladys Wells Crumpacker. *The Complete History of Sullivan County Missouri, Volume II 1900-1979*. Milan, MO: History Publications Inc., 1980.

109 *Omaha World Herald,* Omaha, NE, March 27, 1931, 5.

110 Joe Hunsaker, Jr., True Detective Mysteries, "How Fred Burke Was Captured Through True Detective Mysteries: The Amazing Story of How It Was Done By the Man Who Did It," July 1931.

111 *Detroit News*, Detroit, MI, March 26, 1931, 1, 2.

112 *Detroit News*, Detroit, MI, March 27, 1931, 1, 8.

113 *Joplin Globe*, Joplin, Missouri, March 27, 1931, 7.

114 *Sunday News-Press*, St. Joseph, MO, February 12, 1956, 1A.

115 *Logansport Pharos-Tribune*, Logansport, IN, March 26, 1931, 1.

116 *Sunday News-Press*. February 12, 1956. 1A.

117 *Detroit News*. March 26, 1931. 1, 2.

118 ---March 26, 1931. 1, 2.

119 *Aberdeen Daily News*. Aberdeen, SD. March 26, 1931. 1.

120 *Detroit News*. March 27, 1931. 1, 8.

121 *Spartanburg Herald Journal.* Spartanburg, SC. March 28, 1931. 1.

122 *Sunday News-Press*. February 12, 1956. 1A.

123 *Moberly Monitor-Index*. March 27, 1931. 1.

124 *Jefferson City Post Tribune*. March 26, 1931. 1.

125 *Sandusky Star Journal*. March 27, 1931. 1, 6.

126 *Evening Tribune*. San Diego, CA. March 28, 1931. 18.

127 *Daily Capital News and Post-Tribune*. Jefferson City, MO. March 29, 1931. 2.

128 *News-Palladium*. March 27, 1931.

129 *Chicago Daily Tribune*. March 29, 1931. 1.

130 Dan Kelliher. *Journal-Post*. Kansas City, MO. March 28, 1931.

131 *Sunday News-Press*. February 12, 1956. 1A.

132 State of Michigan Department of Public Safety. *Fred Burke*. Case #2208. "Paw Paw Post, Complaint #PP1763." March 29, 1931. Dec. 14, 1929–July 10, 1940. Michigan State Police. Lansing, MI.

133 *Milwaukee Sentinel.* Milwaukee, WI. March 30, 1931. 3.

134 *Piqua Daily Call.* Piqua, OH. April 21, 1931. 5, 7.

135 *Milwaukee Sentinel.* March 30, 1931. 3.

136 *Detroit News.* March 30, 1931.

137 State of Michigan Department of Public Safety. *Fred Burke.* Case #2208. "Paw Paw Post, Complaint #PP1763." March 29, 1931. December 14, 1929 – July 10, 1940. Michigan State Police. Lansing, MI.

138 *Chicago Evening American.* Chicago, IL. March 31, 1931.

139 ---March 30, 1931.

140 ---March 31, 1931.

141 *Piqua Daily Call.* Piqua, OH. April 21, 1931. 5, 7.

142 *Detroit News.* March 31, 1931.

143 *Cleveland Plain Dealer.* Cleveland, OH. March 31, 1931. 2.

144 *Olean Times.* Olean, NY. April 1, 1931. 1.

145 *Herald-Press.* April 18, 1931.

146 *News-Palladium.* March 31, 1931.

147 State of Michigan Department of Public Safety. *Fred Burke.* "Phillip Hutson and George Waterman." Transcript. Case #2208. April 8, 1931. December 14, 1929 – July 10, 1940. Michigan State Police. Lansing, MI.

148 Stephen Upton. Interviewed by author. September 13, 2013. St. Joseph, MI.

149 State of Michigan Department of Public Safety. *Fred Burke.* "Memo from Commissioner Oscar Olander to A. J. Colby." April 15, 1931. Case #2208. December 14, 1929 – July 10, 1940. Michigan State Police. Lansing, MI.

150 *Piqua Daily Call.* April 21, 1931. 5, 7.

151 *Time Magazine.* "Letters." March 21, 1932. http://www.time.com/time/magazine/article/0,9171,743372,00.html. (Accessed February 21, 2013).

152 State of Michigan Department of Public Safety. *Fred Burke.* "C. C. Branaman in St. Louis, Missouri, memo to Chief Special Agent M. F. Muldoon in Cleveland, Ohio, "Hold-up of Money Truck, Toledo, Ohio April 16, 1928." April 1, 1931. Case #2208. December 14, 1929 – July 10, 1940. Michigan State Police. Lansing, MI.

153 *Chicago Daily Tribune.* April 28, 1931. 5.

154 Berrien County Circuit Court. *State of Michigan v Fred Dane.* "Judge Charles E. White Statement at Sentencing." April 27, 1931. Berrien County Clerk, St. Joseph, MI.

155 *Omaha World Herald.* November 8, 1931. 44.

156 Joseph Hunsaker Jr. "How Fred Burke Was Captured Through *True Detective Mysteries*: The Amazing Story of How It Was Done By the Man Who Did It." *True Detective Mysteries,* MacFadden Publications, July 1931. Reprinted July 1941.

157 State of Michigan Department of Public Safety. *Fred Burke.* "E. A. Westin Letter to Detective Lyle Hutson." Case #2208. May 1, 1931. December 14, 1929 – July 10, 1940. Michigan State Police. Lansing, MI.

158 State of Michigan Department of Public Safety. *Fred Burke.* "Detective Lyle Hutson Letter to E. A. Westin." Case #2208. May 4, 1931. December 14, 1929 – July 10, 1940. Michigan State Police. Lansing, MI.

159 State of Michigan Department of Public Safety. *Fred Burke.* "Cheboygan Post, Complaint #C-864." Case #2208. April 28, 1931. December 14, 1929 – July 10, 1940. Michigan State Police. Lansing, MI.

160 *South Bend Tribune.* South Bend, IN. February 14, 1990. 1, 3.

161 Nelson Foulkes. *Herald-Press.* April 29, 1931.

Fred Burke being led to court by Trooper Carl Kamhout (front), Detective Lyle Hutson (left) and Sheriff Fred Cutler (right). *Author's collection.* **Opposite:** Mugshot of Fred Burke taken at the Marquette Prison in April 1931. *Courtesy of State of Michigan Archives.*

CONSEQUENCE

"It would do the world good if every man would compel himself occasionally to be absolutely alone. Most of the world's progress has come out of such loneliness."

- *Bruce Fairchild Barton*

INMATE NUMBER 5293

ONCE **FRED BURKE BECAME PRISONER NUMBER 5293,** he retired the name Fred Burke. Rather than use his birth name, Thomas Camp, he referred to himself as Fred Dane, perhaps because that is the man he most wished to be—a small-town husband and businessman.

Just a week into his life sentence, he received his first prison visit from police. This time, authorities in St. Louis, Missouri, wanted to question him about an unsolved $38,000 jewelry robbery, so they contacted Detective Fred R. Enius of the Michigan State Police, Marquette Post, to interview Burke at the prison. "Were you ever in St. Louis, Missouri?" questioned Enius.

"Yes," replied Burke.

"Are you familiar with the locality designated as Clayton Road?"

"Yes. I am quite well acquainted in St. Louis," smirked Burke, obviously having spent the early part of his criminal career there.

"I understand you are familiar with the facts surrounding a jewelry robbery committed in St. Louis on November 10, 1929, and that you are willing to give us some facts?"

Burke flashed a wide grin, "Explain it to me; I am credited with so many."

Enius went over the details of the case while Burke stroked his short mustache. After thinking about it for a few moments, Burke sat forward in his chair and replied, "On November 10, I was in St. Joseph, Michigan." He described to the detective how he had purchased his home in late September and lived there continuously until he got into serious trouble, referring to the shooting of Officer Skelly. "I had several men working for me, decorating the house, and doing other general work around the place," informed Burke. "I did considerable business with the bank there at that time and if you would like to verify my statement, all you have to do is get into touch with any of the bankers." Burke encouraged Enius to confirm this with the men whom he had hired.

Detective Enius then read the names of the robbery victims, and asked Burke if he knew any of the five people.

"I have never heard of any of these people," Burke replied. "And as a matter of fact, this is the first time I have heard of this jewelry robbery you speak of."

Enius leaned forward, "Mr. Burke, would you tell me if you *did* know anything about it?" Burke chuckled through his wide-mouthed grin and responded, "I would just as soon take a trip to St. Louis, but really, I don't know anything about this robbery. I was in St. Joseph, Michigan, at that time."[1]

The questioning about other crimes Burke had been accused of never let up. In the case of the still unsolved robbery of the State Bank of Beaver Falls, Pennsylvania, on October 24, 1919, authorities were able to rule out Burke as a suspect once records proved that he was serving a sentence in Jackson Prison at the time of the robbery.[2] The issue of the St. Valentine's Day Massacre and his alleged role in it lingered as well. From time to time, detectives would surface to quiz him, using every tactic imaginable. However, Burke never admitted to anything about the mass killing, usually returning to his cell with a pained appearance, probably realizing that such probing would never end.

On June 18, 1931, Mexican Embassy officials sent a letter to the Secretary of State in Washington, DC, after they learned that in January a man in Atchison, Kansas, believed to be Burke, had alluded to a plan to kidnap the two sons of Mexican president Pascual Ortiz Rubio. Apparently unaware of Burke's incarceration, they requested that the proper authorities open an investigation, pointing out that President Rubio's sons were living in the United States, working for the International Telephone and Telegraph Company in New York. The letter was forwarded to the United States Attorney General, then to the Bureau of Investigation's director, J. Edgar Hoover, for his review. Having survived an assassination attempt after his inauguration on February 5, 1930, President Rubio took the kidnapping threat seriously, as did the Mexican government.

Hoover followed up with a memo to Attorney General Nugent Dodds on July 10, asserting, "The notorious Fred Burke was received at the State House of Corrections and Branch Prison, Marquette, Michigan, on April 28, 1931, to serve a sentence of life imprisonment for murder. In view of this, is it your desire that an investigation be conducted relative to this matter?"[3]

Hoover received a reply from Dodds on July 22, apologizing, "I beg to advise you that the State Department now states that since Burke is serving a sentence of life imprisonment in the State House of Correction and Branch Prison at Marquette, Michigan, it would appear that no further investigation in the matter is necessary."[4]

IT WAS NOT EASY TO FORGET the man known as Burke, even though he now wanted to be called Dane. Warden James P. Corgan hand-delivered a personal letter from Burke's first wife, Theo Marjorie Burke, who left him in 1929 and fled to Washington. Theo must have learned of his incarceration and his apparent marriage to Bonnie Porter and raised the question of divorce, although by her kind words and later actions it was clear that she still loved him. Penning his own response back to her, Fred wrote:

"Thursday, 7-16 1931
My dear Maggie:
      Your letter came several days ago and the Warden has ask [sic] me to answer it. He hasn't been reprehensive toward me in this matter, but has agreeably concented [sic] to lend us his cooperation—in a legitimate way.
      You seem to be the same dear old Maggie, still alibiing [sic] for yourself, but never failing to say something kind about the underdog.
      This is most certainly an unfortunate predicament and I am sincere in saying that I thought you were divorced. You doubtless know that that information was delivered to me three years ago in Chicago.
      You ask in your letter about your status quo, so I'll try to briefly give you the "legal" of it. Your contract surely gives you priority rights, but your rights seem to be more of a liability than an asset in as much as the State of Michigan holds the proverbial nine points, which constitute possession in any court. I am at a loss to know if you are anxious to obtain a divorce or if it is urgent. If so with Mr. Corgan's open mind in the case, and his willingness to cooperate, I am sure such can be obtained with minimum of publicity, which I assume you want to avoid.
      Since my arrest, I have tried successfully to keep your name out of the newspapers. And have tried to protect our worst enemy, your ex-husband, because I cannot see why even he should suffer for my wrongs. As far as Bonnie is concerned, I should feel very badly to disillusion her more than she already is, however through it all she has been very loyal and persists in thinking that something can be salvaged from the wreck. I'm afraid however, I need more of your optimism.
      I am indeed happy to know that you are getting along good and you may be assured that I have often thought of you. I am sure you

will be interested in knowing that I am getting along good here and I haven't the slightest doubt but that I'll continue. I had the assurance of many good friends before I came here of their 100% loyalty. My lawyer in Lower Michigan is capable & square, also any number of people in Detroit and Chicago. But most of all I think old Tom Rowe is the greatest. He was the first on the battlefield after my arrest and I really believe he would have felt no worse had he seen his brother go away.

I shall give this to Mr. Corgan and he will forward to you. In answering, it is best that you write direct to him.

In closing, I'll offer just as a suggestion that if your divorce is not urgent you should hold off until such a time as the public slightly forgets me.

Certainly wish you the best of luck in your business.

Sincerely,

Fred Dane"

Bonnie White, Burke's most recent spouse, would visit her husband in prison periodically, always accompanied by three bodyguards. In mid-August 1931, she spent three days in Marquette, visiting Burke each day, until prison officials finally had to refuse additional visits.

Bonnie moved away from Missouri and began to make a life for herself in Chicago after Burke was locked up. Then, in a somewhat sensational occurrence, on October 9, 1935, a traveler found a note along the highway just north of Walsenburg, Colorado, scrawled out on a Cracker Jack box lid signed by "Mrs. Bonnie Burk of Chicago," reporting that six men had kidnapped her. The note was turned in to Sheriff Claude Swift, who made the connection with the name as possibly Bonnie Burke, the wife of convicted murderer Fred "Killer" Burke. Deputies spent all night searching for suspicious characters and evidence amid the vast coalfields, but could find no sign of a kidnapping victim.[5] Meanwhile, the next day in Chicago, news reporters located the true Mrs. Bonnie Burke, who still went by the surname of White, and they asked her about the alleged kidnapping.

"It was all news to me, boys. You can see for yourself, I'm doing nicely. Thank you."[6] The story quickly faded away.

Bonnie placed approximately $200 a month into her husband's prison account between 1931 and 1936, but then correspondence began to lapse and all forms of communication stopped completely around 1937.[7]

While adjusting to prison life, Burke stepped back to his former life of crime on August 27, 1931, but this time as a witness only. A prison riot broke out resulting in six deaths—four inmates, one trustee, and the prison doctor, Albert W. Horbogen. The prisoners who initiated the plan tried to escape, but after several hours of being barricaded in one of the prison buildings, the four men chose to end their own lives rather than face the consequences.

In the late summer of 1931, attorney Charles Gore and Capone bodyguard Phil D'Andrea visited Burke at the Marquette Prison, possibly to wrap up any unfinished syndicate business or perhaps to deliver a special message from Capone. Once the local press found out about the visit, Gore asked the reporters specifically not to mention D'Andrea's visit, saying, "It isn't important anyway."[8]

While wanting to forget about the past, some of Burke's old cronies kept in touch with him through prison mail. Harry "Brownie" Hendricks, an old pal from the Egan's Rats days in St. Louis, who had been confined in the St. Elizabeth's Hospital for the Insane in Washington, DC, wrote to Burke in November 1931, reminiscing about old times and former pals: "Our old friends Bobby Burns and [John] "Pudgy" Dunn are both in trouble. Burns is serving a life sentence in Joliet, Illinois, and Dunn has a fifteen to thirty year sentence to do in Jackson, Michigan."

Unbeknownst to either man, Dunn had been actually locked up in Marquette Prison with Burke until 1934.

"I sure do miss Johnnie Ryan, as he was always such a good friend to those in trouble," the letter continued, referring to John "Baldy" Ryan, a former Egan's Rat, who ran a popular gambling joint in Detroit. "Danny Sullivan is running a club in Detroit yet and from what I hear he is doing very nicely. I left Dave Kelly down in Leavenworth serving three years and his time is about up this [Christmas]. Do you remember Baldy Smith? He is here doing fifteen years and came from Leavenworth some time ago. He used to hang around Bill Egan's saloon at 14th and Franklin and got into trouble with [William P.] Dint Colbeck and [David] Chippie Robinson in St. Louis. Baldy is in a serious condition and won't last much longer. Jack McGurn is in Leavenworth I hear doing six years." Like his information on Dunn, Hendricks was wrong about McGurn as well, who had been lying low since Capone's tax evasion trial.[9]

Not all of Burke's past associates remained on good terms like Hendricks, however. The mere mention of Burke's name in certain circles conjured up discontent and animosity. Egan's Rat Chippie Robinson was one such associate. He believed that Burke had killed a few of his friends in St. Louis and he wanted to settle the score. John J. "Irish" Bohmer, bank robber and inmate of a prison in Waupun, Wisconsin, felt that Burke left him high and dry after the Jefferson, Wisconsin, bank robbery. Bohmer commented to cellmates, "That was the last run-out powder [I] would ever take."[10]

AUTHORITIES IN SOUTHWESTERN Michigan tried to slip back into routine business after Fred Burke's conviction and incarceration, but another high-profile gangster arrest suddenly thrust the area back into the limelight again.

Mugshot of Fred Burke taken at the Marquette Prison in April 1931. *Courtesy of State of Michigan Archives.*

ROOM FOR TWO

THE MORNING OF AUGUST 5, 1931, MICHIGAN STATE trooper Myron Gillette checked in for duty at the New Buffalo Weigh Station, located at the junction of the newly paved M-60 and U.S. Highway 12. With him was 34-year-old John Hoven, a state highway weigh master whose job was to enforce the weight limits on state roads. The temperature was already starting to soar, eventually hitting the 100-degree mark in New Buffalo and all over the Midwest. After a little small talk with Hoven, Gillette headed out to patrol the area.

Since the early 1920s, the pay for state troopers had been very low. There were no benefits, no civil service credit, no pensions, and no insurance, and the usual shift was 12 to 16 hours.[11] Each post commander ran his daily operations based on need. Schedules would consist of a day off every two weeks and possibly one night off every two weeks, along with a two-week vacation per year.[12] Despite these conditions, morale remained high and the men were eager to work.

One such man was the six-foot-three-inch trooper Myron Gillette, who graduated from the Michigan State Police Academy in Lansing on April 13, 1929. Gillette had learned to fend for himself early in life and certainly could handle surviving in the vast forests and remote areas of the Upper Peninsula, which came in handy when his first post assignment was in Marquette. He was an expert shooter with a steady hand and did the majority of his patrolling on a motorcycle. He transferred to the Newberry Post, also in the Upper Peninsula, to work with the "Sponge Squad" in September 1929.[13] It was around this time when the department first purchased patrol cars—olive green Fords with a white circle on either door. Aside from official squad cars, some cars seized from rumrunners made reasonable substitutes, especially when they were luxury vehicles.[14] In early 1931, Gillette transferred to the new Niles Post, just over 400 miles south of his previous assignment. While the post was under construction, Gillette maintained a temporary office at the New Buffalo Weigh Station, almost 30 miles west of Niles, but he still had a wide coverage area across southern Michigan.

In the summer of 1931, the Michigan State Police began making a much broader presence in Berrien County, due to the increase in crime and the number of notable criminals passing through and taking up residence in Southwestern Michigan. The state established a new police post in Niles, located on East Oak Street near U.S. Highway 31. In fact, planned staff increases were already in the works and there was talk of making Niles the District Headquarters.[15] Prior to this, the closest post was located in Paw Paw, within Van Buren County. Sergeant Leslie V. Maycock became commander of the new post, having previously served as commander at the Jonesville Post, an area known for its heavy rumrunner traffic. Since the location was only a few miles north from the Indiana state line and along the route between Chicago and Detroit, the traffic volume was much higher than in other counties. August 5, 1931, would be no exception.

Trooper Myron Gillette loaded up his squad car and drove to a New Buffalo café, where he enjoyed a cup of coffee. Afterward, he got back in his squad car and began to drive south on U.S. Highway 12. When he glanced out the side window, something caught his eye: a man handling a gun in a Ford coupe passing by in the opposite direction.[16] The glare of the mid-morning sun illuminated the weapon's nickel finish at just the right moment. Gillette quickly turned around to follow the Ford and noticed that it had an Illinois license plate. He passed by the weigh station and signaled to Hoven by sounding his siren. Hoven jumped in his squad car and took after Gillette. Gillette was able to keep the Ford in sight, but it began to pull away after its occupants must have realized the police were in pursuit.[17]

Both cruisers sped northbound on U.S. Highway 12, passing the villages of Union Pier, Lakeside, and Sawyer. Gillette felt adrenaline pumping through his body. With engines revving, and speedometers pegging their limits, the cars kept up the chase. The pursuit continued for 12 miles with speeds reaching 70 miles per hour. Suddenly, just four miles south of the city of Bridgman, in Lake Township, the eluding Ford swerved into oncoming traffic, smashing into a Studebaker sedan. The impact knocked the Ford into a roll, flipping it over twice and pinning the men inside. Gillette and Hoven slammed on their brakes and maneuvered their squad cars to the shoulder of the road. Smoke seeped from the wreckage and the smell of burning rubber and fuel hung in the air. The officers leaped out of their cars to render aid.

The driver of the Studebaker emerged from his vehicle dazed, but uninjured. The occupants of the Ford were not as lucky; the badly injured men were barely conscious. Gillette and Hoven began tossing pieces of metal and debris aside to get to the men. They heard muted groans from inside the wreckage and were able to pull the injured men out of what could have easily been their coffin. Hoven assessed their injuries while Gillette checked their pockets for identification. The driver's licenses suggested that the driver was Jerry Kral, a 34-year-old from Granite City, Illinois, and the passenger was J. R. Moran, also 34, from Chicago, Illinois.[18] Identification provided by the man driving the Studebaker revealed he was C. J. Anderson, a 62-year-old from Chicago.[19]

Soon, Deputies Elmer Hendrix and John Mathieu arrived on scene to assist. While looking over the wreckage, Gillette found two fully loaded Colt automatics: one a .25-caliber pistol and the other a .45-caliber pistol, along with four spare magazines.[20] He also found over $700 in cash and several bottles of whiskey, one that appeared to have been partially consumed. He began to wonder if the men were racketeers of some sort. Interest in the name Moran was one thing, but he also found an aviator's license in Kral's pocket, something the rookie trooper had never seen. Gillette immediately remembered the bulletin he had read before the start of his shift about a stolen bi-plane in St. Louis. He could not help but wonder if this was connected.

The injured passenger identified as Moran became violent as soon as Hoven tried to aid him, thrashing around and refusing to allow anyone to assist him. When he finally submitted, Gillette and Hoven were able to transport him and Kral to the Bridgman office of Dr. William Littlejohn, a 65-year-old native Scotsman, who was no stranger to the mangled and bloody. After some basic assessment and stabilization, Dr. Littlejohn summoned the Fred Hall Ambulance Service, part of the Fred Hall Undertaking Parlor, to transport the men to Mercy Hospital in Benton Harbor, about 15 miles north. It was common for funeral homes to operate a hearse that doubled as an ambulance, in order to transport patients in a prone position, though it must have been disconcerting to the patients.[21]

Dr. Rolland J. Brown, a 28-year-old physician who had recently left general practice in Hamtramck, Michigan, to join the staff at Mercy Hospital, examined the men when they arrived at the hospital.[22] With the assistance of Dr. William C. Ellet, Brown determined that Moran had a fractured jaw, a broken shoulder, and possible internal injuries, while Kral had a broken shoulder and a severe laceration over his eye. Benton Harbor oral surgeon Dr. Leo M. Globensky tended to Moran's fractured jaw, and determined that it would need to be wired shut in order to heal properly.[23] Once doctors stabilized the men, they were moved into a room for two.

The northwest corner room on the second floor of Mercy Hospital bustled with activity well into the next day. Doctors and nurses paraded past the groups of police officers who had gathered. In an effort to determine if either injured man had a criminal record, Trooper Gillette called in Michigan State Police detective Lyle Hutson on Thursday morning to take a set of fingerprints. During the inking process, an unfamiliar man appeared in the doorway. Upon seeing the detectives and hearing the moans, he rushed to the nurse's station and identified himself as Kral's cousin, asking to speak to Dr. Brown. The nurse told him that the doctor had not arrived yet and asked him to wait in the reception room for a few minutes. The man said he needed to return to his hotel room and bolted out of the hospital. Later in the day, Berrien County sheriff Fred Cutler joined the group of detectives gathered at the hospital while Undersheriff Bryan Wise and Deputy William Barry analyzed fingerprint classification files from all over the Midwest. By the end of the day, the results returned for Moran.

Evidently, this was not Moran's first contact with law enforcement. Although no relation to the notorious George "Bugs" Moran of Chicago, John Russell "Babs" Moran had a prior record in Illinois and Missouri. Originally from Mobile, Alabama, Moran was the son of Catherine Clark Clyatt, also known as "Kitty Lewis," who ran a brothel in her one-story house in a rundown area of Mobile. Since her stability was in question, she had sent her son to live with her sister and other relatives in St. Louis, Missouri, when he was quite young.[24] Moran was first arrested for robbery in 1924, but authorities dismissed the charge due to insufficient evidence. Moran became a stolen bond handler in Chicago, St. Paul, and St. Louis, where he befriended many underworld characters. On October 20, 1930, police arrested Moran, along with Thomas P. Connors, Thomas Wilders, and Jack P. Britt, all for attempted kidnapping and murder of the wife of a Peoria, Illinois, gambler, in East St. Louis, Illinois. Moran was again released due to insufficient evidence. He found himself back in the hands of the East St. Louis authorities on March 26, 1931, coincidentally the same day that police captured Fred Burke in Green City, Missouri. Moran and his pals Britt, Wilders, and William Wilbert were arrested for carrying concealed weapons.[25] After being released, Moran continued his crime spree in Belleville, Illinois, where he was charged with robbery and impersonating a police officer. He now faced local charges in Berrien County for carrying a concealed weapon, in addition to the Belleville, Illinois, crimes.

Sheriff Cutler, who had been involved with the apprehension of Fred "Killer" Burke, sensed something familiar about Kral. He looked over some of the items found at the crash site, including the addresses in Kral's personal belongings, notations scribbled on paper, the aviator's license, an expensive pair of eyeglasses, and a set of false gold teeth. Suddenly, he had an idea who Kral really was. He returned to his office, looked through his desk drawers, found a particular mug shot, and headed back to the hospital room to compare the photo to the patient. At that point, he realized that the bandaged man in front of him was none other than Gus Winkeler, one of Burke's close associates and a suspect in the St. Valentine's Day Massacre.

In a brilliant tactic, Cutler confronted Kral with his discovery, hiding the fact that results of his fingerprint check had not yet been completed. "It's useless to keep bluffing," Cutler said emphatically. "Your fingerprints have already revealed the truth."

The sheriff's ruse worked. "Yes, I'm Winkeler, but don't question me now. I'm sick. I'll talk later."

Once the fingerprint check did come in, it verified Winkeler's identity. The *News-Palladium's* later headline, "Sheriff Outwits Winkeler," stunned many.[26] What the readers learned next was even more amazing. Authorities accused Winkeler of the September 17, 1930, robbery of the National Bank and Trust of Lincoln, Nebraska, in which $2.5 million, the largest sum in history, had been stolen. In addition to the St. Valentine's Day Massacre, Winkeler was the most wanted bank robber in the nation.

Within the span of less than a year, Berrien County had prosecuted Fred "Killer" Burke, considered "The Most Dangerous Man Alive," and now his equally dangerous cohort, Gus Winkeler, was in their custody. Shocked by the news of their monumental capture, Trooper Myron Gillette and Weigh Master John Hoven slipped back into the hospital room to confer with Sheriff Cutler. "The big shots are pretty meek when you've got the goods on them," Cutler remarked to the officers.[27]

Rousing in his cot, Winkeler mustered up enough strength to offer Gillette a sizable cash figure for keeping his identity a secret, which Gillette quickly turned down.[28] Still hopeful for another shot, he asked Hoven to come closer. "If you help me get outta here, I'll make it right," Winkeler whispered. Hoven chuckled at the suggestion and politely declined.

Winkeler slept soundly that night, as if relieved to no longer be on the run. Once the word got out, police departments all over the nation began scrambling to tie Winkeler to previous robberies and murders, just as they had with Burke. Winkeler quickly made the robbery suspect lists in Michigan, California, New Jersey, Illinois, Wisconsin, Indiana, Kentucky, and Ohio, and was believed to be tied to the robbery and murder in Piqua, Ohio, that his pal Burke had been accused of. In addition, authorities in Chicago still considered him one of the St. Valentine's Day Massacre killers. With this most famous crime yet unsolved, officers relentlessly probed Winkeler about his associates, which sparked some lively dialogue between the parties. Detective Hutson grilled Winkeler about his dealings with Burke.

"Every time Burke was mentioned by the papers or arrested, I came in for my share of the notoriety," complained the bandaged Winkeler. "Burke is a fine fellow, when he isn't drinking."

Hutson asked when he had last seen Burke.

"I hadn't pulled a job with Fred for more than 12 years."

Hutson quickly discounted his statement because six years earlier, in 1925, Burke, Winkeler, and Ezra Milford Jones were all arrested for robbery and concealed weapons in St. Louis.[29]

Hutson then quizzed him about John Moran and his other associates.

"Moran is not a gangster," replied Winkeler. "Raymond Crane Neck Nugent is dead," referring to Burke's machine-gunner partner in the war, as well as his comrade in crime. "I'll take an oath that he is dead."

"Well, tell me how he died or where he was killed," said Hutson.

"Oh, he just got in the way and some of the boys took care of him."[30]

When asked about Robert "Gimpy" Carey, whom witnesses said they had seen in St. Joseph and Benton Harbor with Burke, Winkeler denied any recent contact. "He and I had an argument a few years back and we haven't seen each other since."

"Say, was that your revolver found in the car?" quizzed Hutson.

"Yeah, that gun belonged to me, but I didn't hammer out the numbers on it," referring to the noticeably marred serial number.

"Where'd you get it?"

"I don't remember."

Detectives kept Winkeler talking while doctors maintained constant watch over Moran, who was in worse condition. On Friday, August 7, Dr. Globensky set his fractured jaw, and then Dr. Brown set his broken shoulder. Even in his semi-conscious state, the feisty Moran disliked the confines and began working the wires on his jaw loose. He mumbled incoherently while a nurse stood by, limiting his efforts to rip off the bandages. Dr. Brown told the officers that Moran's brain had suffered a contusion and that pneumonia was setting in. Meanwhile, Winkeler had x-rays taken, revealing that he also had a fractured skull.[31]

On Friday morning, Winkeler's wife, Georgette, woke up at 4:00 a.m. in their Chicago home to the frantic pacing of their pet Doberman pinscher. Thinking that the dog might be sick, she took her outside for a walk, but the dog continued whining. Georgette already had a sense of foreboding, because her husband had not yet returned from a golf outing in St. Joseph, Michigan. When she and her dog arrived back home, her intuition proved true. She looked at the front page of the morning newspaper and screamed as her coffee cup crashed to the table, spilling coffee in her lap. The paper's headline read: "WINKELER DYING, DOCTORS SAY."

Her screams alerted her neighbors, who immediately ran to her aid. Not knowing what else to do, Georgette asked one neighbor to drive her to Louis Campagna's residence in Berwyn, Illinois. She arrived with tears streaming down her face, prompting Campagna to ask her why she was crying, although he already knew. She sobbingly told him that she had just found out about her husband. He looked her in the eyes and told her that the boys had known since Wednesday and had strict orders to keep her away from the hospital. They were afraid that she would be arrested if she went to see Gus. Campagna suggested that she should contact Burke's attorney, Charles Gore, in St. Joseph, Michigan, before trying to get into Mercy Hospital. Georgette convinced syndicate car dealer and friend Joe Bergl to drive her to Michigan, where they met up with Gore. "He's doing fine and they think he'll pull out of it," reassured Gore when asked about Winkeler's condition.

Gore dissuaded Georgette from trying to see her husband, telling her that the police had surrounded Winkeler and he did not need to worry about her getting into trouble. Bergl agreed, and drove Georgette back to Chicago.[32]

Georgette holed up for the night in her home, still filled with worry. Bergl returned later to see if she needed anything. While he was there, another of Gus's associates stopped by. Georgette knew him only as Jack. "I'm taking a big chance, but you ought to know this. Harvey Bailey, Big Homer Wilson, and the other boys are going up to St. Joseph tonight and try to kidnap Gus out of the hospital. If they can't get him out alive, they'll kill him in his bed. The idea is to get him away from the police one way or another."

Georgette gasped in shock, then pleaded and begged, "No, don't go. Please, no, don't do this!" She knew that Harvey Bailey had given Burke a place to hide out in Green City and together with Wilson, they were committed to keeping Winkeler away from the police.

Believing that Winkeler had been squawking about various crimes, Harvey Bailey and the others devised the scheme. Writhing with fear and anger, Georgette tried desperately to reach Al Capone. She even considered calling the police herself, but she finally got word to Capone and told him about the plan.

"If Harvey Bailey or any of his gang molest Gus, I will wipe them out," promised Capone. Georgette knew that orders from the Boss were law; the hospital plot was then quickly quashed.[33]

Now that Capone was protecting Winkeler, the focus turned to Trooper Gillette, who instantly became gangland's most wanted man. After he received threats on his life, Michigan State Police commanders ordered that Gillette have around-the-clock protection. For the next month, he was confined to an apartment under heavy guard. The only thing he could do was look out the window, to see if any big black sedans were driving by. For the first time in his life, he was in constant fear. Knocks at his door sent chills down his spine, but soon he would feel comfort again.

Gillette had learned his survival instinct at a very young age. He was born on August 14, 1905, in Comins Township, Michigan, the seventh child of Myron Curtis Gillette, Sr. and Mary Marie Burbank Gillette. At the tender age of five, the boy lost his mother, ironically the same way that Charles Skelly lost his–during childbirth delivering her ninth child. Following that, Myron's father became a strict disciplinarian and put high demands on his children, especially his namesake, Myron Junior. When the lad reached his fourteenth birthday he sought out a different place to live, with his Uncle Alonzo Gillette.

Young Myron ended up following in the footsteps of his two older brothers, Alonzo and Otis, who were already troopers with the Michigan State Police. Otis became a detective working in the Detroit area and Alonzo rose to the rank of captain while in Wayne County as part of "The Sponge Squad." After about a month spent in hiding, Myron returned to work but was later transferred back to the Upper Peninsula.[34]

ON SATURDAY, AUGUST 8, Berrien County authorities served two warrants on Moran, although he appeared to be dying. The warrants charged that on July 29, 1931, he and a woman claiming to be Mrs. J. R. Moran had issued $50 checks for purchases at Fetke & Rutkoskie Clothing Store and McAllister Dry Goods, in St. Joseph, signed by Moran and drawn from the Peoples Bank of Lexington, Illinois. The bank returned the bogus checks to each store proprietor, and when Amiel Fetke read Moran's name in the newspaper, he notified the police. Fetke visited the hospital to view both men but did not recognize Moran, who mumbled, "I've never been in Benton Harbor." Instead, Fetke recognized Winkeler as a man who had come in for a $21 trunk purchased by the woman who claimed to be Mrs. Moran. An earlier search of Moran's luggage had produced two laundered shirts wrapped in paper from the American Dry Cleaners in Benton Harbor. Authorities became convinced that Moran and Winkeler had certainly been in the area for at least a week before the traffic accident.[35]

Accusations did not stop there. Four witnesses of the Lincoln, Nebraska, bank robbery and several attorneys arrived at Mercy Hospital to view the injured men. Bandaged and swollen, Winkeler told the Lincoln prosecutor that he did not take part in the robbery but knew who did. "The three men you arrested for the Lincoln job are innocent," he said, referring to Thomas P. Connors, Howard "Pop" Lee, and Jack P. Britt, "and you wouldn't believe me if I did tell you." Unmoved by his statement, the prosecutor maintained that Winkeler was one of the men who took part in the $2.5 million robbery.

Over the weekend, Moran made significant improvement, although his condition remained critical. The deep laceration over Winkeler's left eye was still not healing properly, and Dr. Brown made the decision to remove his eye completely. Already worried about his injuries, Winkeler seemed more upset over the fact that his golf game would suffer by the loss of sight in his left eye. "I was on my way here to play golf with some friends. I shoot an 85 on most courses," remarked the bruised bandit to his guards. "It's hell to think about it. I've always managed to take care of myself and now look at what a jam I'm in all because of a little thing like an auto wreck."

In addition to Winkeler's pain and the loss of an eye, the summer heat started to bother him. He asked if it was possible to purchase fans out of the money recovered at the scene. "I'll give the fans to the hospital when I leave," Winkeler added.[36] Sheriff Cutler approved his request. Winkeler also asked one of his guards if he would bring a barber to his room for a long overdue shave. Soon, Winkeler felt the whipping of cooler air against his tender, hairless face. "I feel fairly good except my head hurts something terrible."

Hospital staff and specially assigned police forces continuously watched over the men, even while they slept. The usually quiet Moran began stirring one night, and his lips began to move. A trooper keeping watch, bent down closer to hear him mumble a woman's name.

"Your sweetie?" whispered the trooper.

"Sweetie?" repeated Moran, in his dream-like state.

"Where is she?"

"She's in..."

Moran fell back asleep and never completed the sentence. Winkeler, however, was awake, lying still and watching with his one eye.

WITH MOST OF THE ATTENTION focused on the injured gangsters, the commanders at the Michigan State Police took the time to celebrate Trooper Myron Gillette's exceptional work. He received a letter dated August 10, 1931, from the district commander, Lieutenant William Bryan Babcock, who expressed his congratulations. "There is no doubt but what these two men are, are major criminals of international reputation, and in bringing about their capture, you have accomplished a difficult task and performed a duty that is envied by every member of the Michigan State Police."

Another letter from Sergeant Wright Meedham, representative of Commissioner Oscar Olander, made light of Moran, "Please accept my congratulations on your good work in the capture of Gus Winkeler and his playmate."

Captain Laurence A. Lyon of the Safety and Traffic Division expressed the same opinion. "I am taking this opportunity to commend you for the excellent piece of work in capturing Gus Winkeler and his play-mate, Moran." Lyon summed up the letter by noting, "Alertness, such as what you displayed in noticing these men on the highway, is what makes a good police officer."

Gillette may have received accolades from his superiors, but soon that honor would be tainted.

The next day, at Mercy Hospital, Dr. Globensky noticed Detective Hutson speaking to Winkeler and stopped abruptly to asked Hutson if he would step out in the hallway for a moment. He wanted to know where the police were holding the golf clubs recovered from the accident, expressing that in payment for services, Winkeler and Moran promised to give the sets to him and Dr. Brown. Hutson was not aware of any golf clubs found at the scene, but called for Gillette to join in the discussion. Gillette indicated that he had never seen any clubs. Not believing him, Globensky pressed further, detailing the payment arrangement. However, Gillette remained adamant.

After Globensky left, Hutson and Gillette returned to the room. Overhearing the conversation, Winkeler asked Hutson if his golf clubs had turned up. Hutson informed him that they would begin a search. "Oh, let them go," replied Winkeler. "It would be impossible to question everyone you saw with a golf bag over his shoulder." He smiled half-heartedly due to the extreme pain he felt whenever he changed his facial expressions.[37]

Intrigued by the golf club mystery, Hutson asked Sheriff Cutler about their whereabouts. Cutler was under the impression that Gillette had found the clubs. With the bold inconsistencies between Winkeler and Gillette, Cutler decided to approach Gillette himself. Once again, Gillette denied finding any golf clubs at the scene. "Myron, I have reason to believe there were clubs taken," the sheriff sternly warned. "I want those clubs or I'll have you called in before the Commissioner,"[38] referring to Oscar Olander, head of the Michigan State Police.

Having just received prestigious honors from his commanders, Gillette now faced an accusation that eclipsed his accomplishments and could easily cost him his job.

A few days after issuing the ultimatum, Sheriff Cutler received a phone call from Gillette, who told him that a man from Chicago had picked up the golf clubs and he would attempt to retrieve them. Within a day, Winkeler's golf clubs arrived in Cutler's office at the jail. To his surprise, though, two drivers and a dozen balls were missing. Fed up with the situation, Cutler paid a personal visit to Weigh Master John Hoven's residence in New Buffalo to inquire further about the clubs. "I've got one of the drivers from Winkeler's set, the longer one," admitted Hoven, not realizing that Gillette had told a different version of the story. "Gillette gave it to me because it was too long for him." Hoven inadvertently implicated Gillette with the taking of property that did not belong to him. Hoven fully cooperated and promised that he would deliver the driver to Dr. Globensky.

A few days later, Captain William Bryan Babcock of the Michigan State Police Paw Paw Post launched an investigation, aided by Detective Lyle Hutson. Babcock interviewed Dr. Globensky, who expressed that he did not want to see Gillette lose his job over this incident but did feel that the topic needed to be addressed. Hutson interviewed Gillette again, who maintained that the golf clubs were put into the Studebaker driven by C. J. Anderson at the accident scene. Gillette told Hutson that once he learned of this, a friend of Anderson's brought the clubs back and Gillette returned them to Sheriff Cutler at the jail.

Babcock then spoke to newspaper reporter Nell Pope, who was at the scene of the crash. Pope told Babcock that he saw the golf clubs in the squad car when Trooper Gillette gave him a ride back to St. Joseph.[39] Babcock and Hutson's consensus was that Gillette had no doubt lied about having the clubs and that the story about someone from Chicago picking them up was entirely false. Gillette was given a final chance to come clean, and it became clear that his conscience finally led him to do the right thing. He admitted what he had done and turned over the remaining property he had recovered from the crash scene: a pair of golf shoes, a diamond stickpin, several guns, and a watch belonging to Gus Winkeler. The once honorable trooper had stumbled into the dark pit of opportunity. Gillette may have thought, *These guys aren't going to need this stuff anymore, and who's to know?* From commendations to denigration in the matter of days, Trooper Myron Gillette continued his career in law enforcement, but never spoke of this incident again.

ON THURSDAY, AUGUST 13, Sheriff Cutler announced to Winkeler and Moran that he would serve them all warrants in his possession, and then asked if either of them desired to have the lengthy warrants read in full.

"No, just tell me what they are," Winkeler answered with a sigh. "I will be able to prove that I'm innocent beyond any doubt and that I was not in Lincoln on the date of the gigantic bank robbery."[40]

Though Winkeler denied his participation, Chicago attorney Elmer J. Smith, representing the Lincoln National Bank and Trust Company, concluded after speaking to him in his hospital room that Winkeler was one of the robbers. "Winkeler is one of the toughest criminals in the country, in a class with Fred Burke, the notorious bank robber and gunman. We scoured the country for him in order that our eye witnesses of the robbery might have a look at him."[41]

Two detectives from the Toledo, Ohio, Police Department arrived at the hospital to view the men along with two witnesses from the U.S. Mail truck robbery in which Officer George Zientara was killed. Neither witness could identify Winkeler or Moran as participants. "I'm glad they're honest," Winkeler remarked after they left the room.

Moran's condition rapidly improved while the alleged leader in the country's biggest bank robbery remained fragile. "I don't feel good at all. My head hurts," moaned Winkeler, "can't get rid of the pain."[42]

In an effort to make Winkeler more comfortable, the doctors decided to perform a surgical procedure that involved scraping the nasal antrum and draining the fluid that had built up. When his pain gradually decreased after the operation, Winkeler often challenged his police guards to games of cribbage. He even felt well enough to begin reading the newspaper with his one eye, sometimes commenting about his own headlines. He objected to one particular article in the *News-Palladium* from August 18, reporting that he carried a five-notch gun, "That stuff is a lot of nonsense."[43]

AFTER SHERIFF CUTLER RETURNED from a Republican Party gathering in Chicago, he went to the hospital to check on Winkeler and Moran. He had a long talk with Moran and convinced him to waive extradition, clearing the way for him to head back to Belleville, Illinois. Moran took the sheriff's advice and was set to leave on Wednesday, August 26. Moran was now 20 pounds lighter than when he had first arrived, three weeks earlier. Still weak on his feet, he cleaned himself up and dressed in an expensive brown suit. Winkeler and Moran carried on a conversation until officers informed them that Moran needed to leave.

"So long, Johnnie, and good luck to you," said Winkeler. "Write me."

"Goodbye, Gus. Yes, I will, old boy," replied Moran. Then in a lowered tone, "I'll take care of that for you."

Winkeler handed him $15; they shook hands, and then parted ways.

As Moran began his departure from the hospital, staff members lined the halls to watch him leave. Moran said goodbye and reached up to tip his hat; however, he was hatless. Realizing the mistake, he grinned widely.

"I was certainly treated fine here," Moran told a reporter outside as he took a seat in the squad car.

Police drove him to the Pere Marquette Train Depot where he and his armed guards boarded the 10:42 a.m. train for the 376-mile, one-way trip to Belleville. Moran would be arraigned the following day.

Now only Winkeler occupied the hospital room for two as he awaited extradition to Nebraska. He instructed Sheriff Cutler to pay the $416 hospital bill for himself and Moran out of the money taken from the wrecked car. As a gesture of kindness, Cutler brought Winkeler a portable radio to listen to, which he truly enjoyed.

A panel of physicians made up of Dr. Brown, Dr. Bert G. Watson, Dr. Edward J. Witt, and Dr. Globensky delayed the extradition process because they felt that Winkeler's condition was still too serious. However, on August 31, they granted authorization to move him into a more secure facility. Under heavily armed escort, the weakened Gus Winkeler was transferred to the Berrien County Jail, just a few miles away. As his former hospital roommate had done, Winkeler dressed himself in a pressed gray suit for the ride. He thanked everyone and said goodbye to the nurses before entering the guarded vehicle. Sitting alongside Sheriff Cutler in the back seat, Winkeler asked, "What do you say if you just take me to a hotel instead?"

The sheriff chuckled, and then denied his request.[44]

Although weak, Winkeler was able to walk into the jail and go through booking procedures. Deputies Vincent O'Neill and William Berk asked him the standard questions, to which he responded that he was married, born in Missouri, and able to read and write. He gave his age as 32 and his address as 4954 Siebert Avenue in St. Louis, Missouri.[45] He listed his occupation as a contractor and his next of kin as his sister, Mrs. Anna Jennewein. Gus Winkeler now became Berrien County inmate number 6855.[46]

BACK IN CHICAGO, the news about Winkeler's move to the jail had reached Al Capone. Gus' wife, Georgette, requested a meeting with Capone at the Lexington Hotel. "They've moved Gus from the hospital to the St. Joseph Jail," remarked Capone. "I am going to fix it for you to get in and see him." Georgette felt relieved to hear this. However, not all was well between Capone and Winkeler.

"The boys all tell me Gus is losing his mind and talking his head off to the police," exclaimed Capone. "They said Gus has refused my help, and if that's true, I don't know what to think about it."

Georgette shook her head "no," while Capone continued divulging what he had been told.

"On the strength of these reports, I haven't done a thing for him. But what I want is some straight dope. You get it, because I can trust you. I think a lot of Gus, and if the boys are wrong I'll do what I can to help him."

Her relief suddenly turned to worry. Georgette knew all of this was untrue.[47]

Capone arranged for bodyguard Phil D'Andrea to take Georgette to visit her husband, but D'Andrea tried to put off the trip. Intent on seeing Gus, regardless, she boarded a train and made the trip to St. Joseph, Michigan, by herself. When she arrived at the Berrien County Jail, the sight of Gus brought tears to her eyes. She never thought for a minute that he had lost his mind or squawked to the police. She was now determined to learn who was behind the lies.

Georgette reconnected with attorney Charles Gore, who took her to see D'Andrea at his St. Joseph estate. She asked both men if they knew who was spreading the lies about Gus. Gore angrily defended himself while D'Andrea seemed tongue-tied. D'Andrea begged Georgette to keep all of this from getting back to Capone. He had already violated Capone's orders to take Georgette to see Winkeler, and now he intended to blame everything on Gore. Gus Winkeler, however, was getting a different version from D'Andrea—that Capone was arranging an escape plot. Georgette could see that D'Andrea was double-crossing her husband.

Now safe for the time being from his fellow gangsters, Winkeler spent the next two weeks in his second-floor cell, attired in a blue gown and slippers. He was thoroughly disappointed when the radio he brought along with him would not function inside the jail. The steel bars caused interference in the reception. A last-ditch effort to keep him from being extradited was lost on Tuesday, September 15. In an almost identical assemblage from Fred Burke's trial five months earlier, Winkeler appeared in Berrien County Circuit Court before Judge Charles E. White and Prosecutor Wilbur Cunningham, accompanied by Gore as his defense attorney. Unlike the Burke spectacle, there were only a few people in the audience.

Following Winkeler's car crash and recovery, guards at Marquette Prison informed Burke that his fellow cohort had suffered severe injuries in his former stomping grounds. "I thought Winkeler was dead," Burke replied, saying that he had not seen Winkeler for 18 months. Although Burke admitted his friendship with Winkeler, he denied any knowledge of John R. Moran.[48]

The most wanted bank robber in the nation, Gus Winkeler, was loaded into a state police squad car at 10:30 a.m. on September 15, 1931, still mildly bruised but able-bodied and shackled. Michigan State Police detective Lyle Hutson and state trooper Laurence Meehan then set off for Chicago, followed by authorities from both Berrien County and Lincoln, Nebraska. Once they arrived in Chicago, Winkeler and his guards boarded the train to Lincoln, Nebraska, where he made them an offer to return the stolen loot. "Bank robbery isn't my racket, for I'm too busy with the liquor racket in Chicago. But I know where these stolen bonds are and I can get them back. It will just cost me $75,000, but it's worth it. What do you say?"

Lincoln authorities accepted Winkeler's offer, but his narcissistic effort would undoubtedly guarantee gangland retribution.

Once again, Sheriff Fred Cutler was relieved to see a gangster led away in shackles. The stress put on him over the last year was taking its toll. Cutler suffered from severe stomach pain but had kept delaying medical intervention during the tumultuous events of the past year that pushed him to the extremes. He knew that his health was declining and that he needed to act quickly.

Gus Winkeler after being extradited to Lincoln, Nebraska in September 1931. *Courtesy of John Winkeler.*

GUARD BANDIT AT MERCY HOSPITAL

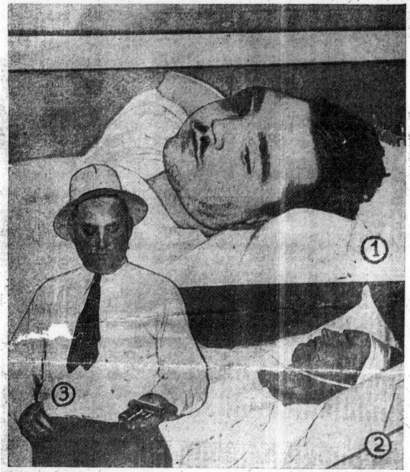

(Pictures by News-Palladium Staff Photographer)

The attention of police authorities in half a dozen states was focused on Mercy hospital here today. In the hospital is a notorious gunman and a companion whose true identity is in doubt. Gus Winkler (1) a former crony of "Killer" Fred Burke, is wanted in several states for murder and bank robbery. John Moran (2) has a broken jaw and internal injuries received when Winkler's skull was fractured in an auto wreck near Bridgman two days ago. State Policeman Lyle Hutson (3) is shown holding an automatic pistol which Winkler was carrying.

Injured Gus Winkeler and John R. Moran, as depicted by the local newspaper, at Mercy Hospital, Benton Harbor, Michigan, after car crash in August 1931. *Courtesy of Herald-Palladium.*

Commissioner Oscar G. Olander, head of the Michigan Department of Public Safety.
State of Michigan Archives.

AL CAPONE'S GRAND EXIT

AS FRED BURKE SETTLED INTO HIS NEW LIFE BEHIND bars in the summer of 1931, painstaking efforts to unravel the criminal enterprise run by Al Capone had paid off, although not in the way that most had hoped. On June 16, Capone pleaded guilty in federal court to tax evasion and liquor law violations, believing that he struck a deal wherein he would only have to serve a two-and-a-half-year sentence. However, Judge James H. Wilkerson, who referred to Capone as "unbelievably arrogant," swiftly made it plain that he was not bound by any agreement, which motivated Capone to change his plea to not guilty. The gangland leader appeared to have no worries and spent the greater part of June and July 1931 in Southwestern Michigan with his associates.

One day in June, Cicero politician and a Capone pal, Edward Konvalinka, the only member of his family involved in the rackets, showed up at the Union Pier home of his brother, Joseph. When Joseph's wife, Emily, heard the knock at the front door, she was scrubbing the porch floor while their four-year old daughter, Ruth, watched from another room. Emily politely greeted her brother-in-law, who was accompanied by another man. He suggested that the man stay with them, but Emily insolently told them to get the hell out, after recognizing that Edward's guest was Al Capone.[49]

Never one to worry, Konvalinka took Capone to Benton Harbor, where the Hotel Vincent became his headquarters. Capone entertained himself with food, spirits, and golf. While hotel proprietor Daniel J. O'Connor rolled out the red carpet, the bellhops lined up to earn their customary $5 tips. Before heading back to Chicago when his October trial was set to begin, Capone threw himself a farewell party of sorts.

On Saturday evening, July 25, 1931, the "Big Fella" and his henchmen returned to the hotel after spending the day playing golf. Capone wanted exclusive access to the Rose Room for his spontaneous celebration, but Mrs. J.

H. Byckford and a group of young women organizing a Twin Cities Chapter of the Epsilon Sigma Alpha sorority already had booked the room. It was soon obvious to everyone concerned which group had more influence. Hotel management quickly escorted the women into a smaller room while Capone commandeered the Rose Room, complete with the floral table decorations and the entertainment as well.[50] Popular WGN Radio singer Wade Booth and pianist Mildred Davis were a highly regarded vaudeville act, hosted by the hotel, and this night they witnessed between 50 and 100 men dine, toast, and honor the head of Chicago's South Side Outfit, Al Capone. From their smaller adjacent room, the young women listened to the clinking of ice cubes and glasses, most likely filled with prohibited alcoholic beverages. It might have been a gala for all to remember but the sorority women considered their event a failure. Mrs. Byckford let her dissatisfaction with hotel management be known when she spoke to proprietor O'Connor.[51] "We had to take our napkins in one hand and our desserts in the other and run off, leaving all our pretty decorations to get smoked up by the awful cigars of those awful hoodlums."[52]

O'Connor backpedaled and remarked, "When Capone comes here he's just a guest and nothing more. We pay no more attention to Capone and his friends than we do to any other guests." O'Connor went on to explain that he had never received a complaint about Capone or any of his friends during their visits. Citing reasons based on good business practice, the proprietor continued to defend Capone's presence, "I don't see how the hotel can make any discrimination so long as he conducts himself as a gentleman. I am sorry if any misunderstandings occurred over Saturday night's incident."[53]

Still trying to downplay the party fiasco, hotel staff member Tom Meehan denied that Capone and his men were drinking alcohol, telling reporters, "There may have been some cracked ice and ginger ale orders."[54] Capone eventually compensated Mrs. Byckford's troubles by returning money owed to the women from his impromptu gala and paying for the group's dinner.

When Michigan governor Wilbur Brucker heard about this pompous affair, he threatened to put a padlock on the doors of the hotel.[55] However, the governor knew that shutting down the leading hotel in all of Benton Harbor and St. Joseph at that particular time would have been a disastrous move for the tourism industry.

Residents of the area certainly understood Capone's power and influence wherever he went, but while an element of fear kept people cautious in his company, the much larger fear probably was of not granting him the privileges he expected. In the face of the economic strife spreading across the country in the 1930s, Capone offered an opportunity of financial gain for doing nothing more than showing him respect. It may have become easier to overlook his improprieties in Chicago when Capone doled out the cash in his playground. Surprisingly, most citizens in the Twin Cities area saw Capone as a Robin Hood character of sorts. He would give an ice cream cone to a child on the street, hand a $100 bill to a hobo, and share his prized spaghetti sauce recipe with his favorite restaurants in "Little Italy": Capone was seen as a giver, not as a killer.

Even while Capone became the first "Public Enemy Number One" in April 1930, courtesy of the Chicago Crime Commission, the Twin Cities were still his playground. The truth, however muddy and ambiguous as it seemed, emerged as Capone thanked those who tended to him. An apt scolding from the pulpit followed as community members bowed their heads in shame. Each resident was a proprietor of Capone's Playground.

Reverend Howard Blanning of the First Congregational Church in Benton Harbor devoted his Sunday sermon on August 2, 1931, to his disgust over the lack of morals that had created Capone's Playground. The *News-Palladium* printed his words the following day:

> "Laxity and low moral force in toleration brought Capone to the area and kept him coming back. This moral force so pronounced in our fathers is sadly lacking today. In Benton Harbor, we have fair illustration right now. A notorious gangster, whose activities in beer and gambling rackets are known to the entire nation, finds a refuge in this city. It has been indicated that our citizens do not object to his presence. He has been designated a 'perfect gentlemen'; although the Webster-Merriam Dictionary defines a gentlemen as a well-bred and honorable man. This man does not care to live in Chicago, where he finds a hostile attitude on the part of sorely maligned and so-called corrupt police.
>
> In Philadelphia a short time ago, when his presence was discovered there, he was arrested for gun-toting and given the maximum sentence in prison of nearly a year, and when released, taken to the outskirts of the city and warned never to return. Yet Benton Harbor people are said to have no objection to his presence here.
>
> This man is a criminal who has made much money out of his crime. He is now awaiting a sentence to Leavenworth. His everyday life is a violation of the laws of the land that tolerates him. In his train, follow debauchery and death. When he muscles in, it is time for decent men and women to move out. His vulgar expenditure of

his ill-gotten gold is a revelation of what this man is. He cannot live in peace in his gang-ridden city across the lake. He must find refuge with people who are not of his brand.

Meanwhile, our city silently frowns, accepts the fabulous tips, gives him quarters in her largest hotel, permits him with his henchmen to carry on his Sodom and Gomorrah tactics and that is all. We do not seem to realize that St. Joseph paid dearly for unknowingly harboring one of these infamous gentleman gangsters. It has apparently not registered that this gang is the enemy of anything or anybody that thwarts its illegal business or racketeering.

The glorification of criminals is not good advertising for any city but among boys and young men it is a most derogatory force. These youngsters watch us knighting bad men and they, too, put a halo on these hoodlums. They are unable to distinguish between popularity and notoriety.

We are unconsciously giving these boys a new platform. Capone has made a marked impression with golf caddies and bellboys with his large tips. Will Nero continue to fiddle while Rome burns, or shall we as children enjoy our precarious pleasure of playing with fire? Will Benton Harbor continue to be a gangsters' rendezvous or have we awakened to the folly of our nightmare?"[56]

REVEREND BLANNING'S brave and honest message served as a wake-up call to many in the community. Only days earlier, an unnamed former Benton Harbor city official had spoken to reporters at the *News-Palladium* about an incident he witnessed at the Twin City Golf and Aviation Club, one he had never mentioned publicly.

"Think of it, Al Capone running around at our hotels and golf courses with armed guards following him. Why don't the officers do their duty and raid Capone and his bodyguards and jail them all for carrying concealed weapons?

Philadelphia wasn't afraid to throw Capone in jail for carrying a gun. If I was running this city, Capone and his henchmen wouldn't be strutting around with the veritable arsenals on their persons. They'd be in jail on charges of carrying concealed weapons.

Benton Harbor has become a popular rendezvous for Chicago's worst gangsters. They come here armed to the teeth and there isn't a single official, local, county or state, apparently that is willing to make a move against them. If that keeps up, you're going to see criminal conditions here a lot worse than they have ever been.

Give the gangsters a break and they'll break any community. Look what they did to Chicago. Chicago is trying to get rid of them, and now I read in the Chicago papers that they're welcome over here and that Capone is a 'perfect gentleman'. What we need is a grand jury and I've already told Judge Charles E. White so."[57]

IN RESPONSE TO the growing scandal, Michigan Supreme Court justice Louis H. Fead spoke at the August 1931 gathering of the Michigan Association of Chiefs of Police. He blamed the acceptance of gangsters on the public's own lack of respect for the law. "Folks can talk all they please about and against gangster rule, but unless he [the gangster] can sell his liquor to so-called law abiding citizens, he cannot exist. So long as Prohibition is a law there should be voluntary obedience to its spirit by those who now provide the incentive and funds for gang activities." He further denounced politicians who meddle in police work by saying that officials could clean up any metropolitan city at any time if they desired.[58]

On October 24, 1931, Alphonse Capone received a sentence of 11 years in federal prison on three felony tax evasion charges, and two misdemeanor charges for failing to file tax returns. Months of appeals followed while Capone sat in the Cook County Jail in Chicago, Illinois. Meanwhile, his bodyguard, Phil D'Andrea, received his own unwanted attention; while escorting Capone into federal court, the bailiff found a .38-caliber pistol in D'Andrea's possession. This earned him six months in jail; however, his hardships were only beginning, as more bad news would come his way.

Finally, on May 4, 1932, guards moved Capone to the U. S. Penitentiary in Atlanta, marking the slow beginning of the end of gangster rule in Chicago during the Prohibition Era.

AS MORE AND MORE people began speaking up about their dissatisfaction with law enforcement, the law countered back in its own defense. Berrien County sheriff Fred Cutler publicly announced to reporters that the Missouri officers and the volunteers who captured Burke were entitled to compensation: "It's no more than right that these Missouri boys be rewarded for their brave accomplishment. So far the only compensation they have received after helping bring Burke 650 miles to St. Joseph has consisted of a boat ride on Lake Michigan, a visit to the House of David, and a two-week paid vacation, courtesy of the St. Joseph, Missouri, Police Department."

Captain John Lard, who participated in the capture in Missouri, told reporters, "We went way out of our territory to make the arrest, driving across eight counties." He had no regrets, saying that they were glad to do this for Michigan.

The Lions Club petitioned the St. Joseph, Michigan, city board in early August 1931 to pay the reward despite the technical language. At a meeting of the city commission, a heated debate ensued. Commissioner Durphy Merrill opposed the petition by saying that it was every citizen's duty to turn in known criminals, regardless of the reward. "Any person who wouldn't is not a real citizen, in my opinion," asserted Merrill.

"Our delay in paying the reward hasn't left a good taste with the public," noted Mayor Theron Yeomans, who endorsed the Lions Club petition. "Public sentiment favors payment of it."

"The same people who want us to pay the reward will be the same ones to protest if their taxes are raised a nickel," scoffed Merrill. "The public wants lots of things but doesn't want to pay the bill."

Commissioner Charles Kingsley did not expect the final burden to rest on the shoulders of St. Joseph. He pointed out, "Other parties were just as much interested in Burke's capture as was St. Joseph, yet they have paid no rewards."

Yeomans asserted, "The city is not legally responsible, but morally responsible to pay the reward."

"I don't think this commission's conscience should be bothered when a bank sees fit to pay only $1,500 for the recovery of $319,000 worth of bonds," Kingsley countered, referring to the reward issued to Berrien County sheriff Fred Bryant by the Farmers and Merchants Bank in Jefferson, Wisconsin.

City Attorney Fremont Evans felt that paying the reward would generate attention that would benefit the city by making it less attractive for lawbreakers. "Gangsters and criminals are beginning to realize that it's rough going for them in this section. It's a good idea to keep them thinking that way."

"After they read how Al Capone is treated," Merrill blasted back, "they probably will think it's pretty easy here for them."[59]

The polarized viewpoints of officials continued throughout the meeting, leading to a motion to give members another week to ponder their decisions. They allowed the motion to pass while the wait continued for Joseph Hunsaker, Allen Morrison, and the Missouri officers.

Al Capone during his tax evasion trail in 1931. *Authors Collection.*

Al Capone with his defense attorney Michael Ahern, taken during his tax evasion trial in 1931. *Author's collection.*

Berrien County Sheriff's Department, 1932. Sheriff Jane Cutler (front row right), Charles Davis (second row right), Bill Hedrick (back row left), William Barry, John Lay, Fred Alden (back row right). *Courtesy of the Berrien County Sheriff's Department.*

FRED BURKE—THE MOVIE

HOLLYWOOD PREPARED TO TELL THE WORLD "HOW Fred Burke Was Captured." A film crew from the Mid-West Film Company flocked to the rural town of Green City, Missouri, to re-enact the capture of Burke for the big screen. The documentary began filming in June 1931 with Fred Lowry serving as the film's producer and director, while Rufus D. Pasquale handled the cinematography. The cast of characters was to include most of the original participants; however, Olen Glenn Webb, a 30-year-old resident of Milan, Missouri, portrayed "Richard F. White," better known as Fred Burke. The filmmakers would soon realize that not all of the Green City residents were happy about the film.

Meanwhile, word reached Green City that the city of St. Joseph, Michigan, had approved granting the $1,000 reward for the capture of Burke, even though the expiration date of the offering had past. In September, Joseph Hunsaker and Allen D. Morrison each received a $250 reward for their roles in the capture of Fred "Killer" Burke. St. Joseph, Missouri, police officers John Lard, Arend W. Thedinga, E. Ray Kelly, and Marvin Sweptson each received $125.[60] The now cynical Hunsaker expressed to the others that it was hardly the $100,000 he had his sights on. "If I had to do it all over again, I would never have reported Burke."

The premiere of "How Fred Burke Was Captured" took place in February 1932 in the cities of Milan, Kirksville, Unionville, and all across the encompassing county of Macon, Missouri. The Lowry production was a four-reel, 32-minute, "talking picture." Gangster cars adorned with advertisement signs drove through each town during the film's debut, even offering a special look at a $50,000 armored car formerly owned by Al Capone. When the film premiered in New York, some audience members broke into laughter at the "corn-fed corpulence of the Green City Constabulary."[61] The film, meant to feature the brave officers and the small-town lifestyle of Green City, only succeeded in instilling fear in the populace of potentially being marked for gangster retribution.

A 52-year-old resident, Missouri Ellen "Zura" Tharp, who had been filmed walking down the street, filed a lawsuit in Macon County Circuit Court on February 21, 1932, shortly after the movie's release. She lived a quiet life on a farm with her husband, George, and their three children, and the sudden notoriety of appearing in a gangster film distressed and humiliated her. She sought $180,000 in damages.[62]

As it turned out, no one asked Joseph Hunsaker to participate in the filming. On July 15, 1932, he filed a lawsuit seeking $10,000 in damages, claiming that an impersonator portrayed him in the movie. The once proud team of participants in the capture of Fred Burke had now become a splintered group. Hunsaker named the following as defendants in his lawsuit: Sullivan County sheriff L. C. Hoover; Allen D. Morrison, his former friend; Leo B. Collins, the actor who portrayed Hunsaker in the movie; Fred Lowry, the movie producer; and the Mid-West Film Company. Hunsaker alleged that Sheriff Hoover, Morrison, and Collins, who all appeared in the movie, were the ones responsible for conspiring to replace him with an actor.

Rather than celebrating the strong values of a community and sharing their brave endeavors with the rest of the nation, the motion picture seemed to divide it. On July 17, 1932, Detective Arend W. Thedinga resigned from the St. Joseph, Missouri, Police Department and began a new career running a poultry house. In realizing the scope of the film and the idea of gangland retaliation, some families moved away. Unable to find work in Green City, Joseph Hunsaker relocated to his brother's farm in Sioux Falls, South Dakota. "Right now, I wouldn't cross the street to catch Burke or any other crook, no matter how much he was wanted," Hunsaker reflected to reporters: "Nobody can be expected to go out of his way to catch crooks these days when cheating and every kind of dishonesty and hornswogglery is exercised to get out of paying rewards." Hunsaker mentioned that the drought made farming conditions very difficult, but amateur sleuthing was much worse. He had even considered pursuing legal action in Berrien County, Michigan, courts if the city of St. Joseph had refused to pay the $1,000 reward.

Fearing for their lives, the family of Allen Morrison moved to Greenbelt, Maryland, and vowed never to speak of the film again. Only upon their deaths many years later would anyone in their families learn about the film's existence.[63] Even though a few chose to leave the area, Barney Porter and his family decided to remain in their Green City farmhouse, but soon realized that they were not safe. One night in September, seven bullets fired from an automobile ripped through the Porter residence, barely missing two children who were sleeping in their beds. Police had little to go on, and despite their investigation, the suspects were never located.

AS THE YEAR 1931 CAME TO AN END, some familiar faces around the Berrien County Sheriff's Department disappeared. Deputy William Barry, previously a captain with the Benton Harbor Police Department and a recent candidate for sheriff, left police work entirely. The 29-year-old had actively participated in more high-profile cases in his four-year police career than most law enforcement professionals had in their entire careers. Rather than continuing to chase criminals, Barry chose a less stressful career as a car salesman.

In early 1932, Berrien County undersheriff Bryan Wise swiftly exited police work, but for a much different reason. The 31-year-old, second-in-command at the Sheriff's Department resigned after he and 17 others were arrested in a bribery scandal involving the county road commission. Then, in late January 1932, Sheriff Fred Cutler entered Taber Sanitarium, at the corner of Colfax and West Britain Avenues in Benton Harbor, due to gallbladder problems. Having put off treatment for so long, he had become extremely weak. Once he regained some strength, his friend, Dr. Roland B. Taber, operated to remove the diseased organ.

By February 4, Sheriff Cutler had improved and was looking forward to returning to work. "We have to go to Florida together after you recover to do some fishing," Taber suggested to Cutler, playfully teasing him.

"My election as sheriff started as a joke among the boys and ended in my election, which is the last thing in the world I expected," confided Cutler. "I wouldn't run again for the world. I have worked hard all my life. What I want to do now is travel with my wife and see the country."

He would never get the chance to do that because, suddenly, at 6:00 p.m. that evening, he suffered a severe heart attack. While still alert, he remarked, "Gosh, Doc, it's been a rough road."

Once family members arrived at the sanitarium, Sheriff Fred Cutler slipped into a semi-conscious state and died peacefully at 8:00 a.m. on February 5, 1932. He was 62 years old.[64]

Burke likely would have read the *News-Palladium* for that day with the front-page headline, "SHERIFF CUTLER DIES." For the businessman-turned-lawman who treated everyone, including Burke, fairly, Cutler's death probably touched the hardened killer in a way that few others had.

AFTER SERVING A STINT in jail for bringing a gun to court during Al Capone's tax evasion trial, Phil D'Andrea sought out the comforts of his vacation home in St. Joseph, Michigan; however, lying low was not on his agenda. On Saturday evening, September 3, 1932, D'Andrea and his extended family left his home and drove into Benton Harbor to eat dinner and celebrate his forty-third birthday.[65] The burning candles that decorated D'Andrea's cake would give a glimpse of what was to come.

At 8:55 p.m., the St. Joseph Fire Department received a report that the D'Andrea house was on fire, and rushed to the scene. Charles Skelly's former coworkers, Fire Chief William Hudson Mitchell and firefighters R. Keane Evans and Frank Thomas, arrived to see the two-story farmhouse engulfed in flames. Not long after the fire broke out, the D'Andrea family arrived back at the residence and were aghast at the sight. Billowing smoke and flames cast an orange glow that had been seen for miles, attracting some 500 curious locals who raced to the scene. Firefighters began pumping 80 gallons of bicarbonate soda to douse the flames while spectators formed a bucket brigade to assist them. The sound of gunfire erupted within the burning house once the flames reached the stockpiles of ammunition. Despite all the assistance, the house was a total loss, with the estimated damage set at $15,000.[66]

The fire not only claimed a home, but a once-clandestine meeting venue for the Capone syndicate. Nevertheless, the cause of the fire was traced to faulty wiring, not revenge as some suggested. Phil D'Andrea seemed most upset by the loss of his beautiful garden.

Months later, after workers cleared away the rubble and debris, D'Andrea announced that he would rebuild the home. In May 1933, he hired Chicago architect Alexander Vincent Capraro, who designed an Italian Renaissance mansion to D'Andrea's liking–an even more extravagant two-story home constructed of brick, with cut stone windows, at a cost of some $40,000. The project seemed somewhat pretentious, considering the economic struggles taking place across the nation; however, the citizens of St. Joseph helped provide the peaceful community he so desired.[67] Though D'Andrea appeared to keep a low profile for the next few years, he would later make headlines again.

EVEN AFTER AL CAPONE WAS imprisoned, Daniel J. O'Connor, the proprietor of the Hotel Vincent, stayed active in hostelry, as well as the political arena. He served as the Benton Harbor Democratic Party chairman and became one of Michigan's delegates at the 1932 Democratic National Convention in Chicago when Franklin D. Roosevelt won the nomination.[68] Nevertheless, with Capone no longer around to guarantee full capacities at his hotel from time to time, patronage dwindled, and the nationwide economic depression, in full swing by 1933, contributed to its problems, as it did at upscale hotels everywhere. One original partner backed out of the investment and another partner died suddenly, leaving O'Connor alone to take on the burden. Without any real means to replace the lost income, he was forced to default on the first mortgage, giving bondholders no choice but to go into foreclosure proceedings. As president and directing manager of the company, O'Connor made an offer to the bondholders in an effort to keep the Hotel Vincent running. Unfortunately, his offer was not accepted, and on May 4, 1933, Sheriff Charles L. Miller served a writ of dispossession upon O'Connor, ordering him to vacate the property immediately, leaving Deputy Charles Davis in charge. O'Connor complied with the order and began moving all of the furniture and equipment out of the building. New investors planned to get the hotel back up and running by June 15, 1933, with brand-new, modernized furniture and equipment and under a new management team.

O'Connor intended to remain in the Twin Cities, taking up an opportunity to sell insurance and real estate with an associate by the name of Ed English. However, he eventually sold the hotel furnishings and began running the Great Lakes Brewery in Calumet City, Illinois, with Johnny Patton, "The Boy Mayor" of Burnham, Illinois; the operation reportedly utilized products directly controlled by the South Side Outfit, now in the hands of Frank Nitti, Capone's successor.[69]

DESPITE THE STRUGGLES taking place in the Twin Cities during 1933, the city of Chicago experienced a spurt of growth. "A Century of Progress 1833–1933" was the theme of the World's Fair held along 427 acres of Lake Michigan frontage on the south side of Chicago. The slogan for the exposition was "Science Finds, Industry Applies, Man Conforms." The fair opened in May 1933 and was scheduled to run through November, but its extraordinary success prompted organizers to reopen it the following May and continue through October 1934.

With groundbreaking advancements in ballistics still at the forefront of scientific progress, experts in criminal investigations set up a display at the Midway Arcade on Northerly Island to share their discoveries with exposition visitors. Colonel Calvin Goddard provided quite a few guns from his collection, which were exhibited in a glass case. Ironically, the law enforcement experts who guarded the display forgot to lock the case one night. On August 27, 1934, 14 guns from Goddard's collection were stolen, including a revolver used by the late North Side Gang leader, Dean O'Banion, and another revolver confiscated as evidence in the St. Valentine's Day Massacre.[70]

The scientific achievement Goddard attained through the comparison microscope and the study of ballistics prompted him to contact the Bureau of Identification Director, J. Edgar Hoover, with an invitation to collaborate on other investigations. Not until 1932, when the microscope had become a virtually standard piece of equipment in metropolitan police departments, did Hoover show any interest. When Goddard conducted a course in crime detection methods at the Scientific Crime Detection Laboratory at Northwestern University, the Bureau sent one of its agents from Washington, DC, and ordered various arms identification equipment, including a microscope and a camera. In the spring of 1934 during a six-week visit to the nation's capital, Goddard telephoned the Department of Justice to see what progress was being made but he was met with roadblocks, as he recounted in the *Chicago Police Journal.*

"I contacted by telephone the operative who had studied under me in Chicago, and expressed a desire to visit his laboratory. Unfortunately, he was 'extremely busy on a case assignment' but would inform me when he was free. Not hearing from him after some days, I called again, and met the same response. And, although I was never flatly denied admission, I was put off by excuses throughout the entire period of my visit.

It began to dawn on me that the Department of Justice, having secured from us in Chicago all the data necessary whereupon to build its own scientific crime detection laboratory, had no further use for us in [any] way, shape or form. Indeed I shall not be surprised to hear, within a few years, that no laboratory ever did exist in Chicago, and that, so far as the United States is concerned, the Bureau of Investigation of the Department of Justice is the Father of all modern scientific crime detection methods!"[71]

The Movie "How Fred Burke was Captured" released in 1932. *Author's collection.*

CHEERS, PROHIBITION ENDS

PROPONENTS OF NATIONAL PROHIBITION DWINDLED AS the Roaring Twenties segued into the Depression Era of the 1930s. Various groups had organized movements to repeal the Eighteenth Amendment, including the Association Against the Prohibition Amendment led by the renowned DuPont family, as well as the Women's Organization for National Prohibition Reform. Even staunch supporters of Prohibition began switching sides after they witnessed the downward spiral the country had taken. Statistics gathered by these anti-Prohibition groups circulated, along with their propaganda, through speakers and advertisements at town hall meetings. Consequently, nationwide interest in maintaining Prohibition lost its momentum on many levels.

The DuPont family's association estimated that $861 million in federal tax revenue had been lost annually to untaxed liquor, while $40 million had been spent annually on Prohibition enforcement. The Women's Reform organization had different statistics, though equally shocking: $11 million in lost federal tax revenue and $310 million spent on enforcement between 1920 and 1931.

In 1929, President Herbert Hoover appointed former attorney general George W. Wickersham to study the current justice system through the creation of the National Commission on Law Observance and Enforcement. For 18 months, the members of the group investigated all aspects of crime and enforcement, including Prohibition. In January 1931, the committee found that the enforcement of Prohibition laws was unsatisfactory, but the majority of the members did not favor repeal of the Eighteenth Amendment as a method of ending liquor violations. They recommended different plans of action to increase awareness and education, as well as to aid enforcement.[72] It was fair to say that no plan could diminish the rise in crime statistics. Polls taken during this period reflected that daily living in America had dramatically changed in many areas. Most notably, homicides increased across the nation. The rate in 1920 was 6.8 homicides per every 100,000 people in the country, but before the Prohibition Era ended, the rate had jumped to 9.7.[73] Far from reducing crime, Prohibition had help fill jails to their maximum capacity.

The amounts of "doctor prescribed" medicinal alcohol soared, while people exploited the "personal use" clause within the law. Police and politicians who were once trusted by the public fell under the spell of greed and corruption. Stories of bootlegging and rum-running operations filled the newspapers. Disease and death rates increased due to lack of quality control or health concerns.[74] In 1921, Prohibition agents seized 95,933 distilleries, and in 1925, that number jumped to 172,537. In 1930, the number of distilleries seized reached a new high of 282,122.[75]

The underworld had taken full advantage by ushering in a highly sought out commodity—alcohol—with plenty of customers. Industrial advancement and economic growth had slowed due to the closure of many commercial alcohol plants. Average law-abiding citizens had turned to bootlegging as a source of income and alcohol for personal use. Police records for those involved with criminal gangs were scarce, to say the least. The Illinois Crime Survey released in 1929 found that this was due to "consideration shown to them on account of their prestige, political influence and their financial ability to command the services of shrewd and indefatigable lawyers."[76] America had a thirst for fermented beverages and there were plenty of illegal suppliers to quench it. Prohibition had created utter chaos.

As more supporters of Prohibition repeal joined ranks over the years, the Democratic Party used it as one of its platforms during Franklin D. Roosevelt's campaign for president in 1932. He won by a landslide. Thirteen years after Americans were first subjected to the "Noble Experiment," the experiment was about to end. On March 22, 1933, Roosevelt signed the Cullen-Harrison Act, which authorized the sale of 3.2 percent alcohol for beer and wine, and gave power to each state to decide whether to repeal Prohibition.

On April 10, 1933, Michigan became the first state in the nation to ratify the repeal of Prohibition. Then, on December 5, 1933, the Twenty-first Amendment was ratified and National Prohibition was officially over. On that day, President Franklin D. Roosevelt declared, "What America needs now is a drink."[77]

Residents in Southwestern Michigan and Northern Indiana celebrated the end of Prohibition with a sigh. "Prohibition was a terrible joke," reflected Skelly's pal, William Barry. "It made millionaires out of guys like Capone. I never took a dime in my life from a bootlegger but I did take a drink once in a while," he admitted.[78]

As the "Noble Experiment" became known as an embarrassing chapter of American history, notorious criminals continued to challenge society, graduating from prostitution and bootlegging to gambling, kidnapping, and bank robbery. As "G-Men" and "Public Enemies" became a part of every American's vocabulary in the 1930s, the war on crime brought forth the "Wild West" antics of desperados against a new breed of enforcers, and new laws on the books. The nation's federal law enforcement agency morphed from the Bureau of Identification (BOI), to the Division of Investigation (DOI), and then, on July 1, 1935, to the Federal Bureau of Investigation (FBI).[79] Criminals began moving out of the big cities and mobilizing in Middle America. Bank robberies had become more sophisticated, steadily rising in number until the mid-1930s. By that time, the stakes were much higher and most outlaws paid the ultimate price: their lives. In 1932, nine bank robberies occurred in the state of Michigan, while other Midwestern states had many more: Wisconsin counted 22; Illinois, 44, Indiana, 26; and Ohio, 42.[80] A wave of crime began to emerge, including the sort of exploits that Fred Burke and his crew had refined during the mid-1920s: kidnapping for ransom schemes, or snatch rackets. Middle America now had something for everyone to fear.

South Bend, in northern Indiana, home of the Studebaker Company and Notre Dame University, was always a city that embraced its achievements, but crime was something entirely different. On January 26, 1932, shortly before midnight, 51-year-old business executive Howard Woolverton, considered one of the wealthiest men in South Bend as the secretary/treasurer for the Malleable Steel Range Company,[81] was returning home from the theater with his wife, Florence, when they were abruptly forced off the road by another vehicle. Once both vehicles had stopped, a man hastily exited the other vehicle, quickly approached the Woolvertons' car, leaped onto the running board, and took control of the car, announcing, "This is a stickup, follow my orders." Then the gunman got in the back seat, directly behind the driver.

Fearing for their lives, Howard Woolverton obeyed the gunman's orders to drive out of town. He steered carefully through the business district, knowing that a gun was pointed at him from the rear seat. Shortly thereafter, a second vehicle met up with them.

As directed, Woolverton pulled over on a deserted road about two miles west of South Bend. The armed kidnapper asked, "You the son of Jacob Woolverton, president of the St. Joe Savings Bank?"

Woolverton answered, "Yes."[82]

The kidnapper, now in the company of another man, pulled Woolverton from his own vehicle, and placed him into the other. The kidnappers handed a ransom note to Woolverton's wife, demanding $50,000. Although neither of the Woolvertons knew it at the time, the two kidnappers were George "Machine Gun" Kelly and Eddie LaRue.

George "Machine Gun" Kelly, born George Kelly Barnes in 1895, got his start with small crimes and bootlegging. In 1927, he met and married his second wife, Kathryn Thorne, a woman who had made several previous trips down the aisle. Kathryn reportedly gave George his first machine gun and later coined the term, "G-Men." Once George Kelly was released from Leavenworth Prison in 1930, he hooked up with his partner, Eddie LaRue, who was an accomplished bank robber. Kathryn Kelly selected the wealthy Woolverton as a kidnapping target by the simple process of randomly flipping through the phone book.[83]

After Florence Woolverton promised not to go to the police, the kidnappers set her free and she nervously drove the couple's car back toward South Bend. She cleverly ran a red traffic light, which brought attention from a plainclothes officer on his way home. The officer hailed her to pull over, and once she did, the South Bend Police Department quickly instigated an investigation of the kidnapping. Detectives worked feverishly through the night, camping out at the Woolverton residence in hopes of receiving any communication from the kidnappers. Authorities decided to hold off paying the ransom.

Meanwhile, "Machine Gun" Kelly and Eddie LaRue were running out of patience. They had driven the blindfolded Howard Woolverton around the area for almost 23 hours, and no ransom payment had been delivered. Perhaps realizing that their plan was flawed, the kidnappers stopped just outside of Michigan City, Indiana, and offered to release their captive if he promised to pay the ransom later. The debacle ended when Woolverton boarded an electric train and reached his home at 11:35 p.m. on January 27, to the complete surprise of his family and the authorities. Although the kidnappers never collected their money or faced prosecution in the botched plot, this was not the typical outcome. Just over one month later, the most sensational kidnapping in the nation occurred.

On March 1, 1932, an infant, Charles Lindbergh, Junior, was snatched from his second-story bedroom at his East Amwell, New Jersey, home. Upon seeing a potential personal benefit for getting involved, Al Capone issued orders from his jail cell to various members in his organization to run down any lead in the underworld, hoping that if his men could find the baby a "special consideration" in his already imposed federal sentence might be forth-coming.[84] Gus Winkeler was especially riled about the crime. Not only was a baby involved, but Charles Lindbergh was an aviator who loved St. Louis, two of Winkeler's passions. "I'd like to get my hands on the rat who would do a stunt like that," Winkeler said bitterly to his wife, Georgette,[85] after reading the newspaper.

Ransom was demanded, and paid, but the kidnapped baby was not re-turned. Unfortunately, baby Lindbergh's decomposed body was found on May 12, 1932, without the aid of Capone or his men. The coroner stated that the child had been dead for about two months, likely killed immediately after the kidnapping. On June 22, 1932, a federal kidnapping statute was enacted, entitled "The Lindbergh Law," making it a felony to take a kidnapped person over state lines in order to collect a ransom. A 32-year-old, German-born thief, Bruno Richard Hauptmann, was eventually convicted of this brutal crime and sentenced to death, which was swiftly carried out on April 3, 1936.

Meanwhile, the man thought to be the prime planner of the St. Valen-tine's Day Massacre had moved from his jail cell at the Cook County Jail to a prison cell at the Atlanta Federal Penitentiary, but it seemed he continued to rule the underworld even while incarcerated. Then, in 1934, Capone was sent to the newest maximum-security facility at Alcatraz, just outside of San Francisco, California, in hopes that a harsher environment would keep him from manipulating the system. His power was still apparent, as his rule never waned, even behind bars.

While showering one day, Capone approached a fellow inmate, "I heard that you were talking about me?" Capone then offered him a bit of advice, "I like you, and I'd hate to have to crush your skull, so I would appreciate it if you kept your mouth shut."[86]

GOODBYE, GUS

A **FTER GUS WINKELER WAS EXTRADITED TO LINCOLN,** Nebraska, for bank robbery, he was allowed to post bond by working out a deal with the authorities to return the $2.5 million stolen cash and bonds. Maintaining that he was not involved with that robbery, the biggest bank robbery in the nation, Winkeler was able to come up with about $583,000 of the loot through his intermediaries. Then he supplied proof to the Lincoln authorities of the destruction of almost $1.9 million in registered bonds so that the bonds could be reissued. Nevertheless, law enforcement authorities would not entirely let him off the hook just yet.

The one constant in his life was Georgette, but no record has been found to confirm that they were legally married. Georgette was rattled by Gus's near-fatal car crash as well as his arrest in Lincoln. After spending almost 10 years together, Georgette insisted that they marry in a traditional Catholic ceremony. Gus agreed, and on December 16, 1931, at the Notre Dame de Chicago Church in Chicago, Illinois, the two became husband and wife.[87] The fact that he was not legally divorced from his first wife was never brought up.

In early 1933, Gus Winkeler had heard about an archaic surgical procedure that would alter fingerprints. While some criminals utilized acid to burn off and destroy the ridges, Winkeler chose to have strips of flesh removed from his fingers, essentially mutilating the pads.

"Look at these hands," Winkeler told his now-official wife, Georgette, holding his palms in front of her face. "See, these lines are completely changed. The next time they [the police] take my fingerprints, I might just as well be Andy Gump (referring to the popular comic-strip character) for all the luck they'll have classifying them. So far as they are concerned, Gus Winkeler is now off the records."

Georgette felt his effort was foolish, in that the process was desperate and excruciatingly painful. This only bought more attention to the plight of criminals, and the science of forensics quickly established the need for the collection of footprints, as well as fingerprints.[88]

Winkeler's crude attempt to alter his fingerprint identity would all be for naught. On October 9, 1933, he stood outside of the Weber Beer Distributing Company, owned by Cook County commissioner Charles H. Weber, at 1414 West Roscoe Street on Chicago's north side. Weber and Winkeler had quietly teamed up to distribute beer once Prohibition ended. Out of nowhere, two men in an old green pickup truck drove up in front of the building and without a word, they dropped the gangster like a rock on the sidewalk, blasting 72 shotgun pellets into his body. A clerk inside the building rushed out to see Winkeler lying face down on the pavement, pleading, "Turn me over on my back so I can breathe." He was quickly transported to John B. Murphy Hospital where he remained conscious, refusing to admit to his identity, although an observant police sergeant recognized him. Winkeler asked for a glass of water and a priest.

Aware of his fate, Winkeler repeated, "I'm going to die. I know I'm going to die," and began to recite the Lord's Prayer. His words trailed off 30 minutes later. He was only 32 years old.[89]

Commissioner Weber denied any affiliation with Winkeler, insisting that the "gunmen should have given Winkeler 175 slugs instead of just 72."

Heartbroken, and at times inconsolable, Georgette Winkeler began making funeral arrangements the next day. "I want Gussie to have the best of everything," she remarked, while choosing a $10,000 silver casket. She had him adorned in diamonds and other flashy gems, with a platinum heart and a silver cross. His final resting place would be in the family plot in St. Louis, Missouri.

Most authorities agreed that Winkeler knew too much and was probably targeted for death; however, the question of who killed him would never be answered adequately. Shortly after his death, the Cook County coroner's office opened an inquest into the brutal slaying. On October 23, 1933, Bonnie Porter White, the wife of Fred Burke, was called to testify. She and Georgette had remained close friends and her testimony, as well as testimony from other witnesses presented during the inquest, proved too much for Georgette. Later that night, she slipped into a deep depression in her palatial Chicago apartment at 3300 North Lake Shore Drive, and attempted to take her own life. She retold the desperate tale later in her memoirs.

"I went to the telephone intending for the last time to hear the voice of a friend. Possibly, it was courage I sought. I telephoned

Bonnie White, the last wife of Killer Burke. 'I have just called to say goodbye,' I said, trying to assume a natural tone. 'I'm going on a long, long, trip, and will never return to Chicago.' She asked me where I would go, but I merely said goodbye again, and returned the receiver to its hook.

I switched off all the lights, then pulled my chair to the stove where I rested my head on my bent arm. Already the odor of gas filled the apartment. It whispered in the kitchen with the voice of my husband, saying, 'I'll be waiting for you.' I took a deep breath, then another, and another.

Something had gone wrong. This was not death. They would not let me die. The doctor came and treated me against my will. Bonnie White had been alarmed at the tone of my voice. She knew that I had been at the breaking point and feared for me. She lived so far away she did not dare waste the time to come to the apartment herself. She telephoned Mrs. Sherman. Mrs. Sherman had come up to my floor, detected the odor of gas, then ordered it shut off in the basement. She summoned the Fire Department, and the crew broke down the door of the apartment, found me drifting from life, and brought me back to the world with a pulmotor."[90]

Georgette Winkeler made a full recovery. Four months after Gus Winkeler's death, he was officially cleared of all charges related to the Lincoln, Nebraska, bank robbery. On February 15, 1934, Eddie LaRue was arrested in St. Petersburg, Florida, for the crime and became known as the "Brains in the Biggest Bank Robbery in the Country."

Crime scene outside of Weber Beer Distributors, 1414 W. Roscoe, Chicago, Illinois, on October 9, 1933, where Gus Winkeler was shot and killed. *Courtesy of John Winkeler.*

Car filled with flowers for the funeral of Gus Winkeler. *Courtesy of John Winkeler.*

The body of Gus Winkeler in his casket. *Courtesy of John Winkeler.*

Georgette Winkeler as she appeared at the Cook County, Illinois, Morgue on October 10, 1933. *Author's collection.*

NEW MASSACRE CLUES

NOT LONG AFTER THE DEATH OF GUS WINKELER, THE still active St. Valentine's Day Massacre investigation received a much-needed jolt from two separate sources. In early January 1935, federal agents arrested Byron Bolton, a onetime pal of Burke, Winkeler, and Goetz, who surprisingly wanted to talk about, of all things, the St. Valentine's Day Massacre. A few weeks later, the *Chicago American* newspaper published an alleged confession by Bolton, which some thought was leaked by an unknown individual in the Division of Investigation. Federal authorities did not have jurisdiction in the massacre case and Director J. Edgar Hoover wanted nothing to do with its investigation. On the heels of Bolton's claims, Georgette Winkeler provided her manuscript detailing her late husband's criminal activity to the Division of Investigation. Remarkably, their independent statements were quite similar and very plausible.

Bolton claimed that the original planning for the St. Valentine's Day Massacre occurred in October or November 1928 at a resort owned by Fred Goetz on Cranberry Lake, six miles north of Courderay, Wisconsin.[91] Those present at the first planning session included Goetz, Bolton, Al Capone, Fred Burke, Gus Winkeler, Louis Campagna, and two corrupt Chicago politicians, Daniel Serritella and William Pacelli.[92] Amazingly, both Bolton and Georgette Winkeler named Fred Goetz, Fred Burke, Ray "Crane Neck" Nugent, Robert "Gimpy" Carey, and Gus Winkeler as taking part in the massacre. Georgette referred to them as "The American Boys," and said most were from St. Louis and part of Capone's special assignment squad, being paid $2,000 a week. Georgette acknowledged that the uniformed men at the massacre were Burke and Goetz. Bonnie Porter White, Burke's young wife, had admitted to investigators in 1931 that her husband and Bolton were close friends and they frequently took trips together to Great Falls, Minnesota, and elsewhere.

CHRISS LYON

Of course, Bolton's alleged confession appearing in the press did not sit well with J. Edgar Hoover and the Division of Investigation. Hoover demanded to know where the story originated: Did a division director not pass along new information? Were the phone lines tapped in the Chicago office? Hoover responded immediately, "There is not a word of truth in it."[93] Editors of the newspaper assumed that the bureau was already investigating the confession; however, the source of the "scoop" was never revealed and the validity of the confession remained in question.

While the Division of Investigation denied the existence of a confession, members of the original coroner's jury thought that Bolton's story from the newspaper rang true. Jury foreman Bert A. Massee responded to reporters, "He seems to have a pretty good knowledge of the whole affair, doesn't he? I don't recall having run across the name of Bolton in the actual slaying, but I do know that Burke was definitely connected as a suspect. We proved that with Colonel Calvin Goddard's ballistics test of the spent shells."

Walter W. L. Meyer, also part of the jury, commented, "This is a wonderful expose after so many years. I'm inclined to believe that Burke was connected with the shooting and I think that Bolton might have had something to do with it. I know Burke was connected with the anti-Moran gang but I don't know just where Capone comes in. Bolton tells a good, well-connected story."

Juror Felix Streychmans was not exactly sold on the statement, responding, "There are some aspects of the story that I don't think are quite accurate. We definitely established the fact that only two machine guns were used, although Bolton claims that four men carried them. However, it is possible that only two of the gun carriers were the actual murderers. We traced the shotgun shells to two guns and afterward located them in Burke's home."

Dr. John V. McCormick reacted in the same manner, "Bolton's hookup with Burke is fairly certain. I first heard Bolton's name mentioned in the slaying about three months after the inquest, but I can't remember in what connection. If Bolton didn't take part in the shooting, I don't see why he has confessed that he did."

Colonel Albert A. Sprague remarked, "I can't imagine what would move a man like Bolton to make such a confession, unless his conscience was bothering him. His name never came into the inquest but that did not mean anything, particularly, because we spent most of our time in endeavoring to trace the bullets found in the bodies."

Lieutenant Otto Erlanson, head of the Chicago Homicide Squad, responded to the confession as well, "I believe the *Chicago American's* story is correct in every line from my investigation, which started right after the murders."[94]

Byron Bolton's confession also included an accusation that in 1929 John Stege, chief of Chicago's Detective Bureau, was on Capone's payroll, receiving $5,000 per week. This point did little for Bolton's credibility and Chicago authorities quietly turned down any further interviews.

J. Edgar Hoover never gave the allegations made by Bolton any credence, and the manuscript that Georgette Winkeler peddled to several publishers was deemed "too hot" and only appeared as installments in a detective magazine.[95] However, Georgette's candid details of not only the massacre, but also of the entire underworld, gave new insight into their dark inner workings. As it turned out, her recollections would explain much of the St. Valentine's Day Massacre as well as the events leading up to Skelly's death 10 months later.

In May 1936, Georgette Winkeler sat down for an interview with special agents in Louisville, Kentucky. By this time, she had married a man named Walter Marsh and was ready to put the past behind her. Agents questioned her as to where she and Winkeler went following the St. Valentine's Day Massacre.

"On April 1, 1929, Gus told me that we're going to Michigan until this heat cools off," Georgette openly recalled, referring to the unwanted attention by police and rivals after the massacre. "We drove to a summer home near St. Joseph, Michigan, which was occupied by the father of Phil D'Andrea. Louis Campagna, Mr. and Mrs. Fred Goetz, Phil D'Andrea, and Robert Carey were already there. I learned the place was a hideout for Italians sought by police in Chicago and other northern cities. Sometimes there were as many as ten there at one time," she said.

She elaborated on the details of one night in late April, when the group got quite the scare during a game of cards. Georgette explained that a strange vehicle had pulled into D'Andrea's driveway. The men suddenly leaped into action, arming themselves to do battle. Georgette heard one of them say, "Police," and then turn off all the lights.

"Mrs. Goetz and I had cleaned the house every day and found only two guns," Georgette remarked, "but in a brief flurry of confusion, guns were produced from dozens of hiding places we had not yet discovered. There were revolvers, sawed-off shotguns, and machine guns. Some had been concealed under the cushions of the divan, others had been in the cabinet back behind the dishes, and some were suspended inside suits of clothes in the closet."[96]

After a short time, Gus Winkeler appeared at the back window and explained to the others that the car was just someone turning around in the driveway. The stress was getting to all of them, so within a week or so the group decided to split up. The Winkelers left for Gary, Indiana, while Carey headed to Hammond, Indiana.[97]

Georgette said they met up with Fred Burke soon after returning to Indiana. Gus Winkeler had run into Burke in Calumet City, Illinois, and learned that he had a new moll named Viola. Wanting to catch up, Burke invited them to a retreat in Grand Rapids, Minnesota, which they gladly accepted. While Gus Winkeler and Fred Burke celebrated the good times, it was obvious that neither Georgette nor Viola cared much for one another. In Georgette's eyes, Viola was a "Dumb Dora," dabbling into a lifestyle she knew little about. Georgette tried to dissuade Viola by telling her about the fear she constantly felt, including the midnight escapes, and always having to worry about every conceivable thing. Knowing that Burke had not been a faithful partner, Georgette tried to point out all of his past relationship failures. Viola only became irritated, telling Georgette that she had been meddling in her business.[98]

Burke consumed plenty of "firewater" over the weekend and enjoyed as much rest and relaxation as he could. Eventually the group left the retreat and headed back to Gary, Indiana. Burke, however, would not stay long as he had his eyes on a certain bungalow near St. Joseph, Michigan, one that he would make his home beginning in September.

The next time that Winkeler met up with Burke was in December 1929. Georgette recalled that Robert Carey had asked Winkeler to take him to Burke's bungalow so he could unload some of the bonds given to him by their friend Harvey Bailey to keep until some "bond fence" men arrived from St. Paul, Minnesota. Winkeler agreed and drove to St. Joseph, Michigan, with Carey on December 14, 1929, with a promise to Georgette to be back in Hammond, Indiana, by 6:00 p.m. However, when they arrived, Burke was intoxicated. They dropped off the bonds, but as they made their way back home, Carey began to regret leaving them with Burke, considering his condition. They decided to call Harvey Bailey the next day to discuss whether they should go back to pick up the bonds; however, before dawn, a phone call came in from the syndicate office that left them all in a state of shock and dismay. As they would all find out, Burke was in big trouble for shooting Officer Charles Skelly.[99]

INVESTIGATORS CONTINUED TO obtain a clearer view of gangster occupation in Southwestern Michigan and Northern Indiana, often referred to as Capone's Playground, where more and more residents were suddenly willing to talk and through the unlikeliest of sources: the gangsters themselves. This was the case of Edward George Bremer, president of the Commercial State Bank in St. Paul, Minnesota, who was kidnapped on January 17, 1934. A relatively new collaboration between misfits Alvin "Creepy" Karpis, Fred

Barker, and Arthur "Doc" Barker gave birth to the newly formed Barker-Karpis Gang, specializing in bank robberies and kidnappings. Even though Bremer was released unharmed a month later after the payment of a ransom, the case was far from being over. New information surfaced when agents in Jacksonville, Florida, interviewed Danny McFarland, a Miami gambler, who told them that he was personally associated with Willie J. Harrison, a Barker-Karpis Gang member who had acquaintances in Benton Harbor and St. Joseph, specifically at the Whitcomb Hotel. Harrison was a friend of Fred Burke and Gus Winkeler, and was even questioned in 1930 by St. Joseph, Michigan, authorities regarding the whereabouts of Burke.

In October 1934, special agents probed reports of gangster activity at the residence of Ed and Rose Konvalinka, in Long Beach, Indiana. Konvalinka was then running his own campaign for the Illinois senate but never distanced himself from the underworld. Prior to the probe, Konvalinka, Ralph Capone, and James Novak were part of a group taken into custody during a raid of Konvalinka's political headquarters in Berwyn, Illinois; however, he denied being affiliated with Capone or using any strong-handed tactics. On more than one occasion, informants discussed Konvalinka's hideout and relationships he had with gangsters.[100] In fact, his friendship with Fred Goetz led not only to an introduction to Willie J. Harrison, but also to gang leader Alvin Karpis in the spring of 1933, when Karpis decided to rent Konvalinka's home for the summer.[101]

Agents spoke with Long Beach postal carrier Clarence W. Sadenwater, pressing him for any information he might know about Konvalinka and his associates. Sadenwater explained that the Konvalinkas resided there, but they often rented out parts of the house. The agent then showed the postal carrier several photos of known gangsters and asked if anyone looked familiar. Sadenwater picked out the photos of Fred Barker and Fred Goetz but could not positively place them in the Konvalinka home. He did elaborate on seeing Jack "Legs" Diamond, a New York bootlegger, visiting the home at one point. Sadenwater had also heard rumors that Al and Ralph Capone visited as well. Likewise, a neighbor, Dr. A. W. Atkinson, gave a relatively similar account and recognized photos of Fred Barker, Goetz, and Arthur "Doc" Barker, who became a key suspect in the Bremer kidnapping along with Alvin Karpis. Another agent added that a confidential informant in the John Dillinger investigation disclosed that Rose Konvalinka was a contact for bank robber George "Baby Face" Nelson.

The Bremer kidnapping investigation resulted in the indictments of 12 criminals, including Willie J. Harrison, Alvin Karpis, Fred Barker, and Arthur "Doc" Barker. Authorities then had the duty of locating these men and bringing them to justice. On January 6, 1935, in what seemed like an unrelated event, a body burned beyond recognition was found in an Ontarioville, Illinois, barn. DuPage County state's attorney Russell W. Keeney revealed that the only clues were an Elgin wristwatch, a gold link bracelet, and a pair of badly damaged, octagon-shaped eyeglasses found next to the charred body.[102] Before the DuPage County authorities could further their work on the case, federal agents requested all the data and subsequently took over the investigation. Two days after the body was discovered, Arthur "Doc" Barker was arrested in Chicago for the Bremer kidnapping, and just days later Fred Barker and his mother, Kate "Ma" Barker, were killed in a shootout with federal agents in Florida.

To follow-up on the potential whereabouts of kidnapping suspects Harrison and Karpis, an agent traveled to St. Joseph, Michigan, in May 1935 and met with St. Joseph attorney Charles Stratton, who noted that Fred Burke had hired him in 1929 to represent his one-time girlfriend, Viola Brenneman. Stratton acknowledged that many Chicago hoodlums had frequented the area, including Phil D'Andrea, who not only owned a large estate along the St. Joseph River but also had a small cottage just north of Benton Harbor in Hagar Township, which was reportedly used by Gus Winkeler and Fred Goetz as a hideout immediately after the St. Valentine's Day Massacre.

The agent then interviewed St. Joseph police chief Ben Phairas, who recalled the business card bearing the name of Willie Harrison that was found among Burke's belongings. A federal informant disclosed that gangsters Homer Wilson, Charles J. Fitzgerald, Fred Burke, Fred Goetz, Ray "Crane Neck" Nugent, Gus Winkeler, Robert "Gimpy" Carey, and Lee Turner would frequent Harrison's tavern in 1929.[103] Phairas also confirmed that the Whitcomb Hotel had been a focal point for Chicago gangsters in the past, but had now become a respectable hostelry. The same was said of the Hotel Vincent in Benton Harbor. The agent also spoke to Richard Wren, a clerk at both of the hotels, who indicated that he had heard about a cottage hideout some 10 miles north of Benton Harbor, on U.S. Highway 31, believed to have been owned by a Danny McFarland and Bill Conner.[104]

The agent continued his quest for information by visiting the Whitcomb Hotel, where he spoke to assistant manager Irving L. Hallett, clerk Carl Ankli, housekeeper/hostess Kathryn M. Thompson, and cigar stand operator, Etta Cohen. When they were shown a photograph of gangster Willie J. Harrison, the only one who recognized him as visiting the hotel was 80-year-old Kathryn Thompson, an employee since 1914. She recalled that Harrison had stayed at the Whitcomb for several days, around 1934, registered under the name of "Harris." She also remembered Harrison specifically from playing bridge with him one evening during his stay. Harrison had a unique look with his ruddy complexion and octagon-shaped glasses.

The investigation then took agents to the residence of Phil D'Andrea, where they noted that surveillance would be difficult to conduct, due to the house being in a very isolated place on the river across from the Berrien Hills Country Club. After checking out the club and speaking with greens keeper Leroy Dustin, agents met up with Berrien County sheriff Charles L. Miller to look over D'Andrea's cottage on Riverside Road in Hagar Township. When the men arrived, the cottage appeared to be vacant, with boarded-up windows. They were able to locate Postmaster Lester Kittell, who verified that no one had lived in the cottage for the past seven months.

In October 1935, the burned body found in the Ontarioville, Illinois, barn was identified as that of Bremer kidnapping suspect Willie J. Harrison.[105] Authorities theorized that fellow Barker-Karpis Gang members were fearful of Harrison's tendency to talk, and saw to it that he would never speak again.

The merging of information collected by local authorities with ongoing federal investigations proved successful, which helped establish a standard for those seeking justice. The activities and movements of criminals within Southwestern Michigan and Northern Indiana continued to be exposed, reinforcing the fact that the trail led back to "Bloody Chicago."

WHILE ASSIGNED TO INVESTIGATE several bank robberies, Detective Lyle Hutson of the Michigan State Police, a native of Niles, Michigan, thought back to the sand dunes peppered among the wooded areas along Lake Michigan between New Buffalo, Michigan, and Michigan City, Indiana. He had become very familiar with these places and would soon learn were perfect sites in which to hide buried treasure. In April 1936, Hutson interviewed Edward Wilhelm Bentz in the Atlanta Federal Penitentiary. An accomplished safecracker and bank robber, a collector of fine art and old coins, and an avid poet, Bentz had been sentenced under the new federal anti-crime laws passed in 1934. Hutson offered him a deal: If he provided detailed information about the Peoples State Bank Robbery in Grand Haven, Michigan, on August 18, 1933, then the state of Michigan would not seek to prosecute him. With some reassurance, Bentz began to talk.

"I rented a cottage on Lake Michigan in Long Beach, in May 1933," Bentz recalled, "and lived there until August 19, 1933." Soon other criminals joined him, including Lester Gillis known as George "Baby Face" Nelson, Tommy

Carroll, Homer Van Meter, Earl Doyle, Charles "Chuck" Fisher, Tom Murray, and another fellow known as "Freddie."[106]

Bentz went on to reveal that "Baby Face" Nelson had inquired about a bank in the vicinity that would be profitable to rob, and since Bentz had already staked out the Peoples State Bank in Grand Haven, he told Nelson that this could be the right one. He admitted to providing Nelson and his crew from St. Paul, Minnesota, with a set of Indiana license plates, a machine gun, a rifle, thumbtacks to toss behind them to prevent a pursuit, and the getaway maps. Bentz drove to Grand Haven the night before to scope out the bank, staying at the Hotel Ferry.

On the morning of August 18, he drove the car back to the cottage, where the men loaded it with the equipment from Bentz. The group then set off for Grand Haven, just over 100 miles north. The robbery occurred at 2:45 p.m. with $30,000 netted; however, Doyle was arrested at the scene. The others all got away and returned to Long Beach, where they split the cash, each one receiving about $260, while Bentz kept the bonds and traveler's checks. Bentz then quickly moved out of the rented cottage in Long Beach and found another rental in Union Pier, Michigan.

Hutson asked Bentz what he did with the bonds and checks. He replied that he had buried everything, and only he knew the location. The detective reminded him of his agreement to come clean, and then Bentz began to describe a site along Lake Michigan, near Long Beach, Indiana.[107] It is unknown if the bonds were ever recovered.

As agents turned up the heat on Edward Bentz for information on the whereabouts of kidnapping suspect and gang leader Alvin Karpis, Bentz hesitated at first, but then conceded. He made clear that he had known Karpis for a considerable amount of time and said he had last spoken with him at their secret meeting place about two miles east of Lake Village, Indiana, along a sand road leading south from Highway 10, known as the "burying grounds." The location was ideal, just east of the Illinois border and south of Michigan's border, in a remote rural area where gangsters buried their loot from robberies until it was safe to retrieve it.[108] Karpis drove a 1933 Dodge outfitted with a secret compartment for guns on the right front side, which opened by turning the radio knob. Members of the Barker-Karpis Gang often hung out at The Big Dutchman in Michigan City, Indiana, where one side of the restaurant served fish dinners and the other side served alcohol.

THE BUSINESS OF BANK ROBBERY and kidnapping continued for some and a few others faced justice behind bars, but the unluckiest ones would be taken for a one-way ride. This was the underworld's version of ridding the organization of disloyal members, and it was nothing shy of brutal. Rumors circulated that Raymond "Crane Neck" Nugent was killed in 1932, but his body was never found. Burke's pal, Robert "Gimpy" Carey, died of a gunshot wound in New York City on July 29, 1932; it was reported as a suicide, but some alleged that he was murdered. A former North Side Gang member turned Capone ally, Ted Newberry tempted fate a few too many times and his body turned up in Baileytown, Indiana, now within the city of Burns Harbor, on January 7, 1933. George "Machine Gun" Kelly was captured on October 12, 1933, and Goetz, another suspect player in the St. Valentine's Day Massacre, died in a drive-by shooting just outside of the Minerva Restaurant in Cicero, Illinois, on March 20, 1934. For those still free, the sand continued to drain from the hourglass when "Baby Face" Nelson met his end during a gun battle with federal agents in Barrington, Illinois, on November 27, 1934. Big Homer Wilson died of natural causes in November 1934, while Charles J. "Big Fitz" Fitzgerald and Alvin Karpis were each captured in the spring of 1936. "Big Earl" Herbert, a member of the Saltis-McErlane Gang, had been convicted of being the second gunman, along with Fred Burke, in the 1930 death of Thomas Bonner; however, the verdict was overturned and Herbert was released in 1935. Capone associate and St. Louis attorney Eddie O'Hare was murdered in Chicago on November 8, 1939.

Now, the war on crime seemed to favor the side of justice, as the number of active gangsters continued to dwindle. However, as in any war, casualties occurred on both sides. On Friday afternoon, February 23, 1934, Benton Harbor two-term mayor John J. Sterling, an attorney, boarded a United Airlines Boeing 247 in Salt Lake City, Utah, returning to Benton Harbor from Los Angeles where he had deposed a witness in a federal case. The aircraft, with a crew of three plus five passengers, lifted off in a rapid ascent to climb above a developing winter storm. Instead of rising, the plane fell vertically, crashing nose-first into the Parleys Summit of the Wasatch Mountains, some 20 miles east of Salt Lake City. Reports of the plane failing to arrive in Cheyenne, Wyoming, triggered an immediate search, one that would last three days. When the wreckage was finally found buried in deep snow, all but one body was mangled behind recognition. Authorities determined that all of the deaths were instantaneous. News of Mayor Sterling's sudden death quickly reached Benton Harbor and the surrounding communities. An outpouring of condolences came from poor farmers all the way up to business owners and government officials. The 57-year-old Sterling had helped lead Benton Harbor out of a dark period and his dreams for the future would never be completely realized.

BESIDES BYRON BOLTON and Georgette Winkeler, others also decided to come forward with what they knew of the South Side Outfit. In an anonymous, two-page, handwritten letter, dated August 11, 1936, and sent to J. Edgar Hoover, the author wrote of a "gang more powerful than the Capone Mob." Members included Frank Nitti and Phil D'Andrea, among others. The letter continued by stating that the gang had "a cottage on U. S. Highway 12 on the outskirts of Benton Harbor, Michigan. They hold their meetings and plan their business, such as killings, shakedowns, and muscling people."[109]

Another handwritten letter sent to J. Edgar Hoover dated November 30, 1936, made similar statements. The author referenced Frank Nitti, Phil D'Andrea, Willie Heeney, Anthony "Mops" Volpe, and Louis Campagna as having "a cottage at Coloma, Michigan, which is near Paw Paw and used as a meeting place."[110] The author continued, "The hiding places are loaded with guns and the police of Michigan are protecting them."[111] The letter noted that the gang members had "connections with deputy game wardens because they would shoot fowl out of season."[112]

Regardless of whether Al Capone still ruled his Twin Cities playground or not, a steady flow of information obtained by investigators continued to implicate both Southwestern Michigan and Northern Indiana as criminal havens. When "Machine Gun" Jack McGurn met his untimely demise on February 15, 1936, inside a bowling alley on the north side of Chicago, authorities sought out members of the underworld in an attempt to find the killer. Two days after the killing, an FBI agent from the Chicago office contacted St. Joseph police chief Ben Phairas concerning Phil D'Andrea. Phairas informed the agent that he had been keeping a close eye on the D'Andrea property in St. Joseph along the river for quite a few years, telling him that D'Andrea never lived regularly in St. Joseph but would spend several weeks at the home there during the summer and at different times in winter.[113]

Phairas mentioned that, coincidentally, usually just before a notable gangster in Chicago would be "bumped off," D'Andrea would appear at his St. Joseph home. In fact, he could pinpoint that D'Andrea arrived in St. Joseph on February 14, 1936, the day before Jack McGurn was killed. When D'Andrea wanted to make a long-distance telephone call, Phairas said, he would use the drug store telephone booth near the police department building in St. Joseph. Representatives at Michigan Bell Telephone Company provided information that at one time D'Andrea had an unlisted home telephone number, but around the year 1934 he had phone service disconnected at the house.

SYNONYMOUS WITH THE Gangster Era, the Thompson submachine gun represented this dark time in American history, but it also became a victim to it. The coroner's inquest held immediately following the St. Valentine's Day Massacre brought to light the ease of obtaining dangerous weapons and the corruption that fueled their sales. In 1930, the Auto-Ordnance Company discontinued all sales to dealers and only allowed sales to military and law enforcement agencies, and then only if a request was submitted on official letterhead. General John T. Thompson was so disappointed in what his invention had become that in 1939 he penned a note to a former engineer at Auto Ordnance expressing his sadness. "I have given my valedictory to arms, as I want to pay more attention now to saving human life than destroying it. May the deadly Thompson submachine gun always 'speak for' God and Country. It has worried me that the gun has been stolen by evil men and used for purposes outside our motto, 'On the side of Law and Order.'"[114]

Years later, in the ultimate expression of the dominance of good over evil, President Franklin D. Roosevelt would adopt Al Capone's armored Cadillac as the presidential vehicle. At the time, the United States government did not own an armored car and rules prevented the purchase of any vehicle costing over $750. Since the Department of the Treasury had confiscated Capone's personal armored 1928 Cadillac Town Sedan years earlier, it was put to good use.[115] Incidentally, Roosevelt would later ride in the Cadillac on his way to the Capitol where he would deliver his most famous address that began, "Yesterday, December 7, 1941, a date that will live in infamy...."

Scene outside of the Chicago World's Fair in 1933. *Courtesy of the James Huber collection.*

33

A SHORT LIFE SENTENCE

FOR THE MAJORITY OF FRED BURKE'S TIME IN PRISON, life was predictable, but seemed to lack the hard labor imposed as his sentence. His routine consisted of an hour of outdoor recreation at noon during the week, but guards allotted four to five hours of recreation time on Saturday and Sunday afternoons. There, along with other inmates, Burke took part in various sports during the summer, such as baseball, softball, pitching horseshoes, handball, and football. The prison even offered boxing matches and special track and field events during the Independence Day and Labor Day holidays. Winter limited the inmates' outdoor activities, but some prisoners were still able to play handball and basketball. On the coldest of winter days, Burke remained in his cell and did some reading. He participated in the various sports offerings at first, but as time passed he opted to become more of a spectator. Burke would kick back in a canvas chair in the recreation area and watch the activities.

Fellow prisoners called Burke "The Sphinx." No longer the dapper dresser, he kept to himself most of the time, wearing his prison-issued, ill-fitting uniform, his cap pulled down over his eyes, with a noticeable wad of chewing tobacco protruding from his cheek. "He's a funny lug, but you can't get a word out of him," remarked one prisoner.

Every so often, Burke chatted with some select fellow inmates, especially Doc Long and "State Street Jerry," who had been a member of the Roger Touhy Gang in Chicago. The men would watch the baseball or football games going on and engage in small talk while enjoying the fresh air. One day, Burke asked him, "How would you like to be in Chicago today, Jerry?"[116]

As the years passed, Fred Burke kept himself busy. The average number of inmates held at Marquette Prison was 733, and all but the most brutal inmates were able to take on a job. Burke started out working in the prison laundry room, and then was a shipping clerk in the factory that made overalls. In 1936, after the overall factory closed, Burke organized a leather concession in which three other inmates also worked. Using Russian calfskin, he designed handbags, purses, cigarette pouches, key cases, suspenders, and billfolds. All of the handmade items were sold at the prison novelty store, just outside the prison gates. As the business grew, Burke had 20 inmates working for him, each receiving approximately $10 a month. Sales of their leather goods reached the $10,000 mark in 1938—about the same amount of money obtained during a bank robbery—but now, for honest work.

Incarceration never kept Burke from finding out what was going on in the outside world. The prison library was available to inmates and contained almost 8,000 books.[117] Censored radio broadcasts were aired in each cell between 4:30 p.m. and 10:30 p.m. In addition to the radio broadcasts, Burke kept current on news and local affairs with his subscription to the *News-Palladium,* the same newspaper that had featured headlines of his crimes and escapes in earlier years. Burke was an avid reader and every Christmas he would send $10 to the *News-Palladium's* Christmas Fund, noting that he wanted to do his part for Benton Harbor's underprivileged people. Burke also subscribed to *Fortune* and *Esquire* magazines. Of course, the generous killer would always share the newspapers and magazines with the other men in his cellblock. Over the years, he lost interest in reading detective magazines, unless there was a story about someone he knew. Occasionally he would mark up a story with various comments. In fact, in one story about Al Capone's days in Alcatraz and subsequent insanity, Burke marked it as "phony."[118]

Some of Burke's routine correspondence with his attorney, Charles Gore, included his opinion on matters of the day. In one letter, Burke denounced Adolph Hitler's gangster tactics. In another letter, he opined on what he thought was the grave state of world affairs.[119] Aside from friendly letters, Gore maintained a cash flow into Burke's prison account. On August 14, 1933, and February 8, 1939, he deposited $1,000 into the account. In addition, an attorney from Calumet City, Illinois, named L. Carmine, deposited $2,000 on August 1, 1932. It was the opinion of Warden Simon R. Anderson that Burke may have hidden away some of his bank robbery proceeds and that Gore might have been forwarding that.[120] Balking at this notion, Gore told the warden, "I had occasional letters from Burke in the years he was at Marquette, but there was no hint of any hidden fortune." Gore continued, "He wrote brief notes mostly, and always at Christmas time he sent a check through the prison office."[121]

Reading about the fate of some of his old pals gave Burke a sense of relief that he was in a much safer place. For instance, Ezra Milford Jones was shot to death at the Stork Club in Detroit, Michigan, on June 15, 1932.[122] In addition, Burke quietly learned that his best friend, Gus Winkeler, had been gunned down in 1933. Although appearing stone-faced at the news, Burke began to transform himself from the hardened prisoner to a much humbler man by way of his interactions with inmates and prison staff and through his correspondence. One friend with whom Burke had lost contact was Harvey Bailey, who subsequently was taken into custody in Kansas City, Missouri, in 1933. Aside from Bailey's own crimes, detectives and reporters were interested in his relationship with Burke, as Bailey recounted after his arrest.

"When were you home last?" the interviewer asked.

"It's been a year and a half, I guess," answered Bailey.

"That must have been shortly before the capture of Burke?"

"Yes, it was in February. Burke was taken in March."

When asked about Burke's stay with him at his mother's farm, Bailey explained, "It was intended to be only for a few weeks, but extended to fifteen months, and in that time Burke found a bride on a neighboring farm. I knew Burke about three months before we took him home."

"Who was with you?" the interviewer asked.

"I'm not telling that. I was running booze from Canada and Chicago, and I met him through a friend; Burke and his friend were working for the Chicago syndicate then."

"What syndicate?"

"The only syndicate in Chicago."

"Capone's organization?"

"Look, I'm not saying it was Capone's. It was the only syndicate there. I was asked by this friend if I knew anyplace they could put Burke for a few weeks. I said I did and we took him to Sullivan County. I don't know why Burke had to hide. I never asked."[123]

BURKE WROTE A SERIES OF letters that seemed to be heartfelt. In mid-December 1933, Jane Cutler opened up a Christmas card and was shocked to see that it was from Fred Burke. It had been almost two years since her husband, Sheriff Fred Cutler, had passed away; by an overwhelming recommendation, she was selected to fill his remaining term as sheriff, the first woman to hold that post in Berrien County.

"If every boy had a chance to come in contact with a man like Fred Cutler, life would be different," wrote Burke.

He also sent a Christmas card to Berrien County deputy Bill Hedrick, who booked him in when he first arrived at the Berrien County Jail. Others on Burke's Christmas card list were the four law enforcement officers who arrested him in St. Joseph, Missouri: Captain John Lard and Detectives E. Ray Kelly, Melvin Swepston, and Arend W. Thedinga. Prison officials thought Burke had experienced a change of heart and wanted to distance himself from his criminal past. Soon, others began to think the same thing.

Newspaper reporter Manthei Howe of the *Daily Mining Journal,* in Marquette, Michigan, interviewed Burke on several occasions. Although she characterized Burke as a killer, she found him to have personal integrity, a talent for leadership, and an innate finesse that made the men in prison respect him. She observed of him, "A man, who if he had made a few different decisions, had a bit more real courage, might have become a highly respected person. For the man had ability and charm of a high order, was an entertaining conversationalist, but was, perhaps, sinfully proud."

Manthei Howe attempted to get Burke to open up, but he would persistently give her the cold shoulder. In one of the interviews in the mid-1930s, Burke told her, "Don't say anything about me. I've been too much in the newspapers. Just let people forget about me. Tell your readers about the work the boys are doing in the occupational department," referring to their leatherworking and the raising of canaries.[124]

Cellblock B was his home, where guards could sniff him out by the plumes of smoke from his cigars. The cell was not the cold cage expected for a murderer, but perhaps one resembling a one-room apartment, including a stove. Burke often donned a white apron, rolled out pie dough, cut apples, and baked the finest apple pie known to his fellow inmates. This was an image seen by few and an aspect of the criminal justice system accepted by even fewer.

The final chapter of Fred "Killer" Burke had begun to play out: His appetite was voracious, his liver was diseased, and his lungs were blackened and tarred from his lavish excesses. The rosy glow of consumption disappeared into a "mask, only the putty of human flesh."[125]

The life sentence for Burke would amount to nine years and two months. As if symbolic of his final breath, a shifting of winds swept over the area, cooling the air and coloring the sky in a corpse-like hue. He died abruptly in his sleep on July 10, 1940, at 5:45 a.m., taking all of his secrets with him.

One man, whose personal sadness lingered even after Burke's incarceration, would never get to see God's justice. Gustav Skalay, the father of Charles, passed away on March 19, 1939, at the age of 59, less than 10 years after his son was killed and over a year before his son's killer died in prison.

In Ike Wood's publication, *One Hundred Years of Hard Labor–A History of Marquette State Prison*, the author, who began working as a guard in February 1943, said this about Burke: "Rumors floated around the prison after his death that he had used some lethal drug to hurry matters along."[126]

They were just rumors. As was customary in cases when inmates suddenly died, Dr. Howard P. Blake, the prison physician, conducted a post-mortem autopsy. He sent Burke's organs to the state laboratory in Lansing and to the University of Michigan in Ann Arbor for examination. Dr. Blake reported that a massive heart attack had claimed the life of this conman, kidnapper, murderer, and "The Most Dangerous Man Alive." Burke's friends, fellow inmates, and the staff he met at the prison were stunned at his passing, captured in a full-page memorial dedicated to him in the July 1940 edition of their in-house prison magazine, *Marquette Inmate*:

> "REQUIESCAT IN PACE
> Suddenly, at 5:45 a.m. on Wednesday, July 10, death took Fred Burke, age 47, since 1931 a resident of this community. A heart attack was the immediate cause of death. Burke, described by officials as 'a model prisoner,' enjoyed the respect and esteem of his fellow men here, in a measure because of his generosity and willingness to assist in material ways in their problems. Few men who die in prison leave behind them a more fragrant memory of life behind walls well lived; by all the measures which may be applied, he was a man."[127]

IN THE END, Warden Anderson said Burke's prison record had been uneventful and described him as a model prisoner with a good attitude and respect for officials, and shunning publicity.

The Oates Funeral home at 213 Blaker in Marquette, operated by undertaker Harold R. Oates, took possession of Burke's body and provided a private funeral service on July 13, 1940. Officiating at the small gathering was Reverend Sidney Smith, the Marquette Prison chaplain. Fellow inmates Norman Burns, Lawrence Fraley, Lewis Korn, James J. Carey, Samuel Lomonaco, and Thomas Hayes acted as pallbearers. Originally, four Great War veterans from the R. M. Jopling post of the American Legion in Marquette were to be pallbearers, but they could not attend since another event had been scheduled for them.

At the cemetery, a few gathered to see the plain wooden box containing the body of Fred Burke lowered into the ground as "Taps" was played by an inmate bugler. The only people who attended were former Burke neighbors Charlotte Crossman, and her mother, Jennie Crossman, of St. Joseph, Michigan, and moll 36-year-old Julia Liskiewicz of St. Louis. His wife, Bonnie Porter White, was unable to be located; her last communication with Burke had been three years prior. His sister-in-law in Kansas City, Maria Spratt, was notified but unable to make the trip due to the expense. Other persons listed as contacts were Duluth, Minnesota, attorney Royal C. Bruen and Calumet City, Illinois, attorney L. Carmine. Neither man was located. Expenses for the funeral were paid for out of Burke's estate.

Park Cemetery[128] in the city of Marquette would be Burke's new confines, far from the streets he once hustled. It was a haven reminiscent of a nature park filled with wildlife, scenic views, and trails, tantalizing to every sense. The crumbled decay of darkness befitting of Burke's deeds, you would not find. A nameless, unknown slice of Earth shall be his. Fred Burke was no longer; Fred Dane was never meant to be. In life, he created who he wanted to become. In death, an unmarked grave was bound to be his legacy.

THE MEMORIES OF THOSE he became close to remained for a short time. "State Street Jerry" said of Burke's prison life, "He ate too much, exercised little, talked seldom, and died as few other men of his type have died–in bed–of natural causes."[129]

Fellow inmate Russell Macklem identified with Burke, having also been convicted of murdering a police officer in 1930. He composed the mournful poem, "Killer" Burke, which appeared in the *Marquette Inmate* in August 1940.

> *"KILLER" BURKE*
> *Oh, "Killer" Burke, he died, they say;*
> *He died within his cell*
> *And what difference, where'er he died,*
> *Could he be deader still?*
> *His was a soul that we may judge;*
> *Yes, by the code of man;*
> *But who are we that we may judge*
> *The soul of another man?*
> *Now, his soul has left his body*
> *And gone beyond this earth;*
> *And maybe there, in the hands of God,*
> *It will have another berth!*
> *So they have carried him away*

From this prison cold and grey,
And buried him on a little hill
So far, far away.
And now he's up in Heaven ~
Away up in the sky;
Yes, he's gone to meet his Maker;
And I'll see him by and by.
  -by Macklem, 46864[130]

PAYING OLD DEBTS

OF THE 313 SENIORS WHO GRADUATED FROM BENTON Harbor High School's Class of 1940, one in particular was ready to set out into the world and make her mark. Eighteen-year-old Mary Emma Moulds had her heart set on a career in nursing. In 1945, she graduated from the St. Joseph's School of Nursing in Mishawaka, Indiana, as one of 11 registered nurses. Undoubtedly, her Uncle Chuck, never far from her mind, was the inspiration behind her career choice.

When Fred Burke passed away in 1940, he left an estate worth $9,000, made up of his sales of leather goods in the prison novelty shop, which he had supervised the last four years of his life. Additionally, $111.13 cash remained in his prison account.[131] Although Michigan governor Luren D. Dickson received complaints from citizens about the wealth accrued by an incarcerated murderer, Warden Simon R. Anderson reiterated that Burke had prospered in the leather-making opportunity granted to him. However, the warden needed to settle the estate, so he contacted Burke's attorney, Charles Gore.

"I had a letter from him in March or April and he appeared to be in good health," remarked Gore. "As for a will, he never asked me to draft one, and I know of no such document."[132]

None of Burke's kin came forward to make a claim on an inheritance. Once funeral expenses were deducted, the remainder of the estate was probated. Herbert J. Potter, an attorney in Ishpeming, Michigan, became the administrator on August 26, 1940, and had 30 days to report to the court with an inventory and potential heirs.

The idea that some of Burke's estate could be used as reward money crossed the mind of Joseph Hunsaker. Having only reaped $250 for Burke's capture, he contacted Green City attorney Robert M. Gifford in September to see if he could help. Gifford inquired with the FBI, who referred him to the Michigan State Police. Seemingly getting the runaround, Gifford finally received a response back from Commissioner Oscar G. Olander, who apparently had forgotten some details.

"I am in receipt of your letter of September 11, and wish to inform you that the State did not offer any reward for the capture of Fred Burke, alias Richard White. I would suggest that you write to the City Attorney of St. Joseph, Michigan, asking if there was any reward at that time."[133]

Hunsaker would have to settle for his $250 because no part of Burke's estate would be used as reward money.

After attending Burke's funeral, former neighbors Jennie Crossman, a 56-year-old widow, and her 30-year-old daughter, Charlotte, both from St. Joseph, Michigan, claimed that Burke had promised to turn over a bank account to them. Warden Anderson checked all local banks for an account in Burke's name, but was unable to locate any such account. The women let it rest after that.

At least two women from Burke's past—his one-time fiancée, Nan Wright, and his former girlfriend, Viola Brenneman—were noticeably missing from his funeral, and various opportunities for them to claim his estate went unanswered. Neither of the women reappeared in the public eye after their short relationships with Burke. However, there were two women who referred to themselves as Burke's sole wife, and both were ready to accept his estate.

The first wife to make a claim was Bonnie Porter White, whom prison officials could not reach at the time of Burke's death; later she had been tracked down living in Chicago and working in a beauty parlor. Theo Marjorie Burke did not come forward until after she received two surprising letters, the first from the probate attorney, Herbert Potter, on February 25, 1941. He had tracked her down in Bremerton, Washington, using the name of Marjorie Burke Wells, and believed she was the only legal heir. After consulting with an attorney, Theo decided to move forward and claim Burke's estate. The second letter was from the Pickaway County, Ohio, treasurer, who was serving legal notice to her regarding delinquent property taxes owed for "now vacant land" that she inherited after the death of her parents. When she failed to answer, the property went on the auction block in June 1941, but it failed to receive any bids.

Having more of an interest in receiving than owing, on July 11, 1941, in the Joseph Vance Building in Seattle, Washington, Theo, as Marjorie Burke Wells, was deposed in the matter of the estate of Fred Burke. A 32-year-old attorney, John Cartano of the Seattle firm of Peyser and Bailey, represented her. Walter Achesen acted as commissioner for the examination, granted by the Marquette County probate judge, the Honorable Carroll C. Rushton. Theo attested to her marriage to Fred Burke, providing a copy of the marriage certificate, her 1927 Pennsylvania driver's license, photographs, and a 1931 letter written to her by Burke while in prison. In typical fashion, Theo was grilled about the details of her first marriage and divorce from William Gephart, her whirlwind romance with Burke, and her subsequent 11-year separation from him without ever divorcing. Cartano asked why Burke had never taken legal steps to secure a divorce.

"In the first place, he was greatly afraid of publicity and the possibility of arrest,"[134] Theo replied.

Although they were separated at the time of Officer Charles Skelly's shooting on December 14, 1929, she explained to Cartano that she did have some limited contact with her husband. "He had given me his promise to 'go straight,' and I found from some men that he was associating with, that he was deceiving me in that respect," she said. "I became angry upon discovering this fact, and went to Detroit without him. While in Detroit, I learned that he had gotten into further trouble in St. Joe, Michigan. Shortly, I received a letter through one of his friends asking me to go to Piedmont, California, because his two sisters resided in California. But instead, I came to Seattle, as I had a relative here."

"Will you state why you dropped the name of Theo on occasions?"

"Because of the spelling, T-H-E-O," she testified, saying each letter aloud. "In business transactions, it was always listed as Mister and confusion sometimes arose as to whether I was a man or a woman."

"Did you ever, at any time, divorce Thomas Camp, alias Fred Burke, alias Fred Dane?" questioned Cartano.

"No, I never have, nor did I ever contemplate such action, nor have I ever discussed such action with anyone," Theo defiantly answered, punctuating her speech. "There is no record of any divorce proceedings connected with myself and Fred Burke, because no action was ever taken by myself, nor was I connected with any proceedings ever instituted by himself."

Theo brought up the fact that she received letters from Burke while he was on the lam, and they were always sent through an intermediary and never with a return address on them. After reading each letter, she destroyed them. Then regular correspondence with him suddenly ceased around January 1931.

As questioning continued, Theo was forthright, "Most of these events have transpired over ten years ago, and I have tried my best to forget this part of my life. However, the dates and answers I have given are correct to the best of my knowledge and belief."[135]

The following month, Bonnie Porter White hired 56-year-old Chicago attorney John A. Pakenham, who made an appearance on her behalf in the Marquette County, Michigan, probate court on August 28, 1941. In the proceedings following Theo's deposition, Pakenham, in trying to discredit Theo Burke's claim, had discovered that a woman using the name of Marjorie Wells in Port Orchard, Washington, was living as the wife of John P. Wells, a stevedore at the Puget Sound Naval Shipyard in Bremerton. Pakenham produced a certified copy of an application to declare her the guardian of John P. Wells, as his wife, on the grounds of his incompetency. A certified copy of joint property ownership had also been uncovered. Furthermore, he learned that this same woman had been the Kitsap County assistant treasurer in 1934. Feeling that these points needed further investigation, Pakenham asked for a continuance of 30 days. "If what I said is true, then fraud is attempted to be perpetrated on this court," blasted Pakenham, suggesting that if Theo/Marjorie had married someone else, then she had no claim on Burke's estate.

Representing Theo Burke in Michigan was Ishpeming attorney Francis A. Bell, the son of a Marquette circuit court judge. Bell insisted that Theo had never remarried.

"Of course we have no way of knowing that this is the same party," Judge Carroll C. Rushton responded to the claim.

"I am only putting this forth to say that this would warrant more time for investigation," expressed Pakenham. "We want to do it for two reasons: One is the value of the estate. But the paramount reason is that the family of this woman, Bonnie Porter, whom Burke or Dane married when she was just a child, is a respectable family and they are very much upset over the thought that there was not a marriage. And we want to try and prove, for good name's sake, that she was legally married to Fred Burke, using the alias of Richard F. White."[136]

The judge granted the 30-day continuance. Pakenham said that on or before September 29, 1941, he would either introduce new testimony showing that Theo Marjorie Burke had become divorced from Fred Burke and married again, or that he would withdraw Bonnie Porter White's claim altogether. The date arrived, but despite great efforts, Pakenham had been unable to locate John P. Wells. Having heard no new testimony, Judge Rushton scheduled the decision to be announced on December 8. In appearance at that time were attorney Bell; Herbert J. Potter, administrator for the Burke estate; and Judge Rushton. The court found in favor of Theo Marjorie Burke, making her the sole heir to Burke's estate.

ON OCTOBER 31, 1941, Potter sent a letter to the Marquette city clerk, Mary Hogan, inquiring about the possibility of erecting a grave marker for Burke upon his burial site in Park Cemetery. He pointed out "there are funds" for this request. Rather than etching one of Burke's many alias names on the marker, the question was posed if there would be any objection to using his birth name instead. Marquette city officials had no objection, so long as it adhered to the specifications set for all markers.

Theo Marjorie Burke shared with her husband that which she had been given. As a final act of love for Fred Burke in his death, his interment site for eternity would be marked with a modest stone that read Thomas A. Camp 1893–1940.

Theo, as Marjorie Wells, continued her low-key life in the state of Washington. Through the years, she moved several times, living in Bremerton, Port Orchard, and Retsil, located on Puget Sound. Mystery surrounded much of her life: her educational achievements that mimicked those of her first husband, her hometown, her name variations, and even her age. Before the end of the decade, though, a Pandora's Box would be opened and the truth about Theo would be revealed.

On August 9, 1947, Theo entered the Northern State Mental Hospital in Sedro-Woolley, Washington, which was not only a home for the mentally unstable and clinically insane, but also where some murderers and sociopaths awaited their day in court. Even after Burke's death, Theo remained united with liberated wrongdoers. As it would turn out, she was a wrongdoer herself. On August 30, 1949, after suffering from bronchopneumonia and toxemia, Theo quietly passed away. The truth of her age was exposed on her death certificate: She died at the age of 70, 15 years older than she had been passing herself as being. Despite her earlier denials, Theo had in fact married John P. Wells in 1931. In all actuality, she had been born Theo May Walston on October 11, 1877, in Deer Creek, Ohio—and not 1892 in Columbus—the only child of John Walston and Mary A. Claridge Walston.[137] Theo probably met her first husband, William F. Gephart, in Deer Creek Township, where they grew up, and married him in 1901, when both of them were 24 years old. They soon relocated to St. Louis, Missouri. When the couple divorced in November 1925, Theo took on a new persona, one of a woman 15 years younger than her true age and one that mimicked the educational attainment of her former husband. After meeting Fred "Killer" Burke in early 1926, the pair were married within two months. Not unlike Burke, Theo lived as a different person all the way up until her death.

AFTER REALIZING THAT HER MARRIAGE to Burke, as Richard White, was not legal, Bonnie Porter White continued to work for a time at the Belmont Harbor Beauty Salon in Chicago, Illinois, and dropped the surname White. Not long afterward, she returned to Kansas City, Missouri, where she met divorcee Wilmot S. Bannon; he enlisted in the United States Army in March 1942. The two became husband and wife in June 1943, but their happiness was short-lived. Not long after their wedding, Bannon was critically injured in the Mojave Desert during a training mission. The wounds proved too much, and Bannon died on the operating table in December 1944, making Bonnie a widow after less than two years of marriage. She found love again when she married William MacGregor Hall in 1951 in Chicago, and they later moved to West Virginia. Bonnie Porter Hall died on June 17, 1994, on what would have been her 64th wedding anniversary with Richard F. White, really Fred Burke. She was 83 years old.[138]

Fred "Killer" Burke's final resting place in Park Cemetery, Marquette, Michigan, with his birth name, Thomas A. Camp. *Author's collection.*

"DO YOU BELIEVE IN SANTA CLAUS?"

NEITHER PRISON NOR DEATH FORMED AN OBSTACLE FOR Chicago's South Side Outfit. Without the bootlegging industry, and the gambling arena too hot, gangs began to focus on other marketable vices. Hollywood was a fresh scene to infiltrate, and while much of the world was wrapped up in the activities of the Second World War, those remaining in the syndicate devised a scheme to shake down and muscle in on the labor unions. When one key player began to flaunt his newfound wealth, authorities caught on and opened up an investigation that named Frank Nitti, Louis Campagna, Phil D'Andrea, Paul Ricca, Charles Gioe, and others in a million-dollar extortion campaign.

All of the men were indicted on March 18, 1943, and the next day Frank Nitti blew his brains out. By then, Nitti's predecessor, Al Capone, was a mere shell of his former self, in a body ravaged by the effects of syphilis since his release from prison in 1939. Capone then moved to his Palm Island, Florida, estate, where he died of bronchopneumonia and a stroke on January 25, 1947, at the age of 48.

D'Andrea still maintained his residence in St. Joseph, Michigan, but sold the property after his indictment in 1943, receiving $30,000.[139] In 1944, he and Campagna, Ricca, and Gioe each received sentences of 10 years in federal prison, but gangland proved it still held the reins, when all four men were hastily paroled in 1947, after serving only three years and four months. Shortly thereafter, this outrage made it all the way to Washington, DC.

Clare Eugene Hoffman, a Republican congressman from Allegan County, Michigan, and a former prosecutor, launched an investigation into these early paroles. He pointed out the unethical conduct of several attorneys who were hired to represent the parolees. One such attorney, Pat Dillon, used his friendly intervention in Washington, DC, having previously managed President Harry Truman's run for the senate in 1934. Hoffman noted that in February 1948, Louis Campagna's wife, Charlotte, admitted that she paid Dillon $10,000 to help her husband obtain parole.[140] Hoffman also discovered that Dallas, Texas, attorney Maury Hughes, a friend of United States Attorney General Thomas Clark, had aided the gangsters in obtaining their early freedom. Hughes testified that a man he did not know in New York gave him "a big bundle of cash on the street," with instructions to take the money to the Federal Court Building and enter motions to quash any outstanding indictments against the four parolees, which he did.

During the Hoffman Committee hearings, two men from Berrien Springs, Michigan, who sponsored Campagna's release, became, in turn, part of the investigation. Guy Frank Heim, a 54-year-old former village president, and 51-year-old Lyle E. Lucas, the editor of the Berrien Springs *Journal-Era* Newspaper, testified during the hearings that their friendship with Campagna was casual and that he appeared to be "a very nice person." Heim added that he met Campagna from his patronage at the drug store he operated, where the members of his family would come in frequently to purchase whatever they wanted without asking the price.

Lucas told a *Chicago Daily Tribune* reporter in September 1947, "I have known Campagna for quite a few years. I didn't know too much, about what he was in jail for. But I've known him for a long time as him being a good citizen. He has a farm up here, always seemed to be a decent sort of chap, so I volunteered to write a letter to the parole board."[141]

Aside from questionable reasons for the early paroles, the lack of income tax payments was another key point brought up during the hearings. Handling the fiscal improprieties for Campagna and Ricca was a Chicago tax attorney and former Internal Revenue Service agent, Eugene Bernstein. Campagna and Ricca failed to file income tax returns for the years 1935 through 1941, owing the Department of the Treasury a total of $468,877 between them. Bernstein arranged a settlement for both men in October 1946; the combined liabilities were disposed of for $120,000 plus $70,000 in penalties, all paid for by anonymous donors.

When Hoffman asked about who the donors were, Campagna responded, "I don't know who made the settlement and I don't know how much had been paid."

"Mr. Campagna," asked Hoffman, "do you believe in Santa Claus?"

"Yes, yes. After all this," Campagna said, "I suppose I do. I mean if you were me, wouldn't you?" The reply prompted a few chuckles within the room.

When Ricca was questioned, he told the committee, "It was a friend of mine. I would put up $190,000 for a friend of mine who needed it."

Attorney Bernstein's secretary, Geneva Cox, recounted that the unidentified donors came into the office between September and October 1946. She said she did not know any of the gentlemen, but did describe one as, "... an Italian about 45 years of age, medium build, and of dark coloring." Cox believed the man was a relative of Louis Campagna, but was not positive.[142]

When it came time for attorney Bernstein to take the stand, he quickly offered, "I am the one who paid the $78,000 tax lien settlement. In fact, eight or nine persons came into my office at different times and plunked down $10,000 or so on my desk and said, 'This is for Louie.' I gave them receipts but I don't know who they were. You don't ask those fellows any questions."

Bernstein described the donors as being "... of different statures, some having a dark complexion." One individual he described as "... rather thin and small, about five-foot-two-inches."

When asked to clarify how he defined a gangster, Bernstein testified, "The word 'gangster' has a different connotation to me than it may have to other people. A gangster is an individual who goes out and, by means of force, duress, obtains sums of money. If you and I go out and do certain things legally, and place funds in his possession without duress, at our own direction, and then he does something with that, that would not be gangsters. Gangsterism is very definitely a form of violence."[143]

In the final Congressional Report, Hoffman concluded that, "The syndicate has given the most striking demonstration of political clout in the history of the republic."

The pressure created by the hearings prompted the parole board to rescind the paroles for Campagna, Ricca, D'Andrea, and Gioe. Ricca appeared in court on June 15, 1948, and Gioe was taken into custody on July 23. In an attempt to locate Campagna at his Berrien Springs, Michigan, estate, United States marshals joined the forces of Berrien County sheriff Erwin Kubath, who had been the wide-eyed deputy serving under Sheriff Fred Bryant during the search for Fred Burke. Working on behalf of the federal court system, three marshals met up with Sheriff Kubath and Deputies Jack Krug, Victor Yost, and Edward Sandara. They took positions outside the iron gates of the Campagna estate while Kubath shouted to be let in. Finally, after 15 minutes of verbal commands, a girl appeared at the gate saying she was Louis Campagna's daughter.

"Do you have a warrant?" the girl asked.

"Yes," Kubath responded.

"A search warrant?"

Admitting they did not have a search warrant, Kubath explained to the girl that they would not hesitate to shoot the lock off the gate if not let in. The seriousness of the situation must have been apparent when the girl asked them to wait while she went into the guard shack to telephone the main house. Finally, the gate opened, and the officers were allowed through. They immediately began searching for Campagna on one of the most impressive properties in the area. The rooms were spacious; the basement included a cold storage facility and storerooms, while the second floor was exquisitely furnished. Bedrooms were on the third floor, and a cabana on the roof overlooked the entire property. Unfortunately, the law enforcement officers did not find Campagna during this search, but later learned that he had fled the residence and surrendered himself in Chicago on that very afternoon.[144]

The enormous scope of information learned during the Hoffman Committee hearings and subsequent court proceedings became the first step in a much larger revelation. Although J. Edgar Hoover insisted that crime was a local problem and refused to admit that a syndicate of mobsters even existed, others had contrary beliefs. Beginning on May 11, 1950, Tennessee senator Estes Kefauver led the United States Senate hearings, coined as the "Kefauver Committee," into organized crime's influence on interstate commerce. Six hundred witnesses would testify in 14 major cities through August 1951 in the first-ever nationally televised hearing, giving Americans their first true glimpse of gangsters and the power they wielded. Over 30 million viewers tuned in to see the likes of Frank Costello, Louis Campagna, Phil D'Andrea, Eugene Bernstein, Charles Gioe, Jake Guzik, Virginia Hill, Meyer Lansky, Paul Ricca, Mickey Cohen, and Tony Accardo.

Time Magazine wrote, "From Manhattan to as far west as the coaxial cable ran, the United States adjusted itself to Kefauver's schedule. Dishes stood in sinks, babies went unfed, business sagged, and department stores emptied while the hearings were on."

One particular witness with potentially explosive testimony never got the chance to speak in front of the Kefauver committee. Lieutenant William Drury of the Chicago Police Department, who had begun moonlighting as a newspaper reporter for the *Chicago Herald American*, and later set up his own private detective agency, had provided much unwanted publicity for the syndicate. Drury helped investigate the case of a woman's body found dumped near Jean Klock Park in Benton Harbor, Michigan, on September 9, 1947. She was later identified as 19-year-old Catherine "Tina" Jacobs of Calumet City, Illinois, a dice girl and prostitute, who had been married just a few days earlier. Working directly with Berrien County sheriff Erwin Kubath, Drury became more of a hindrance by holding witnesses back and never bringing any substantial information to the investigation. Less than a month later, Drury was suspended and ultimately fired from the Chicago Police Department. Drury knew enough about the syndicate to be dangerous and just as he was about to open the floodgates with his testimony in the Kefauver hearings, professional gunmen ensured that he would be a no-show. Police found Drury shot to death in his garage on September 25, 1950, and no one was quite sure what he might have revealed. However, not unlike the former newspaper reporter-turned-mouthpiece for both sides of the law, Jake Lingle, Drury received the same silencing treatment for his ambiguous alliances.[145]

An article in *Life Magazine* captured the energy of the Kefauver hearings: "The week of March 12, 1951, will occupy a special place in history... people had suddenly gone indoors into living rooms, taverns, and clubrooms, auditoriums and back-offices. There, in eerie half-light, looking at millions of small frosty screens, people sat as if charmed. Never before had the attention of the nation been riveted so completely on a single matter."

When the Senate committee members wrapped up their massive investigation into the activities of gangsters all over the country on August 31, 1951, more than a year after it began, Senator Estes Kefauver summed up the findings in a final report:

> "A nationwide crime syndicate does exist in the United States of America, despite the protestations of a strangely assorted company of criminals, self-serving politicians, plain blind fools, and others who may be honestly misguided that there is no such combine. Behind the local mobs, which make up the national crime syndicate, is a shadowy international criminal organization known as the Mafia, so fantastic that most Americans find it hard to believe that it really exists.[146]
>
> The Mafia is based fundamentally on muscle and murder, ruthless destruction of anyone who betrays its secrets and the use of all means available, such as political influence, bribery, or intimidation, to defeat any attempt on the part of law enforcement agencies to touch its top figures or to interfere with its organization."[147]

One by one, death claimed the last of the Gangster Era players. Phil D'Andrea succumbed to an illness on September 18, 1952, in Riverside, California. Charles Gioe served as a top commander in the syndicate after the parole scandal, but on August 18, 1954, gang rivals shot and killed him. Louis Campagna maintained control of the syndicate until May 30, 1955, when he suffered a fatal heart attack after reeling in a 30-pound grouper off the coast of Florida. Death by natural causes claimed Jake "Greasy Thumb" Guzik on February 21, 1956; John "The Boy Mayor" Patton on December 23, 1956; Johnny Torrio on April 16, 1957; Claude Maddox on June 21, 1958; and Anthony "Mops" Volpe in January 1965. Paul Ricca sold his Long Beach, Indiana, residence for $150,000 in 1956 to the Detroit Teamsters. James R. "Jimmy" Hoffa, a vice-president of the International Brotherhood of Teamsters, explained to the press that the union intended to use the Ricca property for training.[148] Ricca eventually relocated to Detroit, where he suffered a heart attack and died on October 11, 1972.

IN 1963, RENOWNED AND OUTSPOKEN syndicated newspaper columnist Drew Pearson wrote an editorial entitled, "Chicago, City of Death, Is Gangland's Dark Den," where he observed, "Since 1919, there have been 976 murders in Chicago. Only two have been solved. It doesn't pay to fight the underworld in Chicago."[149]

By then, most gangsters had met their fate, which helped establish the next generation of underworld figures known as the Mafia. Forensics and ballistics had become standard investigative practice among law enforcement agencies all over the world, while the likes of Capone and Dillinger have become time-forsaken characters of American society. Saint Valentine reclaimed February 14 from its monstrous association of 1929. In 1962, the United States Congress designated every May 15 as Peace Officers Memorial Day, honoring all those who died in the line of duty. St. Joseph police officer Charles Skelly is among those honored each year. His name is carved into the marble walls of the National Law Enforcement Officers Memorial in Washington, DC, and on the Berrien County Fallen Officers Memorial in Lake Bluff Park, St. Joseph, Michigan, just steps away from the spot where Skelly's final act of courage took place.

THERE IS NO GREAT LESSON, only history, to reflect upon.

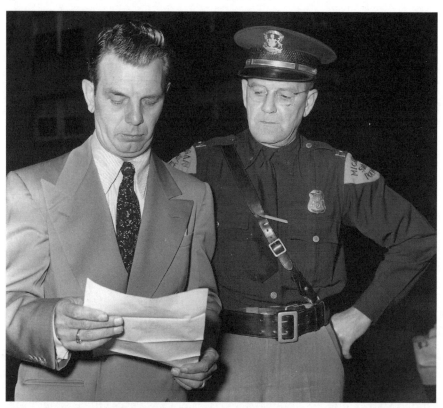

Berrien County Sheriff Erwin Kubath and Fifth District Commander of the Michigan State Police Captain William B. Babcock, 1947. *Author's collection.*

The body of Al Capone in his casket, January 1947. *Courtesy of Mario Gomes.*

Attorney Eugene Bernstein testifying during the Kefauver Committee hearings in 1950. *Author's collection.*

The Berrien County Fallen Officer's Memorial in St. Joseph, Michigan. *Author's collection.*

If you enjoyed *A Killing in Capone's Playground,* consider reading: *OFF COLOR: The Violent History of Detroit's Notorious Purple Gang.*

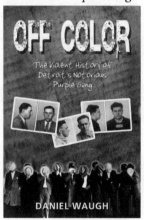

A vivid and compelling chronicle of the life and crimes of Detroit's infamous Purple Gang.

Endnotes

1   State of Michigan Department of Public Safety. *Fred Burke.* "Marquette Post Fred Burke Investigation." Case #2208. May 6, 1931. December 14, 1929 – July 10, 1940. Michigan State Police. Lansing, MI.

2   State of Michigan Department of Public Safety. *Fred Burke.* "Memo to J. C. Sakraida from Commissioner Oscar Olander." Case #2208. May 4, 1931. December 14, 1929 – July 10, 1940. Michigan State Police. Lansing, MI.

3   Federal Bureau of Investigation. *Criminal Record of Frederick R. Burke – FBI #43089 (Deceased).* "Memorandum for Assistant Attorney General Dodds from Director J. Edgar Hoover." Washington, DC. July 22, 1931.

4   Federal Bureau of Investigation. *Criminal Record of Frederick R. Burke – FBI #43089 (Deceased).* "Memorandum for Mr. Hoover from Assistant Attorney General Nugent Dodds." Washington, DC. July 22, 1931.

5   *Salt Lake Tribune.* October 10, 1935. 3.

6   *Oakland Tribune.* October 10, 1935.

7   Federal Bureau of Investigation. *Criminal Record of Frederick R. Burke – FBI #43089 (Deceased)* "United States Department of Justice Letter to J. Edgar Hoover from Special Agent J. W. Vincent." September 11, 1940, Washington, DC.

8   *Ironwood Daily Globe.* October 17, 1931. 5.

9   Michigan Department of Public Safety. *Fred Burke.* "Harry Hendricks Letter Sent to Fred Burke." Case #2208. November 12, 1931. Michigan State Police. Lansing, MI.

10 J. Victor Bate. "Trail's End for the Man Who Murdered 20." *True Detective Mysteries,* July 1941.

11 Joseph S. Kostka. *Early Days with the Michigan State Police.* June 7, 1967. Michigan State Archives, Lansing, MI.

12 Ret/Lt. Kenneth White. *Remembrances.* Michigan State Archives. RG 90-240. Box 55. Folder 11. Lansing, MI.

13 Mary DeMott. "To Preserve, Protect and Defend!" *Wilderness Chronicle,* September 2003.

14 Ret. Lt. Kenneth White. *Remembrances.*

15 *Niles Star.* Niles, MI. January 12, 1932. 42.

16 Donna Gillette Groulx. Interview by author. St. Joseph, MI. September 15, 2008.

17 State of Michigan Department of Public Safety. *Arrest of Jerry Kral (Gus Winkeler) and J. R. Moran (John Clyatt).* New Buffalo Post. August 6, 1931. Michigan State Police. Lansing, MI.

18 State of Michigan Department of Public Safety. *Traffic Accident Report of C.J. Anderson and Jerry Kral.* New Buffalo Post. August 5, 1931. Michigan State Police. Lansing, MI.

19 State of Michigan Department of Public Safety. *Traffic Accident Report of C.J. Anderson and Jerry Kral.* New Buffalo Post. August 5, 1931. Michigan State Police. Lansing, MI.

20 State of Michigan Department of Public Safety. *Arrest of Jerry Kral (Gus Winkeler) and J. R. Moran (John Clyatt).* New Buffalo Post. August 6, 1931. Michigan State Police. Lansing, MI.

21 John Carter, MD. "History of Lakeland Hospital in the Twin Cities." Lecture, The Heritage Museum and Cultural Center. St. Joseph, MI. July 22, 2010.

22 Nineteen Hundred Thirty United States Federal Census. Hamtramck, Wayne, Michigan. Roll 1072. Page 5B. Enumeration District 950. Image 1008.0. http://www.ancestry.com. (Accessed June 26, 2010).

23 Berrien County Historical Association. *Berrien County Dentist's, Registry.* http://www. berrienhistory.org/images/Medical%20Dentist's%20Registry.pdf. (Accessed February 13, 2011).

24 Federal Bureau of Investigation. *Barker-Karpis Gang, Bremer Kidnapping.* http:// vault.fbi.gov/barker-karpis-gang. (Accessed October 24, 2011).

25 St. Louis Police Department. *Bertillon and Criminal Identification Bureau Record No. 21181.* "Memo from Acting Chief John H. Glassco to Sheriff Fred Cutler." August 11, 1931. St. Louis, MO.

26 *News-Palladium.* August 7, 1931. 1.

27 *St. Petersburg Times.* St. Petersburg, FL. August 7, 1931. 2.

28 Groulx, interview.

29 St. Louis Police Department. *Narrative of Arrest, Fred Burke, Milford Jones, Gus Winkler.* June 5, 1925. St. Louis, MO.

30 *Hamilton Evening Journal.* Hamilton, OH. August 8, 1931. 10.

31 *News-Palladium.* August 7, 1931. 1.

32 Georgette Winkeler. *Georgette Winkeler Memoirs.* "Trouble." Federal Bureau of Investigation, Washington, DC. 1934.

33 Georgette Winkeler. *Georgette Winkeler Memoirs.* "His Pal Bailey." Federal Bureau of Investigation, Washington, DC. 1934.

34 Groulx, interview.

35 *Herald-Press.* August 8, 1931. 1, 3.

36 ---August 8, 1931. 1.

37 ---August 11, 1931. 1, 4.

38 State of Michigan Department of Public Safety. *Special Report: Trooper Myron Gillette.* "Report from Captain W. B. Babcock to Captain J. C. Cleghorn." Paw Paw Post. June 21, 1932, Paw Paw, MI.

39 State of Michigan Department of Public Safety. *Special Report: Trooper Myron Gillette.* "Memo to Captain J. C. Cleghorn from Captain W. B. Babcock." Paw Paw Post. June 21, 1932, Paw Paw, MI.

40 *Herald-Press.* August 14, 1931. 1.

41 *News-Palladium.* August 10, 1931. 1.

42 ---August 20, 1931. 1.

43 ---August 20, 1931. 1.

44 ---August 31, 1931. 1.

45 John Winkeler. Interviewed by author. St. Joseph, MI. September 15, 2008. – Address should be 4985 Siebert.

46 Berrien County Jail Ledger Books. "August Winkeler Jail Booking Record." August 31, 1931. Number 8. Page 253. Berrien County Historical Association: Berrien Springs, MI.

47 Georgette Winkeler. *Georgette Winkeler Memoirs.* "And Other False Friends." Federal Bureau of Investigation, Washington, DC. 1934.

48 *Herald-Press.* August 7, 1931.

49 Ruth Magdzinski. Interview with author. St. Joseph, MI. February 15, 2012.

50 Fort Miami Heritage Society of Michigan. "Al Capone and the Society Ladies." *Spring Newsletter,* 1998.

51 Article incorrectly refers to O'Connor as Dennis O'Connor when it should be Daniel J. O'Connor.

52 *Pittsburgh Post-Gazette.* Pittsburgh, PA. July 29, 1931. 24.

53 *Herald-Press.* July 27, 1931. 1.

54 *Chicago Daily Tribune.* July 26, 1931. 3.
55 ---February 1, 1947. 3.
56 *Herald-Press.* August 3, 1931. 1, 3.
57 ---July 27, 1931. 2.
58 ---August 10, 1931. 1.
59 ---August 18, 1931.
60 *Constitution Tribune.* September 15, 1931. 6.
61 *New York Times* Movie Reviews. "How Burke Was Captured." 2011.
62 *Daily Capital News and Post-Tribune.* Jefferson City, MO. February 21, 1932. 1
63 Shirley Price. Interview with author. St. Joseph, MI. September 3, 2010.
64 *News-Palladium.* February 5, 1932. 1.
65 *Herald-Press.* September 6, 1932.
66 St. Joseph City Fire Department. *Daily Log.* September 3, 1932. St. Joseph, MI.
67 ---May 22, 1933.
68 *News-Palladium.* February 1, 1947. 3.
69 Federal Bureau of Investigation. *Barker-Karpis Gang, Bremer Kidnapping.* Part 119(1). http://vault.fbi.gov/barker-karpis-gang. (Accessed October 24, 2011).
70 *Chicago Daily Tribune.* August 28, 1934. 6.
71 Calvin H. Goddard. "A History of Firearm Identification." "Police 13-13." *Chicago Police Journal*, 1936.
72 http://www.drugtext.org/Wickersham-Commission-Report/message.html. (Accessed November 26, 2011).
73 National Center for Health Statistics in 2009 lists the homicide rate for the United States at 6.1 per every 100,000 people.
74 Edward Butts. *Outlaws of the Lakes: Bootlegging & Smuggling from Colonial Times to Prohibition, a Prohibition Primer.* Toronto: Lynx Images, 2004.
75 Internal Revenue Service. 1921, 1966, 1970. 95, 6, 73.
76 *Illinois Crime Survey.* "A Who's Who of Organized Crime in Chicago." Illinois Association for Criminal Justice, 1929.
77 Jeff Burkhart. "Something to Celebrate: Repeal of Prohibition." *Marin Independent Journal*, December 7, 2007.
78 Amy Lee Sheppard. "Officer Down." *Michigan History Magazine*, January/February 2007.
79 http://www.fbi.gov/about-us/history. (Accessed May 5, 2012).
80 Oscar G. Olander. "Michigan State Police, A Twenty-Five Year History: Become State Police." *Michigan State Journal Press.* 1942. 59-60.
81 *Kokomo Tribune.* January 27, 1932. 1, 11.
82 *Kokomo Tribune.* January 27, 1932. 1, 11.
83 Dan Anderson and Laurence J. Yadon. *One Hundred Oklahoma Outlaws, Gangsters and Lawmen, 1839-1939.* "Kidnapping, Inc." Pelican Publishing Company, 2007.
84 Federal Bureau of Investigation, *Report of Agent John L. Madala with Georgette Winkeler Marsh.* May 15-18, 1936. Washington, DC.
85 Georgette Winkeler. *Georgette Winkeler Memoirs.* "Big Mike." Federal Bureau of Investigation, Washington, DC. 1934.
86 William Radkay told to Patty Terry. *A Devil Incarnate: From Altar Boy to Alcatraz.* Leawood, KS: Leathers Publishing, 2005.
87 State of Illinois. County of Cook. "Marriage License for August Winkler and Georgette Bence." December 16, 1931. Chicago, IL.

88   Harold Cummins. "Attempts to Alter and Obliterate Finger-Prints." *Journal of Criminal Law and Criminology* (1931-1951). Volume 25. Number 6. March - April 1935. Northwestern University, 982-991. http://www.jstor.org/stable/1134845. (Accessed on March 5, 2013).

89   Daniel Waugh. *Egan's Rats: The Untold Story of the Prohibition-Era Gang That Ruled St. Louis*. Nashville, TN: Cumberland House Publishing, 2007.

90   Georgette Winkeler. *Georgette Winkeler Memoirs*. "The Torn Curtain." Federal Bureau of Investigation, Washington, DC. 1934.

91   Federal Bureau of Investigation. *St. Valentine's Day Massacre*. Part 001. http://vault. fbi.gov/St.%20Valentines%20Day%20Massacre. (Accessed July 20, 2010).

92   William J. Helmer and Art J. Bilek. *The St. Valentine's Day Massacre*. "The Crime Nobody Wanted Solved." Nashville, TN: Cumberland House Publishing, 2004.

93   *Jefferson City Post-Tribune*. January 23, 1935. 1.

94   Federal Bureau of Investigation. *St. Valentine's Day Massacre*. "*Chicago American*" Part 002. January 24, 1935. http://vault.fbi.gov/St.%20Valentines%20Day%20 Massacre. (Accessed July 20, 2010).

95   *Evansville Press*. Evansville, IN. October 14, 1934.

96   Georgette Winkeler. *Georgette Winkeler Memoirs*. "Hideout." Federal Bureau of Investigation, Washington, DC. 1934.

97   Georgette Winkeler. *Georgette Winkeler Memoirs*. "Hideout." Federal Bureau of Investigation, Washington, DC. 1934.

98   Georgette Winkeler. *Georgette Winkeler Memoirs*. "Fugitives." Federal Bureau of Investigation, Washington, DC.1934.

99   Georgette Winkeler. *Georgette Winkeler Memoirs*. "Trouble." Federal Bureau of Investigation, Washington, DC. 1934.

100   Federal Bureau of Investigation. *Bremer Kidnapping*. Part 45. http://vault.fbi.gov/ barker-karpis-gang/bremer-kidnapping. (Accessed February 15, 2012).

101   Federal Bureau of Investigation. *Bremer Kidnapping*. Part 45. http://vault.fbi.gov/ barker-karpis-gang/bremer-kidnapping. (Accessed February 15, 2012).

102   Federal Bureau of Investigation. *Bremer Kidnapping*. "Summary." November 19, 1936. http://vault.fbi.gov/barker-karpis-gang/bremer-kidnapping. (Accessed February 15, 2012).

103   Federal Bureau of Investigation. *Bremer Kidnapping*. Part 109. http://vault.fbi.gov/ barker-karpis-gang/bremer-kidnapping. (Accessed February 15, 2012).

104   Federal Bureau of Investigation. *Barker-Karpis Gang, Bremer Kidnapping*. Part 119(1). http://vault.fbi.gov/barker-karpis-gang. (Accessed October 24, 2011).

105   *Chicago Daily Tribune*. October 17, 1935. 10.

106   Federal Bureau of Investigation. *Lester Joseph Gillis aka Baby Face Nelson*. Part 1. http://vault.fbi.gov/George%20%28Baby%20Face%29%20Nelson. (Accessed October 29, 2011).

107   Federal Bureau of Investigation. *Lester Joseph Gillis aka Baby Face Nelson*. Part 1. http://vault.fbi.gov/George%20%28Baby%20Face%29%20Nelson. (Accessed October 29, 2011).

108   Federal Bureau of Investigation. *Barker-Karpis Gang, Bremer Kidnapping*. http:// vault.fbi.gov/barker-karpis-gang. (Accessed October 24, 2011).

109   Federal Bureau of Investigation. *Al (Alphonse) Capone*. Part 3C. http://vault.fbi.gov/ Al%20Capone. (Accessed December 6, 2010).

110   Federal Bureau of Investigation. *Al (Alphonse) Capone*. Part 3C. http://vault.fbi.gov/ Al%20Capone. (Accessed December 6, 2010).

111 Federal Bureau of Investigation. *Al (Alphonse) Capone.* Part 3D. http://vault.fbi.gov/
Al%20Capone. (Accessed December 6, 2010).

112 Federal Bureau of Investigation. *Al (Alphonse) Capone.* Part 3D. http://vault.fbi.gov/
Al%20Capone. (Accessed December 6, 2010).

113 Federal Bureau of Investigation. *Bremer Kidnapping.* Part 212. http://vault.fbi.gov/
barker-karpis-gang/bremer-kidnapping. (Accessed February 15, 2012).

114 William J. Helmer. *Al Capone and His American Boys: Memoirs of a Mobster's Wife.*
"Biographies and Historical Notes." Bloomington, IN: Indiana University Press, 2011,
358.

115 Michiel Van Kets. "Limousines of the US Presidency – A Ride Through History."
http://www.articlesnatch.com/Article/Limousines-Of-The-Us-Presidency---A-Ride-
Through-History/930663. (Accessed December 12, 2011).

116 J. Victor Bate. "Trail's End for the Man Who Murdered 20." *True Detective Mysteries,*
July 1941.

117 Marvin L. Coon. Warden. State House of Corrections and Branch Prison State House
of Corrections and Branch Prison – Marquette, Michigan. *Biennial Report Covering
Period from January 1, 1937 to December 31, 1938.* John M. Longyear Research
Library. Marquette Regional History Center. Marquette, MI.

118 J. Victor Bate. "Trail's End for the Man Who Murdered 20." *True Detective Mysteries,*
July 1941.

119 *News-Palladium.* July 11, 1940. 6.

120 Federal Bureau of Investigation. *Criminal Record of Frederick R. Burke – FBI #43089
(Deceased)* "United States Department of Justice Letter to J. Edgar Hoover from
Special Agent J. W. Vincent." September 11, 1940, Washington, DC.

121 *News-Palladium.* July 13, 1940. 10.

122 William J. Helmer and Rick Mattix. *The Complete Public Enemy Almanac.*
"Depression-Era Crime." Nashville, TN: Cumberland House Publishing, 2007.

123 Gladys Wells Crumpacker. Robert Wood Wilson ed. *The Complete History of Sullivan
County Missouri. Volume II, 1900-1979.* Milan, MO: History Publications, 1980.

124 *Daily Mining Journal.* "Fred Burke Not Only One to Waste Talents." Marquette, MI.
July 13, 1940.

125 J. Victor Bate. "Trail's End for the Man Who Murdered 20." *True Detective Mysteries,*
July 1941.

126 Ike Wood. *One Hundred Years of Hard Labor – A History of Marquette State Prison.*
Centennial Edition. KA-ED Publishing Company, 1985.

127 P. J. Kosmoff. ed. "Requiescat in Pace." Volume 8, Number 10. "Killer Burke."
Volume 8, Number 10. *Marquette Inmate.* July 1940. John M. Longyear Research
Library, Marquette Regional History Center.
Marquette, MI.

128 City of Marquette, Michigan. *Park Cemetery.* Cummings Plat #5. Marquette, MI.

129 J. Victor Bate. "Trail's End for the Man Who Murdered 20." *True Detective Mysteries,*
July 1941.

130 P. J. Kosmoff. ed. "Requiescat in Pace." Volume 8, Number 10. "Killer Burke."
Volume 8, Number 10. *Marquette Inmate.* August 1940. John M. Longyear Research
Library, Marquette Regional History Center. Marquette, MI.

131 *Omaha World Herald.* August 21, 1940. 4.

132 *News-Palladium.* July 13, 1940. 10.

133 State of Michigan Department of Public Safety. *Fred Burke.* "Correspondence between Commissioner Oscar Olander and Attorney R. M. Gifford." September 11-13, 1940. Case #2208. Michigan State Police. Lansing, MI.

134 Marquette County Probate Court. *Estate of Fred Dane alias Fred Burke, Deceased.* July 11, 1941. Marquette, MI.

135 ---*Estate of Fred Dane alias Fred Burke, Deceased.* July 11, 1941. Marquette, MI.

136 ---*Estate of Fred Dane alias Fred Burke, Deceased.* July 11, 1941. Marquette, MI.

137 Ohio Births and Christenings Index 1800-1962. "Theo May Walston." http://www.ancestry.com. (Accessed November 27, 2011)

138 Social Security Administration. Social Security Death Index. "Number: 346-09-6804; Issue State: Illinois; Issue Date: Before 1951." http://www.ancestry.com. (Accessed March 14, 2012).

139 Investigation of Organized Crime in Interstate Commerce. "Hearings Before a Special Committee to Investigate Organized Crime in Interstate Commerce." United States Senate. Eighty-first Congress. Second session. Volume 5. Illinois. http://www.archive.org/search.php?query=organized%20crime%20in%20interstate%20commerce%20AND%20mediatype%3Atexts. (Accessed October 9, 2011).

140 ---February 18, 1948. 1.

141 *Chicago Daily Tribune.* September 23, 1947. 9.

142 Federal Bureau of Investigation. *John (Handsome Johnny) Roselli.* Chicago File #58-194. Part 4. http://vault.fbi.gov/John%20%28Handsome%20Johnny%29%20Roselli. (Accessed November 12, 2011).

143 United States Senate. *Kefauver Committee Interim Report #3.* May 1, 1951. "U.S. Senate Special Committee to Investigate Organized Crime in Interstate Commerce." Chicago, IL. http://www.onewal.com/kef/kef3.html#chicago. (Accessed September 26, 2011).

144 *News-Palladium.* July 23, 1948. 1, 8.

145 Federal Bureau of Investigation. *Louis Kutner.* "Drury Killing." https://www.maryferrell.org/mffweb/archive/viewer/showDoc.do?docId=140302&relPageId=7. (Accessed February 20, 2012).

146 Frank R. Hayde. *The Mafia and the Machine: The story of the Kansas City Mob.* "The Kefauver Hearings." Barricade Books, 2007.

147 United States Court of Appeals Sixth Circuit. *Aiuppa v United States.* - 201 F.2d 287. December 11, 1952. http://law.justia.com/cases/federal/appellate-courts/F2/201/287/87991/. (Accessed February 2, 2012).

148 *New York Times.* June 18, 1957.

149 Drew Pearson. *Aberdeen Daily News.* Aberdeen, SD. October 30, 1963. 4.

BIBLIOGRAPHY

BOOKS

Anderson, Dan and Laurence J. Yadon. *One Hundred Oklahoma Outlaws, Gangsters and Lawmen, 1839–1939*. Gretna, LA: Pelican Publishing Company, 2007.

Barton, Bruce. *On the Up and Up*. Indianapolis, IN: Bobbs–Merrill Publishing, 1929.

Bilek, Arthur J. *The First Vice Lord: Big Jim Colosimo and the Ladies of the Levee*. Nashville, TN: Cumberland House Publishing, 2008.

Binder, John J. *The Chicago Outfit–Images of America*. Charleston, SC: Arcadia Publishing, 2003.

Bohn, Michael K. *Money Golf: 600 Years of Bettin' on Birdies*. Dulles, VA: Potomac Books, Inc., 2007.

Butts, Edward. *Outlaws of the Lakes: Bootlegging & Smuggling from Colonial Times to Prohibition, a Prohibition Primer*. Toronto: Lynx Images, 2004.

Chicago Blue Book of Selected Names of Chicago and Suburban Towns. "Year Ending 1915." Chicago, IL: Chicago Directory Company, 1914.

Coolidge, Judge Orville W. *A Twentieth Century History of Berrien County, Michigan*. Chicago, IL: Lewis Publishing Company, 1906.

Cooke, T. G. *Finger Prints, Secret Service, Crime Detection*. Chicago: Finger Print Publishing Association, 1934.

Crumpacker, Gladys Wells. Robert Wood Wilson ed. *The Complete History of Sullivan County Missouri. Volume II, 1900–1979*. Milan, MO: History Publications, 1980.

Dash, Mike. *Satan's Circus: Murder, Vice, Police Corruption, and New York's Trial of the Century*. New York, NY: Crown Publishers, 2007.

Deitch, Scott M. *Cigar City Mafia: A Complete History of the Tampa Underworld*. Fort Lee, NJ: Barricade Books, 2004.

Eghigian, Jr. Mars. *After Capone: The Life and World of Chicago Mob Boss Frank 'The Enforcer' Nitti*. Nashville, TN: Cumberland House, 2006.

Gaines, Larry K. and Roger LeRoy Miller. *Criminal Justice in Action*. Thompson Wadsworth Company, 2009.

Girardin, G. Russell with William J. Helmer. *Dillinger–The Untold Story*. Bloomington, IN: Indiana University Press, 1994.

Gobert, Karen. *Stevensville & Area, Stevensville, Michigan 1884–1984*. Stevensville, MI: Stevensville Village Council, 1984.

Gore, Victor M. *Recollections of the Berrien County Bar*. Benton Harbor, MI: May 1935.

Gusfield, Jeffery. *Deadly Valentines – The Story of Capone's Henchman "Machine Gun" Jack McGurn and Louise Rolfe, his Blond Alibi*. Chicago, IL: Chicago Review Press, 2012.

Haley, J. Evetts. *Robbing Banks Was My Business–The Story of J. Harvey Bailey, America's Most*

Successful Bank Robber. Canyon, TX: Palo Duro Press, 1973.

Hayde, Frank R. *The Mafia and the Machine: The story of the Kansas City Mob*. Kansas City, MO: Barricade Books, 2007.

Helmer, William J. *Al Capone and His American Boys: Memoirs of a Mobster's Wife*. Bloomington, IN: Indiana University Press, 2011.

——— *The Gun That Made the Twenties Roar*. Chicago, IL: The Gun Room Press, 1969.

Helmer, William J. and Art Bilek. *The St. Valentine's Day Massacre*. Nashville, TN: Cumberland House Publishing, 2004.

Helmer, William J. and Rick Mattix. *The Complete Public Enemy Almanac*. Nashville, TN: Cumberland House Publishing, 2007.

History of Sullivan County, Missouri. Chicago, IL: Goodspeed Publishing Company, 1888. Reprint by Hearthstone Legacy Publications, 2008.

Hunt, Cecil. *Word Origins: The Romance of Language*. New York, NY: Philosophical Library, Inc., 1962.

Hunt, Thomas and Martha Macheca Sheldon. *Deep Water: Joseph P. Macheca and the Birth of the American Mafia*. New York, NY: iUniverse, Inc., 2007.

Illinois Crime Survey. Chicago, IL: Illinois Association for Criminal Justice, 1929.

Kahn, Roger. *A Flame of Pure Fire: Jack Dempsey and The Roaring '20's*. San Diego, CA: Houghton Mifflin Harcourt, 1999.

Keefe, Rose. *Guns and Roses–The Untold Story of Dean O'Banion, Chicago's Big Shot Before Al Capone*. Nashville, TN: Cumberland House Publishing, 2003.

Kobler, John. *Capone: The Life and World of Al Capone*. Chicago, IL: First Da Capo Press, 1971.

Lait, Jack and Lee Mortimer. *Chicago Confidential*. New York, NY: Crown Publishers, 1950.

Langland, James ed. *The Chicago Daily News Almanac and Yearbook for 1930*, Chicago, IL: Chicago Daily News, Inc. 1929.

———*The Chicago Daily News Almanac and Year-Book for 1931*, Chicago, IL: Chicago Daily News, Inc. 1930.

Lewis, Lloyd. *Chicago: The History of its Reputation*. New York, NY: Harcourt, Brace and Company, 1929.

Lindberg, Richard C. *To Serve and Collect – Chicago Politics and Police Corruption from the Lager Beer Riot to the Summerdale Scandal 1855–1960*. Carbondale, IL: Southern Illinois University Press, 1998.

Morton, James Stanley. *Reminiscences of the Lower St. Joseph River Valley*. Benton Harbor, MI: Federation of Women's Clubs, 1915.

Moulds, Catharine. *Chips Fell in the Valley 1650–1963*. Berrien Springs, MI: Andrews University Press, 1963.

Myers, Robert C. *Greetings from St. Joseph Historic Photobook Series*. Berrien Springs, MI: Berrien County Historical Association, 2008.

Nash, Jay Robert. *Bloodletters and Badmen: The Definitive Book of American Crime*. Book 2. New York, NY: Warner Paperback Library, 1973.

Pasley, Fred D. *Al Capone: The Biography of a Self-Made Man*. Garden City, NY: Garden City Publishing Company, 1930.

Radkay, William as told to Patty Terry. *A Devil Incarnate: From Altar Boy to Alcatraz*. Leawood, KS: Leathers Publishing, 2005.

Rasmussen, R. L. *A History of Little Paw Paw Lake and Deer Forest Michigan*. Coloma, MI: Southwestern Michigan Publications, 1999.

Reber, Benjamin L. *History of St. Joseph*. St. Joseph, MI: St. Joseph Chamber of Commerce, 1925.

Rubenstein, Bruce A. and Lawrence E. Ziewacz. *Three Bullets Sealed His Lips*. Lansing, MI:

Michigan State University Press, 1987.

Russick, John. *Historic Photos of Chicago Crime – The Capone Era*. Nashville, TN: Turner Publishing Company, 2007.

Stodola, Barbara. *Michigan City Beach Communities–Sheridan Long Beach, Duneland, Michiana Shores––Images of America*. Charleston, SC: Arcadia Publishing, 2003.

Sullivan, Edward Dean. *Rattling the Cup On Chicago Crime*. New York, NY: The Vanguard Press, 1929.

––– *The Snatch Racket*. New York, NY: The Vanguard Press, 1932.

Thomopoulos, Elaine Cotsirilos. *Resorts of Berrien County–Images of America*. Charleston, SC: Arcadia Publishing. 2005.

Tippet, Pam Paden. *Run Rabbit Run–The Life, The Legend, and The Legacy of Edna "Rabbit" Murray, "The Kissing Bandit."* Sallisaw, OK: CreateSpace Independent Publishing Platform. 2013.

Warren, Edward K. *The Region of Three Oaks: 100th Anniversary Edition*. Three Oaks, MI: Edward K. Warren Foundation, 1939.

Waugh, Daniel. *Egan's Rats: The Untold Story of the Prohibition Era Gang That Ruled St. Louis*. Nashville, TN: Cumberland House Publishing, 2007.

Williams, Elmer L. *That Man Bundesen*. Volume 1. Chicago, IL: Elmer L. Williams, 1931.

Wood, Ike. *One Hundred Years of Hard Labor-A History of Marquette State Prison*. Centennial Edition. Au Train, MI: KA–ED Publishing Company, 1985.

INTERVIEWS

Agens, David. Interview by author. Benton Harbor, MI. January 24, 2011.

Bennett, Sandra O'Leary. Email interview by author. January 8, 2012, and February 3, 2012.

Berndt, Neil. Correspondence interview by author. June 15, 2011.

Blunier, Sally Paul. Telephone interview by author. May 18, 2014.

Campagna, Alena. Email interview by author. September 25, 2011.

Cooper, Tom. Interview by John Hodgson. St. Joseph, MI. July 15, 2011.

Daily, Evelyn Vance. Interview by Enfys McMurry. Green City, MO. July 2001.

Deegan, Mary Jo. Email interview by author. February 28, 2013.

Emery, Dr. William. Interview by author. St. Joseph, MI. September 28, 2010.

Ender, Joyce Kool. Interview by author. St. Joseph, MI. September 6, 2011.

Garvey, John. Email interview by author. April 27, 2010, and July 19, 2011.

Gifford, Geoff. Email interview by author. August 1, 2013.

Groulx, Donna Gillette. Telephone interview by author. September 15, 2008.

Keefe, Rose. Email interview by author. August 31, 2011.

Kruck, William. Interview by author. Benton Harbor, MI. February 8, 2012.

Kubath, Tom. Email interview by author. August 13, 2012.

Lievense, Rob. Email interview by author. November 10, 2011.

Magdzinski, Ruth Konvalinka. Telephone interview with author. Feb. 15, 2012, and June 27, 2013.

Mason, Mark. Email interview by author. November 16, 2012.

Moore, Michael. Interview by author. Benton Harbor, MI. August 26, 2011.

Peek, Ramah. Interview by Enfys McMurry. Green City, MO. May 22, 2004.

Price, Shirley. Telephone and email interview by author. September 3, 2010.

Rae, Josette. Telephone interview by author. January 11, 2014

Ratajik, David. Interview by author. Stevensville, MI. June 22, 2010.

Schauer, Chuck. Telephone and email interview by author. September 25, 2011.

Schertzing, Phillip D., PhD. Email interview by author. December 13, 2011.

Schulte, Cheryl. Email interview by author. May 19, 2012.

Sherlock, Bill. Telephone and email interview by author. September 25, 2011.

Skelley, Velma. Interview by author. Benton Harbor, MI.

Skelly, Sharon. Telephone interview by author. St. Joseph, MI. January 13, 2013.

Smietanka, John. Interview by author. St. Joseph, MI. September 20, 2013.

Smith, Robert. Interview by author. Lombard, IL. September 26, 2013.

Smith, Steven W. Email interview by author. May 23, 2011.

Tinsley, Ann Lancaster. Email interview by author. March 4, 2013.

Upton, Stephen. Telephone interview by author. September 13, 2013.

Waugh, Daniel. Telephone interview by author. July 25, 2010, and August 26, 2010.

Williamson, Peg. Telephone interview by author. July 25, 2013.

Winkeler, John. Telephone interview by author. September 15, 2008.

Wulff, Steve. Telephone interview by author. April 13, 2013.

Yetzke, Marge Hess. Email interview by author. November 21, 2011.

JOURNALS

1933: A Century of Progress. Book Series Number 3. Chicago, IL: Exposition Publications and Novelties.

Adkin, Clare E. Jr. "Saying No to War." *Michigan History.* November/December 2007. Volume 9. Number 6. Lansing, MI: Michigan Historical Center, 2007.

Arnold, Amy L. *Southwest Michigan RoadMap: The West Michigan Pike.* Lansing, MI: State Historic Preservation Office, 2010.

Bate, J. Victor. "Trail's End for the Man Who Murdered 20." *True Detective Mysteries,* New York, NY, July 1941.

Berrien County Historical Association. *Fede, Famiglia, e Amici: The Italian Experience in Berrien County 1900–2004.* Berrien Springs, MI, 2004.

Burkhart, Jeff. "Something to Celebrate: Repeal of Prohibition." *Marin Independent Journal,* Marin, CA, December 7, 2007.

Critchley, David. "Goodfellas: Berrien County and Prohibition Era Gangsters." *Historical Society of Michigan Chronicle.* Lansing, MI, April 2008.

Cummins, Harold. "Attempts to Alter and Obliterate Finger-Prints." *Journal of Criminal Law and Criminology (1931–1951).* Volume 25. Number 6. March–April 1935. Evanston, IL: Northwestern University, 982–991. http://www.jstor.org/stable/1134845. (Accessed on March 5, 2013).

DeMott, Mary. "To Preserve, Protect and Defend!" *Wilderness Chronicle,* Ogemaw, MI, September 2003.

Fort Miami Heritage Society of Michigan. "Al Capone and the Society Ladies." *Spring Newsletter,* St. Joseph, MI, 1998.

Foster, L. A. *True Detective Mysteries,* "How Fred Burke Was Captured: High Lights of Burke's Crimson Career." New York, NY: MacFadden Publications, July 1931.

Goddard, Calvin H. "A History of Firearm Identification." "Police 13–13." *Chicago Police Journal,* Chicago, IL, 1936.

––– "The Valentine Day Massacre: A Study in Ammunition-Tracing." *A Crime and its Clues,* Chicago, IL, 1929.

Hess, Eric. "Facial Recognition: A Valuable Tool for Law Enforcement." *Forensic Magazine,* Amherst, NH: Vicon Publishing, Inc., October/November 2010.

Hunsaker, Joseph Jr. "How Fred Burke Was Captured Through True Detective Mysteries: The Amazing Story of How It Was Done By the Man Who Did It." *True Detective Mysteries,* New York, NY: MacFadden Publications, July 1931.

Hunt, Thomas. "Al Capone's Long Stay in Philadelphia." *Informer: The History of American Crime and Law Enforcement.* New Milford, CT: Hunt Publications, October 2010.

James, Ellen. *Chariton Collector*. "Gangster Connections." Spring 1981. http://library.truman. edu/scpublications/Chariton%20Collector/Spring%201981/Gangster%20Connections. pdf. (February 24, 2013).

Kets, Michiel Van. *Limousines of the US Presidency – A Ride Through History*. http://www. articlesnatch.com/Article/Limousines-Of-The-Us-Presidency-A-Ride-Through-History/930663. (Accessed December 12, 2011).

Kosmoff, P. J. ed. "Requiescat in Pace." Volume 8, Number 10. "Killer Burke." Volume 8, Number 10. *Marquette Inmate*. Marquette, MI: July, August 1940.

Merchants, Tradesmen and Manufacturers Financial Condition for Sullivan County, Missouri 1929. R. G. Dun Mercantile Agency Reference, Green City, MO, 1929.

Morrison, Allen D. "The Part I Played in the Trapping of 'Killer' Burke." *True Detective Mysteries*, New York, NY: MacFadden Publications, July 1931.

Myers, Robert and Candace. *A Brief History of the Philip L. D'Andrea House*. 2007.

Olander, Oscar G. "Michigan State Police: A Twenty–Five Year History: Become State Police." *Michigan State Journal Press*. East Lansing, MI, 1942. 59–60.

Smith, Stephen W. "The Battle of Benton Harbor." *Michigan History*. Volume 93. Number 3. Lansing, MI: Michigan Historical Center, May/June 2009.

Stodola, Barbra. "Sands of Time." *The Beacher*. Michigan City, IN, July 17, 2003.

Time Magazine. "Crime: The Most Dangerous Man Alive." December 30, 1929. Vol. XIV No. 27. http://www.time.com/time/magazine/article/0,9171,929144,00.html. (Accessed October 19, 2010).

Von Frantzius, Peter. *P. Von Frantzius Sport Manual*. Peter Von Frantzius. Chicago, IL: 1928.

GOVERNMENT DOCUMENTS
Berrien County Archives. Berrien County Death Records Book E. Benton Harbor, MI.

Berrien County Archives. Berrien County Marriage Records Book M, N, G. Benton Harbor, MI.

Berrien County Clerk. *Complaint and Examination in Murder of Charles Skelly*. December 21, 1929. Berrien County Clerk, St. Joseph, MI.

Berrien County Clerk. *License to Carry Concealed Weapons: Fred Alden*. June 5, 1912. Heritage Museum and Cultural Center. St. Joseph, MI.

Berrien County Circuit Court. *Bill of Complaint for Annulment for Charles F. Steedley v Florence Allen*. November 13, 1929. Box 758, No. 7241, Liber R, Page 425. Berrien County Archives, Benton Harbor, MI.

Berrien County Circuit Court. *Farmers & Merchants Bank of Jefferson and the United States Fidelity and Guaranty Company v Fred Dane*. May 5, 1930, Berrien County Archives, Benton Harbor, MI.

Berrien County Circuit Court. *People v Fred Dane alias Herbert Church*. December 19, 1929, Berrien County Archives, Benton Harbor, MI.

Berrien County Circuit Court. *State of Michigan v Fred Dane*. April 27, 1931. Berrien County Clerk, St. Joseph, MI.

Berrien County Register of Deeds. Liber Book 245. Benton Harbor, MI.

Berrien County Jail Ledger Books. 1927, 1929, 1930, 1931. Berrien County Historical Association: Berrien Springs, MI.

Berrien County Sheriff's Department. *Fred Burke Wanted Poster*. December 1929. St. Joseph, MI.

Chicago Crime Commission. *Inquest on the Bodies of Albert Kachellek, Et Al*. April 19, 1929. May 1, 1929. December 23, 1929. Chicago, IL.

City of Chicago Department of Police. *Report of Murder of Seven Men at Garage at 2122 N. Clark St*. February 14, 1929. 36th District Report #3378. Chicago, IL.

City of Marquette, Michigan. *Park Cemetery*. Cummings Plat #5. Marquette, MI.

Federal Bureau of Investigation. *Al Capone.* http://www.fbi.gov/about-us/history/famous-cases/al-capone. (Accessed October 21, 2012).

Federal Bureau of Investigation. *Al (Alphonse) Capone.* http://vault.fbi.gov/Al%20Capone. (Accessed December 6, 2010).

Federal Bureau of Investigation. *Barker–Karpis Gang, Bremer Kidnapping.* http://vault.fbi.gov/barker-karpis-gang. (Accessed October 24, 2011).

Federal Bureau of Investigation. *Bremer Kidnapping.* http://vault.fbi.gov/barker-karpis-gang/bremer-kidnapping. (Accessed February 15, 2012).

Federal Bureau of Investigation. *Charles 'Pretty Boy' Floyd, Kansas City Massacre.* http://vault.fbi.gov/Charles%20Arthur%20%28Pretty%20Boy%29%20Floyd. (Accessed October 22, 2011).

Federal Bureau of Investigation. *Criminal Record of Frederick R. Burke – FBI #43089 (–Deceased)* Washington, DC: September 23, 1940.

Federal Bureau of Investigation. *George 'Machine Gun' Kelly Barnes.* http://vault.fbi.gov/George%20%28Machine%20Gun%29%20Kelly. (Accessed November 13, 2011).

Federal Bureau of Investigation. *John Dillinger Gang.* http://vault.fbi.gov/John%20Dillinger%20. (Accessed February 18, 2013).

Federal Bureau of Investigation. *John (Handsome Johnny) Roselli.* http://vault.fbi.gov/John%20%28Handsome%20Johnny%29%20Roselli. (Accessed November 12, 2011).

Federal Bureau of Investigation. *Lester Joseph Gillis aka Baby Face Nelson.* http://vault.fbi.gov/George%20%28Baby%20Face%29%20Nelson. (Accessed October 29, 2011).

Federal Bureau of Investigation. *Louis Kutner.* https://www.maryferrell.org/mffweb/archive/viewer/showDoc.do?docId=140302&relPageId=7. (Accessed February 20, 2012).

Federal Bureau of Investigation. *Purple Gang (aka Sugar House Gang).* http://vault.fbi.gov/Purple%20Gang%20%28aka%20Sugar%20House%20Gang%29. (Accessed January 2, 2012).

Federal Bureau of Investigation, *Report of Agent John L. Madala with Georgette Winkeler Marsh.* May 15–18, 1936. Washington, DC.

Federal Bureau of Investigation. *St. Valentine's Day Massacre.* http://vault.fbi.gov/St.%20Valentines%20Day%20Massacre. (Accessed July 20, 2010).

Marquette County Probate Court. *Estate of Fred Dane alias Fred Burke, Deceased.* July 11, 1941. Marquette, MI.

Michigan Legislature. Section 28.282. Radio Broadcasting Stations Act 152. August 28, 1929. Lansing, MI.

Missouri State Board of Health. Certificates of Death. St. Louis, MO.

NOAA Central Library Data Imaging Project. *U.S. Daily Weather Maps Project.* November 7, 1929. http://docs.lib.noaa.gov/rescue/dwm/1929/19291107.djvu. December 17, 1929. http://docs.lib.noaa.gov/rescue/dwm/1929/19291217.djvu (Accessed March 22, 2011).

St. Joseph City Fire Department. *Daily Fire Log.* February 25, 1929, September 3, 1932. St. Joseph, MI.

St. Joseph City Police Department. *Daily Police Arrest Log:* 1926–1931. The Heritage Museum and Cultural Center. St. Joseph, MI.

St. Louis Police Department. *Bertillon and Criminal Identification Bureau Record No. 21181.* August 11, 1931. St. Louis, MO.

St. Louis Police Department. *Narrative of Arrest, Fred Burke, Milford Jones, Gus Winkler.* June 5, 1925. St. Louis, MO.

St. Louis Police Department. *Secret Service Memo and Arrest Disposition of August H. Winkler.* St. Louis, MO. March 30, 1920, April 3, 1920.

State House of Corrections and Branch Prison–Marquette, Michigan. *Biennial Report Covering Period from January 1, 1937 to December 31, 1938.* John M. Longyear Research

Library. Marquette Regional History Center. Marquette, MI.

State of Illinois. County of Cook. *Marriage Licenses.* Chicago, IL.

State of Michigan Department of Public Safety, *Fred Burke,* Case #2208, December 14, 1929– July 10, 1940. Michigan State Police. Lansing, MI.

State of Michigan Department of Public Safety. *Arrest of Jerry Kral (Gus Winkeler) and J. R. Moran (John Clyatt).* New Buffalo Post. August 6, 1931. Michigan State Police. Lansing, MI.

State of Michigan Department of Public Safety. *Special Report: Trooper Myron Gillette.* Paw Paw Post. June 21, 1932, Paw Paw, MI.

State of Michigan Department of Public Safety. *Traffic Accident Report of C.J. Anderson and Jerry Kral.* New Buffalo Post. August 5, 1931. Michigan State Police. Lansing, MI.

State of Michigan Department of State Division of Vital Statistics. Death Certificates 1913– 1920. Lansing, MI.

State of Michigan. *Michigan State Police Fifth District History.* http://www.michigan.gov/ documents/msp/MSP_Fifth_District_History_181277_7.pdf. (Accessed August 16, 2010).

State of New York Department of Health of the City of New York. Bureau of Records. Certificates of Death. New York, NY.

United States Congress. Biographical Directory of the United States Congress. http:// bioguide.congress.gov/scripts/biodisplay.pl?index=h000683. (Accessed October 3, 2011).

United States Court of Appeals Sixth Circuit. *Aiuppa v United States.*–201 F.2d 287. December 11, 1952. http://law.justia.com/cases/federal/appellate–courts/F2/201/287/87991/. (Accessed February 2, 2012).

United States Senate. *Kefauver Committee Interim Report #3.* May 1, 1951. "U.S. Senate Special Committee to Investigate Organized Crime in Interstate Commerce." Chicago, IL. http://www.onewal.com/kef/kef3.html#chicago. (Accessed September 26, 2011).

Washington State Department of Health Public Heath Statistics Section, *Certificates of Death.*

MANUSCRIPT COLLECTIONS

Kostka, Joseph S. *Early Days with the Michigan State Police.* June 7, 1967. Michigan State Archives, Lansing, MI.

Old St. Joseph Neighborhood Preservation Association. *Inventory of Structures in Old St. Joseph Historic District.* St. Joseph, MI. 1980.

White, Ret/Lt. Kenneth. *Remembrances.* Michigan State Archives. RG 90–240. Box 55. Folder 11. Lansing, MI.

Winkeler, Georgette. *Georgette Winkeler Memoirs.* Federal Bureau of Investigation, Washington, DC. 1934.

ONLINE SOURCES

Ancestry, Inc.–http://www.ancestry.com/

Berrien County Historical Association, Berrien County Dentist's, Registry–http://www. berrienhistory.org/images/Medical%20Dentist's%20Registry.pdf

Federal Bureau of Investigation FOIA–http://www.fbi.gov/foia/

Gangsters and Outlaws–http://www.gangstersandoutlaws.com

Lakeside Inn History–http://www.lakesideinns.com/history.htm

Library of Congress–http://www.loc.gov/index.html

Mary Farrell Foundation–https://www.maryferrell.org/wiki/index.php/Main_Page

My Al Capone Museum–http://www.myalcaponesmuseum.com

National Law Enforcement Memorial Fund–http://www.nleomf.org/facts/enforcement/ impdates.html

National Weather Service–Grand Rapids. http://www.crh.noaa.gov/grr/history/?m=12.

Chicago. http://www.crh.noaa.gov/lot/winter/chi_sno_hist.php
Northwestern University School of Law–http://homicide.northwestern.edu/
database/10249/?page==
NRA Museum–http://www.nramuseum.com/the–museum/the–galleries/ever–vigilant/case–
64–world–war–ii–us/us–auto–ordnance–thompson–m1a1–submachine–gun.aspx
Wickersham Commission Report–http://www.drugtext.org/Wickersham–Commission–
Report/message.html

LECTURES

Carter, John, MD. *History of Lakeland Hospital in the Twin Cities*. Lecture. The Heritage
Museum and Cultural Center, St. Joseph, MI, July 22, 2010.

NEWSPAPERS

Michigan
Coloma Courier–Coloma
Daily Globe–Ironwood
Daily Mining Journal–Marquette
Daily News–Ludington
Detroit Free Press–Detroit
Detroit News–Detroit
Herald–Palladium–St. Joseph
Herald–Press –St. Joseph
Holland Evening Sentinel–Holland
Ironwood Daily Globe–Ironwood
Jackson Citizen Patriot–Jackson
Kalamazoo Gazette–Kalamazoo
Ludington Daily News–Ludington
Marshall Evening Chronicle–Marshall
News–Palladium –Benton Harbor
Niles Star–Niles
Owosso–Argus–Owosso
Record Eagle–Traverse City, MI
Tri–City Record–Watervliet
Weekly Press–St. Joseph
Indiana
Evansville Press–Evansville
Hammond Times–Hammond
Kokomo Tribune–Kokomo
Logansport–Pharos Tribune–Logansport
South Bend Tribune–South Bend
Vidette–Messenger–Valparaiso
Illinois
Alton Evening Telegrapher–Alton
Carbondale Daily Free Press–Carbondale
Chicago Daily Tribune–Chicago
Chicago Tribune–Chicago
Daily Register–Gazette–Rockford
Pointer–Riverdale
Rockford Morning Star–Rockford
Southtown Economist–Chicago

Sterling Daily Gazette–Sterling
Ohio
Cleveland Plain Dealer–Cleveland
Circleville Herald–Circleville
Coshocton Tribune–Coshocton
Evening Repository–Canton
Hamilton Evening Journal–Hamilton
Piqua Daily Call–Piqua
Portsmouth Daily Times–Portsmouth
Sandusky Register–Sandusky
Sandusky Star Journal–Sandusky
Times Recorder–Zanesville
Wisconsin
Capital Times–Madison
Manitowoc Herald News–Manitowoc
Milwaukee Sentinel–Milwaukee
Sheboygan Press–Sheboygan
Wisconsin Rapids Daily Tribune–Wisconsin Rapids
Missouri
Daily Capital News and Post–Tribune–Jefferson City
Jefferson City Post Tribune–Jefferson City
Joplin Globe–Joplin
Journal–Post–Kansas City
Moberly Monitor–Index–Moberly
Sunday News–Press –St. Joseph
Iowa
Centerville Daily Iowegian–Centerville
Iola Daily Register–Iola
Moulton Weekly Tribune–Moulton
Waterloo Courier–Waterloo
Telegraph–Herald and Times–Journal–Dubuque
New York
Dunkirk Evening Observer–Dunkirk
Olean Times–Olean
New York Times –New York
New York Times Movie Reviews–New York

Rochester Democrat and Chronicle–Rochester
Syracuse Herald–Syracuse
<u>All Other States</u>
Aberdeen Daily News–Aberdeen, SD
Big Spring Herald–Big Spring, TX
Corpus Christie Times–Corpus Christie, TX
Dallas Morning News–Dallas, TX
Evening Tribune–Albert Lea, MN
Evening Tribune–San Diego, CA
Every Week Magazine–Nationwide
Lowell Sun–Lowell, MA

Oakland Tribune–Oakland, CA
Ogden Examiner–Ogden, UT
Omaha World Herald–Omaha, NE
Pittsburgh Post-Gazette–Pittsburgh, PA
Salt Lake Tribune–Salt Lake City, UT
San Antonio Express–San Antonio, TX
Seattle Daily Times–Seattle, WA
Spartanburg Herald-Journal–Spartanburg, SC
St. Petersburg Times–St. Petersburg, FL
Washington City News Service–Washington, DC

ACKNOWLEDGEMENTS

THERE ARE NUMEROUS INDIVIDUALS, HISTORY CENTERS, and museums that made this book a reality for me, and I truly could not have written this without their help. The one person who started it all for me is MyAlCaponeMuseum.com founder and historian, Mario Gomes, who knows more about Al Capone than anyone else, hands down. He connected me with other "gangsterologists," as we have been referred to. Authors William J. Helmer and the late Rick Mattix mentored me in all things related to Prohibition Era gangsters, sharing their knowledge and expertise on the topic. A huge influence was my uncle, Mike Kline, a lieutenant with the Berrien County Sheriff's Department. He was the first person I shared my findings with and the only person who probably really "gets all of this." His dedication to preserving the history of the two famous Thompson submachine guns is remarkable, and I cannot think of anyone who could fill his shoes when he eventually retires. Berrien County sheriff Paul Bailey supported my research by giving me full access to old files, photographs, and what was left from the raid in 1929, including the Thompson submachine guns. But more so, the opportunity to shoot both guns on a few different occasions ranks as one of my most memorable moments. Others from the Berrien County Sheriff's Department include retired lieutenant Keith Hafer, former Berrien County sheriff Forrest L. Jewell, and the late Berrien County sheriff's deputy Michael Moore, who rallied for me during the writing process, hoping that he could be the first reader. I was only able to send him a few chapter drafts before he passed away, sadly, at only 35 years old.

I have befriended many authors who helped me understand the art of storytelling: Daniel Waugh, John Binder, Jeff Gusfield, Rose Keefe, Thomas Hunt, David Critchley, Valerie van Heest, Robert C. Myers, Kevin McGregor, Janann Sherman, Patrick Downey, Paul Stewart, Michael Jewell, Scott Deitch, Bob Lenthart, and Pam Paden Tippet.

Museums and historical centers played a huge role in the data I found and I am so proud to support their missions: The Heritage Museum and Cultural Center in St. Joseph, Michigan, with curator Caitlin Perry Dial and director Christina Arseneau; North Berrien Historical Museum in Coloma, Michigan, with director Tracy Giarda; Berrien County Historical Association in Berrien Springs, Michigan, with curator Robert C. Myers; Marquette Regional History Center in Marquette, Michigan, with research librarian Rosemary Michelin and historian Laurie Johnson; The Morton House Museum; and Berrien County clerk's office in St. Joseph, Michigan, with retired clerk Louise Stine and archivist Chris Hartman. Archives collections held at businesses and government facilities also proved to be extremely valuable: The *Herald-Palladium* newspaper in St. Joseph, Michigan, with editor Dave Brown, writer Scott Aiken, and photographers John Madill and Don Campbell; Michigan State Police archives in Lansing, Michigan; National Weather Service in North Webster, Indiana, with meteorologists Jeff Logsdon and Sam Lashley; Marquette City Cemetery in Marquette, Michigan, with sexton Paul Albert; historical records maintained by the St. Joseph Department of Public Safety in St. Joseph, Michigan; and Pike Funeral Home with Kraig Pike. Special thanks to Vikkie Wade, current owner of Fred "Killer" Burke's former bungalow; now as Coldwell Banker Advantage, and Bob Willging, antique collector and owner of some of Burke's property.

I sought out the advice of many experts in the fields of law, law enforcement, firefighting, local history, medicine, ballistics and forensics, and beyond, receiving an enormous amount of guidance and understanding: Gary Bruce, Robert A. Smith, Peg Williamson, Rob Reed, Enfys Murray, Janet Horton-Payne, Laura Beach, Chuck Schauer, Bill Sherlock, Neal Trickle, Dr. Phillip Schertzing, Steven W. Smith, John Hogsdon, Neil R. Berndt, Mark Clapp, Deniece Fisher, Donald Taylor, Dan Sullivan, Milt Agay, Steve Petersen, Mark Mason, Larry Wack, Walt Merritt, Odile Loreille, Bill Schnell, Lisa Bradshaw, Chris Garlanger, Debbie Boyersmith, Mary Jo Deegan, Elaine Cotsirilos Thomopoulos, Chris Siriano, and John Smietanka.

The most important aspect of this book is the recollections from family members of those who were involved in the events or knew the people I have written about. David Agens, grandson of William Barry and great-nephew of Fred Alden; Sally Paul Blunier, niece of Ruth Skelly Paul; Alena Campagna, cousin of Louis Campagna; Linda Hackley DeCamp and Gail Hackley Myers, granddaughters of William Bestar; Dr. William Emery, son of Dr. Clayton Emery; Joyce Kool Ender, daughter of Forrest L. Kool; John Garvey, nephew of Phil D'Andrea; Josette Rae and Eric Hulsman, daughter and grandson of Edd Freeman; Geoff Gifford, son of Robert M. Gifford; Donna Gillette Groulx, daughter of Myron Gillette; Jim Humburg, godson of Mary Emma Moulds Gagnard; Tom Kubath, nephew of Erwin Kubath; Ruth Konvalinka Magdzinski, niece of Edward Konvalinka; Linda Mantke-Dolezan and Laura Rosenhagen, nieces of Eugene Bernstein; Shirley Price, granddaughter of Allen D. Morrison; David Ratajik, nephew of Steve Kunay; Jeff Scalf, great-nephew of John Dillinger; Cheryl Schulte, granddaughter of Joseph Kijak; Sharon Skelly, niece of Charles Skelly; Velma Skelley and Patty Skelley-Hopkins, cousins of Charles Skelly; Ann Lancaster Tinsley, cousin of Thomas Camp aka Fred Burke; Neal Webb, nephew of Olen Webb; John Winkeler, cousin of Gus Winkeler; Steve Wulff, nephew of Monroe Wulff; and Marge Hess Yetzke, great-niece of William Bestar.

Thank you to Robert A. Smith for fact checking and early proofreading, and the entire team at In-Depth Editions, including my editor, Sue Olson, who shepherded me through fine tuning my manuscript, and my proofreader, Ann Weller, who had the eye of a sharpshooter in locating those pesky typos. Finally, I owe a great deal of gratitude to my family and close friends who supported me throughout this endeavor.

MAY THE RELEVANCE OF Charles Skelly's sacrifice never become lost through time.

INDEX

Accolades

"Tales of the Gangster Era in Southwest Michigan have circulated for years—truths, half-truths, and lies. Chriss Lyon finally separates fact from legend in this meticulously researched, well-written book."
- Robert C. Myers, Curator, Berrien County Historical Association

"A fascinating book where big city gangsters of Chicago bring tragedy to the small town of St. Joseph, Michigan. You won't be able to put it down."
- Captain Rick Yonker (Retired), Grand Haven, Michigan, Police Department

"A thoroughly researched, well-written account of the gangster going-ons in Southwestern Michigan during Prohibition."
- John J. Binder, author *The Chicago Outfit* and
Philadelphia Organized Crime in the 1920s and 1930s

"Chriss Lyon's new book on the criminal career and capture of The Prohibition Era's most prolific bank robber and gun-for-hire, Fred "Killer" Burke, is a fascinating study of one of the most feared career criminals of the day. Chriss is an indefatigable researcher and has spent years combing through long-forgotten archives and files in local, state and federal archives to uncover documents that paint a picture of an intelligent, yet ruthless, killer that lived a simultaneous existence as a feared gunman and a friendly well-to-do gentleman while hiding from the law in "Capone's Playground." The narrative fills in the blanks on the aftermath of the infamous, "St. Valentine's Day Massacre", and chronicles Burke's odyssey in attempting to stay one step ahead of the many law enforcement agencies seeking his whereabouts. A great read for anyone interested in some little-known facts about one of the most feared gunmen of the Roaring Twenties."
- Chuck Schauer, Certified Latent Print Examination
and retired law enforcement officer.

"Chriss Lyon will amaze readers with this well-written biography and intricate timeline of dates, times, places, quotes, and events that demonstrate exhaustive research and dedication to history and the local community. These historical events explain how the system worked for the enforcers of justice and also for the gangsters who were able to operate, but who were ultimately captured, convicted, and sentenced. This book as an authentic, post-St. Valentine's Massacre accounting of the gangsters' movements and how one community helped put an end to violence and properly shape our nation's history."
- John Winkler, Cousin of Gus Winkler, Fred Burke's partner

in-depth
editions